MERCER
UNIVERSITY PRESS

Endowed by
TOM WATSON BROWN
and
THE WATSON-BROWN FOUNDATION, INC.

GOING BACK THE WAY THEY CAME

GOING BACK THE WAY THEY CAME

A HISTORY OF THE PHILLIPS GEORGIA LEGION
CAVALRY BATTALION

Richard M. Coffman

Mercer University Press
Macon, Georgia

MUP/H800

© 2011 Mercer University Press
1400 Coleman Avenue
Macon, Georgia 31207
All rights reserved

First Edition.

Coffman, Richard M.
Going back the way they came : a history of the Phillips Georgia Legion Cavalry
Battalion / Richard M. Coffman. -- 1st ed.
p. cm.
Includes bibliographical references and index.
ISBN-13: 978-0-88146-187-9 (hardcover : alk. paper)
ISBN-10: 0-88146-187-3 (hardcover : alk. paper)
1. United States—History—Civil War, 1861-1865—Cavalry operations. 2. United
States—History—Civil War, 1861-1865—Regimental histories. 3. Georgia—
History—Civil War, 1861-1865—Regimental histories. 4. United States—
History—Civil War, 1861-1865—Campaigns. I. Confederate States of America.
Army. Phillips Legion. Cavalry Battalion. II. Title.
E559.6.P55C64 2010
973.7'458--dc22
2010045504

CONTENTS

A NOTE TO MY GEORGIA RELATIVES, ANCESTORS, AND DESCENDANTS

This book is a gift to all of you who share descent from the Scots-Irish ancestors of John Fielding Milhollin. We should all be proud to have sprung from these tough people. They stood in the vanguard of the first wave of Irish immigration to the New World. The centrifugal forces of this culture propelled our Milhollin progenitors beyond the edges of early American society. As a result, they grew stronger with each succeeding generation. From the Revolution to the present day, these Scots-Irish ruffians were the guardians and leaders of the Western frontier. They were American soldiers fighting the British, Indians, Nazis, Communists, and, more recently, Islamic Fundamentalists. They are also country bumpkins, rednecks, trailer-park trash, lovers of country music as well as astronauts, Georgia state legislators, and successful entrepreneurs. Like all the patches of the American crazy-quilt, they have their share of felons, losers, and fools. This book is meant to be a beacon on an islet in a tiny portion of our tributary of time. Its purpose is to illuminate the roles played by our Confederate ancestors in that greatest of all American calamities, the Civil War. For us, the man holding the lantern is Major John Fielding Milhollin. He was old enough when he died to have known all about his ancestors from the Irish immigrant James Milhollin, to himself—for him a total of three generations, for the rest of us, many more. He set an example for us all as dedicated son, husband, father, and soldier. His letters to Dearest Ev and the Children tell us about the kind of man he was. Most of them are quoted in part in this book. They are a testament of love, dedication, and bravery to us all.

I hope this book is a good read to all readers, but especially to my Georgia relatives. This is for all of you.

—Richard Milhollin Coffman

I Remember

Major John Fielding Milhollin, Commander, Company B, the Johnson Rangers,
Phillips Georgia Legion Cavalry Battalion
Mortally Wounded in Action on 10 November 1863

Invincible, or so you seemed,
You left your family for a higher cause.
Swaddled in gray, hard and lean.
You swaggered-rattled to the hell of the West Virginia battles.
Wraith-like, you pushed your Rangers, brothers, friends,
Into the apocalypse at Gettysburg and Chancellorsville.
Like meteoric sparkle, they dropped, shattered,
Spent, but you, you set yourself in agony
For the kill.

You led the scout to death's own end near Brandy Station.
For Yankee blood you plunged in wildest Jubilation.
The cannonading left you there, torn askew,
Chest bloody and bare.
You died as did your higher cause,
Drifting smoke from battlefield timber.

I reach through time to touch you, Grandfather,
I don't know why, but you, my Rebel soldier,
I remember.

PREFACE

Going Back the Way They Came is meant to be a "companion volume." It is a shorter piece that will both complement and complete the earlier work, *To Honor These Men, a History of the Phillips Georgia Legion Infantry Battalion.* Once the infantry and cavalry battalions were separated and placed in larger dedicated brigades, the men on horseback and the foot soldiers rarely fought in close proximity to each other. However, the same name designation was maintained; that is, they referred to themselves as soldiers of the Phillips Georgia Legion. Some letters speak of "our Legion." These men trained together at camps Brown and McDonald, came from the same counties of north Georgia, and served together during the western Virginia campaign and the South Carolina respite. In this sense, they were "one" element united by blood, home, and the soldier's life. Although the Macon Light Artillery Battery was never assigned on any permanent basis, the rhetoric in some of their pension applications suggests that the cannoneers thought of themselves as combatants of the Phillips Georgia Legion. In the minds of the foot soldiers, the cavalry troopers, and the artillerymen, they were united by bonds stronger than the puny decision making of generals. They were soldiers of the Phillips Georgia Legion. As a child growing up in Dayton, Ohio, I was regaled with tales of our Georgia family icon, Captain John Fielding Milhollin. His faded ambrotype held center stage on the mantelpiece. I knew he was my great-great-grandfather and was a cavalry officer hero during the Civil War, but for years that was all I knew. I was always impressed, and remain so, whenever I observe the old photograph. He stands stiffly, saber grasped in his right hand, the blade resting on his right shoulder, full-fluted army revolver snug in left hand. He sports a full, Old Testament beard and stares intensely at the camera. I know this rigid stance was necessary to prevent movement that would blur the old photograph and probably not to impress anyone. Nevertheless, it impressed me. Grandfather John was the commander of Cavalry Company B. He was killed while leading a scout near Brandy Station on 10 November 1864 at age thirty-two. My mother chattered about him constantly, always warning me. "He's watching you! You'd better behave or some day you'll answer to him," she shouted every time I brought a note home from grade school demanding my parents do something about my disreputable behavior. Warnings from school and mother continued, but my behavior was unchanged. I was told I was a juvenile delinquent and that if I did not grow up soon I would be sent to a Southern military school. At thirteen years old, I soon found myself a cadet at the Kentucky Military Institute just outside of Louisville, Kentucky, where I resided for four years. I thought very little about great-great-grandfather for the next fifteen years. At age thirty-two, I had an epiphany. While home on leave from the Air Force, I took the ambrotype off of the mantelpiece and stared at it. I wondered, "Who was he? What was he like?" Something clicked somewhere in my reptilian brain. I would investigate this and find out about this man. I called aged relatives in Georgia, wrote letters to the National Archives, and picked my mother's brains. It was like watering a plant that grew into an enormous tree. Years passed. I accumulated an embarrassment of riches in the form of period letters from members of the cavalry battalion, their wives and families, and vast amounts of nineteenth-century documents. Over a dozen file boxes were filled and filed. I needed to write a book. With tutelage from Dr. Richard H. Kohn, I began with an article for a popular but highly regarded journal, *The Civil War Times Illustrated.* Without the training in historiography and historical writing under Dick Kohn, I would never have acquired the literary skills or ability to manage the research.

Letters and diaries told us what these men experienced, how they lived and fought. The letters shared secrets with me. Their fears, the women they loved, the friendships they treasured, the miseries and horrors of combat were all there. I often felt like a voyeur. How did they do it? Exhausted, disease-ridden, covered with vermin, they fought on and wrote home. I tried to trace their combat as well as their personal experiences and bring them to life. I wanted a book about the men. The letters and diaries taught us the same lessons all soldiers come to know: to survive, they had to bond closely with each other. This bond maintained them through the worst fighting at Gettysburg and Trevilian Station. John Fielding Milhollin, John Swan, and William W. Rich yearned for home. The memories of backbreaking farm work drifted to thoughts of Sunday dinners and the price of corn, to gatherings of extended family and Sunday sermons. They begged family members to send boxes of food and clothes and blankets to keep them warm. Some lucky ones were sent home in search of horses so they could return and continue the fight. Before his death, John Fielding Milhollin expressed unbounded love for his wife, Ev, and the children. William W. Rich found humor and shared it with his wife Basheba.

John Swan squabbled with his wife, Bettie, but insisted she was and would always be dear to him.

I have many individuals and institutions to thank. First and foremost, I am indebted to the staff of Mercer University Press. Their patience and kindness for first-time authors as well as unlimited encouragement made all the difference. Many thanks to Marc Jolley, Marsha Luttrell, Kevin Manus-Pennings, and Barbara Kane.

Several distinguished historians gave freely of their time. I am deeply indebted to Keith Bohannon, Eric Wittenberg, Ed Longacre, and Mark L. Bradley. I would also like to thank the following fine people for their help with research as well as encouragement: John J. Fox III, Dr. Donald Hopkins, Libby Buchanan, Wilena B. Branch, Steven Catlett, Dr. Gerald A. Smith, David Vaughn, and Dr. Stephen Wise.

Many libraries and historical societies opened their doors to me, for which I will be forever grateful. They include the United States Army Military History Institute, Atlanta Historical Society, Georgia Historical Society, Georgia Genealogical Society, Cedartown Library, Central Georgia Genealogical Society, Chattanooga-Hamilton Library, Clayton Library, Dalton Historical Society, Emory University's Robert W. Woodruff Library, the Florence County Library, Francis Marion University's James A. Rogers Library, Greene County Library, Ida Hilton Public Library, R. T. Jones Memorial Library, Laurens County Library, Macon Historical Society, Magnus Library, McClung Historical Collection, Monroe-Walton County Library, Norris Library, Newnan-Coweta Historical Society, Richard J. Reardon of the Central Library Local History Department of Los Angeles, California, Rockmart Library, Ringgold Library, Washington Library, and the Public Library of Mecklenburg County, North Carolina. Special thanks to the best researchers I have ever known: Deborah Petite, Amanda Cook, Charlotte Ray, and Jon Deiss.

I will always be grateful for the unflagging encouragement I received from my wife Puggy, my children, Kevin, Rachel, Christopher, and Rebecca, and my grandchildren, Samantha, Hannah, Kevin Richard, and Zachariah. No man is more blessed than I am for the wonderful wife and children who have been granted to me. Thanks also to all those not mentioned but who nevertheless helped me. They were Legion.

ILLUSTRATIONS

Camp Davis, Lynchburg, Virginia
Period Print (1860) of Lynchburg, Virginia, Company C Battle Flag, Cherokee Dragoons
Pass for Captain John F. Milhollin signed by General J. E. B. Stuart
Print by James E. Taylor, Cavalry Battalion at Trevilian Station

MAPS
Camp McDonald
Cavalry and Infantry in South Carolina, January 1862 to 25 August 1862, Western Virginia Campaign
Cavalry Battalion with Stuart, 9–13 October 1862
Legion with Hampton's Charge at Gettysburg, 3 July 1863
Cavalry with Hampton 11 July 1864
Phillips Legion Cavalry Position 12 June 1864
Legion Skirmishes/Battles in the Carolinas Campaign
1865 Topographical Map of Greensboro, North Carolina

IMAGES OF PHILLIPS LEGION CAVALRY
Captain Hugh Buchanan, Company D
Private Nathaniel M. Calder, Company B
Private Josiah Carter (also on CD Rom), Company B
Sergeant John H. Cobb, Company B
Private William Davis Couch, Company A
Private John Calvin Dodgen, Company B, at *Gone With the Wind* Premier in Atlanta, Georgia
Private John H. Dowdy, Company A
Lieutenant Colonel Charles DuBignon, Company A
Captain Samuel S. Dunlap, Company D
Captain Francis Edgeworth Eve, Company G
Captain Al Franklin, Company D
Chaplain William Edward Jones
Private George E. Lavender, companies D and F
Private Middleton Penn, Company F

Captain John Fielding Milhollin, Company B

Lucinda Eveline Dodgen Milhollin (wife of John F. Milhollin)

Private William O. Perry, Company D

Colonel William Phillips, Commander Fourth Brigade, Phillips Georgia Legion

Major W. B. C. Puckett, Field, Staff, and Inspection

Lieutenant Colonel William W. Rich, Cavalry Battalion Commander

Captain Wesley W. Thomas, Company D (also on CD Rom)

Private William Madison "Dock" Trippe, Company C

Captain (Dr.) Robert Leeper Young Long, Company D

Private W. N. Valentine, Company E

Camp Davis, Lynchburg VA. Staging area, here occupied by Union soldiers. Courtesy Lynchburg VA Library.

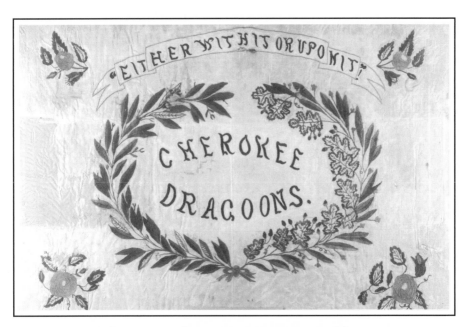

Company C battle flag. Courtesy of Kennesaw Mountain Museum, GA.

Period print (1860) of Lynchburg VA. Courtesy Lynchburg VA Library.

Phillips Georgia Legion Cavalry Battalion at battle of Trevillian Station by artist James B. Taylor. Courtesy of Little Big Horn National Monument Museum (Crow Agency).

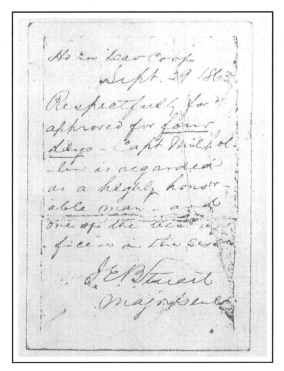

Pass for Captain John Fielding Milhollin signed by
General J.E.B. Stuart. Courtesy of Ms. Susan
Milhollin, Charlotte NC.

Confederate General W. Hampton and Union General Judson Kilpatrick meet at Bennett
House by artist James B. Taylor. Courtesy of Little Big Horn National Monument Museum
(Crow Agency).

(left). Lt. Colonel William Wooford Rich, Commander Cavalry Battalion. Courtesy Mr. Darryl Starnes, Mechanicsville VA. (right) Private W. N. Valentine, Company E. Courtesy Valentine family, Hickory NC.

(left) Private William Couch, Company A. Courtesy of Mr. Mike Couch, Gainesville GA. (right) Lucinda Eveline Dodgen Milhollin, wife of Captain John Fielding Milhollin. Original property of author Richard Milhollin Coffman.

(left) Colonel William Phillips, Commander of the Phillips Georgia Legion. Courtesy of Mrs. R. J. Peardon, Atlanta GA. (right) Captain Samuel S. Dunlap, Company D. Courtesy of Dunlap Family, Bibb County, GA.

(left) Captain Francis Edgeworth Eve, Company G. *Confederate Veteran*, Vol. II, Issue 1, November 1894, p. 342. (right) Captain Major John Fielding Milhollin, Company B. Courtesy Ms. Susan Milhollin, Charlotte NC.

(left) Captain Wesley Wailes Thomas, Company D. Courtesy of Georgia Archives & Mr. Al Camblin, Topeka KS. (right) Sergeant John H. Cobb, Company B. Courtesy Mr. John H. Cobb III.

(left) Private William Madison "Dock" Trippe, Company C. Courtesy Robert E. Davis, Rockmart GA. (right) Private Nathaniel Calder, Company B, Courtesy Calder family.

(left) Captain Hugh Buchanan, Company D. Courtesy Lyn Cay, Bibb County, GA.
(right) Private George E. Lavender, Companies D &F. Courtesy Lavender family.

(left) Private William O. Perry, Company D. Courtesy Perry Family. (right) Private Josiah
Carter. Courtesy of Carter family.

(left) Private Middleton Penn, Company F. Courtesy of Ms. Barbara Penn and Don Penn, Palmdale CA. (right) Private John Calvin Dodgen, Company B, at premier of "Gone With the Wind," Atlanta GA. Courtesy Mr. Herb Bridges, Newnan GA; Author of *Gone with the Wind: The Three Day Premiere,* Mercer University Press.

(left) Captain Al Franklin, Company D. Courtesy Franklin family. (right) Captain/Doctor Robert Leeper Young Long, Company D. Courtesy *Coweta County Chronicles,* Jones and Reynolds, 1928.

(left) Major W.B.C. Puckett. Courtesy Southern Heritage-Old family pictures.
(right) Chaplin William Edward Jones, Cavalry Battalion Chaplin. Courtesy Mr. Bill
Cherapy. Atlanta GA.

(left) Lt. Colonel Charles DuBignon, Company A. resigned due to hearing impairment.
Courtesy Mr. Henry L. Howell, Atlanta GA. (right) Private Elijah Olber Linch, Company
D, Courtesy Al Franklin, East Point, GA.

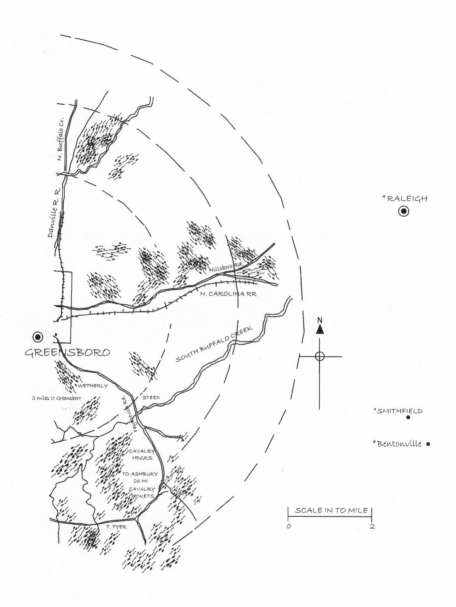

1865 Topographical map of Greensboro. Courtesy of Greensboro, NC Public Library.

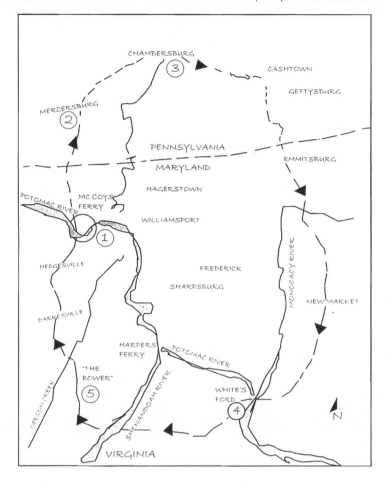

1. LEGION CROSSES WITH STUART OCTOBER 9, 1862 AND REACHES CHAMBERSBURG

2. LEGION AT MERCERSBURG AT NOON

3. LEGION REACHES CHAMBERSBURG AROUND 7:00 P.M.

4. LEGION HEADS BACK, CROSSES POTOMAC AT WHITE'S FORD AT 9:00 P.M., OCTOBER 12, 1862

5. LEGION SETTLES IN AT "THE BOWER" ON OCTOBER 13, 1862

Phillips Georgia Legion Cavalry Battalion with Stuart; 9-13 October 1862.

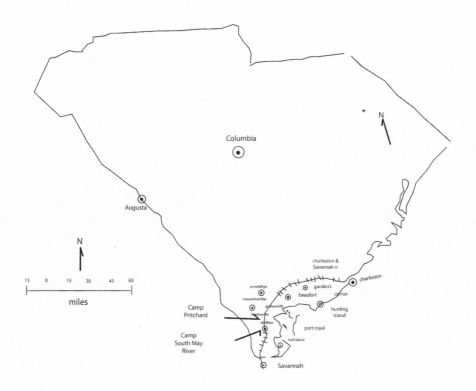

Columbia
⊙

Augusta
⊙

N
↑

15 0 15 30 45 60
miles

charleston &
Savannah rr

pocotaligo
⊙   garden's   charleston
consawhatchie   ⊙ ⊙   corner   ⊙
⊙   beaufort
grahamville
⊙   hunting
Camp   hardeeville   island
Pritchard   ⊙
bluffton   port royal
⊙
Camp   bull island
South May
River

⊙ Savannah

N
↑

Legion Cavalry/Infantry in South Carolina; January 1862 to 25 August 1862.
Map by author.

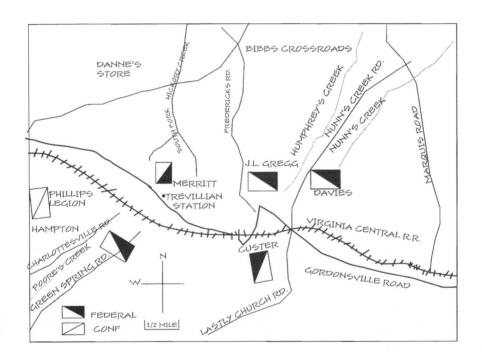

DANNE'S
STORE

BIBBS CROSSROADS

SOUTH FORK HICKORY CREEK

FREDERICK'S RD.

HUMPHREY'S CREEK

NUNN'S CREEK RD.

NUNN'S CREEK

MARQUIS ROAD

J.L. GREGG

MERRITT
• TREVILLIAN
STATION

DAVIES

PHILLIPS
LEGION

HAMPTON

CHARLOTTESVILLE RD.

POORE'S CREEK

GREEN SPRING RD.

N

W

VIRGINIA CENTRAL R.R.

CUSTER

GORDONSVILLE ROAD

FEDERAL

CONF

1/2 MILE

LASTLY CHURCH RD.

Legion Cavalry with Hampton, 11 July 1864. Map by author.

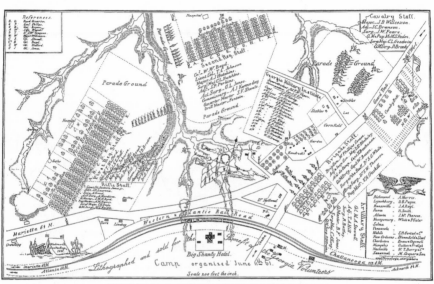

The Georgia Military Institute was organized at Marietta, Georgia, in 1851, by Colonel A. V. Brumby; chartered at the session of the General Assembly in the winter of 1851-1852, and modeled after the U.S. Military Academy at West Point. During the war between the states CAMP McDONALD was established, including the Georgia Military Institute

CAMP McDONALD

A School of Instruction for the 4th Brigade Georgia Volunteers.

His Excellency Governor Joseph E. Brown, Commander in Chief.

grounds and extending to Big Shanty (now called Kennesaw). Here recruits for the Confederate Army were drilled by the cadets and new regiments organized. During the campaign from Dalton to the sea in 1864 the Georgia Military Institute cadets served with great credit. Camp McDonald was destroyed by Sherman and the school was never revived. *Joseph Tyrone Derry.*

Map of Camp McDonald, Big Shanty. Handout for visitors.

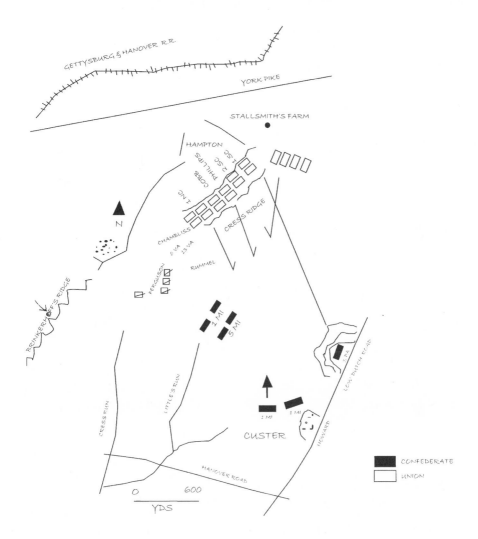

GETTYSBURG & HANOVER R.R.

YORK PIKE

STALLSMITH'S FARM

HAMPTON

COBB
PHILLIPS
1 NC
2 SC
1 SC

CHAMBLISS

CRESS RIDGE

N

6 VA
13 VA

RUMMEL

FERGUSON

BRINKERHOFF'S RIDGE

1 MI
5 MI

STR

LOW DUTCH ROAD

1 MI
1 MI

CUSTER

STEWART

CRESS RUN

LITTLE'S RUN

HANOVER ROAD

0   600
YDS

CONFEDERATE
UNION

Legion Cavalry with Hampton's Charge; 3 July 1863. Map by author.

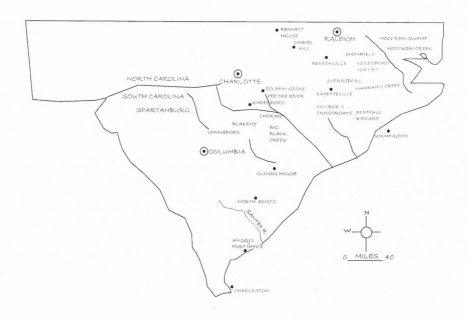

Legion Cavalry skirmishes during Carolina Campaign, January 11, 1865 to Apil 26, 1865.
Map by author.

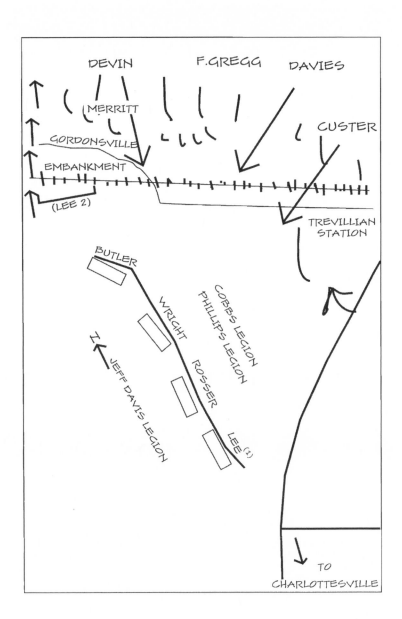

Legion Cavalry position on 12 June 1864. Map by author.

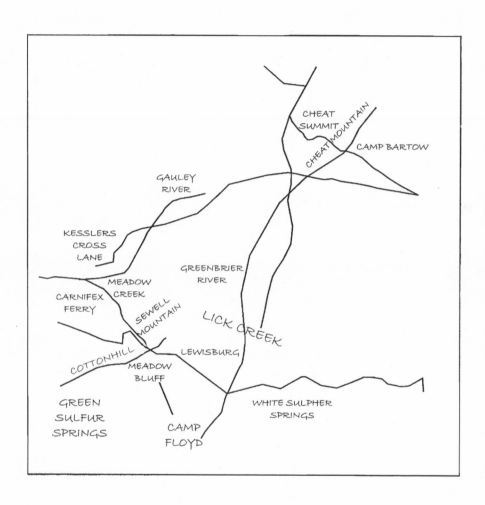

Western Virginia Campaign, 1862.

WE ARE EXPECTING
A BATTLE CONSTANTLY

"I pant for the battlefield as the hart pants for the Water
Brooks. I believe we will leave tomorrow and my heart
rejoices at it."[1]

Mrs. Eliza G. Robarts related the activities of soldiers of the Georgia
Fourth Brigade training near her Marietta, Georgia, home in a letter
dated 20 May 1861 to Rev. and Mrs. C. C. Jones:

> About a week ago there was a large company of officers
> belonging to General Phillips' brigade camped about six miles
> from here on the Atlanta road. Major Capers went out to drill them
> every day. Such a large company so near Marietta drained the
> country of all fresh provisions, such as beef, poultry, eggs and
> butter. They have now gone higher up the country. The ladies here
> gave them a handsome dinner. Their camp ground was a very
> pretty place and the ladies were much amused to ride out
> frequently and see them drilled.[2]

An astute observer, Mrs. Robarts had witnessed the future Phillips
Georgia Legion officers, then of the Fourth Brigade, who had been
training at Camp Brown at the campground in Smyrna, Georgia. Their
next task would be training the brigade enlisted men at Camp McDonald
from 5 July 1861 to 3 August 1861.

The events that preceded Mrs. Robarts's observations set the stage
for the establishment of the Phillips Georgia Legion. Governor Joseph E.
Brown joined with William Phillips and Colonel Henry R. Jackson to
make plans in January 1861 to seize the Federal arsenal at Augusta.

---

[1] H. Buchanan to Mary, 22 September 1861, from Lynchburg, VA. Letters in
possession of Lyn Clay, Seminole, FL.

[2] R. Myers, *The Children of Pride* (New Haven and London: Yale University
Press, 1972) 680.

Georgia was the fifth state to secede from the Union, and officials were busy throughout the state preparing for the coming conflict. Federal forts and arsenals with their caches of arms had to be seized. Fort Pulaski at Savannah had been captured. Now Brown, Phillips, and Jackson demanded that Captain Arnold Elzey, commanding the Second Artillery of the United States Army, surrender the arsenal at Augusta and withdraw his eighty troops from the state. Elzey resisted at first but was directed by the US Secretary of War to surrender with honor in order to avoid casualties. On 24 January 1861, the confrontation ended peacefully when Elzey surrendered and the lone star flag of Georgia wafted in the breeze over the arsenal.[3] The Georgia State Militia needed supplies, equipment, and trained soldiers. The legislature had responded quickly to Brown's request for one million dollars as a military fund to begin the process of building the Confederate forces. Confederate authorities created the office of adjutant general and authorized the governor to accept 10,000 troops.[4]

By mid-March 1861, Governor Brown had begun enlisting troops. He decided to raise two divisions and appointed Colonel Henry R. Jackson to be major general of the first division and Colonel William H. T. Walker as major general of the second division. The governor divided the state into four sections. One brigade of volunteers would come from each section. Brown decided that only one division would be practical and it was tendered to Jackson, who declined in favor of Colonel Walker. Brown offered command of the division's second brigade to Colonel Paul J. Semmes and command of the fourth brigade to Colonel William Phillips. Both men would soon be appointed state brigadier generals. Walker and Semmes resigned before they organized their commands and departed for service under the Confederate government.[5]

---

[3] "Joseph E. Brown to Alexander Hamilton," Governor's Letter Book, 1 January 1847–23 April 1861, Georgia Department of Archives and History, Morrow, GA.

[4] "Governor Brown's Address to the Georgia Legislature, November 7, 1860," in *Life and Times and Speeches of Joseph E. Brown*, 162–69; An Act to Provide for the Common Defense of the State of Georgia, Georgia Law 54, 1860, vol. 1, p. 49, Georgia Department of Archives and History, Morrow, GA.

[5] Phillips was appointed brigadier general on 8 March 1861 pursuant to the Georgia Act of 18 December 1860. His brigade was denominated the Fourth by

Governor Brown and Confederate President Jefferson Davis found themselves locked into their own private war at this time. Both were strong, self-willed men. Brown intended to maintain Georgia sovereignty and fiercely protected his views of states' rights throughout the war. Davis knew better. To fight the United States, the Confederacy had to be a consolidated nation or it would surely fail. State governors could not be commanders in chief of their own armies, but Brown meant to have exactly that role.[6]

One of many confrontations between Brown and Davis involved the governor's refusal to send troops to defend Pensacola, Florida. During the coming year, the governor attempted to confer military titles on many Georgians by forming as many skeleton regiments as possible. He intended to appoint all officers through colonel and even general officers and planned to allow the state's soldiers to elect their company-grade officers rather than accept commanders appointed by the Confederacy.[7]

General Order No. w issued by the Georgia adjutant general's office on 16 January 1861. This also directed recruitment from the Cherokee, Blue Ridge, Western, and Tallapoosa judicial circuits. The organization included two regiments of infantry, one battalion of riflemen, one battalion of cavalry, and one battalion of artillery. Henry Wayne "To William Phillips," 8 March 1861, Adjutant's Letter Book, 18 February 1861 to 25 April 1861, vol. 2, 163, in Georgia Department of Archives and History, Morrow, GA; Rev. George Smith, *The Atlanta Journal*, 15 June 1907. On 28 March 1861, Brigadier General Phillips received instructions to report to Major General W. H. T. Walker of the Irish Division of Volunteers in accordance with the Act of 18 December 1860. Henry Wayne, "To William Phillips," 28 March 1861, Adjutant's Letter Book, 18 February 1861 to 25 April 1861, 419, in Georgia Department of Archives and History, Morrow, GA. Avery, State of Georgia, 186; S. Temple, *The First Hundred Years: A Short History of Cobb County in Georgia* (Atlanta: Walter W. Brown Publishing Co., 1935) 235-36, "Message from Governor Brown to the Georgia Legislature, November 1861," in *Confederate Military History*, ed. Evans, 6:53–55.

[6] W. Bragg, *Joe Brown's Army: The Georgia State Line, 1862–1865* (Macon GA: Mercer University Press, 1987) 2–3; T. Bryan, *The History of the State of Georgia from 1850 to 1881* (New York: Brown & Derby, 1881) 48–49; T. Bryan, *Confederate Georgia* (Athens: University of Georgia Press, 1953) 80–85.

[7] Ibid.

Brown's close friend William Phillips soon found himself in the eye of the storm swirling around him at the behest of Governor Brown and President Davis over who had the right to organize military units, control their use, and appoint their field officers. The Phillips Georgia Legion cavalry battalion was born from the unstable marriage between these two leaders.

A legion was intended to be a small field army with all three combat arms: infantry, cavalry, and artillery; that is, the modern equivalent of a regimental combat team or combined arms unit. Unfortunately, this was an idea ahead of its time. Cavalry tactics changed later in the war. Cavalry action in the "mounted charge" mode shifted to the "mounted infantry" action preparatory to fighting on foot so that the cavalry provided its own infantry. Perhaps the attachment of a mounted company to each infantry regiment was what was intended to create a legion so the two arms could work together. This type of cooperative combat action, which suited the legion concept, probably occurred on numerous occasions. Prior to and during the Civil War this was probably what a legion was designed for, but this tactical experiment never came to fruition. Cavalry and infantry remained two unique services and seldom cooperated tactically. Exceptions to this did occur. Griffith described Captain Samuel Barron's last fight for the Third Texas Cavalry in which the infantry opened the action and the cavalry charged, forcing the Federals back two or three miles. Unfortunately the legion concept died on the vine for lack of central direction or interest in this tactical experiment.[8]

Second Lieutenant Hugh Buchanan of Company D, Phillips Georgia Legion Cavalry Battalion, was not shy. At age thirty-seven, he possessed more self-confidence and maturity than other legion officers. In the midst of intensive training at Camp McDonald in April 1861, he confronted Governor Joseph Brown with questions about his plans for the legion cavalry. In a letter to his wife, Buchanan recounted his disagreement with the stubborn governor:

---

[8] Paddy Griffith, *Battle Tactics of the Civil War* (New Haven CT: Yale University Press, 1989) 185.

The Governor of the state was with us and the cavalry were detailed as guard of honor to escort the Governor from the cars to the camp and from the camp to the cars. The Governor made two speeches and your humble servant made one in which it was my misfortune to differ with the Governor as to his policy. The Governor proposes to keep the Brigade [Fourth Brigade] at home until Georgia is invaded, my proposition is to give the enemy enough to do on the Border and thus prevent an invasion of the state and leave our wives and children exempt from invasion.[9]

Buchanan was probably unaware of the acrimonious squabbling between Brown and Davis that was just getting underway. He had all he could handle with training, confident that he and his troopers would soon be in the inevitable fight. Logistics would quickly prove to be the Confederacy's greatest concern but at this early stage, officers like Buchanan were consumed with short-term problems, such as the availability of writing materials, horses, and forage.

On 22 July 1861, Corporal Elisha J. Humphries of Company A, the governor's horse guards, complained bitterly to his wife. He hadn't heard from any family members, and the primitive Confederate postal service might have misplaced his trunk. To make matters worse, Confederate authorities ignored his pass and promptly arrested Humphries and his comrade Private Henry A. Wise when they arrived at the depot to inquire about the missing trunk:

> I went down to the Depot the other day and got arrested with a pass in my jacket and sent to the Guard tent but I would not go in and I then sent for Dr. White to come and release me and they would not let him he then went to General Phillips who released me as soon as he got there and told them they had no right to arrest me with a pass. I send you the pass so you can see it.[10]

---

[9] H. Buchanan to Dear Molly, August, 1861.

[10] E. J. Humphries to Dear Wife, 22 July 1861. Dr. Samuel G. White was the Fourth Brigade Surgeon of the Staff. Dr. White was later assigned to the Cobb's Georgia Legion.

At the conclusion of training at Camp McDonald, four companies of the legion cavalry, commanded by Lieutenant Colonel Seaborn Jones, Jr., of Polk County, mustered into service on 11 June 1861. While on their way to Virginia from training camps, they passed through Knoxville, Tennessee. Here, Lieutenant John Fielding Milhollin of Company B found time to pen a brief note to his wife, dated 14 August 1861, describing the turmoil in eastern Tennessee at Knoxville:

We [cavalry battalion] arrived here safe about 11:00 o'clock and will leave for Bristol, Virginia at 6 P.M. Everything came off well on the way. There are, I am told, about 20,000 armed Tories in East Tenn. But, I have a host of warm friends here. I learned that five hundred Tories left Louden a very few days since for Kentucky to get arms and supplies...immense secret excitement prevails here. Brownlow [William Gannaway Brownlow was a leading Tennessee Unionist and Methodist Minister as well as editor of the *Knoxville Whig*] submits—Pres. Davis released Tom Nelson [Thomas A. R. Nelson was also a prominent Unionist candidate and leader of the Whig party. When attempting to flee East Tennessee he was captured by southern troops and sent to Richmond where he took the oath of allegiance to the Confederacy and was permitted to return home. After Lincoln suspended the writ of habeus corpus and issued the Emancipation Proclamation he turned his back on the Union altogether stating that the last link binding him to the Federal government was broken.] yesterday. We are all on the lookout for bread...we are told that one of our 4 brigade boys was poisoned here yesterday. We don't know particulars...& one regiment now in camp here...but should Lincoln succeed as well in getting men in here as he has arms we may yet see trouble in East Tenn.[11]

---

[11] J. Milhollin. to Dear Ev, 14 August 1861; Milhollin letters in Georgia Archives, Morrow, GA 30260-1101; "Parson" William Gannaway Brownlow was an east Tennessee unionist, a Methodist minister, strongly proslavery but opposed to secession, who was imprisoned by Confederate authorities for several months; Thomas Ames Roger Nelson, congressman and attorney from Tennessee, Union sympathizer, was arrested by Confederate scouts and taken to Richmond as a prisoner, later paroled and allowed to return to his home.

From there they proceeded to their staging area at Lynchburg, Virginia. Lynchburg, a city located in the geographic center of the state and bordered by the eastern edge of the Blue Ridge Mountains, is only about 180 miles southwest of Washington. It had its origins in the mid-1750's when John Lynch decided to establish a ferry service on the James River (then Fluvanna) and in doing so, established the colonial town of Lynch's Ferry. In 1786, the General Assembly granted a charter, creating the town of Lynchburg. During the Civil War, Lynchburg was a logistical and medical complex that avoided the total destruction experienced by many other Virginia cities, although it did see some battle action later in the war. Camp Davis was established in the city in order to maintain and train Confederate troops.[12] Lieutenant Buchanan related his experience at Camp Davis in August 1861 in a letter to Dear Molly:

> We have just got our tents up and are comfortably fixed up so far as can be comfortably fixed in tents. I drew a new tent the day I left the best on the ground for Matt and myself. Daniel and Sam [slave attendants] have the old one and have the horses to attend to and cook cheaper than we could buy the provisions...we do not know where we are to go from here but I hope not to Western Virginia. I. E. Conyers [probably Christopher B. William J. Conyers of Company B or a relative] is here and John...from the description Mr. Conyers gives of the country in Western Virginia it will be a hard place to winter.[13]

Hugh Buchanan was right on the mark; the legion cavalry halted in western Virginia serving under General Floyd, and the region's severe weather would prove to be the worst ever experienced by the legion riders.

Jefferson Davis determined to maintain control of western Virginia. This part of the state of Virginia, ranging west of the Allegheny

---

[12] Phone conversation between Mr. Lewis Averett of Jones Memorial Library, Lynchburg, VA, and Richard M. Coffman on 11 January 2006.

[13] H. Buchanan to Dear Molly, August 1861; I. E. Conyers of Company B is probably Christopher B. Conyers or William J. Conyers.

Mountains, consisted of a mass of rugged mountains and deep, crevasse-like valleys with rivers all flowing northward. Both branches of the Potomac River flowed into western Maryland and veered toward the Atlantic via the Chesapeake Bay. The Tygart and Cheat rivers intercepted the Monongahela then headed into western Pennsylvania and then to the Ohio River. The Ohio River drained the Kanawa, which was filled by the Gauley and New Rivers. Western Virginia varied from the eastern part of the state in all dimensions: culturally, geographically, and economically. Scots-Irish peoples, contemptuous of the Patrician east and loyal to the Union, populated this part of the state. They considered themselves to be more like Pennsylvanians and Ohioans and were for secession; that is, secession from the state of Virginia. They would get their wish. The Rebels hoped to head north then westward and capture or destroy the Baltimore and Ohio Railroad. This track brought troops and materiel from Ohio, Indiana, Illinois, and Michigan. After western Virginia became West Virginia, a new Union state, the Southerners desperately wanted to grab the new capitol at Wheeling and obtain complete control of the northwestern area of the state.[14] The north had other ideas. Whereas the mountains were opportune sites for the South to launch possible invasions into the North, Northern strategists viewed them as points to launch attacks into the Shenandoah Valley and threaten to destroy or capture the Virginia Central Railroad and the valley breadbasket at the same time. The campaign would become a source of confusion and distress for the legion troopers. The freezing mountain weather, unsoluble leadership problems among general officers, and logistical nightmares, made their tenure in western Virginia miserable.

The legion cavalrymen did not head west until late September 1861. The date 1 September 1861 did not bode well for the cavalry riders at Camp Davis. Some of the first signs of camp sickness began to appear at this time. W. D. Harris of Company C penned a short note to his wife: "I drop you a few lines to let you know that I am well at this time we are all well except a few complaining with diarrhea. There are two of our men

---

[14] Campaign for western Virginia (3 June 1861–12 December 1861).

sick, Lt.[2d Phillip J.] Evans and [W. D.] Rusk are both right sick. G. B. Chastain has been sick a few days, but he is better today."[15]

Still at Camp Davis on 15 September, John F. Milhollin received some information that seemed to be more than the usual camp rumor mill:

> We go to aid Floyd—four thousand Troops will leave here this week...our Legion and the Mississippi Regiment go to Floyd's Division. Col. Boyd goes to Manassas [Colonel William Wade Boyd commanded the Nineteenth Regiment, Company A, originally known as the Second Regiment, Fourth Brigade, Georgia State Troops] and the other Georgia [troops/troopers] are ordered into battle—Field too [probably Private Henry F. Fields of Company A] but I won't know until tomorrow where th[ey] go to.[16]

Buchanan was anxious to leave the tedious duty at Camp Davis and lead his men to glory on the battlefield. In a letter to his wife, Mary, dated 22 September 1861, he described his feelings:

> We are still here contrary to my wishes and expectations. I have been chewing the Bit of impatience for the last eight days. The Railroads have been unable to furnish us transportation and I have advocated leaving our tents and baggage behind and going across the country one hundred and fifty miles and sleeping on our blankets and meet our baggage and tents by railroad at the end of the route...we have the best company in the world and every man is a jewel. I do not expect to find as good a place as this and yet I am anxious to leave. I pant for the battlefield as the hart pants for

---

[15] W. Harris to Dear Wife, 29 September 1861; First Lt. Phillip J. Evans of Company C resigned 12 January 1864; Pvt. William D. Rusk, also of Company C, was KIA on 11 June 1864; Pvt. G. B. Chastain of Company C surrendered at Greensboro, NC, 1 May 1865.

[16] J. Milhollin to Dear Ev and Children, 15 September 1861; "Field" is probably Pvt. Henry F. Fields of Company A, who was paroled at Greensboro on 1 May 1865, also see www.clanboyd.info.

the Water Brooks. I believe we will leave tomorrow and my heart rejoices at it.[17]

Just a week later the legion troopers left Lynchburg on 26 September for Charlottesville, then took the Virginia Central Railroad through Stanton and Jackson River, and finally arrived at Big Sewell. They rode over muddy roads in unrelenting rain before arriving at Green Sulfur Springs (a natural spring probably named after a William Green, who owned the farm on which it is located) on Lick Creek, Greenbrier County, on 4 October.[18] At Camp Floyd at Meadow Bluff, Greenbriar County, western Virginia (so named because most of the surrounding area is meadowland near a steep hill or bluff) on 28 September 1861, W. D. Harris described the march from Lynchburg in a letter to his wife:

> We are expecting a battle constantly. It will come tomorrow or in a few days. At least we have been on a forced march one time…last Thursday we marched fifty miles through the mountains. It took us till in the night and it was dark and rainy. We see some of the hardship of soldiers. Now we would have been fighting by this time if the waters had not been so high that we could not march to get to the battlefield. You all need not think our officers are too big-headed, for they will all stand by us in all trials. Colonel Phillips does even take and give up his horse to the boys [on foot], roll up his pants and wade the mud and water and tote the sick on his back…we will leave here tomorrow morning at five o'clock to go within two miles of the enemy. They are on Sodels [sic; Sewell] Mountain and we will be with them by twelve o'clock tomorrow.[19]

---

[17] H. Buchanan to Mary, 22 September 1861.

[18] S. Cohen Historic Springs of the Virginias, Pictorial Histories Publishing Company, Charlestown, WV, 189. Green Sulfur Springs was a natural spring probably named after a William Green, who owned the farm on which it is located. Meadow Bluff, Greenbriar County, is so named because most of the surrounding area is meadowland near a steep hill or bluff.

[19] W. Harris to Dear Wife, 28 September 1861.

By early October 1861, the legion horsemen had experienced their first bitter taste of war. The legion riders would soon experience blood-and-honor combat that would make their time in western Virginia pale in comparison.

2

MOUNTAIN MISERY TO COASTAL CAROLINA

"As I have little of interest to write until I have the pleasure of
killing a Yankee and not much paper to write on I will close and
walk up the mountain and take another look at
the Yankee camps."[1]

Major General Robert E. Lee's reputation suffered due to his mediocre performance during his three-month tenure in western Virginia. A large part of Lee's problems centered on critical newspaper editors as well as timid and often cantankerous generals who seemed more concerned with one-upmanship than success in battle. Few would have guessed that Lee would become a God-like figure over the next few years in the eyes of his soldiers and his countrymen as well as future generations of Americans. At least some of the legion troopers were more interested in fighting than in carping about General Lee. Lieutenant John Fielding Milhollin of Company B, legion cavalry, was exuberant in a letter dated 3 October 1861 to his family:

> I am glad we came to the mountains as we have learned a great deal and seen more than we could by having gone to Manassas— and we will have harder fighting to do here than was at Manassas as the Yankees have fortified their post and will have the advantage of us in their fortifications as we will have to storm them and perhaps lose many valuable lives—our Army here is strong and all ready and willing, yes even anxious to see the battle begin and if we succeed in whipping out the Yankees and I think General Lee and Floyd—also other generals with such a force as ours can do it.[2]

W. D. Harris reported a skirmish with the Federals and his feelings about western Virginia in a letter to his wife:

---

[1] J. Milhollin to My Dear Ev and Children, 3 October 1861.
[2] Ibid.

Our Legion is about 16 miles from here. We expect to push on after the enemy as they have all retreated from Sewell Mountain. They destroyed lots of their provisions, flour, coffee, soap and other things. Our company ran them. They got news that the Cherokee Indians had come into Floyd aide [*sic*], but it was the Cherokee Dragoons in place of the Indian…some of our men went out the other day on a scouting party got into a skirmish with the enemy and taken two of their horses. Nobody killed on our side…it is no use to try to tell you what sort of country this is. This is the damndest hole I ever saw and how people live, God only knows, for it is nothing but mountains.[3]

Good spirits and good health prevailed throughout the encampment except for several cases of typhoid fever and measles. The legion horsemen had set up camp at Green Sulfur Springs on Lick Creek, one of several curative springs in Greenbrier County, on 13 October 1861. Four other curative springs in the area included the Blue, White, Red and Salt.[4]

Over twenty-five of the horsemen were sick with the measles. Rotten weather prevailed, and no baggage trains had arrived to distribute blankets or other comforts for the sick men living in mud and squalor. Although the Yanks camped only about twelve miles from them, the bluecoats did not attack, and by 6 October, the Unionists had departed. On Monday, 7 October, the legion cavalry rode out of their muddy camp to reconnoiter and locate the enemy. After a twenty-mile ride over mountainous terrain, the Southerners ran head on into the Yankee foe. Buchanan recalled the whistling of bullets, one striking a chestnut tree near him. In the lead, Buchanan's troopers dismounted and rushed into the woods, driving the Yankee pickets away and chasing them as they ran down a road that fronted the Rebels. The Yanks left behind two overcoats, two blankets, one knapsack, a bayonet, several canteens, and three horses. This brisk exchange of shots continued with a chase. The

---

[3] W. Harris to Dear Wife, 10 October 1861.

[4] Stan Cohen, Historic Springs of the Virginias, (Charleston WV: Pictorial Histories Publishing Company, n.d.) 142–44, 188–89.

legion riders came upon several Yankee tents but no Yankees. They returned to camp, rose early the following day, and rode out in hopes of finding the Northerners, getting behind them, cutting off their supplies, and forcing them to fight, but they were unsuccessful.[5]

Lee failed to perform as expected. General Wise had been sacked earlier, and Robert E. Lee, now known as "Granny Lee," followed Wise back to Richmond. Lee's army would leave the western Virginia mountains then head south to the Carolina coast.[6] General Lee traveled south to Coosawhatchie, South Carolina, where he established his headquarters. Near Beaufort, this tiny settlement was named after the "Kussah" Indian tribe. Coosawhatchie was a commercial stagecoach stop between Charleston and Savannah as well as a railroad station on the Charleston-Savannah Railroad. Secretary of War Judah Benjamin assured Lee he would be reinforced by numerous artillery, infantry, and cavalry units for the coming campaign along the Carolina coast. By 8 December 1861, all of Floyd's forces, including the legion, had been withdrawn from western Virginia and were on their way to General Lee.[7] An inspection of Floyd's brigade near Newbern, Virginia, on 14 December 1861 revealed some alarming information. Although Floyd's overall strength was around 3,500, over 1,500 of these soldiers were absent, sick in hospital, or located at various unknown places throughout western Virginia. Some were returning to their commands every day and Floyd was confident he would receive most of them in the near future.[8]

Assistant Inspector General George Deas recommended to Adjutant General S. Cooper that the Phillips Legion and Twentieth Mississippi

---

[5] H. Buchanan to Dearest Mary, 13 October 1861.

[6] Shelby Foote, *The Civil War: A Narrative. Fort Sumter to Perryville*, vol. 1. (New York: Random House, 1958) 131; also see a letter to General S. Cooper in the OR, Confederate Correspondence, etc., ser. 1, vol. 5, S #5, p. 995–96, that states, "The troops have suffered a great deal of hardship and exposure during their active campaign in Western Virginia, and now feel the effects of the measles and its consequences; but they are evidently improving, and with a little rest they will soon be able to engage in any service which may be required of them."

[7] J. P. Benjamin, secretary of war, to Maj. Gen. R. E. Lee at Coosawhatchie, SC, 8 December 1861.

[8] Report of the Adjutant and Inspector General for 14 December 1861.

Regiment be moved to a milder climate and that Dublin Depot, Virginia, not be considered for a winter camp. Any considerations of maintaining these men in the severe winter of western Virginia would not be advisable. In some cases, it would probably be fatal. The men of Floyd's brigade had been worn down by their arduous experience and had suffered terribly from camp diseases, such as typhoid and measles, but discipline was good. All the Southerners needed was a short respite in a warmer climate to be reinvigorated and ready to fight once more.[9] Deas soon realized his recommendations, but the fighting would be minimal. The legion cavalry was on its way to Hardeeville, South Carolina, by 12 January 1862. An article in the *Southern Confederacy* on this date revealed their movements and condition. The writer was either uninformed or overconfident about the health of the legion soldiers: "The four Cavalry Companies attached to Phillips' Legion arrived here on Friday, and are encamped at the Fair Ground [in Atlanta], awaiting transportation to Hardeeville, S.C., where the Legion is now stationed [Infantry battalion]. The men are in fine health; but their horses look like the climate of Western Virginia was altogether unwholesome."[10]

The legion cavalrymen had settled at Hardeeville, South Carolina, by 31 January 1861. Hardeeville populated the southernmost tip of South Carolina just a few miles above Savannah, west of Hilton Head Island. Thomas and Pearson Hardee settled this hamlet in the eighteenth century. The legion officers stationed the troopers around twenty miles from the seaside in order to protect railheads and scout the adjacent areas for any signs of Yankee incursions by sea. Hardeeville was the first station north of Savannah on the railroad.

Lieutenant Milhollin's health was rapidly improving, as was his appetite for oysters. In a letter to his family dated 31 January 1862, he sent a capsule report of his troopers' day-to-day activities and the activity of the ever-present rumor mill:

> This leaves me in common health. Though my cold troubles me yet...some excitement had prevailed about Savannah for a few days as 12 or 13 Yankees on Federal War Steamers ran above Fort

---

[9] Assistant Inspector General George Deas to Adjutant S. Cooper, 14 December 1861 in OR, ser. 1, vol. 5, S #5, p. 995.

[10] Southern Confederacy, 12 January 1862.

Pulaski and our people I believe were in daily expectation of the city being shelled and burnt. But they have gone back to Quarantino [*sic*] and now lie out to sea. I guess there will be a lively time down this way if they try to take Pulaski and burn the city...I am of the opinion however that General Lee whom I saw on the way to Savannah during the cannonading the other day will have better officers than have been in order to save the city. As to the fighting I do not think we will have any change here as the Yankees in my opinion will rely on affecting their purposes from ships and not attempt a land fight. Our camp is in a piny flat country, as a friend says, our...would not be drowned if he fell into two or three wells, we get water close to the surface...one of the new recruits is sick, Waters [Private John R. Waters of Company B] has bad cold. Grady [Private John M. Grady of Company B] is unable for duty—Lt. Franklin [First Lieutenant Augustus M. Franklin of Company B] is officer of the day...Capt. Rich is reading Old Man Gilhams. [William Gilham, a noted American soldier, teacher at Virginia Military Institute, and graduate of West point, authored *Manual of Instruction for the Volunteers and Militia of the United States* in 1860.]"[11]

Perhaps to improve his flagging morale, Milhollin ordered a 1/2 gallon of whiskey on 3 February 1862.[12] On 13 February, he wrote his wife mocking the local black dialect:

Rest, eat, drink. Not whiskey but sandy plains, water and den we reads liclacs. De fact is, I is given to know a whole lot of em liclacs afore dis war am closed and den you know we is de crack company all about what has left Old Cass [Cass County, Georgia] and we intend to be the crack drilled company in Southern Federacy too. O, Shaw I must tell you we gets lots oysters in the shell. Sweet potatoes in the skin and a whole heap of good fixins in the..., what de widow Rich [Captain W. W. Rich's mother] sended to the Cap'n, and I speck we go down to de coast as

---

[11] J. Milhollin to My Dear Ev and Children, 31 January 1862.

[12] Special Requisition for 1/2 Gal Whiskey dated 3 February 1862: J. Milhollin to Wife, 13 February 1862.

vedettes, to stay two or three weeks and den I get some oysters and send to Jack and Jimmy and de shell what be about de ocean to you and de children—well, as I spose you is getting tired of my stuff I will close.[13]

The legion cavalry shifted their encampment a few miles east of the attractive village of Hardeeville, known for its impressive manor homes and churches, to a more nondescript hamlet known as Bluffton by 13 February 1862. Bluffton's claim to fame was its location. Founded in the early 1800's on high bluffs facing directly into the prevailing cool, southeast summer breezes, it became an ideal setting for plantation owners wishing to escape the summer heat as well as malaria and yellow fever mosquitoes.[14] Lieutenant John F. Milhollin's health was showing signs of improvement as a result of exposure to the warm, humid air from the Atlantic coast and improved diet. In a letter to Dear EV, dated 13 February 1862 from Bluffton, South Carolina, Milhollin asked his wife for news about the latest addition to the Milhollin family:

> I received yours of the 7th yesterday also the one from Jack— you did not state the date of the baby's birth, and as you have kindly confirmed upon me the honor of selecting the name I shall try to find a pretty one if within the limits of the Confederacy [the baby was named Anna Corra]...I have written all about our comfortable quarters, etc, but I have no doubt that the Yankees will land some gun boats here before long and shell us out. I further think that from the information received there will in a few days be a fight at Savannah. I guess you have heard of Fort Roanoke on Roanoke Island, South Carolina by the Yankees with 3,000 prisoners—our boys killed about 1,000 and we had about 300 killed. [Milhollin's figures were incorrect. See endnotes.][15]

---

[13] Ibid.

[14] Bluffton Historical Preservation, Inc., Heyward House Historic Center; No. II, a Longer History of Bluffton, (*Bluffton, South Carolina and its Environs*: Bluffton Historical Preservation, Heyward House Center, No. II, 1988) 7–8.

[15] J. Milhollin to Wife, 13 February 1862. The Battle of Roanoke Island, North Carolina, (not South Carolina) took place on 8 February 1862. Federal

A few cavalry operations involving the legion troopers occurred from 19–24 March 1862 and centered around Bluffton and Buckingham Ferry in the low country of South Carolina. The legion cavalry battalion commander reported a Yankee foray at Buckingham Ferry and one at Hunting Island on 20 March 1862. Hunting Island was a term given to a peninsula that extended into Skull Creek in a northeastern direction from Bluffton.[16] Confederate troops were stationed there to prevent the Federals from threatening Bluffton. The Yanks had landed a regiment at both locations as well as a battery of artillery. When the legion riders prepared to attack Hunting Island, the enemy fired on them with artillery. The fire was intense enough to prevent them from moving any farther. On 23 March, Major John Butler Willcoxon clarified the situation in a report to General Drayton, the brigade commander. Late in the morning, pickets stationed at Hunting Island claimed to have seen ten or twelve boats or barges, each of which contained fifty to 100 bluecoats.

General Ambrose E. Burnside led a flotilla of 100 ships with 13,000 men against Confederate General Henry Wise. Wise, who had only 1,900 effective men to oppose Burnside, lost 23 men killed and 62 wounded. Union losses were 37 killed, 214 wounded, and 13 missing. Colonel H. W. Shaw, who led the Cofederate forces in the field because of Wise's illness, surrendered. The result was a Union victory, and the capture of an important outpost on the Atlantic Coast, tightening the blockade. See http://.us-civilw-ar.com/roanoke.htm. Also see John S. Bowman (ed.), *The Civil War Day by Day* (Greenwich CT: Dorset Press, Brompton Books, 1991) 57–58.

[16] Conversation between Richard M. Coffman and Stephen R. Wise, museum director, 24 January 2002, Marine Corps Museum, Parris Island, South Carolina and letter of the same date, Stephen R. Wise to Richard M. Coffman: "Hunting Island was a term given to a peninsula that extended into Skull Creek in a northeasterly direction from Bluffton, SC. Skull Creek runs between Hilton Head and the mainland. After the occupation of Hilton Head by the Federal forces, the Confederates maintained a picket line on the mainland opposite Hilton Head and Pinckney Islands. Troops stationed here were to prevent Federal advances toward Bluffton. Most likely, as in the case of the Phillips Legion, actual units were located there in early 1862. Later the Confederates pulled the majority of their troops farther inland, leaving only pickets and signalmen to watch enemy activities. There were some minor raids carried out between the two sides, but nothing major." Also, information pertinent to Buckingham or Buckingham Ferry from The Bluffton Historical Preservation Society, Inc.

Supposedly, they were advancing on Bluffton in two columns by the Ferry gate and one around the bluff. Simultaneously, another picket reported four boats landing at Baynard's Negro quarters. Willcoxon then sent Captain Charles DuBignon's company to confront the Third New Hampshire Infantry regiment on Hunting Island Road and also sent Captain William B. C. Puckett's company to Seabrook Church. DuBignon's and Puckett's troopers were met by a superior force and were forced to fall back after exchanging musket fire with the enemy. Willcoxon himself arrived on the scene and ordered all legion troopers to retreat to the end of Mr. Crowell's lane.[17] Lieutenant Milhollin, of Rich's company, in the rear of the fighting, fell back. Following orders, he tracked the enemy and reported his movements. After returning to Bluffton late in the evening, Milhollin reported no enemy in the Bluffton vicinity. This was a minor skirmish with a cheap price tag: two horses were wounded, one of which died, and one horse was captured. A storehouse and dwelling house were broken into as well as the post office. No legion troopers had been wounded or killed. Further reconnoitering found no Federals.[18]

The brigade commander, Brigadier General Thomas Fenwick Drayton, must have been doubtful of the accuracy (and perhaps veracity) of these reports. In his report from Hardeeville, South Carolina, dated 24 March 1862, Drayton stated: "The examination of witnesses was made by Captain Carlos Tracy in the presence of Major Willcoxon without any contradiction by that officer of the testimony given by the officers and men eye-witnesses of the facts and circumstances stated."[19] The following statement in Drayton's report seems to belie his previous one: "Major Willcoxon no longer occupies a separate command, and I trust that under a new and severer discipline no such confused reports of the position and numbers of the enemy will again be forwarded like those

---

[17] OR, ser. 1, vol. 6, Chapter 15 [#6], The Civil War CD-ROM, 104, *The War of the Rebellion, A Compilation of the Official Records of the Union and Confederate Armies* (Zionsville IN: Guild Press of Indiana. 10665 Andrade Drive, 2000).

[18] Ibid., 103.

[19] Ibid., 105.

which have so lately ended in harassing marches and disappointment to the troops."[20]

The legion cavalry battalion remained in coastal Carolina until late August 1862 after which they returned to Virginia. Letters from Captain Milhollin and Private Swan of Company F reveal minimal combat activity during this period. From Camp Pritchard, located between Bluffton and the New River Bridge near Captain Pritchard's house, Milhollin offered fatherly advice to his oldest son, James, on 25 May 1862: "James, I do trust that you will be kind to your Ma and your little brother and sisters. I do not want you to have any fusses or fights with those bad town boys—but if you behave yourself and any boy wants to impose on you then you must knock him down with a rock and frail him right. But I do not want any bad boys to keep your company. If they do wish to do so, you must tell them that you have not time to play."[21]

By 6 June 1862, the legion riders had shifted to a new camp called Camp South May River, located near Bluffton just fifteen miles from Hardeeville and six miles from Foot Point. John T. Swan wrote his wife, describing his trip to Savannah and issue of new arms and equipment:

Well, Bettie, I will tell you something about our travails. We left Atlanta [2 June] Tuesday morning at 7 o'clock and got to Macon at 4 P.M. that is I never got there until 4 there was 6 men out of our Crowd detailed to go on the freights with the horses and the rest went on the pasinger. They go there at 2. I preferred going with my horse we left Macon at 9. We then saddled our horses and rode out to camps about 15 miles...the boys are all tolerable well; we drew part of our arms this morning; a Sharps rifle is all I got. We will get more in a few days. J. H. Christian [Private J. H. Christian of Company F] is sick this morning but not dangerous. We have not drew our bounty [reenlistment] yet we will get that in a few days.[22]

---

[20] Ibid., 104, 108.

[21] J. Milhollin to My Dear James, 25 May 1862.

[22] J. Swan to Dear Wife, 6 June 1862.

Major John Butler Willcoxon, commander of the cavalry battalion, resigned his commission effective 4 July 1862, as did Captain DuBignon because of deafness. In a letter to his wife dated 26 June 1862, Hugh Buchanan speculated on the reasons for Willcoxon's departure: "Major Willcoxon I think resigned for several reasons, one was I think he did not like the Colonel [Phillips], another was as is currently reported that his wife acts 'Tarter'and abuses his children and perhaps there is one or two other reasons of his own."[23]

Lieutenant Colonel William Wofford Rich replaced Willcoxon and retained command of the cavalry battalion from then until late in the war.[24]

The cavalry battalion and Company A of the infantry were camped at Camp Willcoxon from 26 June to 19 July 1862. This camp was situated two miles above Bluffton on the bluff itself, just ten feet from the May River.[25] June and July had been good months for the Confederacy. General Lee had pushed McClellan off the peninsula between the James and York rivers. The war news was encouraging and would continue so throughout the coming months. Private Swan and the legion troopers managed to spoil the Fourth of July for the Yankees. They took two prisoners and killed another in a minor skirmish. They were shelled by Yankee gunboats but suffered no casualties.[26] On 17 July 1862, Major General John C. Pemberton directed General Drayton, then at Hardeeville, to proceed to Richmond:

---

[23] H. Buchanan to Dear Mary, 26 June 1862.

[24] J. Willcoxon and W. Puckett, officers senior to Rich, had resigned, leaving Rich the next in line for command of the cavalry battalion; Organization of the Army of Northern Virginia for 23 July 1862 shows Rich in command; William M. Phillips does not appear as overall commander on this date; Governor Brown accepted Phillips's resignation effective 1 August 1862.

[25] OR, ser. 1, vol. 6, Chapter 15 [#6]; see 15 above; also see W. Smedlund, *Camp Fires of Georgia's Troops, 1861–1865* (grant provided by the R. J. Taylor, Jr., Foundation, 1995) 714, 713.

[26] J. Swan to Dear Bettie from Camp South May River, 8 July 1862.

You will proceed to Richmond, Va., in command of Phillips' Legion, Slaughter's [Colonel William M. Slaughter] Fifty-First Georgia Regiment, from Charleston; Manning's [Lieutenant Colonel Seaborn M. Manning] Fiftieth Georgia Regiment, from Savannah; DeSaussure's [Colonel Wilmot G. DeSaussure] Fifteen Regiment South Carolina Volunteers, from Charleston; James' [Lieutenant Colonel James Strother James] Third Battalion South Carolina Infantry from Summerville. Phillips' Legion and Manning's Regiment will go by Augusta.[27]

Their sojourn was over. By 23 August, John Milhollin was at Camp Phillips, which was located a few miles from Richmond in Henrico County. Milhollin was searching for his older brother, Dr. James Theopholus Milhollin. What he witnessed in a letter to his wife while in the Confederate capital prefigured the legion's future: "Troops & trains of artillery have for days past been passing by the thousands. Strung out by the mile. Many as you say in your letter never to return but like the thousand a few miles from Richmond scattered o'er the field of Honor, Victory, Glory & Death."[28]

---

[27] OR, ser. 1, vol. 2, pt. 3, p. 644.

[28] J. Milhollin to Dear Ev. from Camp Phillips, Richmond VA, 23 August 1862.

3

A LONG RIDE TO CHAMBERSBURG

"One old woman ran out in the streets, and said Lordy! I thought they had crooked horns and curly tails!"[1]

The legion reorganized during spring 1862. The original four companies of G, H, I, and K added two companies designated N and P. The two additional companies compensated for trooper and horsepower shortages. When the cavalry and infantry battalions separated in the following year, the cavalry companies were re-lettered A, B, C, D, E, and F. The legion would remain in this pattern until May 1864 when the four-company Fourth Alabama Cavalry Battalion was temporarily assigned to the legion cavalry and Richmond authorities attached the Richmond Dragoons, a spare company from Cobb's Legion, commanded by Captain Francis Edgeworth Eve. On completion of training at camps Brown and McDonald, Confederate authorities assigned the legion to the Department of Georgia. This command, renamed the Department of South Georgia, Georgia, and Florida, expanded in numbers and range. The legion transferred to Virginia in the late summer after completion of duty in western Virginia and South Carolina. Authorities also assigned the legion cavalry to the South Carolinian general Wade Hampton's brigade of the Cavalry Corps of Major General James Ewell Brown Stuart of the Army of Northern Virginia. The legion horsemen remained in the Army of Northern Virginia until the Carolinas campaign of 1865. Confederate authorities then attached the legion riders to the Army of Tennessee for the last few months of the war.

The Federals also reorganized in the summer of 1862: three Yankee armies consolidated into a corps under Major General John Pope of the Federal Army of Virginia. Pope shifted most of his army near Fredericksburg. On 14 July 1862, he moved closer to Gordonsville and Charlottesville. Stuart took careful notice of this movement. After the Seven Days Battles, General Robert E. Lee (no longer "Granny Lee"

---

[1] W. Mapp letter, n.d.

after his success during the Seven Days) marched the majority of his infantry and artillery from the area near Richmond to Orange County and settled his troops behind Clark's Mountain in preparation for the Battle of Second Manassas.

By 20 August, the Confederate cavalry under Fitz Lee and Robertson had engaged in fierce struggles at Kelly's Ford and Brandy Station. The legion was not involved. Glaring at each other, both armies settled in on opposite sides of the Rappahannock River. On 21 August, General Stuart's troopers galloped off on a raid across the Rappahannock. Their goal was to cut the Orange and Alexandria Railroad behind Pope. None of his 1,500 troopers ran into a single enemy. After his approach to Warrenton and Auburn, Stuart reached Catlett's Station and overran the Federal camp stationed there. Rainy weather prevented further fighting of any consequence, but Stuart's men did find Pope's baggage trains and captured several Federal officers who were members of Pope's staff as well as money, a dispatch book, and important papers. Stuart captured over 300 Yankee prisoners and withdrew. Stuart displayed Pope's uniform in a store window at One Main Street in Richmond. The Southern commander had covered over sixty miles in twenty-six hours, and aside from the extreme embarrassment inflicted on the Federal army, Stuart gained vital information that boded poorly for Yankee general Pope. Lee learned the details of Pope's plan and put this information to good use. On 25 August, Hampton's brigade rode to Culpeper Court House and Brandy Station in order to join Stuart's cavalry. On the way, they skirmished off and on with small detachments of Federal cavalry.[2]

In a letter to his wife, Captain John Fielding Milhollin related some details of the fighting leading up to the Second Manassas battle: "There are rumors here occasionally of fighting between some of Jackson's & Pope's armies. I heard yesterday that the infantry of our Legion had a bout and lost some men, did not learn names. I also learn that the Yanks are particular to keep out of the way of our Rebel army."[3]

---

[2] M. Boatner, *The Civil War Dictionary*, rev. ed. (New York: David McKay Co., 1988) 813–14; D. Hopkins, *The Little Jeffs* (Shippensburg PA: White Mane Books, 1999) 80–86.

[3] J. Milhollin to My Dear Ev, 28 August 1862.

On Friday morning, 29 August, the Second Battle of Manassas was underway. Both sides suffered heavy casualties. Lee's Confederates defeated Pope and forced him to withdraw toward Washington.[4] On 1 September, the legion was in Richmond. Cavalryman Humphries had not heard about Pope's defeat at Second Manassas. He wrote to his wife on 1 September, assuring her he had plenty of clothes and that the legion cavalry would be on its way to Jackson the next morning: "As for the clothes all that I need is a pair of pants one pair is enough as I can not carry anything along only what I put in my saddle bags. I have got at this time as many shirts and drawers as I can carry along. We will leave in the morning for Stonewall Jackson. How far we have got to go or where we go I can not tell you."[5]

The Battle of Antietam (also known as the Battle of Sharpsburg) took place from 17–19 September 1862 near Sharpsburg, Maryland. The fight was preceded by the fierce struggle at South Mountain in which the legion infantry took a savage beating (detailed in chapter 8 of *To Honor These Men: A History of the Phillips Georgia Legion Infantry Battalion*.) Although these battles were fought by infantry troops, the legion cavalry attempted to involve themselves only marginally, as attested to by legion rider E. J. Humphries in a letter to his sister-in-law. Humphries described the legion cavalry as joining Hampton at dawn on 19 September at a place called Hard Scrabble and then riding for Williamsport, arriving there at 5:00 P.M. They chased some fifty Federal horsemen away and bedded down for the night. The following morning they pushed into Maryland and confronted a body of Federals about four miles out and then headed back to the Potomac.[6]

Lee made a fateful decision during fall 1862 when he decided to move the war into Yankee territory in Maryland and Pennsylvania with hopes of seizing Washington itself. John Swan found himself in Winchester, Virginia, on 24 September after his few weeks at "Rapped Ann Station, Va." [*sic*]:

---

[4] Boatner, *Civil War Dictionary*, 814; Hopkins, *The Little Jeffs*, 86.

[5] E. Humphries to Wife from Richmond, VA, 1 September 1862.

[6] E. Humphries to "Well Puss" from Tick Mills, Berkeley County, VA, 25 September 1862.

I have no war news to write you more than you have heard for you can here [sic] more about the war than I can. I saw 500 prisinors [sic] that was taken at Harpers Ferry, they looked fat and sassy but they say they are very tired of this war...our army is all on this side of the Potomac...they had to get out of Maryland...they was too hot for them over there. [Swan referred to the Battle of Antietam, or Sharpsburg.] They say we whipped them there but from what I can learn we did not make very much...they are fighting every day or two.[7]

On 4 October 1862, Swan was on picket on arrival at camp near Martinsburg. He mentioned a small "scrumish"[sic] that he did not participate in but provided the details of the fight:

I was on picket when they come over the river...about 2,000 cavalry & 6 pieces of Artillery made a dash into Martinsburg but did not stay long...our Cavalry charged them and they left us with the bag to hold...they killed 3 of our men and wounded several...we killed some of them but do not no how many. I had to get out the best way I could. Gen. Hamton sent us word to get out if we could or we would be cut off...you ought to saw us make our horses get. We struck a lope and kept it for about 4 miles. We had to go about 30 miles to get 10 but by the time we got there they had the Yanks all out of Martinsburg. Next morning we went up to town.[8]

On 9 October 1862, General J. E. B. Stuart implemented his Chambersburg Raid. Before dawn, with a force of 1,800 troopers, he crossed the Potomac near the mouth of Black Creek, which was some twenty miles west of Williamsport. His prodigious force included detachments of select men from Fitz Hugh Lee's, Wade Hampton's, and W. E. Jones's brigades, as well as four guns of John Pelham. Company A, the Governor's Horse Guards of the Legion, constituted of some of the 150 hand-picked horsemen who participated in Stuart's famous raid. Captain James H. Nichols of the Governor's Horse Guards was sick on the day of selection, and the next in line, Lieutenant George Beecher,

---

[7] J. Swan to Dear Bettie, 24 September 1862.
[8] J. Swan to Dear Bettie, 4 October 1862.

was absent. Lieutenant William T. Mapp, Company A, was third in command and was lucky enough to become the leader of the legion detachment. Captain Samuel S. Dunlap, commander of Company N, the Bibb Cavalry, and a few of his troopers, also participated. Stuart's troopers captured two or three horses of the Yankee pickets and headed northward to the turnpike at Hagerstown and on to the National Road, capturing ten prisoners, then proceeded to Mercersburg, Pennsylvania, intending to capture Hagerstown. Unfortunately, General Hampton discovered that the Yankee enemy had word of their approach and changed course to Chambersburg, reaching this point after dark. Stuart attacked immediately and received a flag of truce. His next step was to appoint General Wade Hampton the military governor of the city.

The following day Stuart seized more horses, paroled sick and wounded in the local hospital, cut telegraph wires, and obstructed the railroad. The day after that, Stuart appropriated many small-arms, muskets, and munitions from the local railroad depots. Stuart moved ahead on the following day to Emmettsburg, Maryland, where the locals welcomed him and his men. They passed through open country, avoiding any heavy contact with enemy troops. Federal general McClellan suffered utter humiliation, and Stuart captured prisoners and much-needed munitions and weapons. None of the Rebel raiders were killed and only a few were wounded. Lieutenant Mapp stated that they captured 1,600 horses "from a fat Dutch farmer in Pennsylvania" and seized enough revolvers to rearm the entire company: "Their owners [of the horses] protested most strenuously against such proceeding, but our boys referred them to Pope in Virginia and Hunter in South Carolina...the stolen Negroes were much more valuable than horses. At Chambersburg we took $150,000 in specie, besides arms, Commissary stores, clothing, boots, &c., in the greatest abundance. I equipped myself with overcoat, boots, hat, &c."[9]

Stuart's successful raid received kudos for himself and Hampton. At one point Stuart claimed to be surrounded by some 15,000 Yankees but slipped out of the trap and made his way back to the Potomac, traveling eighty-three miles in one day. Mapp elaborated briefly:

[9] W. Mapp letter to wife, n.d.

27

One of the Yankee farmers whose horse I took told me he was going to report he was talking to—he replied yes: he supposed we were Union me to President Lincoln for pressing so many of his horses. I asked him if he knew who soldiers, gathering up horses for the government. I quickly undeceived him by informing him that we were the same, ragged, starving rebels that the North had been abusing so long. One old woman ran out into the streets, and said "Lordy, I thought they had crooked horns and curly tails."[10]

The raid lasted three days, from 9–12 October 1862, and was a great morale booster.[11]

Barbee's Crossroads, or Southeast Manassas Gap, Virginia, was a busy place for Rebel and bluecoat cavalry on 5 November 1862. A major skirmish occurred on 5 November when Federal general Pleasonton attacked Hampton's cavalry of 3,000 troopers with 1,500 of his own. Three Federal units under General Pleasonton attacked Hampton's troopers, right, left, and center. The Confederate riders retreated and no pursuit occurred. This brutal skirmish cost only fifteen Union casualties and thirty-six Confederate.[12]

On 28 November, Hampton was at it again. Not known as a raider, he nevertheless conducted a foray into country he knew well from his experiences there in the previous year. Hampton forded the Rappahannock with 158 Carolinians and Georgians and a small detachment from the legion. He surprised the enemy pickets at Hartwood Church and captured over 100 horses and ninety-two Yankee prisoners. There were no casualties on the Confederate side. Lee was elated over Hampton's success.[13] In a letter to his wife on 29 November, William D. Harris witnessed the results of Hampton's Hartwood Church raid: "This

---

[10] Ibid.

[11] Governor's Horse Guards in Pennsylvania, Confederate Union, Milledgeville, GA, for Tuesday, 4 November 1862, 3, col. 2; OR, ser. 1, vol. 14/2 [S#28], *The Civil War* CD-ROM, *The War of the Rebellion* (Cincinnati OH: Guild Press Emmis Books, 2000).

[12] Ibid.

[13] OR, ser. 1, vol. 14/2 [S#28], Lee stated: "His expedition was eminently successful, and accomplished without other loss than the wounding of 1 man. He obtained many remounts for his cavalry and artillery, and deserves much credit for his prudence and enterprise."

leaves me in tolerable health. I have no news in camp save that a scouting party of our Brigade brought in 80 Yankees, horses and arms on yesterday that they captured some 15 or 20 miles from camp with that exception everything is quiet in Camp."[14]

Twelve through 15 December 1862 marked a disastrous period for the Union infantry forces under General Burnside at Fredericksburg. The Yanks suffered one of the worst defeats of the Civil War as Burnside launched charge after charge against the Rebel forces behind the stone wall at Mary's Heights. (See chapter 9 of *To Honor These Men: A History of the Phillips Georgia Legion Infantry Battalion*). Hampton decided on another raid on 19 December while the Federals dug in for the winter just north of the Rappahannock. Yankee horsemen patrolled the Telegraph Road intensively, but the Carolina troopers surprised one picket after another and captured forty-eight Northerners. A regiment of Federal cavalry appeared on the scene and forced Hampton to turn back from Occoquan but not before he had successfully captured 150 prisoners and twenty wagons loaded with delicacies. Eighty legion troopers under Major W. B. C. Puckett engaged the Yankees in the 19 December raid.[15]

At year's end a colorful raid on Dumfries and Fairfax Station, Virginia, caused real embarrassment for the Lincoln administration. In a letter dated 3 January 1862 to his wife, Captain John F. Milhollin shared his adventures:

I was on an eight days scout we left camp 25 December and returned 1 January '63. We went all round the Yankees in 12 miles of Washington City—General Stuart sent a dispatch from Burk Station [some seven miles this side Alexandria City] to President Lincoln that he had taken charge of the...and C. O. - C. [Covington & Ohio Railroad Co.] I did not see Abe's reply—we

---

[14] W. Harris to My Dear Wife from Madison County, VA, 29 November 1862.

[15] Boatner, *Civil War Dictionary*, 43; W. Blackford, *The War Years With Jeb Stuart* (New York: Charles Scribner's Sons, 1945) 101–105; OR, ser. 1, vol. 14/2, [S#28]; M. Wellman, *Giant in Gray* (New York: Charles Scribner's Sons, 1949) 101.

then went within a short distance of Fairfax C. H. at which place a large force of infantry were camped Stuart and Hampton and the two generals Lee had a number of campfires built the Yankees sent a truce flag to know if we were Rebels or Yankees. General Stuart replied that they would find [out] at daybreak next morning who were there and then marched off—the Yankees then shelled the campfires while we marched on—we marched all night—I often found myself asleep on my horse—as you will have the full account of the same in the Standard [*The Cartersville Standard and Express*] I will not give it we sent our prisoners to Richmond 250 or 300.[16]

The last good year for the Confederacy, 1862, finally ended. The coming year would bring death and misery for families of both sides at two previously little-known sites: one in Virginia at a crossroads and country inn called Chancellorsville and the other in a Pennsylvania town known as Gettysburg.

---

[16] J. Milhollin to My Dear Wife from Camps, 3 January 1863, OR, ser. 1, vol. 21 [S#31], also see Robert C. Black III, *The Railroads of the Confederacy* (Chapel Hill: University of North Carolina Press, 1998) 163. Burkes Station was named after Silas Burke (1796–1854), a nineteenth-century farmer, merchant, and local politician who built a house on a hill overlooking the valley of Pohick Creek in approximately 1824. See http://en/wikipedia.org/wiki/Covington_and Ohio Railroad.

4

FIND US SOME HORSES

"Gen Stewart [sic] *had a fight one day last week; they worsted him the first day."*[1]

It was New Years day 1863, and the commander of legion cavalry Company B, Captain John Fielding Milhollin, must have been in high spirits The thirty-one-year-old officer and his Johnson's Rangers compatriots had just returned from an eight-day scout with his commander, Major General James Ewell Brown Stuart. They had captured many Yankee prisoners and even sent a humiliating message complaining about the quality of captured mules to President Lincoln. They were cocksure, confident of their coming success in combat.[2]

The morale of the ragtag Confederate army was improving and would be at its pinnacle after the battle of Chancellorsville. The good mood distracted them from concern for their rumbling stomachs. During their three-month winter quarters, the horsemen and foot soldiers entertained themselves with regimental theatricals and minstrel shows as well as prayer meetings, which were a part of the religious revival that seemed to mesmerize the soldiers throughout the Rebel army. They organized (with near-combat enthusiasm) brigade-sized snowball fights and had glorious fun. The Confederates had fought in over thirteen battles and skirmishes. General Ambrose Burnside had been totally humiliated at Fredericksburg, relieved by Lincoln on 25 January and replaced by General "Fighting Joe" Hooker. The future seemed bright for the Rebels. General Wade Hampton's Brigade, along with the Phillips legion, had camped near Culpeper Court House and manned freezing picket posts along the upper Rappahannock River and easterly toward Alexandria. Swan expressed his confidence in a letter to his wife dated 12 January 1863: "Dear Bettie, I have no news to write to you much. We

---

[1] J. Swan to Dear Betty from Camp Rockingham, VA, 23 March 1863.

[2] D. Hopkins, *The Little Jeff* (Shippensburg PA: White Mane Books, 1999) 119; also see Sparkman Diary, US National Military Park, Manassas, VA.

are not doing very much now but Picket; the army is still now. Some thinks we will have peace in a short time, and I can't think myself it can last much longer. It is the general opinion that we will have an Armistus [*sic*] of five or six months and if we can get that I think we will have Peace sooner and then we can all go home like people ought to live."[3]

A few bad omens haunted the legion troopers: recruiting shortages because of the harsh terms of the Conscription Act and lack of suitable mounts. The legion troopers heard constant rumors that there would be a short period of recruiting and then Hampton's brigade would be reassigned to North Carolina. For the moment, the latter proved to be only rumor.

Meanwhile, enemy forces planned to resume the offensive in early February. General Meade instructed General Franz Sigel to send a reconnaissance party on the following day to Rappahannock Station near Morrisville by way of the Falmouth and Warrenton road. Sigel posted one brigade near Grove Church near the turn-offs to Ellis's and Kelly's fords. Another brigade proceeded to the crossing of Deep Run and one more to Hartwood Church. Yankee general Sigel fired the Orange and Alexandria Railroad Bridge and picketed all fords. Elements of units from Massachusetts, New Hampshire, New Jersey, New York, and Pennsylvania, as well as regular artillery units of the United States Army, participated in this expedition. A heavy snowfall interfered with the success of the operation, but the Yankees pushed on by 5 February. Unfortunately, they collided with the Confederate horsemen of General Wade Hampton's Brigade. Fighting raged around the Orange and Alexandria Railroad Bridge on 7 February. The Yankee riders had moved up on the Marsh Road during the previous two days. Three of their brigades had camped near Grove Church while a cavalry unit settled at Kelly's Mills with but one gun. The Yanks attacked Hampton's pickets at the bridge and attempted to destroy it but failed. As night came on, some of the Federals insinuated themselves and, hiding behind the abutments, cut some of the posts and attempt to burn them. The Confederate pickets hunched down in their rifle pits and held their ground. By two in the morning, it was all over. Hampton could not give chase because of the pitiful condition of the horses but drove the Yanks

---

[3] J. Swann to Dear Wife from Camp near Culpeper, VA, 12 January 1863.

off and suffered only one wounded rider. Hampton's troopers, which included elements of the legion cavalry, captured twenty-five Yanks and killed six. This minor affair served notice to the Union forces in the area that they could expect more of the same was in the future.[4]

Swan reported his impressions of events in a letter to his wife on 7 February 1863. He was probably not involved in the fight:

I think the prospect is not so good for peace as it has been. They are looking for Gen. Hooker to make a move as soon as the wether [sic] will admit of it. The roads is so bad now it is impossible for either side to make a move though the Yanks are reported to be about 12 miles from here this morning down below Stephensburg. Gen. Hamton [sic] is gone down to look after them. I think we will move from here soon. Some say we will go to Hanover Junction about 20 miles from Richmond; some say we will go the N.C. coast. I think we will go to the coast.[5]

While General J. E. B. Stuart was busying himself with finding accurate intelligence and skirmishing with the Federal enemy along the line of the upper Rappahannock during the Chancellorsville campaign, and earlier, at Kelly's Ford, General Wade Hampton's Brigade with the legion cavalry searched for fresh mounts in southern Virginia. The

---

[4] OR, ser. 1, vol. 25/1 [S#39], 5–7 February 1863, Operations at Rappahannock Bridge and Grove Church, VA; also Dyer's Compendium, Pt. 2 (Campaigns, etc.); also see OR ser. 1, vol. 25/2 [S#40], Geo. G. Meade to Maj. Gen. Franz Sigel: "General: In compliance with orders from the headquarters Army of the Potomac, I enclose copies of the instructions received this P.M. from the commanding general, in regard to a reconnaissance ordered to be made to Rappahannock Station. I have also to add that I have ordered on this reconnaissance tomorrow two regiments of cavalry and a battery of artillery, and to support them I shall advance a division of infantry on the Falmouth and Warrenton road, posting one brigade in the vicinity of Grove Church [where the roads to Ellis and Kelly's Fords turn off], another brigade at the crossing of Deep Run, and the third at Hartwood Church. I have also placed under the command of the division commander a regiment of cavalry, with which he will picket all the fords and approaches to them, from the United States to Kelly's Ford."

[5] J. Swan to Dear Bettie from Culpeper C.H., VA, 7 February 1863; also see Hopkins, The Little Jeff, 81.

shortage of suitable horses would only worsen.[6] The fight at Kelly's Ford on 17 March accomplished little. The Federal cavalry outnumbered the Confederate troopers. After an all-day brawl, the Yanks had fewer casualties than the Rebels. The gallant artillerist Major John Pelham's death spread despair in the ranks. By 23 March, Swan had heard about the Kelly's Ford fight. In a letter to his spouse, he commented: "Gen. Stewart had a fight one day last week; they worsted him the first day. They cut the 1St & 2nd Va cavalry all to smash; killed and taken about half of them but we run them back the next day."[7]

The weather improved considerably by early April. It was still cold but at least the snow and rain that stopped Hampton's troopers hovered stubbornly over the Virginia interior through much of April. The two generals Lee held a long picket line from Chesapeake Bay to the Blue Ridge Mountains. General Robert E. Lee established his headquarters near Fredericksburg, facing the Federal army across the Rappahannock River.[8]

Hampton rejoined Stuart in May 1863 in time to confront Union general George Stoneman during the Chancellorsville campaign. Stoneman, anxious to establish his troopers as the equal of Stuart's Dragoons, commanded the newly established Federal Cavalry Corps. From 9 April to 8 May 1863, General Hooker ordered Stoneman to operate in advance Hooker's planned turning movement and raid Lee's lines of communications. Stoneman's cavalry outnumbered Stuart's by a three-to-one ratio, or roughly 11,500 Yankee horsemen to 3,500 rebel riders. Hooker's plan involved placing 60,000 Union infantry and artillery in Lee's immediate front to block Lee's retreat while his cavalry battered his lines of supply and communications in his rear. Lee had achieved success by splitting his forces, so why could not Joe Hooker do the same? Stoneman proved to be a disappointment to both "Fighting Joe" and Lincoln. Mother Nature, the harshest of enemies, foiled his best intentions. A pounding rainstorm turned the roads to mud the consistency

---

[6] S. Foote, *The Civil War: A Narrative: Fredericksburg to Meridian* (New York: Random House, 1963) 245–47; M. Wellman, *Giant in Gray* (New York: Charles Scribner's Sons, 1949) 105.

[7] J. Swan to Dear Bettie from Camp Rockingham, VA, 23 March 1863.

[8] Hopkins, *The Little Jeff*, 121.

of pudding and halted the rolling stock. The vicious weather stalled Stoneman for the next few weeks. When the Yanks finally started and attempted a crossing of the Rappahannock River, Stuart's cavalry thwarted them. By April's end, the blue riders crossed in spite of opposition from the butternuts. Union general Alfred Pleasonton replaced Stoneman on 3 May. Hooker destroyed the James Canal and part of the Virginia Central Railroad from the South Anna River to Richmond as well as a section of the Fredericksburg Railroad. The Yankees suffered few casualties, but in spite of their best work, Stuart's cavalry found Hooker's exposed flank. The Rebels acted on this intelligence and damaged the Federals severely at the battle of Chancellorsville.[9] The legion troopers marched to Pennsylvania a few weeks later. Less than a hundred years earlier, James Getty of Scots-Irish heritage inherited 116 acres of land from his tavern-owner father Samuel Getty. James, an entrepreneur, organized his property into 210 lots. By 1785, settlers occupied enough of Getty's lots to create a new town, named Gettysburg after its founder.[10] The men of the legion cavalry had no idea that they would soon take their place in history while fighting in and around this small settlement—founded with such hard work and hope, such enterprise—only to be nearly demolished by two marauding armies in early July 1863 in an orgy of violence unparalleled in American history.

---

[9] Ibid.

[10] M. Boatner., *The Civil War Dictionary*, rev. ed. (Bel Air CA: David McKay Co., 1987) 803; also conversation between Richard M. Coffman and Sara Edmiston, reference librarian of the Adams County Public Library, Gettysburg, Pennsylvania.

5

ROUGH ROADS TO GETTYSBURG

"Whither have ye made a road today?"

*"We have been through a great deal of hardship and hard
fighting since we have been here."*[1]

General Stuart left the legion cavalry with Hampton's brigade behind to
hold the line farther south, posting vedettes along the south side of the
Rappahannock, and to rejoin Stuart after 20 June. The legion skirmished
this same day near Warrenton. Hugh Buchanan described the fight: "On
the same day on Sunday near Warrentown when on the march, we met a
squad of Yankee cavalry. Our company and Thomas's Company
[Company F] charged them and captured twenty-three men with their
arms and horses. Nobody hurt on our side. We are now with the Brigade
and on very active service indeed."[2]

Swan's account of this action differed from Buchanan's in that he
mentioned taking "2 prisinors, one Zouave."[3] Perhaps he is referring to
prisoners taken by his company and not the entire brigade.

The brigades of Major General Fitzhugh Lee and Brigadier General
W. H. F. (Rooney) Lee were screening Longstreet's right flank as he
rode from Culpeper to the Blue Ridge Mountains. One of Fitz Lee's
brigades under Brigadier General Thomas Taylor Munford and a brigade
of Rooney Lee's under Brigadier General John Randolph Chambliss, Jr.,
were on their way to occupy a gap in the Bull Run Mountains at Aldie.
Chambliss headed toward Thoroughfare Gap while Robertson halted in
place at Rectortown. Later that afternoon Union general Pleasonton
reached the town of Aldie. His force included Kilpatrick's brigade of

---

[1] W. Harris to Dear Wife, 9 July 1863, from Maryland.

[2] H. Buchanan to Dear Mary, 24 June 1863, from Loudon County, VA.

[3] J. Swan to Dear Bettie, 20 June 1863 from camp on the Rappahannock,
VA.

Gregg's division. One of the first major fights of the Gettysburg campaign occurred on 17 June 1863 around Aldie. This tiny settlement was founded in 1807 and named after Aldie Castle in Perthshire, Scotland.[4] In a charge of flashing sabers and hand-to-hand fighting, the fighting began in earnest as the Confederate pickets were pushed back and Rosser's Fifth Virginia pushed the Federals back in turn. Four hours of fighting continued with the Unionists attacking in mounted and dismounted modes. Finally, Munford was forced to withdraw. Union casualties were around three times those of the Confederates. The First Rhode Island Cavalry, commanded by Union colonel Alfred Nattie Duffie, suffered near-annihilation on the same day at nearby Middleburg. Duffie had been ordered by General Judson Kilpatrick to push ahead through Thoroughfare Gap to Middleburg. Simultaneously, Gregg was to advance on Aldie. Duffle succeeded in routing Stuart and his entourage out of Aldie and was promptly surrounded by the units of Munford, Robertson, and Chambliss. Duffie, a Union officer of French birth, lost 268 men. By dark, the mounted assaults by regiments and squadrons finally ended with inconclusive results.[5]

General Stuart had amassed Robertson's, Chambliss's, and Rooney Lee's brigades at Middleburgh on 18 June 1863. The pickets he posted in the east were pushed in, but fortunately the Yankees didn't try to snare them. The Federals attacked Stuart and he withdrew to the west and camped near Middleburg, near Upperville.[6]

Sometime during the next few days, Hampton skirmished with the Federals near Warrenton while trying to locate Stuart. His brigade camped at Rector's Cross Roads, close to Upperville. Swan described his experience near Warrenton in a letter:

---

[4] E. Scheel, in *Loudon Times*, 22 January 1976.

[5] E. Longacre, *The Cavalry at Gettysburg* (Lincoln: University of Nebraska Press, 1986) 90–92, 109–13, 119; also E. Longacre, *Lee's Cavalrymen* (Mechanicsburg PA: Stackpole Books, 2002) 193–94, 199; D. Hopkins, *The Little Jeffs* (Shippensburg PA: White Mane Books, 1999) 133.

[6] Middleburgh (VA) Library, "Forming Upperville," 1. This oddly named place was created in 1797 by Joseph Carr and called Carr Town. Records are not clear on the change of name to Upperville, but it may derive from the fact that present-day Upperville is "up" from Middleburgh, which is the midway point from Alexandria and Winchester.

I guess you have heard of our raid by this time, we have had some hard times and some very good. I will now tell you a little about our trip as much as I can think of. It was such a round I can't recollect all but I recollect very well every fight I was in. We started from Brandy Station 21st June [probably a day earlier] and went on by Warrenton and down to a little town called New Baltimore. There we jumped a squad of about 100 Yanks as soon as we saw them about 100 of us drawn our sabers and put out after them as hard as our horses could go. We run them about 4 miles. The head of our column was in about 100 yds of them you ought to seen them get beating there horses with their sabers every hill they went up they would wheel and fire on us but we never stopped until they got in about 1 mile of their camp and taken the woods and got behind trees and there they tried to stop us agin but failed. We did not have anything to do there & we then went on to Mouth Minster [probably Westminster] and got many things— oats, bacon and a little whiskey. They knocked the head of a barrel and I got my canteen full. It went right well.[7]

Upperville was a sleepy hamlet in 1863. It had one street with a few scraggly shade trees and several boxy houses. The village nestled between tributaries of Goose Creek. A road from the east ran into the town, undulating between stone walls and proceeding to Ashby's Gap. A few fields north of the town were also bordered by stone walls. The hamlet abutted another road from Union near Snicker's Gap.[8] Hampton

---

[7] J. Swan to Dear Bettie, n.d.; also see OR, ser. 1, vol. 27/3, [S# 45] from *The Civil War* CD-ROM (Cincinnati OH: Guild Press Emmis Books) in a letter from Jul. Stahel at Gainsville, VA, to General Butterfield, 23 June 1863: "The whole rebel cavalry passed through Warrenton during Thursday and Friday last, and was only a portion of Hampton's division called Phillips Legion, which was in front of New Baltimore on Sunday, and had the skirmish with a portion of the Eighth Pennsylvania Cavalry which is now attached to General Hancock's command." Also see Robert F. O'Neill, *The Cavalry Battles of Aldie, Middleburg and Upperville: Small but Important Riots*, (Lynchburg VA: H. E. Howard, Inc., 1993) 165.

[8] Hopkins, *The Little Jeffs*, 138–39.

linked up with Stuart on 20 June. Stuart's next step was to assign Chambliss and Jones to the north near Union and Robertson with Hampton close to Upperville. Stuart's strategy called for a slow withdrawal toward the Blue Ridge Mountains and maintaining his cavalry at Upperville.[9]

J. E. B. Stuart was a devout Christian and hoped to spend 21 June, a Sunday, quietly, perhaps pondering otherworldly matters. Union lieutenant William D. Fuller's cannon, of Gregg's command, disrupted Stuart's pious mood for the day. Fuller's goal was to clear a path for Colonel Strong Vincent's Brigade, marksmen of the Sixteenth Michigan, the Forty-fourth New York, and the Twentieth Maine. All of these Federal units were to enfilade Stuart's right. The attack was successful: Stuart's troopers headed for Upperville. Yankee general Pleasonton was pleased—so far. The road was emptied. Judson Kilpatrick's Brigade could now attack.

Hampton's gunner, James Hart, blasted the Federals with canister but lost one of his Blakely rifles. Rebel troops leapfrogged around each other and headed toward the rear, doing their best to delay the bluecoats. It was no use. The Yankees managed to muscle Stuart's cavalrymen closer to Upperville. Robertson's brigade was pushed back while attempting to hold the pike and fields near the town. It was forced to withdraw through Upperville with Hampton's Brigade as his rear guard. The men of the legion cavalry were busy escorting their wagons through town while Hampton's remaining four regiments settled on either side of the turnpike. There was no letup as Buford's blue troopers smashed into Robertson's Brigade on the west side of the tiny village. Undeterred, all of Hampton's regiments pushed on but were shoved back. Hampton tried again twice. The second time, his men crashed head-on into the enemy troopers in Upperville itself. Graycoats and Yankees slashed at each other with sabers and fired their pistols and carbines at point-blank range, all punctuated by shouted obscenities and the crackling of firearms.[10]

When the battle finally ended, the Rebels and Yankees installed themselves on each side of Upperville. The tiny town was strewn with

---

[9] H. McClellan, *The Campaigns of Stuart's Cavalry* (Secaucus, NY: Blue & Gray Press, 1993) 30.
[10] Hopkins, *The Little Jeffs*, 141.

dead animals and men. Stuart headed toward Ashby's Gap. The Federals remained in control of the field. Both sides were able to tend to their wounded and bury their dead on the following morning. General Stuart found his troopers in the same position they were in before the three fights at Aldie, Middleburg, and Upperville. Stuart praised Hampton in his report.[11] On 22 June, the following day, the legion cavalry camped near Rector's Cross Roads along with the remainder of Stuart's battered cavalry troopers.[12]

Lee gave Stuart more than the usual latitude in his orders for his mission at Gettysburg. This was just as Stuart wanted it. His first task was to link up with Ewell's infantry near York, Pennsylvania. Lee ordered Stuart to leave two brigades to keep an eye on the Blue Ridge Mountain passes if the Yankees decided to head north from Virginia. This, Lee hoped, would stop them from attacking the rear of his army. The remainder, Hampton's, Fitz Lee's, and Chambliss's brigades, would ride with Stuart.[13] Stuart moved his cavalry to Salem, Virginia. They stayed there until the morning of 25 June, when they departed around 1:00 A.M. Stuart's march began in a blinding rainstorm and a maneuver to avoid Federal infantry near Gum Springs. When they arrived at Fairfax Court House, the legion with Hampton's Brigade ran into the Eleventh New York Cavalry. Stuart was nearly captured before Hampton's troopers beat off the Yankees. Because the horses were exhausted, Hampton stopped for a short time to feed the animals then moved ahead to Dranesville, where they were lucky enough to stumble onto sutler's stores. Stuart's troopers gorged themselves and frolicked over other items, such as gloves and new boots.[14] By early evening 27 June, Hampton's Brigade, now in the van, was situated on the Potomac River at Rowser's Ford near Seneca Creek. In spite of the mile-wide river, the troopers were able to cross and avoid confrontation with any marauding Federals. They destroyed around thirty canal boats on the Chesapeake and Ohio Canal and captured over 300 Federals. Hampton

---

[11] OR, Armies, vol. 27, pt. 2, 690; also see Hopkins, *The Little Jeffs*, 143.

[12] Ibid.

[13] Longacre, *Lee's Cavalrymen*, 154.

[14] E. Thomas, *Bold Dragoon: The Life of J. E. B. Stuart* (New York: Harper & Row, 1986) 242.

stayed in the van to Rockville, Maryland, where his troopers battered a small Federal unit.[15] By noontime, most of Stuart's troopers were settled around Rockville. Just five miles away, Hampton's men found a train of wagons and drove off the wagoneers, pursuing and capturing most of them.

A major change occurred in the Federal army around this time: Major General George Gordon Meade replaced General Joseph Hooker.[16]

Stuart continued the march. On 29 June, Fitz Lee, heading northward from Cookesville ahead of Stuart's main body, came upon the Baltimore and Ohio Railroad while near Sykesville. Here, they destroyed track and telegraph lines. The rest of Stuart's brigades joined in the destruction the next day. Later the same day, the Confederates headed toward Westminster, arriving in the afternoon when the First Delaware Cavalry attacked them. The Federals took a beating, losing thirty prisoners. Stuart's Confederates camped at Westminster.[17]

Stuart's intelligence was inadequate. He did not know exactly where the Confederate army was located as it moved toward Gettysburg. He was unaware that he himself was somewhere in the center of the Federal army. His scouts did learn that Kilpatrick was only seven miles away at Littlestown, Pennsylvania. Both Stuart and Kilpatrick were searching for Ewell's army for different reasons. After a five-mile march, Stuart entered Pennsylvania and continued on toward Hanover. On approaching the outskirts of Hanover with Fitz Lee's Brigade to the left, Stuart saw the Yankee troopers already passing through the town. About this time, the Second North Carolina of Chambliss's Brigade ran into the rear guard of the Yankee riders. Hampton, with the legion, was encumbered by the captured wagons and not able to repulse a Yankee attack, but later in the day was able to unload the wagons and dislodge the Yankees. Fitz Lee was then able to move up and join the fight where they were heavily engaged by Brigadier General George Armstrong Custer's Michiganders. Stuart pushed his troopers on in an exhausting night march on 30 June

---

[15] Ibid., 146.

[16] M. Boatner, *The Civil War Dictionary*, rev. ed. (New York: David McKay Co., 1987) 409.

[17] Hopkins, *The Little Jeffs*, 147.

toward York, Pennsylvania. Passing through Jefferson, they grabbed every horse they came upon, paying hapless civilians with Confederate currency.

Unknown to Stuart, the Confederate infantry had already made their way through York, so he continued on west to Dover and arrived on 1 July. He left around noon and went on toward Carlisle, just north of Gettysburg. Later in the evening, he shelled Carlisle. He demanded surrender, but militia of Union general William F. Smith stubbornly refused, so Stuart burned the barracks and depot. About this time, Lee's couriers found Stuart. Lee directed Stuart to move by way of Heidlersburg and Hunterstown, the latter only five miles from Gettysburg. Later in the afternoon, Hampton heard from Stuart. He was to push his troopers in a circuitous route to Heidlersburg and arrive just behind Stuart's main body. All of Stuart's brigades would then head south on the Heidlersburg-Gettysburg Road. Hampton's Brigade was detached after passing Heidlersburg and ordered east to Hunterstown, where it arrived in the late afternoon. At the same moment, Stuart was in Gettysburg reporting to General Robert E. Lee. Some sources suggest that Lee was furious over Stuart's absence and upbraided him.

Longacre disagrees with these sources.[18] When Lee's and Stuart's meeting adjourned, Lee gave Stuart his orders for 3 July. Stuart was to circle north of Gettysburg toward the right rear of Meade's army and then take the offensive.[19]

General Wade Hampton could see the steeples of Gettysburg around 4:00 P.M. A courier found the general with orders from Stuart to return to Hunterstown and deal with the blue cavalry that was certain to be there and ready for a fight. When Hampton arrived back at Hunterstown, no Yankee riders were on hand to greet him, but they appeared in force as Hampton was departing the premises. With the boy-general George Custer in the lead, the bluecoats slammed into Colonel P. M. B. Young's troopers. A nasty fight began as Young countercharged the Federals. Hampton moved quickly, stationing Cobb's Legion in the center of the road with the legion cavalry on the right, the First South Carolina in the

---

[18] Longacre, *Lee's Cavalrymen*, 216.

[19] M. Wellman, *Giant in Gray* (New York: Charles Scribner's Sons, 1949) 116.

center, the First North Carolina on its left, and the Jeff Davis Legion on the right of the First North Carolina. The brawling seesawed back and forth, finally concluding at sundown. The Federals left the area around 11:00 P.M. While Hampton's men were battling the Federals, Stuart stationed his last two brigades on the banks of Rock Creek just to the west of Hampton's camp.

Lee's battle strategy at this time involved attacks by Ewell's and Longstreet's infantries on the Federal right and center. Lee ordered Stuart to position his 6,000 troopers well beyond the Federal right flank. Stuart was now equipped with Hampton's, Fitz Lee's, Rooney Lee's, and A. G. Jenkins's brigades as well as elements of C. A. Green's Louisiana Guard Battery of Mounted Artillery. Stuart was to interfere with an expected Yankee retreat.[20]

On the morning of 3 July 1863, Hampton's riders had moved back toward Hunterstown and were ready with ample ammunition. He was to join Stuart on the York Pike. Hampton found Stuart's men at Daniel Stallsmith's farm on the north of Cress Ridge. Stuart placed Hampton on the right, then Chambliss on Hampton's left, followed by Stuart and Jenkins' brigade under Colonel Milton J. Ferguson. Jenkins had been wounded the previous day. Stuart had one cannon shot fired at this time followed by the roar of cannonading on Meade's center, which was preparatory to an attack by Rebel general George Pickett's 12,500 infantry. Stuart focused his attention on a grassy plain around the Hanover-Low Dutch Road junction. Yankee troops moved forward toward the Rummel Farm, which was northwest of the crossroads. Stuart's men held up the bluecoats, pinning them down. The Rebel troopers were forced to retire. Fighting began again at around 2:00 P.M. Fitz Lee was now on the Cress Ridge with his entire brigade. He attacked immediately but was forced to pull back when confronted with superior numbers and firepower. At this point, Federals under the brigades of McIntosh and Custer pushed forward against Stuart's troopers and the fight increased in intensity with swarms of blue and gray men battering each other.[21]

---

[20] Hopkins, *The Little Jeffs*, 150–51.
[21] Longacre, *Lee's Cavalrymen*, 219–20.

Fitz Lee then launched a mounted attack on Federals hunkering down behind a split rail fence. Custer's Michiganders crashed into the Rebels head-on. The Rebels, the First Virginia, were forced back with Custer in pursuit who, in turn, was flanked by two of Wade Hampton's brigades. Vicious brawling continued until the Ninth and Thirteenth Virginia forced Custer's men into retreat.

Hampton was in pain from wounds received at Hunterstown but was in high spirits—until he noted the remainder of his brigade departing their positions at Cress Ridge and advancing. Hampton's adjutant, Captain T. G. Barker, was the culprit. He had mistakenly ordered Lieutenant Colonel Twiggs's First South Carolina, Major Thomas J. Lipscomb's Second South Carolina, and the legion cavalry under Lieutenant Colonel William W. Rich all to proceed to Hampton's side. Too late to be called back, the gray riders charged ahead only to be met by a countercharge by Custer's First Michigan. The horsemen headed toward each other and collided with extreme force, resulting in somersaulting horses and horribly injured riders. Nevertheless, those who survived recovered and engaged their enemies in hand-to-hand fighting. At first, Hampton's men had the advantage, but soon other Federals arrived and joined the fray. A squadron of Pennsylvanians hit the Rebel left. Yankee troopers of Gregg's First New Jersey also smashed the Rebel left flank. Hampton himself received a ball in the thigh and a saber slash to his head. A half hour later both sides pulled apart, leaving countless dead and wounded men and horses. By 4:00 P.M., General Robert E. Lee's attack on Cemetery Ridge had failed, and the Yankee generals were certain they had won a signal victory against Stuart's horsemen.[22]

Independence Day, 4 July 1863, arrived with drenching rain showers, which only added to the sour mood of Stuart's horsemen. Stuart had been ordered to begin the movement back to the Potomac River and pushed his battered Rebels over Seminary Ridge. He was to screen the withdrawal of two wagon trains. Stuart appointed Brigadier General John D. Imboden to safeguard the larger train for the trek back to Virginia. This plan was fraught with danger. The Confederates were to proceed to Cashtown, then Greencastle, Williamsport, and on to the Potomac.

---

[22] Ibid., 222.

Stuart's brigades would cover the left flank of the column while two of its brigades held mountain passes on the east. Kilpatrick's division set out in hot pursuit. Its commander had learned that a Rebel-held wagon train was approaching Fairfield Gap. They galloped west and reached Jack Mountain by evening. This small train, conducted by Ewell, had already passed by, so Kilpatrick pursued in hopes of finding the wagons on the other side of the mountain. Brigadier General William Edmonson "Grumble" Jones battered part of Kilpatrick's command while the rest, near Monterey Pass, met a portion of the First Maryland battalion. This small group of twenty Marylanders under Captain G. M. Emack was able to stop a far larger group of Yankees for over five hours. The Unionists finally caught up with the Southerners, destroyed dozens of the wagons, and took several prisoners. Emack managed to save the majority of the wagons. Jones's Brigade arrived and chased off civilian vandals and Yankee troops.[23]

Lieutenant Colonel William Wofford Rich, commander of the legion cavalry battalion, wrote with optimism to his wife on 5 July 1863:

> We are now guarding the eastern flank of the army as we return to our lines after the great battle in Pennsylvania. The Legion fought well and covered themselves with honor. I led charge after charge against the Union cavalry and not once were we compelled to retire until they brought up the infantry against which no cavalry could advance. The Union cavalry which [will] approach us on our return to Va. [will] quickly retire when we draw up in line of battle. I will write again soon.[24]

Imboden's larger train twisted through the tortuous mountain passes and turned west at Cashtown. Kilpatrick had abandoned his position, freeing Stuart to push ahead toward Williamsport by way of Hagerstown. Imboden reached Williamsport in the afternoon of 5 July ahead of Stuart and was met by the forces of Yankee general John Buford on the afternoon of 6 July. Imboden's guns went into action. They consisted of four cannons of Eshelman's battery with two rifles and two twelve-pounder howitzers recently assigned to Hart's battery. Another battery

---

[23] Longacre, *The Cavalry at Gettysburg*, 250.
[24] W. Rich to Dearest Basheba, 4 July 1863.

45

went into position facing north along the Greencastle Road, while the cannon attached to Imboden's own brigade, the Virginia battery of Captain J. H. McClanahan, took post on both flanks of the river.[25] All these guns blasted away at the astonished Buford, and he was able to capture only a few wagons. Buford, with Kilpatrick, abandoned his positions upon learning that Fitz Lee was near Williamsport.

W. D. Harris described his travails from his Williamsport camp in a letter to his wife dated 9 July 1863:

> I sit down this morning after a fatiguing trip into Pennsylvania of twice this week, to let you know a little of the news. We have been through a great deal of hardship and hard fighting since we have been here. We have been fighting ever since we have been over here and lost a great many men, although we have killed a sight of Yankees. Our battalion has suffered severely. We lost five men yesterday killed and several wounded severely. The killed is Alfred Allen, Albert Gains, Joe Ingrew, John Waters, Joe Ray, Sgt. R. Bailey. The wounded are Capt.Dunlap, Lt. Evans, Sgt. Avant, Pearing Brown, Gus Roberts, Frank Cole, Clayton Hood, and the fight is still going on. Allen and Bailey were shot through the head. We are all well at present, although G. Chastain is ill.[26]

Stuart had battled with Kilpatrick at Hagerstown, prevented him from reinforcing Imboden. Stuart's men suffered numerous casualties but Stuart, joined by Jones's Brigade, pushed all of Kilpatrick's blue riders out of Hagerstown. By 7 July, the rear of the Rebel army had reached Hagerstown, a few miles from Williamsport. General Robert E. Lee was busy building a pontoon bridge while waiting for the rain-swollen and high-rising Potomac River to recede. He was able to ferry bridge-building materials across as well as pioneer parties to complete the bridge. Stuart was assigned the job of keeping marauding Yankees from interfering with the bridge and the crossing. Over the next week, blue and gray riders fought several inconclusive skirmishes at Hagerstown, Boonsboro, and Funkstown. Stuart was able to protect Lee's infantry

---

[25] Longacre, *Lee's Cavalrymen*, 229–30.

[26] W. Harris to Dear Wife, 9 July 1863, from camp near Williamsport.

from Hagerstown to the Potomac River. Stubbornly, Buford continued harassing Stuart's cavalry for the next few days.

Stuart continued his protective screen on 13 July. The fording and crossing of the Potomac got underway. On the morning of 14 July, Stuart received word to go ahead and cross behind the infantry. A couple of his regiments crossed on pontoons at Falling Waters, but most forded at Williamsport. Most of the Southern cavalry were on the Virginia side by the early morning of 14 July. The last of the gray riders under Fitz Lee were over by around 8:00 A.M.[27]

Sources available to determine casualties for the Gettysburg campaign are often confusing, but it is clear that the riders of the legion cavalry suffered severely as the following data suggest: Company A: two captured, two WIA, one POW; Company B: two captured, one WIA, one POW, one KIA, one died later of dysentery; Company C: two captured, three WIA, one exchanged, two POW, two KIA, one MWIA; Company D: one surrendered later at Greensboro, three captured, two WIA, one exchanged, one POW; Company E: four captured, four WIA, three exchanged, one died of natural causes; Company F: one WIA. Sergeant Jesse W. Avant of Company E was wounded and credited for saving the life of his commander, Captain S. S. Dunlap, and later promoted to lieutenant for his bravery.[28]

The soldiers listed below never appeared on a legion muster roll but are men mentioned in Federal prisoner of war records. Errors may account for this, or the men many have given their captors false names, or they could be troopers who joined in late 1862 or early 1863 and never appeared in legion records because the muster rolls from September 1862 to November 1863 have been lost.

George Chance of Company E, captured at Gettysburg on 3 July 1863 and sent to Point Lookout, no further record; T. J. Chatham, captured at Gettysburg 3 July 1863, died at Point Lookout in 1863; J. E. Franklin, captured at Gettysburg 3 July 1863, exchanged from Point Lookout 18 September 1864; P. A. Harris, WIA and captured at

[27] Hopkins, *The Little Jeffs*, 159.

[28] Compiled Service Records of Confederate Soldiers who Served in Organizations from the State of Georgia, Record Group 109, War Department Collection of Confederate Records, M266-; Reels 592–600.

Gettysburg on 3 July 1863, lost arm and sent to provost, no further record; Company F; R. F. Dale, captured at Fairfield on 3 July 1863, exchanged from Point Lookout on 18 February 1865; Thomas W. Jenkins, captured at Gettysburg 3 July 1863, took oath of allegiance in 1863, and joined Third Maryland (US) cavalry as a "Galvanized Yankee."[29]

A frustrated General George Armstrong Custer fired a useless few cannon volleys while Lee's men cut the pontoon bridge away. The exhausted Confederates must have breathed a collective sigh of relief. They were home again and away from the past two weeks' nightmare. They were going home to recuperate, heal their physical and spiritual wounds, and await the next bloodletting.

---

[29] Federal Prisoner of War Records.

6

I USED TO THROW MY PILLOW OUT ON THE FLOOR AT NIGHT

"J. R. Sewell was very badly wounded—the ball entered the right side of his face and came out at his mouth knocking out several of his teeth and tearing his lips to pieces."[1]

The Fourth of July, 1863, Independence Day, brought bad news for the Confederacy: Vicksburg had fallen. This disaster combined with the Gettysburg slaughter produced a depressive mood that infected many Rebel soldiers and civilians alike. In spite of the black atmosphere, though, the ragged scarecrows continued to fight.

Swan reported a clash with Yankee cavalry around 16 July in a letter to his wife: "There has been some little fighting about Martinsburg. Our Brigade was in it but I was not there. I have no horse fit to ride now."[2] Swan was referring to Fitz Lee's and Chambliss's attack on the brigade of Union Brigadier General J. Irvin Gregg on the Martinsburg Road. Fitz Lee's men drove the Federals toward the river, but Gregg's men rallied and pushed the Confederates back. Lee expected support from Colonel Milton Ferguson and Brigadier General William Edmondson (Grumble) Jones, but some of the Rebel troops arrived late and the attack came to naught.[3]

Between 16 and 22 July, the Northerners pushed Hampton's brigade back around Hedgeville, Virginia. The Rebel riders fought small pockets of Yankees almost daily while Lee was busy massing his Army of

---

[1] H. Buchanan to Darling Wife, 18 September 1863, from Camp Phillips Legion.

[2] J. Swan to Dear Bettie, 22 July 1863, from Martinsburg.

[3] E. Longacre, *Lee's Cavalrymen, A History of the Mounted Forces of the Army of Northern Virginia* (Mechanicsburg PA: Stackpole Books, 2002) 239; see also E. Longacre, *Lincoln's Cavalrymen, A History of the Mounted Forces of the Army of the Potomac* (Mechanicsburg PA: Stackpole Books, 2000) 207–18.

Northern Virginia in Culpeper County. The Federals assembled a bridge that crossed the Shenandoah near Charleston. The Rebel vedettes fell back as the blue riders crossed the Shenandoah and shuffled through the Blue Ridge gaps, then headed south on the east side of the mountains in the Loudoun Valley. The deep Shenandoah River at flood stage prevented the Confederate soldiers from crossing, and the troopers could not follow the enemy soldiers who were attempting to insert their troops between the graycoats and Richmond. Stuart's cavalry rode parallel to the Rebel infantry moving up the Shenandoah Valley to intercept the Yankees. On 23 July 1863, a heavy skirmish erupted at Manassas Gap in Warren County. Meade ordered Federal General William H. French to halt the retreating Confederate columns at Front Royal by pushing through Manassas Gap and intercepting them. Brigadier General James A. Walker's brigade of Anderson's division slowly retreated into the mountain gap. By late afternoon 23 July, the Yankees had battered Walker's troopers back until they were successfully reinforced by Rodes and some artillery units. The Federals halted their awkward thrusts and the Southerners fell back to the Luray Valley. The Yankees occupied Front Royal the next day, but Lee's army was well out of range by this time. Casualties were high on both sides.[4]

Swan was one of many troopers complaining of unfit mounts, and shortages of cavalry mounts approached emergency status. General Stuart used a few quiet days at Culpeper to attempt to deal with horse shortages as well as personnel problems. He hoped to reduce the population of the horseless Company Q. Company Q was composed of cavalrymen without mounts. They occasionally served as infantry until a remount was received. General Hampton, wounded in several fights, had been sent to Charlottesville for medical treatment, and Brigadier General Laurence S. Baker had replaced him. (Baker was later wounded and replaced temporarily by Colonel Dennis Ferebee.) Stuart promoted some of his most reliable general officers and disposed of General Beverly Robertson, who had long been a thorn in his side. The Federals interrupted his recommendations on 1 August 1863 when Union general John Buford's cavalry again crossed the Rappahannock River for a reconnaissance at Beverly Ford and then attacked the leading troops of

---

[4] Ibid., 239–40.

Baker's Brigade. Baker had been patrolling the south bank near Brandy Station when a second party of Yankees smashed into the Confederate right flank. Baker's troopers had to retreat and Baker was badly wounded. Swan reported on this bitter fight in a letter to his wife:

> Well, Bettie, I have no news to write you much more than our Brigade had a heavy fight here the 1st of Aug. though I was not in it. [Because he was a member of Company Q.] Three Brigades fought ours all day. They was compelled to pull back near Culpeper where the infantry came to our relief. They made them get back faster than they come. We lost several men out of the Brigade but none was killed out of our Battalion, but several was taken prisoners. They wounded the last Col. We had a Lieut. Col. [who] is now in Command of the Brigade. Col. Baker of the first N. C. and Col. Black of the first S. C. and Col. Young of the Cobb Legion was all wounded. I have no horse that is fit to ride.[5]

The Federals battered the Rebels relentlessly, pushing them south. Around 3:00 P.M., Jones's riders counterattacked with infantry from General Richard H. Anderson's division and reversed the course of the fight. The Yankees were forced to retreat. More skirmishing between Buford and Baker occurred on the evening of 4 August resulting in some hand-to-hand fighting and an artillery exchange. Buford was forced to pull back to his infantry.[6]

For a few weeks after 5 August, both sides seldom skirmished. A kind of tacit stalemate seemed to settle in. On 22 August, Rosser's Fifth Virginia joined with a force of Confederate marines and captured two Yankee gunboats and three transports on the Rappahannock River. The Federal crews were sent to Richmond as prisoners of war. On 2 September, most of Kilpatrick's division moved to a point near the captured gunboats and blew them to pieces.[7] From 9 September through 15 September, several skirmishes involving Stuart's troopers took place around Stevensburg, Raccoon Ford, and Robertson's Ford.

---

[5] J. Swan to Dear Bettie, 6 August 1863, from camp near Culpeper Court House.

[6] Longacre, *Lee's Cavalrymen*, 242.

[7] Ibid., 243.

On 9 September, hundreds of miles from Virginia, Union general William Starke Rosecrans marched into Chattanooga, Tennessee, with his Army of the Cumberland. He was following the retreating army of Major General Braxton Bragg. As a result, General James Longstreet joined Bragg to deal with the situation. Yankee general George Gordon Meade's cavalry discovered the movement and informed Meade. The Yankee general crossed the Rappahannock with his cavalry, intending for his riders to probe Lee's positions. Stuart's scouts had informed him of Meade's actions by 12 September. He prepared immediately for a quick retreat. At 7:00 A.M. the next morning, Union major general Alfred Pleasonton attacked Stuart's left and center with the blue horsemen of Buford and Gregg. Kilpatrick's troopers circled around the Confederate right. Stuart readied Rooney Lee's and Jones's brigades as well as the artillery batteries of colonels Roger Preston Chew, Marcellus M. Moorman, and William M. McGregor, to meet the assault. It did not go well, and Stuart's men were forced back to Culpeper Court House. The Northern troopers had struck hard and smashed into the Confederate cannoneers. The Rebels fought hard, and Stuart moved his line of defense back to Rapidan Station. By 16 September, the Federal horsemen had fled to the north and Stuart's line stabilized.[8] Hugh Buchanan told his wife all about his experience in this fight in a letter dated 18 September 1863:

Last Sunday we were in a cavalry fight nearly all day. We aroused Sunday Morning before daylight in the rain with the news that the enemy were crossing the Rappahannock. In full force we went out to meet them. Our Brigade held them in check on the right, but the Yankees drove Jones Brigade, Wm. H. Lees back to Culpeper Court House. We were ordered to fall back. About two miles to the right of Culpeper we attacked them and had a very severe fight. The Yankees, besides three brigades of Cavalry, had a heavy infantry and Artillery force all against our brigade. We kept fighting and falling back the balance of the day in perfect order. We had two horses shot in our company Joe Brown's [Private J. L. Brown] and James Johnson's [Private James C. Johnson]. J. R. Sewell [Private John R. Sewell] was very badly

---

[8] Ibid., 249.

wounded—the ball entered the right side of his face and came out at his mouth knocking out several of his teeth and tearing his lips to pieces. Poor fellow he is disabled for the war. We all had narrow escapes. A watchful providence spread his protecting shield around us and sheltered us from the death dealing missile of the enemy.[9]

The Army of the Potomac was bearing down on the Rapidan River by 20 September. A head-on collision between the blue and gray riders seemed inevitable. The fight began on 22 September 1863 when Stuart's scouts noted the advance of Buford's cavalry coming from Madison Court House. Stuart rode north to meet the Yanks with a large portion of Hampton's badly depleted division. The fight started when Stuart ran into the head of Buford's column on a road leading to a blacksmith's establishment known as Jack's Shop. Stuart attacked in both mounted and dismounted modes, resulting in heavy casualties throughout his brigades. To add to Stuart's woes, Kilpatrick had crossed the rapids around Liberty Springs and headed straight for the Confederate riders. Buford's troopers pressed Stuart relentlessly. The Virginian had no choice but to fight both Yankee groups simultaneously. Rebel sharpshooters and artillery blasted away, and Major General John Brown Gordon and Colonel Dennis Dozier Ferebee attacked the Yankees in mounted mode and managed to hold Buford in check. Stuart then ordered the Laurel Brigade under Colonel Oliver Funsten to assault Kilpatrick. The Eleventh and Twelfth Virginia joined in, shoved the Yankees out of the way, and cleared the road. Buford pursued the Southerners across the river but halted and immediately departed the premises. Clearly, the Union cavalry had improved dramatically, and General J. E. B. Stuart's riders had been battered but not defeated.[10]

In a letter from D. C. Latimer (Second Lieutenant Robert C. Latimer) to Will, dated 25 September 1863 from Camp Phillips Legion, Latimer extolled the fighting spirit of the cavalrymen of the legion:

---

[9] H. Buchanan to Darling Wife, 18 September 1863, from Camp Phillips Legion.

[10] Longacre, *Lee's Cavalrymen*, 249–50.

I am rejoiced to see that there is a spirit of religion pervading throughout the army. We, however, have no chaplain. We would like very much to get one...doubtless ere this, you have heard of our recent fight in this county. It was a cavalry fight. The enemy attempted a raid, but in this they failed. We have just recd circular from Stuart congratulating our Brig[ade] for their gallantry displayed on that occasion, [22d inst]. Our boys fought well—never could men do more. We have a number of brave boys in our company. The enemy with superior force succeeded in surrounding us, but we fought them to the last. Our Legion charged in front, while others charged in our rear & the enemy's front. Col Gordon [John B. Gordon] commanding gives us credit for capturing 30 prisoners...We had but few of our company with us. Only one wounded in Legion. The loss of our Brig[ade] was small. But the loss of others rather heavy. The total loss on our side over 200. We captured 160 prisoners in all I suppose...our Legion is to go on picket the Bugle calls me to mount. The Major wants me...with him. No picket by Regts now. Adjt. Wofford [First Lieutenant John W. Wofford] is home on furlough. I am act[ing] in his stead...[11]

The fight at Jack's Shop roused the ire of Captain John F. Milhollin, commander of B Company. In a letter to his wife, he discussed his selection of those troopers who, in his opinion, deserved credit for their bravery and implied that some who were credited for valor did not deserve it:

A similarly...numbers of our Cavalry circled on the 22nd. As we had a desperate struggle with enemy in Madison County at Jack['s] Shop. Lt. Delaney Cobb Legion—and left in enemy's hands—other noble fellows were left dead and wounded on the field but we licked the said and saved the railroads and fought them all day. They flanked us [Kilpatrick] and got in our rear—the Phillips Legion charged at our end and drove them back. Said to be the most brilliant charge known—we brought off several

---

[11] D. Latimer to Will, 25 September 1863, from Camp Phillips Legion. Roster for Company B shows Second Lieutenant Robert C. Latimer.

54

prisoners and lost several of the Rangers [Company B]. I desire to mention specially the names of R. P. Jones [Rutherford P. Jones] and Billy Light [William P. Light] as noble fellows who in the hottest part of the fight remained firing their carbines when few remained to witness their valor. These two and Edd Waldrop [Edward P. Waldrop]…false statements have been made at home giving credit to some who did not deserve it. I am naming others who did. I intend hereafter to give the names of all engaged and each his dues. Sgt. Oaks [Private William Oaks, Company C], McReynolds [John G. McReynolds], and A. P. Wofford [Private A. P. Wofford] were on scout at the time, but both boys have returned safe—I during time wheeled my horse [in the woods] to see who was flanking us and when I found a Yankee devil firing at some of us—about 20 or 25 steps off but when I brought my big Colts Cav. [which Captain Conwell captured at Gettysburg] to bear on him he surrendered. I got his horse, bridle, saddle, and equipment complete, good sabre belt and pistol. Col. Gordon…[probably Colonel John Brown Gordon] brigade said I was worthy of my prize and could keep it. I find him to be an excellent horse and just in time. I now have two good horses and saddle.[12]

Captain Milhollin wrangled a leave around this time. Stuart approved his leave request, which reads: "Hqrs Cav. Corps, Sept. 29, 1863, Respectfully for'd approved for four days. Capt. Milhollin is regarded as a highly honorable man—and one of the finest officers in the service. JEB Stuart, Major Genl."[13]

Just prior to the onset of the Bristoe Campaign and following the skirmish at Jack's Shop, the legion fought a minor skirmish around Robertson's Ford. Somewhere about this time, Captain Milhollin's rangers experienced a minor affair in the Orange Court House area. In a letter to his son from Camp Orange County, Virginia, Captain Milhollin described a humorous event:

---

[12] J. Milhollin to My Dear Ev, 25 September 1863, from camp. No record available for "Captain Conwell."

[13] Leave request signed by JEB Stuart, major gen., 29 September 1863, from hq. cav. corps for Capt Milhollin for four days.

Although we are only 4 miles from Orange C. H. ....you have doubtless ere this received several letters from me as I have written several. There is no news of importance on our lines at present. Our legion was relieved this morning and we will be on again within about 3 days. There are some 65,000 Yankee infantry reported between here and Rappahannock River by our scout C. M. Reynolds [this is probably Lieutenant Clay Reynolds]...returned from Stephensburg yesterday and six others passing been through the Yankee camp with Capt. Farley [Captain William Downs Farley] of Hampton's staff They had the misfortune to get an artillery sergeant wounded as they lay concealed in a barn under hay, a Yankee came in at night to steal hay and pulled the hay off this fellow who raised up and was instantly shot by the Yankee who ran at once to camp. They boys then rushed out and aroused the boys but they [our boys] knew the hog paths too well for Mr. Yank to pick em up in the night. They start back to Culpeper this evening to steal Yankee horses. I should like to be along but I cannot get permission. We are at all times ready for an attack from the enemy but I do not think it will occur at once, but likely in a reasonably short time.[14]

Stuart moved Hampton's division to Madison Court House southwest of Culpeper Court House on 9 October 1863. They bivouacked here while Young's and Gordon's Brigades positioned vedettes toward Robertson's River, which was just a mile from Madison Court House.[15] Daylight the following morning marked the beginning of the Bristoe Campaign. Stuart pushed Young's and Gordon's brigades across the Robertson River at Russell's Ford with Young bringing up the rear as the men rode toward James City and Culpeper Court House.

---

[14] J. Milhollin to My Dear James, 31 September 1863, from Camp Orange County, VA; also see http://nps.gov%seac/ferydawnich8.htm for information on Confederate scout Lieutenant Clay Reynolds.

[15] OR, Armies, vol. 29, pt. 2, 457–59; also see D. Hopkins, *The Little Jeff, The Jeff Davis Legion, Cavalry Army of Northern Virginia* (Shippensburg PA: White Mane Books, 1999) 173.

Stuart hoped to keep Meade's attention while the Rebel infantry continued toward the northwest to the Blue Ridge.[16]

Stuart's troopers found Yankee pickets in their front while crossing the river. The pickets were part of a regiment of infantry and a detachment of cavalry. The Federals established a line near Bethesda Church. Gordon attacked in their front immediately as Stuart stationed Young's Brigade, which included the legion through woods on the enemy's left. Young's troopers smashed into the Federal flank, capturing eighty-seven prisoners. They pursued the Yankees as they retreated toward James City just a mile and a half away. Stuart ran into Meade's main body and moved his troopers into the little town of James City.[17]

On 12 October, Stuart ordered Young to meet him at Culpeper Court House. Stuart headed north toward Jefferson covering the infantry on his front while the troopers skirmished with scattered groups of Federals. Rosser, though forced from his position, steadied his troopers and fought a delaying action while falling back toward Culpeper Court House. At Culpeper, Rosser observed commissary and quartermaster personnel loading wagon trains. He knew that loss of these wagons would impose severe logistics problems on the Confederate army, so to counter this possibility, Rosser asked General P. M. B. Young for help. Young reacted immediately, moving his troopers to a ridge known as Slaughter's Hill. The Yankees pushed Rosser back toward Young and ran into a line of dismounted troops and artillery. They were thrown back with great loss. General Young did not know he had faced a full corps of infantry and a division of the Federal cavalry.

While this action was going on, Stuart's troopers skirmished with the Federals near Jefferson and at a ford of the Rappahannock River.[18]

Young departed Culpeper Court House on the morning of 13 October. Later, he received orders from Lee to head east by way of Bealeton Station on the Orange and Alexandria Railroad and stay on the right flank of the Rebel army. Simultaneously, cavalrymen were holding the roads to the east of the Federals. Stuart reconnoitered from Warrenton toward Catlett's Station and, in the process, his entire

---

[16] Hopkins, *The Little Jeff*, 173.

[17] Ibid., 173–74.

[18] Ibid.

command was almost captured when they discovered themselves in the middle of the Federal army in the early evening.[19]

General Robert E. Lee had been keeping pressure on the withdrawing Federal army while it headed south toward Bristoe Station on the Orange and Alexandria Railroad between Catlett's Station and Manassas Junction. Stuart repositioned Hampton's division by the eastern flank of the army. Young's Brigade moved east along the line of the Orange and Alexandria Railroad, and Fitz Lee was situated well to the west near New Baltimore. By the time the Confederate infantry came to Bristoe Station, the largest part of the Federal army had withdrawn back toward Manassas, and the Yankees had left an entrenched rear guard stretched out along a railroad embankment. General Ambrose Powell Hill's troops attacked immediately and suffered heavy losses. This unfortunate act on Hill's part gave Meade the time needed to establish his defenses near Centreville in the north. However, the Confederates had destroyed the Orange and Alexandria Railroad from the Rappahannock crossing to the far north. This action made resupply a serious problem for the Federals. By 14 October, Stuart had moved north to Manassas and harassed the bluecoats when they crossed Bull Run at Blackburn's and Yates's fords. Stuart sent word to Young to meet him near Bristoe Station, and Young arrived the evening of 15 October.

On 16 October, Stuart, with Hampton's division, moved against Meade's right flank and had a hard fight at Groveton while riding through a blinding rainstorm.[20] Stuart reconnoitered near Frying Pan Church on 16 October. Young captured several Yankee pickets in the morning and engaged a regiment of Federal infantry while Stuart headed out through Gainesville on 18 October, and gathered supplies and forage at Haymarket. They camped at Buckland, southwest of Manassas. Yankee cavalry smashed into Stuart's vedettes. In response, Stuart sent Young to Haymarket with orders to hold there.

The next morning, 19 October, Stuart slowly retreated while being chased by Federal cavalry from the east. Young found Stuart at Buckland with Hampton's division in line of battle. Young's Brigade filtered

---

[19] Ibid., 175.

[20] J. Cooke, *Wearing of the Gray: Being Personal: Portraits, Scenes and Adventures in the War* (Bloomington IN: P. V. Stern, 1959) 265.

through the Rebel lines and was immediately attacked by artillery and cavalry. This proved to be a brilliant move on Stuart's part, since he had lured the Yanks into a trap with Fitz Lee's help. The Federals followed Stuart closely while Fitz Lee tailed them. Stuart moved on to Chestnut Hill, about two-and-one-half miles from Warrenton. The Yankees had been led to believe that Stuart was retreating. Fitz Lee's artillery blasted the rear of the pursuers. Stuart turned his troopers around and had Gordon charge the head of the Yankee column. Young's and Rosser's troopers engaged the astonished Federals on their flanks and rear. All order for the blue riders disintegrated, and they retreated en masse down five miles of turnpike. This was an "every-man-for-himself" retreat that became known as the Buckland Races. The Rebels captured numerous prisoners, wagons, and ambulances, including the baggage of Union general George Armstrong Custer.[21]

By 19 October, most the Army of Northern Virginia had settled south of the Rappahannock with cavalry as vedettes. Young was camped on either side of the Orange and Alexandria Railroad near Culpeper Court House with pickets to the east near Stevensburg.

During November 1863, the Confederate cavalry had been keeping a sharp eye out for the next move of the enemy. In the late evening of 7 November, the Federals repaired the railroad on the north of the Rappahannock River and headed south, making their way across the river at Kelly's Ford and the railroad bridge. The Northerners caught the Confederate infantry off guard and hit them hard. The Yankees captured more than 1,600 men. While this fight was in progress on 8 November, General Wade Hampton returned amidst several rounds of cheers.[22]

Company B of the legion cavalry suffered a heavy loss on 10 November 1863 after the fighting around Rappahannock Station: its commander, Captain John Fielding Milhollin, succumbed after being wounded on 8 November while leading a scout near Brandy Station, Rappahannock Station, and Culpeper Court House. According to an interview with Milhollin's wife, Lucinda Eveline Milhollin, entitled "Grandma's War Memories," the Georgian was "shot down by grape at

---

[21] Longacre, *Lee's Cavalrymen*, 260–61; Hopkins, *The Little Jeff*, 177.
[22] M 269 Rolls 66, 71, M. Wellman, *Giant in Gray* (New York & London: Scribner's, 1949) 130; also see Hopkins, *The Little Jeff*, 179.

the head of his command." He had been taken to a Federal hospital at Brandy Station where he died. Milhollin's oldest son, James, had picked up the notification letter from the War Department on his way home from school in Cassville, Georgia. Ten days later, the casket arrived. Family lore suggested that Milhollin's small unit was ambushed and some were captured. Milhollin's brother-in-law and a soldier of the legion in Cavalry Company B, James M. Dodgen, was permitted to accompany the body home by private conveyance along with Milhollin's saber, pistol, uniforms, and accoutrements. (Later, they were pilfered by a Union soldier when found buried in the Confederate cemetery under a grave marker at Cassville, Georgia.) The pistol and saber were probably obtained from the Gettysburg battlefield as mentioned in Milhollin's letter to "Dear Ev" dated 25 September 1863. (These arms have never been located in spite of the author's best efforts.) For Lucinda, a tiny woman, just over five feet tall, her husband's death was shattering news. Like so many lonely and stressed widows of the time with overwhelming family responsibilities, she had six children and her youngest sister, Jane, to care for. She often identified with her husband's travails: "I used to throw my pillow out on the floor at night...it seemed wrong for me to be in a good bed and John out all night in the rain and snow."[23]

John T. Swan commented on Milhollin's death and the fight in a letter to his wife: "The boys had a fight last Sunday about Culpeper. Robt. Roop of our company got wounded in the knee. Cap. Milholland got killed. Several horses was shot. They are looking for a fight every day. I can not tell but I hope there will not be much more fighting this winter."[24] James Dodgen of Company B felt compassion for his recently widowed sister, Lucinda Eveline Milhollin. In a letter to her dated 21 December 1863, he promised always to be by her side:

> Sister, you must try to take it as easy as you can for he died willingly. He said he felt like he was doing his duty when he received the wounds. I stayed with him one day and night. Left before he died. He talked a great deal before he died. He said he

---

[23] Interview with Lucinda Dodgen Milholland by Lily Milholland Dodgen in *The Bartow* (Cartersville GA) *Herald*, entitled "Grandma's War Memories," 9 April 1931.

[24] J. Swan to Dear Bettie, 14 November 1863, from camp near Orange C. H.

did not regret dying if it was not for his family but I hope I will live to get home and I will help you as long as I live so I will close for this time. I learned that A. J. Cottens [no records to identify this man, he was probably a late-war enlistee] was killed right by me. Whether it is so or not give my love to all inquiring friends.[25]

The next year promised more fighting for the men of the legion. The Bristoe Campaign had ended inconclusively. John Swan complained about lack of sleep and a fight with a regiment of Yankee cavalry in a letter to his wife dated 19 November 1863:

I was up all night and I have not caught up yet for sleep. We went on scout Tuesday and got back yesterday. We crossed at Ellie's [Ely's] Ford and went in about six miles of Stephensburg where we run into a Regt. of Cavalry about Sun up about the time they was puting on there breakfast but we fooled them out of it one time. You ought to seen them running through the woods, some a foot and some barback. One man had not got his pants on. You ought to seen him running through the woods with his shirt tail out. We got many horses and 60 prisoners, there wagons and ambulance. We then crossed back at Madden Ford. We did not stay there long. The alarm stired up the hole army. No body got hit. We killed several of them. Bettie I was in hops they would not fight any after I got here but they keep knocking at us. There is picket fighting evry day most.[26]

Another inconclusive campaign ensued on 26 November 1863 near a tributary of the Rapidan River known as Mine Run and extensive Confederate fortifications situated on high ground. Union general Meade attempted to sneak his troops through the wilderness and maneuver Lee out of his position by smashing the right flank of the Rebel army south of the Rapidan River. Meade hoped to keep Lee in the dark but failed, and Lee beat him to the punch. Confederate major general Early, commanding Ewell's Corps, moved eastward on the Orange Turnpike to

---

[25] J. Dodgen to Dear Sister, 21 December 1863, from camp near Hamilton's Crossing; A. J Cottens remains unidentified.

[26] J. Swan to Dear Bettie, 19 November 1863, from camp near Orange C. H., Virginia.

confront Union general William French's corps situated near Payne's Farm. Union General Eugene Asa Carr's division attacked first, and Rebel general Edward "Allegheny" Johnson counterattacked, but his graybacks were scattered by heavy fire and confusing terrain. Considerable skirmishing occurred on the following day but no major attack followed.

On the morning of 26 November, Rebel general Rosser picked up some important intelligence. He learned that Union general David Gregg had crossed Ely's Ford and headed toward Chancellorsville. Rosser was certain Gregg intended to prepare the way for the Union infantry. Lee began an eastern movement to strike Meade, who, Lee believed, was on the road, and met him in a fight at a little-known place called Locust Grove. This was mainly an infantry clash, but one of Meade's columns moved more slowly than the others and collided with Stuart at New Hope Church, south of Locust Grove. The legion, with the rest of Young's Brigade, arrived late on the scene and participated in the fight. Because infantry troops augmented the Yankees, the graybacks could not halt the westward thrust of the Federals under Meade. Both sides hardened their positions and stayed put for several days.

On 28 November, Lee decided the stalemate had to be broken and ordered Stuart to get in Meade's rear and divine his intentions. Stuart moved quickly, reaching Hampton's headquarters on the Catharpin Road the next day and was infuriated when he found Hampton absent. Stuart sent Rosser's Brigade along a trace to Parker's Store (a general store) on the Orange Plank Road. When Hampton caught up with Stuart, the two officers settled their differences and Hampton joined with Rosser and routed the Federals. General Gouverneur Warren's troops reinforced the Federals. Warren observed the Confederate fortifications the following morning and decided against an assault. Meade was furious but began withdrawing to the north side of the river on 2 December. Swan commented on the fighting in a letter to his wife:

> Well, Bettie, I have no news to write you more than they have been fighting a little ever since last Thursday. Sonday and Monday they fought right smart. They are in line of Battle now. They crossed Friday morning at Ellies [Ely's] and Diamond's Fords and came up the plank road about Chancellorsville. They are now

above Chancellorsville. The center of both armies is on the plank road. Our division is on the right wing. I think there will be a general engagement to day or tomorrow though I cannot tell any thing about it. I have not been in it this time. I was detailed to unload cars as luck would have it. I came to camps last night. I may go down where they are tomorrow, if they don't come in today. Our Brigade is at Madariesville [*sic*; probably Madisonville]. They have been fighting some but no body got hurt as I have heard of. I think this will close the winter campaign.[27]

Swan was correct.

Lee's position was far too strong for Warren's taste, and Meade, in a sulk, retreated on the night of 1 December 1863, which effectively ended the winter campaign for the legion infantry battalion. The Yankee soldiers went into winter quarters near the Rapidan River.

Only part of Stuart's cavalry wintered near Orange Court House. On 11 December 1863, most of Fitz Lee's command (Wickham and Chambliss) camped near Charlottesville. Yankee general William Woods Averell launched his troopers on a raid on the Virginia and Tennessee Railroad. Rebel general John Daniel Imboden was unprepared and asked General R. E. Lee for help. Lee reacted by sending part of Hill's corps to Staunton and Fitz Lee's cavalrymen to the valley on 14 December. Rosser followed suit but little was accomplished. The Yankee forces escaped, as attested to by John Swan in a letter to his wife, and fighting

---

[27] J. Swan to Dear Bettie, 2 December 1863, from camp near Orange C. H., Virginia: also see OR, ser. 1, vol. 29, pt. 2, ch. 41, Mine Run, Virginia, Campaign, 906–907, report of Brig. Gen. Pierce M. B. Young, C. S. Army, commanding, Headquarters Cavalry Brigade, 29 December 1863: "Major: I have the honor to submit this my report of the operations of this brigade on the morning of November 29...I received an order from General Hampton to move my brigade, following Generals Rosser and Gordon...I immediately dismounted two regiments [the Cobb and Phillips Legions] bringing them up on the enemy's right flank, charging on foot. The First South Carolina I carried up the plank road at a trot, hoping to have an opportunity to charge. We moved on briskly under a pretty warm fire, but which did me little damage. I soon found myself in possession of the field. I was still pushing the enemy when I was ordered to withdraw my troops and cover the rear of the column. We encamped that night near Antioch Church. My loss in this engagement was 2 killed and 3 wounded."

abated:[28] "In my last letter I told you I thought there would be a fight but the Yanks went back without fighting much. Everything is still now. We have to go on picket about every ten days is all the duty we have to do now and that is very light to what we have to do some times. I don't think there will be any more fighting here this winter though I can't tell."[29]

By 17 December, Swan's unit had camped about three to four miles from Hamilton's Crossing between the crossing and Guiney's Station. The brigade had relieved General Rosser's Brigade after it went to the valley. The legion was then on the extreme right of the entire Rebel army. Swan concluded his correspondence with his wife on 10 December 1863. He was apologetic to Bettie. He had not inquired about her health:

> You seemed to think from your letter that I did not care much for you as regard your condition and state of health. Bettie I am sorry that you have formed such an opinion of me as that for I am sure that you don't know how much I think of such things or you would not write to me that way—I no that I have not inquired into your present state of health but Bettie the reason I did not I did not no whether it was so or not and I thought you would tell me yourself. Bettie as it hurts your feeling so bad and disturbs your mind so it would be the best for me not to come home any more but I no that you would not be willing to that nor neither would I for I want to see you every chance and I intend to come evry chance if you have no objections. Bettie I know that you are not satisfied and you being so dissatisfied makes me more dissatisfied than I would be if I new that you was so satisfied. Bettie it grieves me to think that my lovely companion is so dissatisfied and I can't help it. I hope the time will come when I can return to you to stay and I think then we will both be better satisfied but Bettie it does seem to me that you ought be better satisfied with me. My present

---

[28] Longacre, *Lee's Cavalrymen*, 265–66.

[29] J. Swan to Dear Bettie, 17 December 1863, from camp near Hambletons (Hamilton's) Crossing.

task is a much harder one than yours—though I guess you think the same way by me.[30]

Swan's letters of 1864 suggest that this minor marital spat was forgotten. Swan also noted the death of a Company D trooper named Edward A. Fambro. Fambro was killed by a local citizen on Christmas night when he demanded supper at the man's house and was refused. Fambro went after the man, intending to strike him on the head with his pistol, but the man relieved him of his weapon and shot him. Fambro is listed as killed in action in the company roster on 26 December 1863.[31]

Many of Stuart's men disbanded for the winter, especially those who were near their family and homes. Hampton's troopers braced themselves for the hard work of picketing and scouting, although Hampton was deeply resentful on behalf of his men but unable to alter the situation. The horsemen lacked basic supplies and equipment, and their horses were in sorry shape. A pall of gloom settled upon the Rebel cavalry and the entire Confederacy at year's end.

The coming year would herald a change in overall command of the Union army to a western general known for fighting and winning. Lieutenant General Ulysses S. Grant would fight and keep on fighting to the end. He would do whatever it took to finally corner and defeat Robert E. Lee. One of his favorite officers was a short, bandy-legged Irishman named Major General Phillip Henry Sheridan. His name would become synonymous with the ascendancy of the Federal cavalry.

For the Confederacy, the gloom would only deepen in 1864.

---

[30] J. Swan to Dear Bettie, 28 December 1863, from camp near Hambleton's (Hamilton's) Crossing.
[31] Ibid.

7

THE LAST FULL YEAR OF THE WAR

"The Yanks have been very kind in furnishing me equipment since I have been out here. They have furnished me with saddle, Bridle, Halter, gun pistol and anything I wanted in that line. They also furnished me with a nice piece of shell in the left arm above the elbow, night before last."[1]

Hampton's Brigade suffered the travails of a hard winter in late 1863 and early 1864. Picketing, scouting, and searching for sustenance for themselves and their overstressed horses kept them busy enough to have little time for rest and preparation for the coming bitter campaigns of the final full year of the war.

On 6 February, the Federals crossed the Rapidan at Ely's Ford, Morton's Ford, and Raccoon Ford. The Yankees intended to destroy all of the important facilities they could find. Rebel lieutenant general Richard S. Ewell's infantry resisted the crossings. The fighting was intermittent but severe at Morton's Ford as the Federals pushed back the Confederate pickets. The legion, with General P. M. B. Young's brigade, had moved closer to brigade headquarters. Major General Arnold Elzey, commander of the Department of Richmond, requested help from General Robert E. Lee. Lee ordered Stuart to support Elzey. Stuart complied by sending Hampton's exhausted brigade to the capital. By the time they arrived, the crisis was over.

Amid rumors the following day that the Federals were once more on their way to strike Richmond, Stuart tasked Hampton to move in support once again. Hampton refused and was finally supported by Lee. The Union attack had stalled, and the Yanks withdrew during the night of 7

---

[1] E. Humphries to Dear Sis, 30 June 1864 from Stony Creek Depot between Petersburg and Walden.

February.[2] John Swan related the legion's role in this minor event in a letter dated 11 February 1864: "We had a bust up a few days ago. The Yanks was coming up behind us and we was ordered down there and got as far as Milford Station and was turned back to our old camp."[3]

In spite of the unusually cold weather, the Federals did not sit idly by. They moved quickly, attacking bridges and fords, and even with reports of four-inch-thick ice in some areas, generally caused much mischief. On 8 February, Hampton's troopers were also on the move trying to intercept the Yankees. They were unsuccessful and camped on the Mattapony River near Milford.[4]

Stuart's men had experienced continuous shortages of horses. Company Q was destined to grow in size, so much so that by 28 February, Hampton's division, which included Butler's Brigade, then commanded by General P. M. B. Young and General James B. Gordon's North Carolina troopers, all stationed near Fredericksburg, were equipped with a total of only 719 horses, many of which were probably spavined or close to starvation.[5]

> The Yanks have been very kind in furnishing me equipment since I have been out here. They have furnished me with saddle, Bridle, Halter, gun pistol and anything I wanted in that line. They also furnished me with a nice piece of shell in the left arm above the elbow, night before last.[6]

Hampton's Brigade suffered the travails of a hard winter in late 1863 and early 1864. Picketing, scouting, and searching for sustenance for themselves and their overstressed horses kept them busy enough to

---

[2] E. Longacre, *Lee's Cavalry Men: A History of the Mounted Forces of Northern Forces of Northern Virginia, 1861-1865* (Mechanicsburg PA: Stackpole Books, 2002) 169.

[3] Swan to Dear Bettie, 11 Feburary 1864.

[4] Waring Papers, Southern Historical Collection, UNC Chapel Hill, NC.

[5] On this day a division-sized force of more than 4,000 Yankee troops under command of General Judson Kilpatrick and Colonel Ulric Dahlgren galloped out of their winter camps heading straight for Richmond.

[6] E. Humphries to Dear Sis, 30 June 1864, from Stony Creek Depot between Petersburg and Walden.

have little time for rest and preparation for the coming bitter campaigns of the final full year of the war.

On 6 February, the Federals crossed the Rapidan at Ely's Ford, Morton's Ford, and Raccoon Ford. The Yankees intended to destroy all of the important facilities they could find. Rebel lieutenant general Richard S. Ewell's infantry resisted the crossings. The fighting was intermittent but severe at Morton's Ford as the Federals pushed back the Confederate pickets. The legion, with General P. M. B. Young's brigade, had moved closer to brigade headquarters. Major General Arnold Elzey, commander of the Department of Richmond, requested help from General Robert E. Lee. Lee ordered Stuart to support Elzey. Stuart complied by sending Hampton's exhausted brigade to the capital. By the time they arrived, the crisis was over.

Amid rumors the following day that the Federals were once more on their way to strike Richmond, Stuart tasked Hampton to move in support once again. Hampton refused and was finally supported by Lee. The Union attack had stalled, and the Yanks withdrew during the night of 7 February.[7] John Swan related the legion's role in this minor event in a letter dated 11 February 1864: "We had a bust up a few days ago. The Yanks was coming up behind us and we was ordered down there and got as far as Milford Station and was turned back to our old camp."[8]

In spite of the unusually cold weather, the Federals did not sit idly by. They moved quickly, attacking bridges and fords, and even with reports of four-inch-thick ice in some areas, generally caused much mischief. On 8 February, Hampton's troopers were also on the move trying to intercept the Yankees. They were unsuccessful and camped on the Mattapony River near Milford.[9]

Stuart's men had experienced continuous shortages of horses. Company Q was destined to grow in size, so much so that by 28 February, Hampton's division, which included Butler's Brigade, then

---

[7] E. Longacre, *Lee's Cavalrymen: A History of the Mounted Forces of the Army of Northern Virginia, 1861–1865* (Mechanicsburg PA: Stackpole Books, 2002) 169.

[8] J. Swan to Dear Bettie, 11 February 1864, from camp Near Hambletons Crossing.

[9] J. Waring Papers, Southern Historical Collection, University of North Carolina, Chapel Hill, NC.

commanded by General P. M. B. Young and General James B. Gordon's North Carolina troopers, all stationed near Fredericksburg, were equipped with a total of only 719 horses, many of which were probably spavined or close to starvation.[10] On this day, a division-sized force of over 4,000 Yankee troopers under command of General Judson Kilpatrick and Colonel Ulric Dahlgren galloped out of their winter camps close to Stevensburg, heading straight for Richmond. They made their way across the Rapidan at Ely's Ford, capturing pickets of Young's Brigade, including John Swan. Yankee troops surprised Swan and several other Rebel troopers while on picket. Two of the men arrived late and avoided capture. J. M. Housworth, one of Swan's legion mates, related Swan's fate:

> The Yankee Capt. came in the room that the Capt. from the Cobb Legion was in and told him to surrender which he did. They took him and the Lieut. out and missed these two that come in yesterday. These two that come in yesterday told me that John was in the big room with a big light so the Yankees got John and all the rest of them. There was 17 at the post. Got all of them too. I will say to you John was well when he left Camps and I know John will make a good thing of it. If I get any more news from John I will let you hear from him. Tell my wife that I am well.[11]

Swan headed off to Old Capitol Prison in Washington so quickly that he left his leggings and hand towel behind. John Swan, faithful soldier and devoted husband and father, would spend the remainder of the war in a Yankee prison. Prison authorities moved Swan to Fort Delaware later in August.[12]

Kilpatrick and Dahlgren planned to enter Richmond, release prisoners of war, kidnap and perhaps kill Confederate officials, including Jefferson Davis, and destroy as much of the city as possible. An unfordable river and a slapdash force of government clerks in local defense battalions stymied Dahlgren's attempt to enter the city while

---

[10] D. Hopkins, *The Little Jeff,* 186 (Confederate requisition for forage, Gulfport MS).

[11] J. Housworth to Mrs. Swan, 3 March 1864, from Hamilton's Crossing, Virginia.

[12] Ibid.

Confederate cavalry, including Hampton's command, pounced on Kilpatrick. Dahlgren's force met disaster when Federal troops killed Dahlgren and captured many of his raiders. The Yanks found papers on his body that suggested that the raid had two purposes: to free the prisoners of war and to kidnap and/or assassinate Jefferson Davis and his cabinet. After Kilpatrick was turned back from Richmond, he and his troops camped at Atlee's Station, where Hampton's men attacked him but Kilpatrick managed to escape to Williamsburg.[13] Little skirmishing occurred from the repulse of Kilpatrick's raiders in early March to spring. Authorities in Richmond worked to reorganize and refit Young's Brigade. On 14 March, Major Samuel L. Melton, assistant adjutant general, proffered suggestions to build up Young's Brigade. Major Melton proposed that additional Georgia troops from the Twentieth Georgia Cavalry Battalion, the Georgia company of the Jeff Davis Legion, and the Phillips Legion's three Georgia companies all be added to Young's Brigade. Adjutant General Samuel Cooper was agreeable to these changes.

By 20 March, the weather had worsened. Snow covered the various campgrounds, and the troopers engaged in snowball fights on April Fool's Day. The legion troopers picketed, scouted, and settled in at their camp at Hamilton's Crossing through 26 April. On 30 April, Confederate authorities transferred Young to North Carolina for a few weeks, leaving Colonel Gilbert (Gib) Wright in charge of his brigade. On 5 May, authorities saw fit to reorganize Stuart's cavalry again. These same authorities transferred Gordon's North Carolinians out of Hampton's division, leaving Young's and Rosser's groups as Hampton's remaining brigades.[14]

The emotional climate throughout Virginia improved. Farmers put in larger than usual crops of corn, but all food supplies for the Confederate army remained scarce. Officers even detailed some of the troopers to fish to add to the depleted larder. Lieutenant General Ulysses

---

[13] E. Longacre, *Lee's Cavalrymen*, 270–72; also see E. Longacre, *Lincoln's Cavalrymen: A History of the Mounted Forces of the Army of the Potomac, 1861–1865* (Mechanicsburg PA: Stackpole Books, 2000) 243–45; Hopkins, *The Little Jeff*, 187–88.

[14] Longacre, *Lee's Cavalrymen*, 273, 274; Hopkins, *The Little Jeff*, 189–90.

S. Grant's dark countenance loomed menacingly on the Confederate horizon at this time. He had been reassigned to the east, promoted, and assigned command of all Federal operations in Virginia, as well as all the armies of the United States. Grant elected to maintain his headquarters with the Army of the Potomac. By early May, Hampton's scouts had observed the movement of Grant's army on its way to cross the Rapidan River at Ely's and Germanna fords. Grant planned to turn the left flank of the Army of Northern Virginia near the Chancellorsville battlefield. This ominous sign portended what came to be known as Grant's "Overland Campaign." The first major confrontation between the two Titans, Grant and Lee, took place in a seventeen-square mile area of brambles, marshes, creeks, and ravines called "The Wilderness." The series of battles that comprised the Overland Campaign proved to be the most brutal contests of the Civil War.

The Wilderness was strategically located: the northern position of the battlefield ran along the side of the Rapidan River close to its confluence with the Rappahannock. Rapidan River crossings included Germanna's and Ely's fords. Chancellorsville lay to the east with Mine Run to the west. One road ran east to Fredericksburg and the Orange-Fredericksburg Turnpike, which went on to Orange Court House, while a branch to the left of the turnpike called the Catharpin Road headed south of Brock Road and crossed the Po River at Corbin's Bridge above Shady Grove Church. Beyond Chancellorsville, the turnpike forked to the south becoming the Orange Plank Road. Both the turnpike and Orange Plank Road led to Orange Court House.[15]

The carnage began on 4 May 1864, when Meade, closely scrutinized by Grant, crossed the Rapidan River fords and halted to allow his supply wagons to catch up. Stuart's excellent scouting served Robert E. Lee well. Just before midnight of 4 May, Stuart noted that the Yankees had paused in the heart of the gloomy Wilderness. Lee planned to slam into the Federals before they could clear the tangled foliage. Late on the morning of 5 May, Ewell moved toward the Army of the Potomac's Fifth

---

[15] Hopkins, *The Little Jeff*, 192–93; Longacre, *Lee's Cavalrymen*, 276–77; Longacre, *Lincoln's Cavalrymen*, 256–58. Also see P. Mason, *The Plank Road Craze: A Chapter in the History of Michigan's Highways*, Michigan Historical Center, Department of History, Arts and Libraries, Wayne State University MI.

Corps, which attacked his men first. Hill moved to assist Ewell. After 4:00 P.M., the Federal Sixth Corps, accompanied by Hancock's Second Corps, attacked the Rebel Third Corps. The bloody fighting continued throughout the day, seesawing back and forth, ending with little gain for either side by day's end. Eleven Union and Confederate cavalry skirmished on the right of the Confederate army, but no major mounted battles took place on 5 May. On the morning of 6 May, the Army of the Potomac advanced across the front limits of the battlefield. The poorly timed and poorly planned Yankee assaults triggered enormous casualties, including wounded of both sides burned to death in raging fires kindled by the dry foliage. On 7 May, Sheridan and Stuart collided with each other at Todd's Tavern. This fierce, slashing cavalry battle lasted until darkness. Although Stuart succeeded in impeding the movement of the Federals, the Yankees held the field. The legion cavalry, near Spotsylvania Court House all day, could hear the rumbling battle. The conflict ended with no clear gain for either side, but Lee lost over 7,500 men, which he could ill afford to lose.[16]

Grant proceeded to sidle around the Rebel right flank and move on toward Richmond via Spotsylvania Court House. Lee divined Grant's intentions and both armies raced toward Spotsylvania Court House. If the Federals could beat Lee to Spotsylvania, they would be able to insert themselves between the Rebel army and Richmond to the south. Gib Wright, leading Young's Brigade past Shady Grove Church, found that the Yankee cavalry was close behind him. He wheeled about and skirmished with the Federal riders, driving them away. The Confederate infantry marched out of the burning wilderness and headed toward Spotsylvania Court House, passing by the cavalry pickets that night.[17]

General Sheridan was determined to gain control of the bridges over the Po River near Spotsylvania Court House. On 8 May, Gib Wright's

[16] J. Sparkman, diary, US National Military Park, Manassas VA; Longacre, *Lee's Cavalrymen*, 276–81; Longacre, *Lincoln's Cavalrymen*, 256–58.
[17] Longacre, *Lee's Cavalrymen*, 281–82; E. Wittenberg, *Glory Enough for All: Sheridan's Second Raid and the Battle of Trevilian Station* (Dulles VA: Brassey's Inc., 2001) 17; M. Boatner, *The Civil War Dictionary*, rev. ed. (New York: David McKay Company, 1987) 840–41; S. Foote, *The Civil War: A Narrative: Red River to Appomattox*, vol. 3 (New York: Random House, 1974) 199–200.

troopers ran into Sheridan's skirmishers embedded in the woods above a bridge near Shady Grove. Wright struck hard and drove the Federals out of the brambles and thickets for over a mile. Federal infantry arrived on the scene forcing Wright's men to pull back. The race to Spotsylvania Court House was on, with Robert E. Lee in the lead. Confederate infantry had successfully entrenched themselves in Grant's front north of the Court House.[18] General Phillip Sheridan had something to prove. On 9 May 1864, with his complete cavalry corps, he set off to defeat Jeb Stuart in an action that became known as the Richmond Raid. His total force included roughly 9,300 men, a brigade of horse artillery comprised of around twenty guns and 300 men. In turn, Stuart's forces consisted of 6,000 mounted troopers, four batteries of horse artillery, which included 400 men and fifteen guns, for a total strength of about 6,400 men, far fewer than Sheridan's. Sheridan intended to head straight for the Confederate capital and, in the process, force Stuart to follow him into a battle. In this, Sheridan was successful. Skirmishing between Wright and the Yankees continued on the south side of the Po River until the Federals finally withdrew across the river, departing with a sharp blast of artillery at the Rebel riders. Between 11 and 13 May, General Stuart placed a portion of his cavalry between the Yankee horsemen and Richmond. A grueling battle took place at Yellow Tavern, where Stuart was mortally wounded. Sadly, the legendary cavalier died the following day. Although Sheridan won the battle at Yellow Tavern, the raid accomplished little else except to leave a difficult problem of command for the Army of Northern Virginia's Cavalry Corps that would not be resolved until August. In the interim, all cavalry division commanders reported to Lee, acting as independent commands.[19]

On 12 May, the legion troopers heard the roaring artillery and crackling rifle fire some distance away as Union infantry assaulted the "mule shoe" salient at Spotsylvania Court House. On 13 May, Grant attempted another flanking movement, hoping to sidle around the Rebel right. Grant disengaged and continued moving toward Richmond. By 15 May, the Yankees had positioned troops and an enormous support complex of supply bases, hospitals, and transportation facilities in front

---

[18] Hopkins, *The Little Jeff*, 195.
[19] Ibid.

of the Confederate right. On 16 May, Wright's troopers, which included the legion cavalry, headed north on a scout by way of Germanna Ford. The road was covered with blankets, clothing, and personal materials left by the marching Federals, who had moved away from the Spotsylvania area.

The day 19 May was a difficult one. Hampton's division, including the legion, accompanied Ewell's Second Corps on a reconnaissance in force on the Confederate left. Ewell ran into Federal troops and engaged them in a bloody fight in the afternoon. Hampton's dismounted riders and horse artillery helped to hold the Federals back after Ewell's men had taken a savage beating. Hampton's troopers then pulled back to their supply base on the Orange and Spotsylvania Road near Germanna Ford.[20]

Grant did not stay idle. He prepared to shift a force of infantry and cavalry toward Hanover Junction. He would place his men just north of Richmond near the junction of the Virginia Central and Richmond and Fredericksburg and Potomac Railroads. Just north of this position the North Anna River flowed from the northwest and splashed under the Chesterfield Bridge heading toward its confluence with the Pamunkey River.[21] On 22 May, Hampton's riders, including Wright's Brigade, rolled over the Chesterfield Bridge with their wagon train. The Southern army was also marching to meet the threat to the south. They fed their starving horses in a rich field of clover near Pole Cat Creek before heading back to the North Anna River and camping there. Confederate officials decided to reorganize part of the Confederate cavalry during the latter days of May 1864. These actions would prove to be beneficial for the legion.

On 22 May, Major Andrew P. Love's Fourth Alabama Cavalry Battalion, composed of companies A, B, and C and totaling around 160 men (often referred to affectionately by their Phillips Georgia Legion mates as "the lovelies"), arrived in Danville, Virginia. They joined the Phillips Georgia Legion Cavalry Battalion as companies A, B, C, and D.

---

[20] Ibid., 197; also see General Theo F. Rodenbough, *Sheridan's Richmond Raid in Battles and Leaders of the Civil War*, vol. 4 (New York: The Century Co, 1884, 1887, 1888) 188–94.

[21] J. Sparkman, diary.

They served with the legion until they merged officially with the Jeff Davis Legion on 11 July 1864.[22] At this time, the legion also added a company under Captain Edgeworth Eve from the Cobb's Georgia Legion Cavalry Battalion designated as Company G.[23]

Grant hoped to lure Lee out to assault his army while he moved to the right, but Lee again divined his plans and did not take the bait. By the time Grant reached Hanover Junction, Lee's men were dug in along the North Anna River. Lee was in an excellent position. He could attack the Yankees any time they moved or he could remain in a nearly impregnable defensive position in front of Richmond.[24]

At the same time, there was active skirmishing on the north bank of the river about four miles away on the opposite bank on the left of the Confederate line. A major fight took place at Jericho Mills. Union infantry crossed to the south side of the river and collided with a smaller group of Rebels. Both sides suffered heavy casualties, but the Federals held their position. Lee's well-laid battle plan earned the admiration of military historians for generations. Lee's defenses occupied several miles of the south bank of the North Anna, with its center at Ox Ford, and took the shape of an inverted "V." The line was changed so that the only Confederate strong point on the North Anna River was at Ox Ford, and the two wings angled backward from that point, one southwest and one southeast. The line was shaped somewhat like a "hog's snout." Grant's men would have to cross the river twice to set up for an effective attack. Grant decided to withdraw both wings of the Federal army back across the North Anna River, and he withdrew to sidle around Lee's right once more. Grant stole a march on Lee by heading downstream toward Richmond then marching to the point where the North Anna River flowed into the Pamunkey River, to continue down the north side of the Pamunkey crossing over at Hanovertown Ferry. This plan brought on an unexpected but severe cavalry fight at a nondescript place called Haw's Shop on 28 May. The legion cavalry probably served picket duty with

---

[22] Hopkins, *The Little Jeff*, 198.

[23] Ibid., 199.

[24] OR, ser. 1, Vol. 40/3, [S#82], Special Orders #161, 11 July 1864, Adjutant and Inspector General's Office from Samuel W. Melton, assistant adjutant general.

the Little Jeff on the South Anna River and didn't participate in the Battle of Haw's Shop. Charles Paine Hansell of the Twentieth Georgia Cavalry Battalion, who had the good fortune to run into Captain James Nichols of the legion cavalry a few days later, commented in his diary on Union brigadier general Horace Porter's erroneous assessment of the tactical environment the Twentieth Georgia Infantry Battalion and other cavalry units must have faced: "Gen Horace Porter in his 'Campaigning with Grant' says that at Hawe's Shop they drive the enemy from their entrenchments. If there were any entrenchments anywhere around there they would have been a welcome sight to us. Even small saplings were greedily sought as some protection.[25]

This battle was a precursor to the slaughter at Cold Harbor a few days later. The Haw family machine shop sat adjacent to the handsome Haw home, which remains an active residence. It served as a field hospital during the battle. The machine shop was later merged into the Tredegar Iron Works at Richmond. The Enon United Methodist Church on Studley Road is also still active as a house of worship at its original site.[26]

On the morning of 28 May, Hampton's troopers neared Hanovertown Ferry. A new pontoon bridge across the Pamunkey River suggested to Hampton that Grant was about to cross. Hampton pushed on for a few miles and ran directly into the head of Sheridan's marching cavalry column. Neither Grant nor Lee had any idea as to each other's respective positions. Lee ordered his cavalry to go to Mechanicsville to locate the enemy cavalry. The two cavalry forces smashed into each other near the Haw machine shop and crossroads. Federal brigadier general David M. Gregg's Second Cavalry Division arrived first. Before Gregg could gain control of the crossroads, Hampton's riders arrived on the scene driving in the Yankee pickets who retreated to some high ground west of Haw's Shop. Hampton busied himself constructing breastworks and barricades beside Enon Church and then positioned his dismounted men behind them. The numbers engaged were about even, and for approximately six hours, the opposing forces banged away at

---

[25] Hopkins, *The Little Jeff*, 199–200.
[26] Charles Paine Hansell, diary, 8; also see Sparkman diary, US National Military Park, Manassas, VA, and Hopkins, *The Little Jeff*, 203.

each other with rifles and carbines. The arrival of Brigadier General George A. Custer's Michigan Cavalry Brigade shifted the advantage to the Federals, as the Wolverines overran a Confederate position. Hampton noted that he had taken many prisoners who were mainly infantrymen. The South Carolinian took this to mean that the Federals were crossing the Pamunkey at Hanovertown Ferry. He believed he had learned all that he needed to know from his reconnaissance and then ordered his men to withdraw. After the fight, the Yankees fell back to the Pamunkey and reestablished contact with Meade's army. The legion cavalry did not participate in the Haw's Shop battle because they were stationed with their Jeff Davis comrades as vedettes on the South Anna River.[27]

On 29 May, Young's Brigade, including the legion, rode to the northeast and bumped into a few Yankee pickets. Young surmised that the Federals were on their way to Hanover Court House so he moved his men beyond Ashland and camped for the night. Several skirmishes followed near Ashland later in the day. General Young received a serious chest wound in one of them and handed command over to Gib Wright. Young would be hors de combat for several weeks.

On the next morning of 30 May, a courier informed Colonel Gib Wright that the Yankees were again advancing toward Hanover Court House. The Federals were on their way, hoping to destroy the railroad bridges over the South Anna River. In the short skirmish that followed, the Federals pushed the Rebels back to a point along Mechump's Creek.[28]

On 1 June, Sheridan was ordered to move his cavalry corps to the important road junction at Old Cold Harbor, so named for a local tavern. Sheridan deployed his dismounted troopers on a north-south axis near the old Gaines Mill battlefield from McClellan's 1862 Peninsula Campaign. Sheridan's determined horsemen held off a number of determined attacks by Major General Robert Hoke's Confederate Infantry Division until Union infantry came up to reinforce and relieve Sheridan's wary horsemen. On this same day, Hampton and W. H. F. Lee engaged Wilson's cavalry division, while Union general George Henry Chapman

---

[27] Longacre, *Lee's Cavalrymen*, 294–95; Hopkins, *The Little Jeff*, 203.
[28] Longacre, *Lee's Cavalrymen*, 295–96; also see Hopkins, *The Little Jeff*, 203 and the Sparkman diary, US Military Park, Manassas VA.

moved to destroy two railroad bridges on the South Anna and Union general John Baillie McIntosh's First Brigade headed to Ashland to assist and to destroy the railroad. Hampton and Rosser attacked McIntosh from the east and W. H. F. Lee attacked him from the south. The bridges were destroyed and a stalemate soon developed that degenerated into the brutal bloodletting that became known as the Battle of Cold Harbor. Both sides suffered heavy losses.

Years later, Captain Bethune B. McKenzie of Love's Fourth Alabama Cavalry (then serving with the Phillips Georgia Legion Cavalry Battalion) recounted a harrowing incident that took place around 1 June involving the near capture of two of his men just prior to the beginning of the battle of Cold Harbor:

> We got in position about sunrise, relieved a South Carolina regiment. My instructions were not to advance but hold the position as long as I could until ordered to retire. The two skirmish lines, ours and the Yankees, were about a hundred yards apart and at first there was but little firing on either side...in placing the men along this line J. T. Kendall and W. M. Locke were placed upstairs in a two-story log house which happened to be on our right at the edge of the field where they could see better and were well protected from bullets by the logs of the house. I received orders to slowly withdraw my men. I at once extended the order to the men and we began slowly to fall back. When we had gone about fifty yards I discovered that Kendall and Locke were not in their position on the line and on inquiry found that the messenger, not knowing that they were up in the house, had failed to notify them to fall back...I sent A. A. Dorman to notify Locke and Kendall to get out quick. Just then a squadron of cavalry all mounted on black horses charged down amongst the Yankees we were fighting and created a diversion that enabled Dorman to notify Kendall and Locke to join their commands which they did safely.[29]

The Union and Confederate armies jockeyed for position around Richmond. The battle that followed was one that Ulysses S. Grant lived

---

[29] Ibid, 205–206, also see Hopkins, *The Little Jeff*, 204; Longacre, *Lee's Cavalryman*, 297; Boatner, Civil War Dictionary, 163-64.

to regret. Colonel William W. Rich reported on the combat activity of the legion riders around Cold Harbor in a letter to his wife dated 14 June 1864 from Near Mechanicsville, Virginia:

Please forgive me for not writing sooner, but the Legion has been engaged in considerable action in the past several weeks. I am sure the news of the army's great victory at the recent battle of Cold Harbor, Virginia has reached you by now. The Legion was one of the first units engaged in this battle. Being on patrol to the North of our main infantry force we were engaged by a superior number of Union Cavalry. After the stampede of those new recruits, explained in my previous letter, I was most determined that an orderly withdrawal be made. This proved difficult at times, as there was constant danger of our being flanked. We were however fortunate enough to be able to withdraw to the cover of wood lines several times. This prevented flanking movements and enabled us to inflict losses on the enemy as he approached across open fields. We withdrew to a crossroad that was in full view of many of our infantrymen. In order to regain the confidence of our fellow soldiers and redeem the pride of the Legion, I turned the Legion and mounted a counter attack in full view of the infantrymen. We caught the Union Cavalry by surprise as they were coming out of a tangle of briars and vines in a swampy area and momentarily threw them back. However this attack could not be sustained due to our inferior numbers. We then fell back in splendid order, down the road by twos and through the infantry lines. Our infantry immediately closed the road behind us and opened upon the Union Cavalry with a most effective volley.[30]

The majority of the cavalry of the Army of Northern Virginia was positioned near Atlee's Station to the north of Mechanicsville on the Virginia Central Railroad. Hampton, with Rosser's and Wright's brigades, was in the center. Fitz Lee's division was on their right, and Rooney Lee's division held the left. At dawn on 3 June, Wright moved his men through Atlee's Station to the left of the Rebel infantry while the slaughter at Cold Harbor was starting to die down. On 4 June, the legion

---

[30] W. Rich to Dear Basheba, 14 June 1864 from near Mechanicsville, VA.

and Rooney Lee's division participated in a skirmish near Totopotomoy Creek. The troopers then returned to Atlee's Station and moved farther south near the Meadow Bridge over the Chickahominy River swamp, camped for a few days, and rested their precious mounts. Wright continued active scouting on 6 June. On 7 June, the brigade headed out to Bethesda Church.[31] After failing to break Lee's lines at Cold Harbor, Grant realized that he had run out of room to maneuver around Richmond, just as McClellan had in 1862. He came up with a brilliant plan: he would send off two divisions of his cavalry on a raid to distract the Confederates, then steal a march on Lee, cross the James River, and move on the critical railroad junction town of Petersburg, twenty-one miles south of Richmond. If Grant could seize Petersburg, he would cut the last remaining supply lines from the Deep South and force Lee to come out and fight on ground of Grant's choosing. The fall of Petersburg would also make Richmond untenable and it would inevitably fall. Grant ordered Sheridan to take two divisions of cavalry, march along the north bank of the North Anna, cross the river near Gordonsville, fall on the critical railroad junction at Gordonsville, and then march west along the route of the Virginia Central Railroad to Charlottesville, where he would link up with the army of Major General David Hunter, operating in the Shenandoah Valley. The combined force would then march to Petersburg, where it would join Grant's army for the coup de grace. It was an excellent plan if it could be made to work. Success would sever the flow of supplies and equipment for the Rebel forces in the area.

However, Sheridan's departure on 7 June did not go unnoticed, and reports of the movement westward of a large body of Union cavalry quickly made its way into the Confederate lines. General Lee, divining Sheridan's intentions, ordered Hampton to march with his division and Fitz Lee's division to intercept the Union raiders. Young's brigade, still commanded by Gib Wright during Young's recuperation, was on the move before sunup on 9 June. At Hampton's behest, Wright took the lead to investigate this matter. Hampton intended to interpose his men between the Federals and their objective to the west near Gordonsville and Charlottesville with Fitz Lee right behind. The day 9 June was a sweltering, gloomy one. The Rebel troopers stumbled through the heat

---

[31] Hopkins, *The Little Jeff,* 207.

and dust and slept hardly at all. The following day, 10 June, after taking advantage of interior lines of march and friendly locals, Hampton's troopers found themselves squarely across Sheridan's line of march on the Virginia Central near Green Spring Valley. This was just three miles west of Trevilian Station, an obscure stop on the Virginia Central, named for Louisa County's wealthiest resident, Charles Goodall Trevilian. Hampton was confident he was positioned properly to surprise and attack the Yankee raiders. Fitz Lee's division halted at Louisa Court House, six miles to the east of Trevilian Station. Hampton's scouts had reported the enemy crossing the North Anna River ten miles from his encampment. Sheridan camped near a general store called Clayton's Store, named for Arthur Clayton, an early resident of Louisa County who had been county court justice and county sheriff from 1831 to 1832.[32] There were two routes to the Virginia Central Railroad from the store and south of the river: one that led directly to Trevilian Station and one that led to Louisa Court House. Hampton decided his best bet would be to advance on Sheridan's troopers at Clayton's Store from the direction of Trevilian Station while Fitz Lee's division advanced from Louisa Court House. He would be outnumbered, two to one, but he would smash into the coming Federal enemy anyway.[33]

Butler had picketed the road from Trevilian Station to Clayton's Store. Early in the morning of 11 June, the head of the Federal column encountered Butler's pickets at a place called Bibb's Crossroads, located on the road connecting Trevilian Station and Clayton's Store. Butler brought up the rest of his brigade and Wright's brigade to meet the threat, and a general engagement developed along the road. In the meantime, Brigadier General George Custer's Michigan Cavalry Brigade, moving on Sheridan's flank along the Gordonsville Road, spotted Hampton's entire wagon train parked and Custer ordered the Wolverines to pitch in. They captured the wagon train as well as the

---

[32] Ibid, 208; Louisa County, Virginia Deed Records-Book K, Arthur Clayton died in 1832; Louisa County Historical Society Magazine, 23/1 and 24/1; telephone conversation between Patty Cook and Richard M. Coffman on 19 October 2005.
[33] Ibid, 208–209; Longacre, *Lee's Cavalrymen*, 299–303; Hopkins, 209; Waring Papers, Southern Historical Collection, University of North Carolina, Chapel Hill, NC

attention of Rosser, whose brigade was positioned to guard against any potential movements by Hunter's army from the west. Without waiting for orders, Rosser ordered his brigade to draw sabers and charge. His Virginians crashed into Custer's men near Trevilian Station and a melee broke out. When Fitz Lee's division finally came out from Louisa and engaged, Custer found himself completely surrounded and cut off from the rest of Sheridan's command.

Colonel W. W. Rich related this situation to his wife:

> The past week has seen your husband and the Legion almost constantly in the saddle. We were engaged near the Trevillon [*sic*], Virginia Railroad Depot in a large cavalry engagement on the twelfth. [The correct date was 11 June 1864.] General Custer's unit over ran us at one point and captured a number of men, horses and supplies, however by skillful maneuvering General Hampton abetted the advance, recaptured all that had been lost and forced the withdrawal of the Union Cavalry. The Legion fought both on foot, near the Depot, and mounted in the fields about the area, giving a good account of its self all day. Hampton was forced to withdraw to deal with the problem in his rear.[34]

Confusion reigned for a short time but Hampton quickly restored order. The setting degraded into chaotic shouting and cracking rifles. A determined attack by the Federals finally cut through and freed Custer from his trap. A final attack by Butler's and Rosser's brigades quickly ran out of steam when Rosser received a severe leg wound, and the day's fighting ended with the Federals in possession of the train depot and the day's battlefield. Hampton's division camped a couple of miles to the west, astride the road to Gordonsville, and spent the night and the next morning preparing a strong defensive position. Fitz Lee's division fell back to Louisa for the night.[35]

Sergeant Charles P. Hansell of the Twentieth Battalion of Georgia Cavalry of Wright's Brigade related a frightening experience that occurred on 11 June 1864. When Hansell and his men were lost and

---

[34] W. Rich to Basheba, 14 June 1864 from near Louisa Court House.
[35] Hopkins, *The Little Jeff*, 209.

confused, Captain James Hall Nichols of legion cavalry Company A appeared and provided direction and leadership:

> The next morning, Saturday, June 11th, at an early hour this Reg't was formed in the Pike near us, and I there recognized Capt. Frank W. Hopkins by his resemblance to others of his family then in Thomasville. They moved off down the pike over the same route we had come the P.M. before and in a few minutes the rest of the Brig. followed. We left the pike and turned square off to the left or northward, rode by a large two story house, through a small piece of woods, and then halted and remained here for some time, sitting on our horses and listening to the firing in front where the dismounted 7th and Butler's Brig. were engaging the enemy, and listening with still sharper interest at the singing of the minie balls as they went over or by us at short intervals. While waiting here quite a number of prisoners passed by going to the rear and some wounded men. Anyone who has been situated just that way or anywhere that the minies were whistling can tell you that even an ordinary horse feels like he might be 15 feet instead of 15 hands high. After a while, much to my relief, our squadron was ordered to dismount and report to Capt. Jimmie Nichols of the Phillips Legion. This gallant and clever officer led us through the woods and across a small field to the fence nearest to where the fight seemed to be progressing. We could not see any distance in front of us because the woods were too thick. We had scarcely taken our position behind this fence when we were ordered to fall back. We returned to where we had dismounted and Capt. Nichols mounted his men and left us, we were told to mount and did so, but were at a loss where to go.[36]

Captain Hugh Buchanan of company D was wounded in the chest on 11 June 1864. The wound damaged his left lung. He was later

---

[36] Charles Paine Hansell, diary, 16, Georgia Department of Archives and History, 5800 Jonesboro Road, Morrow, GA 30260.

furloughed for sixty days and made his way home to Newnan, Georgia, with the help of his servant.[37]

Some of Sheridan's men spent the morning of 12 June destroying the Virginia Central between Louisa and Trevilian Station. The rest of his command spent the morning resting while Fitz Lee's division made a long flank march around the Federals to join Hampton. His command arrived late in the afternoon after fighting was already underway. Sheridan, still determined to reach Gordonsville, ordered a sortie by Brigadier General Alfred T. A. Torbert's First Cavalry Division. Sending Custer's Wolverines forward dismounted along the railroad, the heavy fire laid down by Butler's South Carolinians soon drove them back. Torbert committed the reserve brigade and a brigade of Gregg's Second Division, and the Confederates repulsed seven separate attacks by the Federals. Before long, the two sides battered each other from a distance of forty feet or less in places. Lee's division arrived during these attacks, and he dispatched one of his brigades to flank Torbert's position.

After the Rebels repulsed the seventh Federal attack, Lee's men launched their flanking attack, which triggered a frontal attack by the rest of the Confederate cavalry. The combined force crushed Torbert's command, rolled up its flank, and sent the Yankee horsemen fleeing. They fell back to Clayton's Store. Low on ammunition and finally persuaded that he would be unable to fulfill his mission, Sheridan decided to fall back. His men began crossing the North Anna River late that night, utterly defeated. The legion suffered ten casualties during this battle.

That night, dead and wounded men littered the battlefield. That same night, Lieutenant Colonel William W. Rich and a detachment of his troopers from the legion cavalry scoured the battlefield for loose horses and boots. Rich reported a humorous incident:

Later that day, near dark, myself and a detachment entered some woods looking for stray horses when we came upon a young

---

[37] Report of the examining board in Gen. Hosp. #4, at Richmond for furloughs s Shows date of injury 6/11/64-"V.S. through left lung much debilitated-given 60 day furlough, Destination, Newman, GA; Newnan Herald, 1982; telephone conversation between Richard M. Coffman and Libby Buchanan, 1998.

Union Lieutenant and five of his men dashing about the woods, apparently cut off and lost from their unit. We quickly surrounded the group who apparently had no further cartridges for their weapons. They backed into a tight circle and drew their sabers. As I approached the group the young Lieutenant advised me they intended to fight us to the death. I assured him that was not necessary. I told our men to draw their pistols and aim them at these men. I then called on the Lieutenant to surrender. He informed me that he had heard Rebels were afraid to fight with sabers. I ask[ed] the men to holster their pistols, draw their sabers and advance on these men at a walk. Suddenly the Lieutenant walked his horse forward and with great pomp and arrogance, offered me his sword in surrender, advising that his position was untenable due to the superior numbers about him and his men. I told the Union men to dismount, lay their sabers and guns on the ground and remove their boots, which they did after much grumbling and oath swearing. I had our men to retrieve their weapons, boots and horses. I advised the Lieutenant that he was free to go. We were not interested in any more Union prisoners, that Richmond was full, but we were interested in horses and boots. We then turned and walked away. Looking back I could see the Lieutenant and his men, disarmed, dismounted and in their stocking feet running through the woods, where they most assuredly would be captured again within the hour. The story was told all about the camp that evening and the men were much amused by the event.[38]

On 13 June, skirmishers patrolled near the station at dawn and discovered that the Yankees were gone. Sheridan's raid was a failure. He had smashed the Virginia Central, but the Rebels quickly repaired the damage. Hampton dogged Sheridan's retreat across the Virginia countryside. Sheridan's command did not rejoin the Army of the Potomac until 24 June.

---

[38] W. Rich to Dear Basheba, n.d., from near Louisa Court House.

In the meantime, Grant's army began crossing the James on the morning of 13 June, successfully stealing a march on Lee's army. By 16 June, he had reached Petersburg and only a determined defense by a scratch force commanded by General P. G. T. Beauregard prevented Grant from seizing the Cockade City and cutting the supply line to Richmond. By the end of the third week of June, the Yankee attack had failed and Lee's army had taken position along the lines at Petersburg, which was secured for the Confederates by 18 June.

From 20 through 22 June, Wright's brigade of Hampton's cavalry corps pursued Sheridan. On 21 June, Sheridan's command arrived at White House Landing on the Pamunkey River, where it took on an additional burden. Since the Federals had shifted their base of operations to Petersburg, there was no reason to maintain a huge supply depot at White House Landing. Confederate authorities ordered Sheridan to escort more than a thousand wagons and a division of United States Colored Troops from White House Landing to join the rest of the Army of the Potomac at Petersburg. Sheridan's wagon train crossed the James River near Charles City Court House on 24 June. Sheridan left David M. Gregg's cavalry division near Samaria (St. Mary's) Church to act as a rear guard. Hampton, with six brigades of cavalry, saw an opportunity to pounce on Gregg's two isolated brigades. Gregg's men took position near a sawmill at Nance's Shop while Hampton planned his attack.

The legion riders remained in readiness for a short time. At first they were to support a charge by the Seventh Virginia Cavalry, but the Virginians did not move ahead, so the legion was ordered to throw up breastworks. A nasty fight ensued between the dismounted Rebels and Yankees, which was supported by a saber charge by the mounted elements of Hampton's command. The Phillips Legion cavalry was in the lead with the Little Jeff close behind. In all, the Rebels charged three more times and drove the Yankees back toward Charles City Court House in a wild rout. Once they reached Charles City Court House, the Federals blocked the road and made a successful stand by early evening. The Confederates finally backed off and camped for the night. General Hampton praised the Phillips' and Jeff Davis legions' performances: "As soon as the enemy gave way, I brought up the Phillips and the Jeff Davis Legions [mounted] and ordered them to charge. This they did most gallantly, driving the enemy three miles in confusion." The Rebels bagged several hundred Federal prisoners and General Gregg narrowly escaped capture.

Cavalry tactics changed in mid-1864 because of the availability of repeating rifles and carbines. Advances in technology drove the evolution of tactics. Brave and spectacular as they were, old-fashioned cavalry charges were no longer the order of the day for one solid reason: they were suicidal. For the legion cavalry, more fighting was in the offing, but it would be primarily in dismounted mode. On the command "dismount to fight," three of four troopers would dismount and pull the reins of the horses together and the one remaining trooper would take the reins of all four horses and move them to the rear for instant remounting. This tactic deceived the Federals into thinking there were more Rebels than there actually were. However, the Confederate cavalry did not possess the technological advantages enjoyed by their Union counterparts. Only a handful of Southern horse soldiers carried repeaters, and most of those were captured. The majority of the Confederate cavalry rode with two-band Enfield rifles, which were at a distinct disadvantage when compared to the firepower laid down by the rapid firing breechloaders carried by the enemy. The focus of further cavalry action moved southward into the brambled and wooded areas south of Richmond.[39]

Confederate positions at Petersburg consisted of a semi-circular chain of breastworks over ten miles long (also known as the "Dimmock" line, named for Captain Charles Dimmock, the Confederate engineer who designed and built them several years earlier). The line began and ended east and west of Petersburg on the banks of the Appomattox River. The eastern and western portions circled back to the river. Petersburg was the junction of several major incoming and outgoing railroads. Union cavalry under General James H. Wilson made every effort to damage or destroy these railroads and set off on an extended raid on the Weddon and Southside Railroad on 24 June. On the morning of the 28th, the legion passed Reams Station and headed toward the Stony Creek Depot with the rest of Hampton's division. Fitz Lee remained at Reams Station and around noon Hampton's riders reached Stony Creek Station.

---

[39] Edward L. Wells, *Hampton and His Cavalry in '64* (Richmond VA: Johnson, 1988) 220.

The Federals were not there. This put the South Carolinian in an ideal position to intercept Wilson and Hampton sent Colonel Gib Wright's and General John Randolph, Jr., Chambliss's troopers ahead. Their orders were to engage the enemy at the first opportunity. Supported by their artillery these dismounted Rebels attacked the Yankees near Sappony Church. The Federals, under Wilson, fell back to Sappony Church immediately and placed themselves in a strong defensive position behind Little Sappony Creek and brought their own artillery into action. .

Wilson realized he was in grave danger. Hampton might cut him off and destroy him if he attempted to cross the railroad at Stony Creek Station. So Wilson shifted to the left, moving toward Reams Station. The Federals tried their best to break through the Rebel lines to the east but failed. Wright's and Chambliss's dismounted troopers assumed prone positions and fired one volley. The Yankees refused to charge, then firing ceased, and the Rebel troopers built breastworks. Rebel infantry was called on to shore up the defenses at Reams Station in the event Wilson attacked the Confederate cavalry there.[40]

Sporadic firing continued throughout the night as Confederate dismounted troopers moved up to find the Federal trenches in their front abandoned. At daylight on 29 June, General Matthew C. Butler's dismounted gray troopers struck Wilson in flank and rear. Hampton and Fitz Lee attacked Wilson's and General August V. Kautz's combined divisions near Reams Station at the same time. Wilson and Kautz lost 1,500 of their 4,500 men plus all of their artillery and wagons. The others were lucky to escape at all. Hampton had good reason to be proud of himself and his troopers, because the Yankee riders had suffered due to his leadership at Trevilian Station, Samaria Church, and now Ream's Station. A letter from Captain James H. Nichols of Company A of the legion cavalry said it well: "I think Gen. Hampton has convinced them that raiding is an unprofitable investment."[41]

---

[40] Hopkins, *The Little Jeff*, 214. Captain Nichols, 9 July 1864 from Stony Creek Station, between Petersburg and Weldon R. R. in *Southern Recorder*, p. 2, column 3.

[41] Ibid, 217-19.Captain Nichols to wife 9 July 1864 from camp near Stony Creek Station, Petersburg, and Weldon R. R. in *Southern Recorder*, page 2, column 3.

Legionnaire E. J. Humphries provided his sister with a poignant account of his experiences at this time:

As I don't expect any of my letters have gone through from Richmond, I thought I would give you a few lines to let you know that I am able to eat all my rations although the Yanks have tried a good many times to put me East eating every since I left home. The first was on the 22nd, the second time on the 24th, third was on night of 28th and morning of 29th. (At Reams Station.) The last was the heaviest fire I was ever under. I worked harder that night than I ever did in my life trying to get us some breastworks fixed which we succeeded in doing after whipping the Yanks back twice. They charged us four different times that night but never got nearer than forty yards of our breastworks before we drove them back. Yesterday morning was the time that we caught it. After waiting a while for them to advance on us and they not doing so, we concluded to advance on them. When we had advanced about half a mile, we found them behind their breastwork waiting for us and the way they did pour balls into our ranks was a sad sight. They were giving us fits. Butlers Brigade took them on the right flank completely routing them. The Yanks have been very kind in furnishing me equipment since I have been out here. They have furnished me with saddle, Bridle, Halter, gun pistol and anything I wanted in that line. They also furnished me with a nice piece of shell in the left arm above the elbow, night before last. It is only a slight wound, merely bruising my arm enough to keep me from fighting them for three or four days.[42]

About 15 August, General P. M. B. Young returned to resume command of his brigade. Hampton was stationed at Taylor's Farm near the Chickahominy River at this time. The following day, Rooney Lee was involved in a skirmish some eight miles up the Charles City Road.

---

[42] E. Humphries to Dear Sis, 30 June 1864 from Stony Creek Station, between Petersburg and Walden.

Hampton flanked the Yankees by moving over White Oak Swamp to the Williamsburg Road then crossed the White Oak Bridge and attacked the Federals' rear on Charles City Road. The Federals suffered severe losses. Most of Young's Brigade camped near Bottoms Bridge after the fight. No major contact took place during the next few days. The legion's mounts needed replacements, fodder, and rest.

On 20 August, the Yankees, located south of the James River, moved against the Weldon Railroad at Globe Tavern, south of Petersburg. This movement cut the railroad supply lines to Petersburg from the south, which meant that supplies now had to be offloaded at the Stony Creek Depot and then hauled west by Flat Foot Road to Dinwiddie Court House, and then east by Boydton Plank Road and on to Petersburg.[43]

The Northerners readied themselves for another raid from their position at Globe Tavern. Two days later, Major General Matthew C. Butler's troopers of Young's Brigade fought enemy cavalry near the intersection of the Vaughn and Stage roads. The gray troopers pushed the Yankees back to their breastworks near the Weldon Railroad. Hampton believed he had found an opening but needed more men from the defenses around Petersburg in order to exploit it. General R. E. Lee agreed and sent several of Hill's Brigades to help Hampton on 24 August. Young's Brigade spent 25 August marching. The Confederates received reports indicating that the Yankees had established outposts just south of Reams Station. At sunup, Hampton's men smashed into the Yankee outposts and drove them back into their fortifications. Hill's infantry had arrived and joined Hampton and his horse artillery in two major attacks against the Federal positions at Reams Station. At 5:00 P.M., Hampton's troopers charged the southernmost point of the enemy fortifications and routed the Yankees. The Rebel cavalry then screened the withdrawal of Hill's infantry back to Petersburg and picketed Reams Station. Lee was pleased and notified the Secretary of War: "One line of breastworks was carried by the cavalry under General Hampton with great gallantry, who contributed to the success of the day."[44]

---

[43] D Hopkins, *The Little Jeff*, 229–30.
[44] OR, vol. 42, pt. 1, 942–46.

On 4 September, E. J. Humphries described this fighting in a letter home. "Everything seems to be quiet around here now. I have not heard one gun in twenty-four hours—which is something that has not happened before in the last two months—always a calm before a storm they say. But I am in hopes it will not come so this time, not before I get off I am in hopes at least."[45]

On the home front, Lucinda Eveline Milhollin had her own problems. Her husband Captain John Fielding Milhollin, commander of Company B of the legion cavalry, had been killed on 10 November 1863 while leading a scout during the fighting around Rappahannock Station. His body, accompanied by his brother-in-law James M. Dodgen, had been conveyed back to his home in Cassville, Georgia, and buried there. John's cavalry saber (probably manufactured by the Confederacy) and full-fluted cylinder, six-shot, .44 caliber, eight-inch barrel, Colt 1860 model Army revolver had been hidden under the grave marker but were discovered by soldiers of the Fifth Ohio Volunteer Cavalry. One unhappy day brought a Federal officer to Lucinda's house. He claimed to have orders to burn the house and told her she had twenty minutes to remove her furniture. The Yankees burned the house to the ground, and Lucinda, her six children, and youngest sister, Jane, had to sleep under a shelter over her husband's grave. To add insult to injury, a Yankee officer offered to take her and her children with him and his wagons to Ohio. In no uncertain terms, she refused his offer. This tiny, brave woman lived to be 83 years old, never remarried, and successfully raised her little sister and all of her surviving children.[46]

Another incident on the home front that occurred in late November 1864 must have caused enormous distress for the ubiquitous Captain James H. Nichols of the legion's Company A, Governor's Horse Guards. His wife, Kate Nichols (nee Latimer), had been residing at the isolated Midway Community (commonly referred to by the locals in Milledgeville, Georgia, as "The Asylum"). She had been confined to her

---

[45] E. Humphries to Dear Puss, 4 September 1864 from near Petersburg.

[46] Interview with Lucinda Dodgen Milholland by Lily Milholland Dodgen in *The Bartow* (Cartersville GA) *Herald*, entitled "Grandma's War Memories," 9 April 1931. Also Herb Peck to Dear Buck, 16 March 1976, 3332 Love Circle, Nashville, Tenn. 37212.

bed with an unknown illness when two Federal soldiers threatened to shoot a Negro guard, forced their way into her room, and allegedly raped her. This unfortunate woman had a history of mental illness, having been admitted to the Asylum in April 1858 and June 1860. She later died in a mental institution. The nature of her illness is not known, although it could have been a case of clinical depression and/or post-traumatic stress disorder.[47]

During the remainder of November 1864, the legion continued picket duty and prepared winter quarters. The availability of suitable horses remained a serious problem to the end of the war.

General Young's detached troopers, including the legion in Georgia, stayed busy during the month of December. Those men able to remount at Waynesboro reported to Captain Francis Edgeworth Eve, Company G commander, formerly of Cobb's Legion. They then traveled by rail to Pocotaligo, South Carolina, on 6 December. E. J. Humphries, with Young's command at this time, wrote a letter to his wife dated 11 December 1864:

> We were fixing to go up there to Savannah when word came that the Road was cut up here by the Yanks, so we made about wheel and come here to drive off the Yanks & hold open the Road. We did not find things as bad as reported but found the Yanks close enough to shell the trains as they pass to & from Charleston & Savannah. We can hear very heavy Cannonading in the direction of Savannah this morning. I think either Savannah or Sherman will go up by tomorrow night. I am fearful for Savannah but I hope Sherman.[48]

---

[47] *The Journal of a Milledgeville Girl 1861–1867*, ed. J. Bonner (Athens: University of Georgia Press, 1964) 61–63; K. Walters, *Oconee River*, 307; J. Bonner, *Milledgeville, Georgia's Antebellum Capital*, (Athens: University of Georgia Press, 1978); R. Davis, *The Georgia Black Book: Morbid, Macabre & Sometimes Disgusting Records of Genealogical Value* (Easley SC: Southern Historical Press, 1982) 199–201, 46. E. Humphries to Dear Wife, 11 December 1864, from between Pocotaligo and Coosawhatchie.

[48] E. Humphries to Dear Wife, 11 December 1864 from Pocotaligo SC.

On 27 December, Young's riders were ordered to march to Grahamsville, South Carolina, to join Major General Joseph Wheeler's Cavalry Corps of General P. G. T. Beauregard's army. The legion suffered several casualties there. E. J. Humphries related his thoughts as well as the movements of the legion cavalry in a letter dated 30 December 1864:

You must excuse me for not writing sooner as I have been on the move and have not had a chance of sending letters off. I thought we were off for Georgia some five days ago but got sadly disappointed. We started from Hardeeville last Tuesday and went about thirty miles when we received orders to come to this place. I don't know how long we will stay here but I don't think more than a few days before we will go up farther toward Charleston. A portion of our Command has gone on to Augusta. I am in hopes the balance of us will get to go on there in a few days. This leaves me in good health & I am in hopes may find you all in good health & fine spirits. Speaking of spirits puts me in mind that I have not had a drink this Christmas. Wish I had one to day as it is sprinkling of rain & we have to go some four or five miles on picket to night. This paper is some of the wreck of old Savannah, which you know went up a spout on the morning of the 20th inst. We had a small fight with the Yanks on the 19th. We lost four men killed on the field and some twenty wounded. Two since died. We tried to charge the Yanks out of a small skirt of woods but failed in doing so. They come very nigh to hitting of me. They sent a ball so close to me that it struck my gun on the lock and it flattened so that it did not hurt me when it struck on the cap. If it had not struck my gun first it would have sent me up a spout.[49]

---

[49] E. Humphries to Dear Wife, 30 December 1864, from Grahamsville SC.

By the end of 1864, the three divisions of Hampton's cavalry corps had been scattered from Virginia to the Carolinas. The end of this year marked the beginning of the four-month Carolinas campaign for the Phillips Legion dragoons and 1864 as the last full year of the war.

8

GOING BACK THE WAY THEY CAME

"Such a thing as surrender, and the idea of Lee's surrender, was unthinkable! But it proved to be a fact and was soon verified, as his men came plodding by footsore and weary. Paroled! What a shock! I was nineteen years of age, color bearer for the Phillips Legion, I dropped down my flag, and for two days and nights I rolled in the dust, kicked, and cussed and vowed, neither ate nor slept much."[1]

The Phillips Georgia Legion cavalry battalion suffered a great loss of leadership on 9 January 1865 when its popular and much-respected commander, Lieutenant Colonel William Wofford Rich, resigned his Confederate army commission. The legion cavalry's surgeon, J. W. Coxe, examined Rich and diagnosed him as ailing from chronic hepatitis and apoplexy. Major Wesley Wailes Thomas, former commander of legion cavalry Company F, succeeded Rich. Rich's application did not become effective until 27 January 1865.

Rich's trip back to his home in Cassville, Georgia, was nightmarish. Several recently freed, marauding slaves attacked and seriously injured him, but in spite of the pain, he was strong enough to push on to his home, recuperate, and begin a new life. He served two terms as sheriff for Bartow County, worked as a railroad agent for nearby Cartersville, and opened a mercantile store.

Rich often played with two black orphans who loitered around his Cassville office when he arrived in the morning. The children touched his heart. The local community had not cared for them, so he took them into his own home. Family lore has it that his wife, Basheba, saw him coming home with the children and asked him what he had for her. He replied that he had two children. She told him to bring them to her home,

---

[1] J. Evans, "With Hampton's Scouts," *Confederate Veteran* 1.

where they were nurtured and spent their playtime with Rich's biological children for over a decade until Rich died at the age of sixty-nine.[2]

During the Carolinas Campaign, which lasted from 1 February to 26 April 1865, the Federal force commanded by Major General William T. Sherman heavily outnumbered the Confederates under General Pierre Gustave Toutant Beauregard. One of Beauregard's subordinates, Lieutenant General William Joseph Hardee, commanded the small corps that had evacuated Savannah and then marched to Charleston. Hardee had departed Charleston in February and managed to keep one step ahead of Sherman's army, hoping to link up with the remainder of the Confederate forces in North Carolina. In addition to Hardee's Corps, Beauregard's scattered force consisted of Major General Matthew Calbraith Butler's cavalry division (including the Phillips Legion cavalry) recently transferred from Virginia, General Joseph Wheeler's small cavalry corps, and elements of the Army of Tennessee's infantry. Beauregard's forces totaled roughly 22,500.[3]

Grant's overall strategy called for the combined armies of Sherman, Meade, and Union major general Edward Otho Cresap Ord to destroy Lee's Army of Northern Virginia. To provide Sherman an alternate base if needed, Grant ordered the capture of the port city of Wilmington. The Federal troops under Major General John M. Schofield took the city on 22 February. In February 1865, Union general Sherman then divided his

---

[2] See Court of Ordinary Bartow County at Chambers, 23 June 1869, W. W. Rich to Lavinia Johnson and Charles Gresham, Application to have Minors Bound Out, telephone conversation between Richard M. Coffman and Darryl Starnes, great-grandson of Colonel William Wofford Rich and Rich Family historian. Lavinia married at fifteen or sixteen, moved to Richmond, and became an expert horse breeder/trainer. Charles tended Colonel Rich's grave until his own death. Also see letter dated 9 January 1865 from W. W. Rich to gen. hdq. Phillips Legion Cav. then forwarded to Gen. S. Cooper at Hdq. in Richmond and endorsed by J. W. Coxe, maj. surg. in charge Phillips Legion.

[3] D. Hopkins, *The Little Jeff: The Jeff Davis Legion, Cavalry Army of Northern Virginia* (Shippensburg PA: White Mane Books, 1999) 253; also see M. Bradley, *This Astounding Close* (Chapel Hill: University of North Carolina Press, 2000) 1, 2; also see M. Bradley, *Last Stand in the Carolinas, The Battle of Bentonville* (Mason City IA: Savas Publishing Company, 1996) 20, 54, 61, 409, and 410; and M. Boatner, *The Civil War Dictionary* (New York: David McKay Company, 1988) 123–25.

army into two wings, as he had done on the March to the Sea, and advanced into South Carolina. He intended to push through the Carolinas and combine with Grant's forces in Virginia.

Sherman's left wing marched overland from Savannah, crossed the Savannah River into South Carolina, and then proceeded forty miles to Robertsville. One corps of the Federal right wing had been shifted north from Savannah to Beaufort, South Carolina. Rivers overflowing their banks and logistical problems delayed their advance until early February. Once on the road, however, Sherman marched through South Carolina in two parallel columns with Brigadier General Judson Kilpatrick's cavalry division covering his left flank. After the fall of Wilmington, Sherman directed Schofield to advance from Wilmington and New Berne and join him at Goldsboro, North Carolina, the junction of two coastal railroads: the Atlantic and North Carolina and the Wilmington and Weldon. After resting and resupplying his army at Goldsboro, Sherman would march into Virginia and combine with the forces under General Grant.[4]

By 9 January 1865, the legion cavalry had been split up, with some of the legion troopers in Augusta, Georgia, and some in Charleston, South Carolina. The legion cavalrymen in Augusta made up a portion of the dismounted cavalry that had been sent to Georgia under General Young in September 1864. Sergeant Humphries had been assigned to the Charleston group. Humphries was in fine health and described his living conditions to his wife from his quarters on the corner of Society and Meeting streets. "We have a plenty of house room here," Humphries wrote, "as the people all deserted the houses down here when the Yanks used to shell the place. They have not shelled the place any, for about a month."[5] On the night of 17 February, the Charleston contingent of the legion cavalry evacuated Charleston with the rest of Hardee's Corps.

During this late period, several skirmishes took place at several remote locations. Little is known about these clashes except that they involved the legion troopers. The first action occurred on 4 February 1865 at Angley's Post Office, seventy-five miles southwest of Columbia,

---

[4] Hopkins, *The Little Jeff*, 253–54, R. C. Black, *The Railroads of the Confederacy* (Chapel Hill: University of North Carolina Press, 1998) 14, 20.
[5] E. Humphries to Dear Wife, 9 January 1865, from Corner Society and Meeting streets, No.154-Charleston, SC, 12m.

South Carolina. On 8 February, they skirmished with the Federals at Williston, South Carolina, twenty-two miles southwest of Orangeburg. On the same day, the legion riders collided with the Federals at White Pond, five miles west of Williston.

On 11 February, Young's small body of cavalrymen that had accompanied him to Georgia (including a portion of the legion) skirmished with elements of Sherman's army as it neared Orangeburg. The next day Federal soldiers sacked and burned Orangeburg. This was a portent of the grim fate in store for the rest of the Palmetto State in Sherman's path.[6] John Hammon of Company G was killed at Orangeburg on 11 February. Hammon was probably a late-war enlistee since he does not appear on any unit rosters.[7]

Minor cavalry skirmishes continued as Sherman's forces headed north from Robertsville toward the South Carolina state capital. On 12–13 February, the Southern cavalrymen fought a force of the bluecoats at the North Edisto River, a few miles above Orangeburg.

By the evening of 14 February, the legion troopers had arrived at Columbia. They passed through the city and camped on the outskirts. On the same day, Beauregard realized that Sherman intended to strike Columbia. His army was then around twelve miles from the capital, and the troops marched as rapidly as their aching feet would take them.[8] Only Butler's and Wheeler' cavalries and a small infantry unit from the Army of Tennessee stood in Sherman's way, and they were no match for 60,000 veteran Federal soldiers. On 16 February, Wade Hampton, who had just arrived at Columbia, was promoted to lieutenant general and appointed commander of all Confederate cavalry confronting Sherman.

---

[6] Hopkins, *The Little Jeff*, 254–55.

[7] "Civil War: Sherman in Orangeburg, Various Incidents (Cont.), Confederate Killed Here…," *Orangeburg Democrat*, 10 March 1881; "Killed in Orangeburg Action," *Times and Democrat*, 26 June 1884. "Confederate Killed Here. We are requested to state for the benefit of the survivors of the Confederate dead, that John Hammon, Young's Brigade, Georgia Cavalry, Company G, Phillips Legion, was killed on 11 February 1865 near the Railroad Depot at Orangeburg by the forces of Gen. Sherman. His body is buried at the Cemetery of the Protestant Episcopal Church of the Redeemer near the place where he fell."

[8] Hopkins, *The Little Jeff*, 257.

The Federals were rapidly massing near Columbia. The legion riders observed their deployment from the Congaree River. On 16 February, the legion cavalrymen settled in the city center with other units under Hampton. The date 17 February was a day of sorrows. Soldiers discovered supplies of liquor, and many of Hampton's men became heavily intoxicated. However, the men did not shirk their duties when they heard that Sherman had entered Columbia and that the mayor had surrendered the city. Hampton's men headed north, and his rear guard burned the bridges over the Congaree River. On 18 February, the legion cavalry formed a line of battle along a ridge near the Charlotte and Columbia Railroad. On the same day, General Butler came into possession of an excellent map of South Carolina, which he entrusted to the care of Ulysses Robert Brooks, a trooper of Company B, Sixth South Carolina Cavalry, and the future author of a volume on General Butler's army career. Distracted by several charming ladies, Brooks forgot to take the map with him. Shortly thereafter, Butler called for the map and an embarrassed Brooks, riding an exhausted horse, returned to his lady friends and retrieved it. Brooks also recounted an incident that occurred about this time that involved a rash comrade named McDaniel:

A private soldier belonging to the Phillips Legion named McDaniel, being possessed with more pluck than judgment, charged fourteen Yankees in the Campbell House. Well do I remember how poor old Mrs. Campbell looked when she ran out of the house and said, "My gracious alives, men, if you don't stop that shooten somebody is gwine to git hurt." I soon discovered she was right. My horse was shot, and so was I, but the poor horse had enough strength to take me to the swamp, where McDaniel and I held a council of war and decided to separate at once. Poor fellow, I hope he is doing well—I have not heard of him since.[9]

---

[9] J. Sparkman, diary, US National Military Park, Manassas, VA.; U. R. Brooks, *Butler and His Cavalry in the War of Secession, 1863–1865* (Columbia SC: The State Company, 1909) 419–20. The name McDaniel does not appear on any of the legion cavalry company rosters. Perhaps Brooks was mistaken about the name of the legion cavalry man, or his memory may have failed him over the years since the book in which it appears was published in 1909, forty years after the war.

Stalled by floods, the Yankees advanced only a short distance by the next day. That night the legion riders headed out toward Winnsboro.[10] The morning report for 19 February laid bare the manpower limitations of the legion. Only thirteen officers and 131 enlisted men were mounted. A total of thirty-four enlisted men were dismounted. Fourteen were sick and twelve were on extra duty.[11]

Riding with Butler's division, the legion cavalry arrived near Winnsboro just after midnight on 19 February. They passed through the town, continued for about eight miles, and then camped at McCoy's farm. At this time, part of the Confederate army moved north along the railroad toward Charlotte, North Carolina, its rear protected by elements of Wheeler's cavalry. On 21 February, Butler received orders to place his two brigades around Sherman's right and harass his flanks and rear. Beauregard assumed that Sherman was heading toward Charlotte. On 21 February, Butler sent scouts to determine if his movement to Sherman's right could be made through Winnsboro. Because the roads were too well guarded, the scouts were forced to alter their line of march and head east toward Camden. The legion participated in several poorly documented skirmishes with little effect and few casualties. The Confederates were forced to detour even farther because increasing numbers of Federals were blocking their movement. The Rebels now knew that Sherman was not heading toward Charlotte but was proceeding eastward at a right angle.[12]

On 25 February, General Joseph Eggleston Johnston assumed command of the Confederate forces opposing Sherman with General Beauregard relegated to second in command. Johnston's command included all troops in Hardee's Department of South Carolina, Georgia, and Florida, the Army of Tennessee contingent, and Hampton's cavalry. As of early March, Johnston also commanded the Department of North Carolina troops under General Braxton Bragg in North Carolina.[13]

---

[10] Hopkins, *The Little Jeff*, 258; Sparkman diary, US Military Park, Manassas, VA.

[11] Ibid., 258.

[12] Ibid., 259.

[13] Hopkins, *The Little Jeff*, 260. OR, *The Civil War in South Carolina*-Index, 10, also see Brooks, *Butler and His Cavalry*, 470–71.

Meanwhile, on 23 February, Butler's Division crossed the Catawba River. The next day, the gray riders trotted south toward Lancaster and then veered toward Camden, attacking enemy foragers and taking several prisoners. On 25 February, the troopers assaulted Sherman's wagon train at Cantey's Plantation near Little Lynch's Creek. The bluecoats lost nineteen wagons and teams as well as 200 prisoners. The prisoners and wagons were rushed to the bridge over Little Lynch's Creek. As the legion troopers were clearing the bridge, a large body of Federal infantry descended on Young's Brigade under Colonel Gilbert J. "Gib" Wright but did little damage. The trouble didn't end there. The legion riders had to ride through a swampy area on the north side of Lynch's, and a squad of mounted bummers attacked them. The legion as rearguard killed, captured, or wounded seventeen Yankees. Butler's troopers skirmished with the Federals at West Cross Roads. A minor skirmish took place between Butler's men and the Yankees at Stroud's Mills on Rocky Creek near the road from Rossville to Rich Hill.[14]

On 27 February, scouts from the Jeff Davis Legion learned from Yankee prisoners that Wilmington, North Carolina, had been evacuated. The gray riders also skirmished with the enemy at Cloud's House. Meanwhile, Hardee was in Cheraw, just a few miles south from the North Carolina border, attempting to save a large stockpile of supplies and equipment.[15]

General Butler decided to push his two brigades to the northeast on 28 February and join Hardee. He was directed to place his troopers in a picket line along Thompson's Cree, about eight miles west of Cheraw. On 1 March, Butler's scouts found the Yankees on the Old Stage Road, twelve miles from Cheraw. The gray riders withdrew from their positions and headed toward Chesterfield, arriving there at first light the next morning only to find that the enemy had advanced to the outskirts of town from the west, forcing Butler back across Thompson's Creek. Later that night Butler headed toward Cheraw, with the Yankees following close behind in the darkness. On the evening of 2 March, Hardee decided to evacuate Cheraw and Butler's cavalry followed as rear guard. At

---

[14] Hopkins, *The Little Jeff*, 4. OR, *The Civil War in South Carolina*-Index, 10, also see Brooks, *Butler and His Cavalry*, 470–71.

[15] Ibid., 262.

sunup on 3 March, the legion cavalrymen approached Cheraw, where they learned that a Federal force was near enough to cut them off from Hardee. General Butler described his perilous situation:

> I scarcely had time to get in one of my brigades from up the Chesterfield Road before the enemy reached the outskirts of Cheraw on the Camden Road. I halted a Georgia battalion of infantry in the forks of the two roads to hold the enemy in check until Young's (Wright's) Brigade could get in on the Chesterfield Road. As it was forty-six men were cut off, but they managed to make their way across the river higher up and escaped.[16]

The legion troopers galloped along the road toward Cheraw, arriving there before the Federals. Two skirmishes took place on 3 March at Big Black Creek (now Black Creek Church Road) southeast of Blakeny (also referred to as Blakeny's Crossroads), and at Blakeny itself (now Pageland), fifty miles south of Charlotte. Another minor set-to between the gray riders and the Yankees took place at Himsborough. (This is probably modern Hornsboro, near Chesterfield. The Official Records describe "Himsborough" as a confused location because it does not appear on any modern or period maps.)[17] On Saturday, 4 March, Hardee's Corps, closely followed by Hampton's cavalry, marched toward Fayetteville, North Carolina. Meanwhile, the Confederate army's general in chief, Robert E. Lee, assigned General Braxton Bragg's Department of North Carolina troops to Johnston's command. Sergeant E. J. Humphries recounted his changing locations and miserable marching conditions around this time in a letter written to his wife later on 12 March:

> I am now in the rear of the Yanks with a portion of our regiment trying to make our way around Sherman's left flank to get in his front. I expect we will have a lively time of it when we get there. When we left Charleston we were in front of Sherman

---

[16] Ibid., 263, U. Brooks, *Butler and His Cavalry*, 473.

[17] OR, *The Civil War in South Carolina*-Index 6, A Guide-Index to the OR, vol. 3, sect. M; Dyers Compendium, pt. 2, Campaigns, etc. Battle Index-NC, John F. Walter, Capsule History of Phillips Legion, Institute for Civil War Research, Dept. 1, 79-1367 Drive, Middle Village, NY 11379.

but he out-marched us and got ahead—if you will look on the map of North Carolina and find Wadesborough you will see where we are or rather to-night. We are camped ten miles from the right on the Pee Dee River.[18]

Butler's troopers battled Yankee cavalry near Rockingham while serving as rear guard for General Hardee. On 7 March, Kilpatrick took possession of Rockingham while Wade Hampton, who had been with Wheeler's riders for the previous two weeks, joined Butler near Rockingham. Kilpatrick hoped to cut off Hampton while he was heading to Fayetteville by blocking roads in the South Carolinian's front. Heavy rains made the roads virtually impassable. By 9 March, Gib Wright had marched his brigade toward Love's (Blue's) Bridge, where he planned to attack Kilpatrick's cavalry. They skirmished with Union horsemen and captured an entire squad of thirty Yankees. On the evening of 9 March, Hampton and Butler laid plans to avoid Kilpatrick and rejoin Hardee at Fayetteville.[19]

Kilpatrick's cavalry had crossed the Lumber River during the evening of 8 March, and on 9 March, they smashed into the rear of Hardee's column at Solemn Grove. Kilpatrick succeeded in capturing several prisoners and learned from them that Hampton was then in Kilpatrick's rear and heading for Fayetteville. Hoping to trap Hampton's column, Kilpatrick recklessly spread out his brigades to cover all possible approach routes. The Yankee general camped that night with Colonel George Eliphaz Spencer's Brigade at Monroe's Crossroads. Having located Kilpatrick's encampment, Hampton prepared his command to attack the Yankee camp at daylight 10 March. Just before sunup, Colonel Gib Wright of Butler's Division had positioned his brigade north of Kilpatrick's camp in hopes of bagging "Kilcavalry" himself. Wright's troopers roared into the Yankee camp and the Federals ran for their lives. Blankets flew everywhere as men in blue fled into a

---

[18] E. J. Humphries to wife, 12 March 1865, Waring Papers, Southern Historical Collection, University of North Carolina, Chapel Hill, NC.

[19] Ibid., 264–65, OR, *The Civil War in South Carolina*-Index, 6; A Guide Index to the Official Records of the Union and Confederate Armies, 1861–1865, vol. 3, sect. M; Byers Compendium, pt. 2, Campaigns, etc., Battle, Index-North Carolina.

nearby swamp for shelter, but most had the presence of mine to carry their weapons with them. Kilpatrick was able to avoid capture but lost his headquarters, camp, and animals. Unfortunately for Wright, his troopers were scattered and thus unable to follow up their surprise attack. The Federals rallied and, firing their seven-shot Spencer carbines, recaptured the camp and artillery. The Confederates' attack on Kilpatrick's camp nevertheless reopened the road to Fayetteville, enabling Hampton to rejoin Hardee. Each side lost around 100 killed and wounded, and the Confederates rescued most of their comrades who had been captured by Kilpatrick's cavalry. On the morning of 11 March, Hampton was surprised by Federal cavalry at Fayetteville and, in turn, surprised some Yankees as they entered the town by a little-known side road. Hampton rallied his men and charged the Federals, killing eleven and capturing twelve.[20]

A few days later Sergeant E. J. Humphries witnessed a horrifying incident involving the execution of a black slave and reported it to his sister-in-law. The unfortunate slave was "so insolent that she [his mistress] could not do anything with him." This attitude sealed his fate. "The Yanks had got him in the notion that he was as free as any body. They made a detail of six men to take him out & and shoot him, which they did in short order. I reckon the Negroes around there will mind how they do here after. If they would all opt that rule over the south it would be better for all hands, both Negro & master."[21]

Sherman occupied Fayetteville on 11 March and rested there for four days before resuming the march to Goldsboro. On 15 March, in a feint toward Raleigh, Kilpatrick's cavalry, in advance of Sherman's left wing, crossed the Cape Fear River and headed north on the Plank Road. Four divisions of Yankee infantry followed behind Kilpatrick. Hardee's Corps attempted to cover the approaches to Raleigh. Sherman neared Smithfield. On 15 March, Kilpatrick's cavalry and artillery advanced up the Raleigh Road pressing Hardee's rear guard, which was attempting to slow Sherman's advance and buy time for the concentration of

---

[20] Waring Papers, Southern Historical Collection, University of North Carolina: Chapel Hill, NC.

[21] E. Humphries to Sister-in-Law, 13 March 1865, from Anderson County, NC.

Johnston's forces at Smithfield. Hardee decided to halt and give battle four miles south of Averasboro on the Cape Fear River. Heavy rain and darkness intervened and put a stop to the skirmishing between Kilpatrick's and Hardee's men.

On 16 March, Kilpatrick attacked Hardee's infantry on a narrow neck of land between the Black River to the east and the Cape Fear River to the west. The fight lasted all day with the Federals driving the Confederates from their first two fortified lines before nightfall halted their attempt to carry the third and main line. After dark, Hardee began his withdrawal toward Smithfield with Wheeler's troopers covering the retreat. Hardee's effort delayed Sherman by only one day, but it gave Johnston enough time to launch an attack before the Federals could reach Goldsboro.

While Hardee battled the Federal left wing at Averasboro, the legion cavalry participated in the Confederates' attempt to delay the Union right wing's advance. By 13 March, Gib Wright had repositioned his men (including the legion), facing them eastward on the Clinton Road to guard the bridges over the South River. He learned that he was in danger of being intercepted by Union Major General Oliver O. Howard's men near Blockersville. Wright detoured through some woods and was able to reach the bridges, destroy them, and deny their use to the enemy, who now had to build pontoon bridges. Wright was then directed to cover the Smithfield and Raleigh roads. Smithfield stood roughly midway between Goldsboro to the east and Raleigh to the west. General Johnston selected Smithfield as his base of operations because he believed that Sherman's destination was either Raleigh or Goldsboro.

On 15 March, Johnston formed the Army of the South from Hardee's Corps, Major General Robert Frederick Hoke's Division, the Army of Tennessee contingent under Lieutenant General Alexander Peter Stewart, and Hampton's cavalry, amounting to around 20,000 troops. In a few days Johnston would lead his new army against Sherman's much larger force in the Battle of Bentonville.[22]

---

[22] Bradley, *This Astounding Close*, 17, 80 and B. Ridley, *Battles and Sketches of the Army of Tennessee* (Dayton OH: Press of Morningside Bookshop, 1978 and 1906 edition) 452, in which Ridley reports: "March 16, 1865, I have just reached camp from Oxford, North Carolina where I went on

On 15 March, fighting along the South River continued throughout the day. One of Howard's columns attacked Wright's pickets. Wright made a stand at a mill and held the enemy for about two hours until he was forced to withdraw. As Howard's wing marched toward Goldsboro, Wright's Brigade—including the legion cavalry—attempted to delay their advance.[23]

On 17 March, Kilpatrick and an infantry division feinted north toward Averasboro while the rest of the Federal left wing turned east and headed toward Goldsboro.[24] At dawn on 18 March, Hampton notified Johnston that Sherman was approaching Goldsboro, with the two wings of his army separated by a day's march. Johnston decided to attack the closest Federal column, which was the left wing commanded by Major General Henry W. Slocum. Heeding Hampton's advice, he opted to launch his attack at the Willis Cole Plantation a few miles south of Bentonville using Hampton's cavalry to delay the Federal advance until he could deploy his forces. Hoke's Division and the Army of Tennessee contingent had an eighteen-mile march to make from Smithfield, while Hardee's march from Elevation was several miles longer.

Hampton planned for his cavalry to delay the enemy's advance and then fall back through the Confederate infantry hidden in the woods at the Cole Plantation on the Goldsboro Road. Hampton's men would then circle around and hold the far right of the Confederate line of battle.[25]

The Unionists made the first move. On Sunday, 19 March, Federal skirmishers attacked Hampton's pickets and drove them back. Hampton was then about two miles from Bentonville. The bluecoats formed line of battle and attacked Hampton's riders. As the gray cavalry vanished into the woods, the Yankees were astonished to find that they were fighting not only Hampton but also a large body of Rebel infantry. About noon,

---

two days leave to visit my father's mother. Found Lieutenant General A. P. Stewart commanding the Army of Tennessee by order of General J. E. Johnston who took command yesterday of the Army of the South-Hardee's, Bragg's and Stewart's [formerly Hood's Army] consolidated making 'the Army of the South.'"

[23] Hopkins, *The Little Jeff*, 266–67.

[24] Ibid., also see Waring Papers, Southern Historical Collection, University of North Carolina: Chapel Hill, NC.

[25] Hopkins, *The Little Jeff*, 268–69.

the Union troops attacked and were easily repulsed. The Southerners then attacked three hours later and drove the Federals back. The fighting south of the Goldsboro Road was savage, with the bluecoats having to fight on both sides of their earthworks. At dusk, the Confederates launched several desperate attacks in an effort to dislodge the Union Twentieth Corps but were repulsed. Darkness brought a halt to the fighting. The Confederates buried their dead and withdrew to the positions they had held earlier in the day. Johnston's exhausted men slept on the swampy ground with their rifles at the ready. Thus ended the first day of fighting in the Battle of Bentonville.[26]

The Rebel lines redeployed several times to meet the expected arrival of the Union right wing on 20 March. Skirmishing continued all day as the Federals extended their line northeast toward Bentonville, the site of Johnston's headquarters and the Confederates' only avenue of retreat across a flooded Mill Creek.

On 21 March, a Federal division attacked the extreme Confederate left, overrunning Johnston's headquarters and threatening the Mill Creek Bridge at Bentonville. Hampton directed Wright's Brigade to charge the front and right flank of the advancing Federal line. The fighting raged until the Northerners fell back to their earlier position. While directing the fighting at Bentonville, Johnston learned that General Schofield's Federal force had captured Goldsboro.

On the night of 21 March, amid a steady rain, Johnston withdrew his army across Mill Creek and returned to Smithfield. The legion troopers headed across the creek with infantrymen following close behind. At sunup on 22 March, the Yankees discovered the withdrawal, and their skirmishers ran into the Confederate infantry rear guard. The Rebels then unleashed rifle-musket blasts, which forced the blue soldiers to fall back, but Wheeler failed to burn the bridge over Mill Creek after crossing. The Rebels later halted the Federal pursuit when they skirmished with the Twenty-Sixth Illinois Infantry at Hannah's Creek where it crossed the Smithfield Road.[27]

By 23 March, Sherman had joined Schofield at Goldsboro and concentrated his forces. On 24 March, the legion cavalry crossed

---

[26] Ibid.
[27] Ibid., 270.

Moccasin Creek while galloping toward the enemy. The Northerners lost several black troops. In spite of some of these troops' allegedly tossing their rifles away, these soldiers of the United States Colored Troops (USCT) repulsed Wright's attack. Wright's men suffered no casualties.[28]

The Southerners rested the next day at Atkin's Farm and awaited the arrival of supply wagons. They scrubbed filthy clothing and wrote letters to loved ones back home. The regimental Chaplain preached a provocative sermon on Sunday, 26 March. The next day, the Rebel troopers crossed Cox's Bridge and made camp at Crew's Bridge, setting out pickets along the Smithfield-Goldsboro Road. Monday, 28 March, began with occasional alarms as Federal foraging parties ran into Rebel pickets.[29] The Rebel riders skirmished with Union Fourteenth Corps foragers at Gully's Station, which later became the site of Sherman's headquarters.[30]

On 1 April, the sweaty legion troopers dug rifle pits but the work proved unnecessary. The following morning, they marched off with their brigade. They left their position near Smithfield and headed up the railroad to Raleigh. The high morale that had characterized Gib Wright's Brigade was strained when rumors of Richmond's fall spread throughout the ranks. Desertions, which for the legion cavalry, had never been a serious problem, increased and attitudes worsened. Late the same day, Wright headed back to Smithfield. On 7 April, Wright's Brigade passed through Smithfield and pushed on by the railroad until it reached a spot about eight miles from Goldsboro where it made camp.[31]

In mid-April, rumor had it that Lee's army had met with disaster. The army grapevine was accurate for once: on 9 April 1865, General Robert E. Lee had surrendered the Army of Northern Virginia at Appomattox Court House, Virginia. While the disturbing rumors spread, General Johnston reorganized his army. The cavalry corps remained under the command of Lieutenant General Wade Hampton. His command consisted of Major General Joseph Wheeler's Corps and two

---

[28] Ibid.; Dyers Compendium, pt. 2, Campaigns, etc., Battle Index, NC.
[29] Hopkins, *The Little Jeff*, 271, Waring, J. Papers, Southern Historical Collection, University of North Carolina, Chapel Hill, NC.
[30] Ibid., Bradley, *This Astounding Close*, 114.
[31] Ibid., 273.

brigades of cavalry under Major General Matthew C. Butler. Logan's new command comprised five South Carolina regiments. Young's Brigade, under Colonel Gib Wright, consisted of the Phillips Georgia Legion, Cobb's Georgia Legion, the Jeff Davis Legion, and the Tenth Georgia Cavalry.[32]

Searching for forage, Logan's Brigade moved out toward Wilson, North Carolina, on 9 April. After crossing the Little River, they were directed to return to Smithfield. General Hampton had learned that Sherman was heading toward Raleigh. Early the next morning, Rebel scouts reported that a Federal advance was in the offing. Soon afterward, the Yankees appeared on Smithfield Road and drove in Logan's pickets. The gray riders skirmished with soldiers of the One-Hundred-Twenty-Third and One-Hundred-Forty-Third New York infantries at Moccasin Swamp.[33] The shocking news of Lee's surrender at Appomattox reached Johnston on 11 April. Hampton rejected the information, calling it no more than rumor. After sunup the same day, the Yankees again drove in Logan's pickets. Around noon, Logan's men rode into Smithfield, dismounted, and skirmished with the Yankees for a short time. On 12 April, Logan marched his men off in the early morning after learning that Kilpatrick's cavalry was camped between them and Raleigh. The Rebels dismounted about four miles from Raleigh near the Swift Creek Bridge, where they dug shallow entrenchments and prepared breastworks of fence rails next to a large farm. Some found cover in deep woods along the road. The enemy advanced and the fighting began. The legion cavalry and Jeff Davis Legion troopers were ready. Around 10:30 A.M., the Ninety-Second Illinois Mounted Infantry of Atkins' Brigade collided with the Jeff Davis Legion riders.

Unfortunately for the Yankee troopers, they found the bridge over Swift Creek torn to pieces and filed off the road to ford Swift Creek on horseback. Colonel Wright reacted quickly and ordered the Phillips Legion riders to attack. The Georgia men charged with drawn sabers and

---

[32] Ibid., Dyers Compendium, pt. 2, Campaigns, etc., Battle Index, NC; J. Barrett, *The Civil War in North Carolina* (Chapel Hill: University of North Carolina Press, 1963) 374; J. Barrett, *Sherman's March through the Carolinas*, (Chapel Hill: University of North Carolina Press, 1956) 214, 215, 217, 222.

[33] Bradley, *This Astounding Close*, 101.

stalled the Illinoisans' advance, but the Federals' Spencer repeating rifles forced the Georgians to move out of danger while the Jeff Davis Legion opened fire on the Ninety-Second, who then charged. The Cobb's Legion troopers came onto the scene to cover the Confederates' right flank but it was not enough. The Illinois men overran the Rebels, and the fight went to the Federals. Wright's Brigade then passed through Raleigh and headed west on the Hillsborough Road toward Greensboro.[34]

On 14 April, Logan's troopers shifted back to a position about seven miles from Hillsborough. They marched into Hillsborough the following day and met paroled soldiers from Appomattox Court House. There could no longer be any doubt that Lee had surrendered and the end was near.[35]

Union and Confederate soldiers met under a flag of truce on Sunday, 16 April, and arranged a conference between generals Sherman and Johnston for the next day. On 17 April, General Joseph E. Johnston met Major General William T. Sherman at the James Bennett farm about five miles west of Durham Station. On 18 April, the day after President Lincoln's assassination was announced in Raleigh, Sherman drafted a preliminary surrender agreement, which he immediately sent to Washington for President Andrew Johnson's approval. Lincoln's murder had thrown the soldiers of both sides into a frenzy, and the Southerners feared that disastrous results would follow. On 24 April, Logan's brigade sent off its wagons. Many of the men believed that the assassination had ended the truce. They felt certain that this was true the next day when they learned that President Johnson had rejected the surrender terms. General Hampton decided to fight on rather than surrender and set out after President Jefferson Davis and his party, who were in Charlotte. Wright's Brigade was in Greensboro when the final surrender agreement became official on 26 April. Johnston and Sherman signed the document at the Bennett farmhouse, and generals Butler and Logan were present.[36]

---

[34] Hopkins, *The Little Jeff*, 273; also see Bradley, *This Astounding Close*, 298; OR, Armies, vol. 46, pt. 1, p. 453.

[35] Hopkins, *The Little Jeff*, 278.

[36] Dyers Compendium, pt. 2, Campaigns, etc., Battle Index, NC; Barrett, *Sherman's March through the Carolinas*, 203–204.

On 27 April, General Johnston announced the sad news that the Confederate army had agreed to lay down its arms. Logan's Brigade filled out its final muster rolls at Greensboro, North Carolina, on 1 May. Major Wesley Wailes Thomas formally surrendered 254 legion cavalrymen and Federal authorities paroled them at Greensboro.[37] They then headed out the Yanceyville Road toward Jamestown and camped around seventeen miles from Greensboro. A few days later, it was all over—they had disbanded and were going their separate ways. All complications regarding surrender terms had been laid to rest, and the men of Gib Wright's brigade, with the Phillips Legion cavalry battalion, headed homeward. They were going back the way they came.

---

[37] Hopkins, *The Little Jeff*, 274; Bradley, *This Astounding Close*, 105–106, Waring Papers, Southern Historical Collection, University of North Carolina, Chapel Hill, NC; H. Hendricks "Imperiled City: The Movements of the Union and Confederate Armies toward Greensboro in the Closing Days of the Civil War in North Carolina," M.A. thesis, University of North Carolina at Greensboro, 1987, 149–51; Muster Rolls and Lists of Confederate Troops Paroled in North Carolina, M1781-Reel 1, Cavalry Battalion, Phillips Legion.

AFTERWORD

SEARCHING FOR COLONEL PHILLIPS

A haunting article appeared in the *Augusta Chronicle* and appeared just a few weeks later on the 25 July 1874 front page of the *Thomaston Herald*: "A Colored Confederate. A colored man named John Phillips, who says he was a body servant of Col. Phillips, of Phillips Legion, during the war, passed through our city yesterday en route from Virginia. He was wounded in the head in one of the battles in Virginia, and the ball was but recently extracted, leaving the unfortunate man totally blind. He goes to his relatives in Atlanta now, to which place a pass was given him. He ought to be kindly cared for."[1]

Colonel William Phillips contracted typhoid fever early in the war and returned to his home in Marietta, Georgia, to convalesce. Phillips may have been separated from his servant, John Phillips, on or about that time. Perhaps John Phillips was left at a private home or hospital after his wounding. One can only speculate since none of the descendants of Colonel William Phillips, except for Ms. Peardon's sister, have any recollection or documentation relating to John Phillips.

---

[1] *Augusta Chronicle*, 7 July 1874, 3. Also on front page of The Thomaston Herald; 25 July 1874. Confirmed via telephone conversation between Richard M. Coffman and Ms. Betty Peardon, granddaughter of Colonel William Phillips, on 9 February 2007 and through letter from Ms. Peardon to Richard M. Coffman dated 11 February 2007, in which Ms. Peardon's sister recalls this incident as being accurately described.

ROSTERS

10 August 1861–4 January 1862
ARMY OF THE KANAWHA
PHILLIPS GEORGIA LEGION
Cavalry Battalion under command of
Colonel William Monroe Phillips

Field and Staff Officers:
Major John Butler Willcoxon
Reverend William E. Jones, chaplain of cavalry
Dr. Levi J. Willcoxon, surgeon of cavalry/infantry
Dr. Iverson Lewis Harris, assistant surgeon of cavalry

Cavalry Companies
Major John Butler Willcoxon
G. DuBignon's Cavalry
(Governor's Horse Guards)
H. Johnson Rangers
I. Cherokee Dragoons
K. Coweta Rangers

Captain Charles DuBignon
Captain William Wofford Rich
Captain William B. C. Puckett
Captain Robert Leeper Young Long (physician)

4 January 1862–25 August 1862

DEPARTMENT OF SOUTH CAROLINA, GEORGIA, AND EASTERN FLORIDA
General Robert E. Lee

DEPARTMENT OF SOUTH CAROLINA, GEORGIA, AND FLORIDA
Lieutenant General John Clifford Pemberton
FOURTH MILITARY DISTRICT
Brigadier General Thomas Fenwick Drayton
PHILLIPS GEORGIA LEGION
Colonel William Monroe Phillips

Field and Staff Officers:
Lieutenant Colonel William Wofford Rich, cavalry
Major John Butler Willcoxon, cavalry
Captain William B. C. Puckett (promoted to major 1 September 1862)
Cavalry
Reverend William E. Jones, chaplain of cavalry
Dr. Iverson Lewis Harris, assistant surgeon of cavalry

Cavalry Companies—Major John Butler Willcoxon (resigned 4 July 1862)

Lieutenant Colonel William Wofford Rich (replaced Willcoxon)

A. DuBignon's Cavalry	Captain Charles DuBignon (resigned 19 August 1862)
(Governor's Horse Guards)	Captain Charles H. Nichols (Replaced DuBignon)
B. Johnson Rangers	Captain William Wofford Rich (promoted to lieutenant colonel 6 July 1862)
	First Lieutenant John Field Milhollin (promoted to captain 26 September 1862, replaced Rich)
C. Cherokee Dragoons	Captain B. C. Puckett (promoted to major 1 September 1862)
	Captain Eli C. Hardin (replaced Puckett)
D. Coweta Rangers	Captain Robert Leeper Young Long (physician before war)

Two companies of cavalry were added to the Phillips Georgia Legion in spring 1862.

116

Cavalry:
N. Bibb Cavalry mustered 12 May 1862 Captain Samuel S. Dunlap
P. (Unknown) mustered 16 May 1862 Captain Wesley W. Thomas

There being no brigade or division organization at this phase of the conflict, the Phillips Georgia Legion (both infantry and cavalry battalions) were loosely assigned as one discrete component of the Army of the Kanawha under Brigadier John Buchanan Floyd.

25 August 1862–1 September 1862

SECOND MANASSAS

ARMY OF NORTHERN VIRGINIA
General Robert E. Lee

CAVALRY DIVISION
Major General James Ewell Brown Stuart

CAVALRY BRIGADE
Brigadier General Wade Hampton

PHILLIPS GEORGIA LEGION
Colonel William Monroe Phillips

The cavalry battalion was assigned under Major General James Ewell Brown Stuart at this time. They were engaged in scouting/reconnaissance activities and were not engaged at Second Manassas.

Cavalry Companies	Lieutenant Colonel William Wofford Rich
A. DuBignon Cavalry	Captain James H. Nichols
(Governor's Horse Guards)	
B. Johnson Rangers	First Lieutenant John Fielding Milhollin
C. Cherokee Rangers	Captain Eli C. Hardin
D. Coweta Rangers	Captain Robert Leeper Young Long (physician before war)
N. Bibb Cavalry	Captain Samuel S. Dunlap
P. (Unknown)	Captain Wesley W. Thomas

4 September 1862–20 September 1862

SOUTH MOUNTAIN AND SHARPSBURG

ARMY OF NORTHERN VIRGINIA
General Robert E. Lee

PHILLIPS GEORGIA LEGION
Colonel William Monroe Phillips

The cavalry battalion was located north of Richmond and did not participate in the battles of South Mountain and Sharpsburg (Antietam).

Field and Staff Officers:

Lieutenant Colonel William Wofford Rich, cavalry
Major William B. C. Puckett, cavalry
Reverend William E. Jones, chaplain of cavalry

Cavalry Companies	Lieutenant Colonel William Wofford Rich
A. DuBignon Cavalry	Captain James H. Nichols
(Governor's Horse Guards)	
B. Johnson Rangers	Captain John Fielding Milhollin
C. Cherokee Dragoons	Captain Eli C. Hardin
D. Coweta Rangers	Captain Robert Leeper Young Long
	(physician before war)
N. Bibb Cavalry	Captain Samuel S. Dunlap
P. (Unknown)	Captain Wesley W. Thomas.

12 December 1862–19 December 1862

HARTWOOD CHURCH TO OCCOQUAN

ARMY OF NORTHERN VIRGINIA
General Robert E. Lee

Cavalry Companies	Lieutenant Colonel William Wofford Rich
A. DuBignon Cavalry	Captain James H. Nichols
(Governor's Horse Guards)	
B. Johnson Rangers	Captain John Fielding Milhollin
C. Cherokee Dragoons	Captain Eli C. Hardin
D. Coweta Rangers	Captain Robert Leeper Young Long (physician)
N. Bibb Cavalry	Captain Samuel S. Dunlap
P. (Unknown)	Captain Wesley W. Thomas

The Legion cavalry under Hampton did not participate directly in the Fredericksburg battle. With Hampton's brigade, the Legion troopers picketed the upper Rappahannock.

A History of the Phillips Georgia Legion Cavalry Battalion

20 September 1862–4 May 1863

SECOND RIDE AROUND MCCLELLAN AND DUMFRIES RAID
ARMY OF NORTHERN VIRGINIA
General Robert E. Lee

CAVALRY DIVISION
Major General James Ewell Brown Stuart

CAVALRY BRIGADE
Brigadier General Wade Hampton

PHILLIPS GEORGIA LEGION
Colonel William Monroe Phillips:
The legion existed in name designation only after Army of Northern Virginia Special Order No. 104, March 1863, separated infantry and cavalry battalions. With the resignation of William Monroe Phillips, no overall commander existed.

Field and Staff Officers:
Lieutenant Colonel William Wofford Rich, cavalry
Major William B. C. Puckett, cavalry (promoted to major 11 September 1862)
Reverend William E. Jones, chaplain of cavalry

Cavalry Companies	Lieutenant Colonel William Wofford Rich
A. DuBignon Cavalry	Captain James H. Nichols
(Governor's Horse Guards) Promoted captain 9 August 1862	
B. Johnson Rangers	Captain John Fielding Milhollin
C. Cherokee Dragoons	Captain Eli C. Hardin
D. Coweta Rangers	Captain Robert Leeper Young Long (physician)
N. Bibb Cavalry	Captain Samuel S. Dunlap
P. (Unknown)	Captain Wesley W. Thomas

The implementation of Army of Northern Virginia Special Order No. 104, March 1863, was a benchmark for Phillips Georgia Legion, since the infantry and cavalry battalions were separated and each integrated into operationally dedicated units. The cavalry battalion was assigned to Major General James Ewell Brown Stuart's cavalry division, Brigadier General Wade Hampton's cavalry brigade. Colonel William Monroe Phillips resigned 13 February 1863 because of chronic illness (probably typhoid fever).

1 January 1863–4 May 1863

KELLY'S FORD THROUGH THE CHANCELLORSVILLE CAMPAIGN

ARMY OF NORTHERN VIRGINIA
General Robert E. Lee

CAVALRY DIVISION
Major General James Ewell Brown Stuart

CAVALRY BRIGADE
Brigadier General Wade Hampton

Field and Staff Officers:
   Lieutenant Colonel William Wofford Rich, cavalry
   Major William B. C. Puckett, cavalry
   Reverend William E. Jones, chaplain of cavalry
Cavalry Companies   Lieutenant Colonel William Wofford Rich

A. DuBignon Cavalry   Captain James H. Nichols
(Governor's Horse Guards)
B. Johnson Rangers   Captain John Fielding Milhollin
C. Cherokee Dragoons   Captain Eli C. Hardin
D. Coweta Rangers   Captain Robert Leeper Young Long (physician)
N. Bibb Cavalry   Captain Samuel S. Dunlap
P. (Unknown)   Captain Wesley W. Thomas

Less than a week after the battle of Fredericksburg, General J. E. B. Stuart sent
General Wade Hampton behind the Federal lines on a raid that netted 150
prisoners and twenty wagonloads of booty. The Phillips Georgia Legion cavalry
battalion had little involvement with the Chancellorsville campaign. Shortage of
suitable mounts became a serious problem. General Wade Hampton's brigade,
which included the Legion, had to be sent south below the James River, where
they would remain until the spring.

9 June 1863–14 July 1863

GETTYSBURG

ARMY OF NORTHERN VIRGINIA
General Robert E. Lee

CAVALRY DIVISION
Major General James Ewell Brown Stuart

CAVALRY BRIGADE
Brigadier General Wade Hampton

Field and Staff Officers:
Lieutenant Colonel William Wofford Rich, cavalry
Major William B. C. Puckett, cavalry
Reverend Willliam E. Jones, chaplain of cavalry

Cavalry Companies	Lieutenant Colonel William Wofford Rich
A. DuBignon Cavalry (Governor's Horse Guards)	Captain James H. Nichols
B. Johnson Rangers	Captain John Fielding Milhollin
C. Cherokee Dragoons	Captain Eli C. Hardin
D. Coweta Rangers	Captain Robert Leeper Young Long (physician)
N. Bibb Cavalry	Captain Samuel S. Dunlap (resigned 22 September 1863)
P. (Unknown)	Captain Wesley W. Thomas

27 August 1863–20 October 1863

BRISTOE CAMPAIGN

ARMY OF NORTHERN VIRGINIA
General Robert E. Lee

CAVALRY DIVISION
Major General James Ewell Brown Stuart

CAVALRY BRIGADE
Colonel Pierce Manning Butler Young

Field and Staff Officers:
Lieutenant Colonel William Wofford Rich, cavalry
Major William B. C. Puckett, cavalry
Reverend William E. Jones, chaplain of cavalry

Cavalry Companies	Lieutenant Colonel William Wofford Rich
A/G DuBignon Cavalry (Governor's Horse Guards)	Captain James H. Nichols
B.H Johnson Rangers	Captain John Fielding Milhollin
C/I Cherokee Dragoons	Captain Eli C. Hardin
D/K Coweta Rangers	Captain Robert Leeper Young Long (physician)
E/N Bibb Cavalry	Captain Samuel S. Dunlap (resigned 22 September 1863) Captain Arthur F. Hunter (promoted captain 22 September 1863, replaced Dunlap)
F/P (Unknown)	Captain Wesley W. Thomas

A History of the Phillips Georgia Legion Cavalry Battalion

21 October 1863–27 November 1863

MINE RUN

ARMY OF NORTHERN VIRGINIA
General Robert E. Lee

CAVALRY CORPS
Major General James Ewell Brown Stuart
CAVALRY DIVISION
Brigadier General Wade Hampton
CAVALRY BRIGADE
Brigadier General Pierce Manning Butler Young
PHILLIPS GEORGIA LEGION
Cavalry Battalion

Field and Staff Officers:
    Lieutenant Colonel William Wofford Rich, cavalry
    Major William B. C. Puckett, cavalry
    Reverend William E. Jones, chaplain of cavalry

Cavalry Companies   Lieutenant Colonel William Wofford Rich
A/G DuBignon Cavalry   Captain James H. Nichols
    (Governor's Horse Guards)
B/H Johnson Rangers   Captain John Fielding Milhollin
                          (KIA 10 November 1863 near Brandy Station)
                          Captain Thomas G. Wilkes
                          (Promoted captain 10 November 1863,
                          replaced Milhollin)
C/I Cherokee Dragoons   Captain Eli C. Hardin
D/K Coweta Rangers   Captain Robert Leeper Young Long (physician)
E/N Bibb Cavalry   Captain Arthur F. Hunter
F/P (Unknown)   Captain Wesley W. Thomas

The Phillips Georgia Legion cavalry battalion was assigned to Hampton's
division,Stuart's cavalry corps, effective September 1893.

Going Back the Way They Came

1 May 1864–7 May 1864

WILDERNESS SKIRMISHING

ARMY OF NORTHERN VIRGINIA
General Robert E. Lee

CAVALRY CORPS
Major General James Ewell Brown Stuart (MWIA 5 November 1864 at Yellow
Tavern, Virginia, Major General Wade Hampton replaced Stuart.)

CAVALRY DIVISION
Brigadier General Matthew Calbraith Butler (replaced Hampton)

CAVALRY BRIGADE
Brigadier General Pierce Manning Butler Young (WIA Ashland, Virginia,
replaced temporarily by Colonel Gilrt J. Wright)

Field and Staff Officers:
   Lieutenant Colonel William Wofford Rich, cavalry
   Major William B. C. Puckett, cavalry
   Reverend William E. Jones, chaplain of cavalry
   Dr. Calhoun Sams, surgeon of cavalry

Cavalry Companies   Lieutenant Colonel William Wofford Rich

A. DuBignon Cavalry   Captain James H. Nichols
   (Governor's Horse Guards)
B. Johnson Rangers   Captain Thomas G. Wilkes
C. Cherokee Dragoons   Captain Robert Leeper Young Long (physician,
                         resigned 26 April 1864 because of poor health)
E. Bibb Cavalry   Captain Arthur Hunter
F. (Unknown)   Captain Wesley W. Thomas.

Commanded by Captain A. P. Love, the 4th Alabama Cavalry Battalion,
consisting of three companies, was officially attached to the Phillips Georgia
Legion cavalry battalion from May 1864 to 11 July 1864. These three

companies were organized in August, September, and October 1863. After the ending date of 11 July 1864, these same three companies were officially reassigned to the Jeff Davis Legion and relettered as shown below:

Company A. "Morehead Rangers," Pike County, commanded by Captain A. P. Love. Later became Company H of the Jeff Davis Mississippi Legion.

Company B. Barbour and Montgomery counties, commanded by Captain Bethune B. McKenzie, became Company I of the Jeff Davis Mississippi Legion.

Company C. Barbour County, commanded by Captain G. A. Roberts, became Company K of the Jeff Davis Legion Mississippi Legion.

All three companies fought side by side with their Phillips Georgia Legion brothers at five major engagements. They were affectionately referred to as the "Lovelies" by the Legion veterans.

The Battle of the Wilderness: 5, 6 May 1864 Spotsylvania Courthouse—8, 12 May 1864 North Anna—1, 3 June 1864

Cold Harbor: 1, 3 June 1864

Petersburg Siege: June–July 1864

A company roster dated 11 June 1910 of Captain Love's company, 4th battalion of cavalry, Jeff Davis Legion, lists a total of four officers, six sergeants, five corporals, and 55 privates. This roster was copied from the Confederate Monument in Troy, Alabama. Some of these Alabamians were probably assigned to Company F, Captain Wesley W. Thomas's company of the Phillips Georgia Legion cavalry battalion.

Going Back the Way They Came

8 May 1864–19 May 1864

BATTLE OF SPOTSYLVANIA

ARMY OF NORTHERN VIRGINIA
General Robert E. Lee

CAVALRY DIVISION
Brigadier General Matthew Calbraith Butler

CAVALRY BRIGADE
Colonel Gilbert J. Wright

First and Staff Officers:
Lieutenant Colonel William Wofford Rich, cavalry
Major William B. C. Puckett, cavalry
Reverend William E. Jones, chaplain of cavalry

Cavalry Companies	Lieutenant Colonel William Wofford Rich
A. DuBignon Cavalry	Captain James H. Nichols
(Governor's Horse Guards)	
B. Johnson Rangers	Captain Thomas G. Wilkes
C. Cherokee Dragoons	Captain Eli C. Hardin
D. Coweta Rangers	Captain Hugh Buchanan
	(WIA shot through lung 11 June 1864 at Trevillian Station)
E. Bibb Cavalry	Captain Arthur H. Hunter
F. (Unknown)	Captain Wesley W. Thomas

128

21 May 1864–3 June 1864

NORTH ANNA AND COLD HARBOR
ARMY OF NORTHERN VIRGINIA
General Robert E. Lee

CAVALRY CORPS
Major General Wade Hampton

CAVALRY DIVISION
Brigadier General Matthew Calbraith Butler

CAVALRY BRIGADE
Colonel Gilbert J. Wright

PHILLIPS GEORGIA LEGION
Cavalry Battalion
Field and Staff Officers:
Lieutenant Colonel William Wofford Rich, cavalry
Major William B. C. Puckett, cavalry
Reverend William E. Jones, chaplain of cavalry
Dr. Calhoun Sams, surgeon of cavalry

Cavalry Companies   Lieutenant Colonel William Wofford Rich

A. DuBignon Cavalry   Captain James H. Nichols
    (Governor's Horse Guards)
B. Johnson Rangers   Captain Thomas G. Wilkes
C. Cherokee Dragoons   Captain Eli C. Hardin
D. Coweta Rangers   Captain Hugh Buchanan
    (WIA at Louis Courthouse, Trevillian Station, 11
    June 1864, shot through lung)
E. Bibb Cavalry Captain Arthur H. Hunter
F. (Unknown)   Captain Wesley W. Thomas

11–12 June 1864

TREVILLIAN STATION
ARMY OF NORTHERN VIRGINIA
General Robert E. Lee
CAVALRY CORPS
Major General Wade Hampton
CAVALRY BRIGADE
Colonel Gilbert J. Wright
PHILLIPS GEORGIA LEGION
Cavalry Battalion

Field and Staff Officers:
   Lieutenant Colonel William Wofford Rich, cavalry
   Major William B. C. Puckett, cavalry
   First Lieutenant James W. Christian, quartermaster
   First Lieutenant Robert C. Latimer, commissary
   First Lieutenant John W. Wofford, adjutant of cavalry
   Reverend William E. Jones, chaplain of cavalry
   Dr. Calhoun Sams, surgeon of cavalry

Cavalry Companies	Lieutenant Colonel William Wofford Rich, cavalry
A. DuBignon Cavalry	Captain James H. Nichols
(Governor's Horse Guards)	
B. Johnson Rangers	Captain Thomas G. Wilkes
C. Cherokee Dragoons	Captain Eli C. Hardin
D. Coweta Rangers	Captain Hugh Buchanan
	(At home after WIA at Louisa Courthouse/Trevillian Station, probably replaced by First Lieutenant William J. Ransom.)
E. Bibb Cavalry	Captain Arthur F. Hunter
F. (Unknown)	Captain Wesley W. Thomas

A company of cavalry was later transferred from Cobb's Legion to Phillips Georgia Legion on 11 July 1864 in accordance with A and I GO No. 161. This 11th company became Company G of the cavalry battalion commanded by Captain Edgeworth Eve.

October 1864–2 March 1865

BATTLE OF CEDAR CREEK/SHENANDOAH VALLEY
AND SIEGE OF PETERSBURG
ARMY OF NORTHERN VIRGINIA
General Robert E. Lee

CAVALRY CORPS
Major General Wade Hampton

CAVALRY DIVISION
Brigadier General Matthew Calbraith Butler

CAVALRY BRIGADE
Brigadier General Martin Witherspoon Gary (Young's brigade under General
Gary was assigned to the Department of Richmond for the defense of
Richmond, Lieutenant Richard Stoddert Ewell commanding, September and
October 1864)
PHILLIPS GEORGIA LEGION
Cavalry Battalion
Field and Staff Officers:
Lieutenant Colonel William Wofford Rich, cavalry (resigned 27 January 1865)
Major William B. C. Puckett, cavalry (detailed back to Georgia with dismounted
men to procure horses, September 1864. No surrender or parole record
found, so probably never returned.)
First Lieutenant James W. Christian, quartermaster
First Lieutenant Robert C. Latimer, adjutant of cavalry
Reverend William E. Jones, chaplain of cavalry

Cavalry Companies   Lieutenant Colonel William Wofford Rich
A. DuBignon Cavalry   Captain James H. Nichols
                           (On horse detail September 1864; not known whether
                           or not he returned to duty.)
    (Governor's Horse Guards)
B. Johnson Rangers   Captain Thomas G. Wilkes
                           (Detailed for special duty at Lynchburg, Virginia, late 1864; did not
                           surrender at Greensboro; probably never returned.)

C. Cherokee Dragoons   Captain Eli C. Hardin
(Home sick after September 1864 through end of war.)
                             Second Lieutenant Benjamin Franklin Freeman
                             (Promoted First Lieutenant 10/51864; probably
                             replaced Hardin.)
D. Coweta Rangers   Captain Hugh Buchanan
                             (At home after WIA Louisa Courthouse/Trevillian
                             Station 11 June 1864.)
                             First Lieutenant William Ransom
                             (Probably succeeded Buchanan.)
E. Bibb Cavalry   Captain Arthur H. Hunter
                             (Not officially present for duty 11 July 1864;
                             examining board recommended him for retirement.)
                             First Lieutenant G. M. Davis
                             (Replaced Hunter.)
F. (Unknown)   Captain Wesley W. Thomas
                             (Surrendered legion at Greensboro.)
G. Richmond Dragoons   Captain Edgeworth Eve
                             (Ordered to Georgia with General Young 23
                             November 1864; no further record; Eve's
                             replacement not known.)

1 February 1865–1 May 1865

CAROLINAS CAMPAIGN/BENTONVILLE AND SKIRMISHING AND SURRENDER AT GREENSBORO/END OF THE LINE
ARMY OF TENNESSEE
General Joseph Eggleston Johnston

CAVALRY CORPS
Major General Wade Hampton

CAVALRY DIVISION
Brigadier General Matthew Calbraith Butler

CAVALRY BRIGADE
Brigadier General Thomas Muldrup Logan

PHILLIPS GEORGIA LEGION
Cavalry Battalion commanded by Colonel Gilbert "Gib" Wright

Field and Staff Officers:
Major Wesley W. Thomas
(Succeeded Rich, paroled at Greensboro, North Carolina, 1 May 1865.)
First Lieutenant James W. Christian, quartermaster
First Lieutenant Robert C. Latimer, adjutant of cavalry
Reverend William E. Jones, chaplain of cavalry

Cavalry Companies   Major Wesley W. Thomas
A. DuBignon Cavalry   Captain James H. Nichols
                         (On horse detail September 1864; not known whether
                         or not he returned to duty.)
    (Governor's Horse Guards.)
B. Johnson Rangers   Thomas G. Wilkes.
C. Cherokee Dragoons   Second Lieutenant Benjamin Franklin Freeman
                         (Surrendered at Greensboro, North Carolina, 11 May
                         1865.)
D. Coweta Rangers   First Lieutenant William J. Ransom
                         (Surrendered at Greensboro, 1 May 1865.)

E. Bibb Cavalry   First Lieutenant G. M. Davis
(Surrendered at Greensboro, North Carolina, 1 May 1865.)

F. (Unknown)   Captain Wesley W. Thomas
(Surrendered at Greensboro, North Carolina, 1 May 1865.)

G. Richmond Dragoons   Captain Francis Edgeworth Eve
(Ordered to Georgia with General P. M. B. Young, 23 January 1864; no further record; Eve's replacement unknown.)

PHILLIPS GEORGIA LEGION
Cavalry Battalion

Field, Staff, Inspection, and Unassigned Soldiers

Commissioned Officers

Christian, James W. Enlisted as a private, Company B., on 3 August 1861 in Cass County, October 1864; last muster showed absent; detached by order of Gen. Lee 21 September to get horse; quartermaster of cavalry battalion paroled Greensboro, NC, 1 May 1865.

Coxe, John H. Enlisted 1 January 1864, date of rank 2 June 1864, assistant surgeon, first muster 1 April 1864; 11 October 1864 to present, appeared on list of CSA prisoners in charge of Captain John C. Marvin, 17th Corps, captured 16 February 1865 at Columbia, SC; paroled 18 February 1865, shown as deserter.

Harris, Iverson Lewis. Enlisted as sergt. in Company A; asst. surgeon on 4 July 1861 at Camp McDonald; appointed asst. surgeon, 17 April 1862, in effect 24 February 1862; resigned 1 August 1862.

Hines, J. C. Assistant surgeon; appeared on a roll of prisoners of war belonging to the Confederate Army; surrendered by Major General Sam Jones, commanding Confederate forces in Florida to Brigadier General E. M. McCook, U.S.V., commanding U.S. forces at Tallahassee, Florida, and vicinity in compliance with the terms of a military convention made on 26 April 1865 at Bennett's House, near Durham's Station, NC, between General J. E. Johnston of the Confederate armies and Major General W. T. Sherman, U.S.A., approved by Lieut. Gen. U.S. Grant, U.S.A.; paroled at Madison, FL, on 23 May 1865.

Jones, William E. William Edward Jones was born 7 January 1836 at Elberton, Elbert County, Georgia, to Reverend Samuel Gamble and Elizabeth Edwards Jones. William, one of six brothers, followed in his father's footsteps and became a minister. He married Martha Evelyn Hampton on 1 May 1856. When the Civil War broke out, Jones enlisted as a private in Company G of the 22nd Georgia Infantry on 4 August 1861. Company G., known as "The Fireside Defenders," was organized by William's older brother Robert Harris Jones at Silver Creek near Rome, GA, and became its captain. On 16 November 1861, William was elected to the position of regimental chaplain.

He served with this unit until transferring as chaplain to the Phillips Georgia Legion's cavalry battalion in November 1863. He remained in this position until surrendering with the battalion on 26 April 1865 at Greensboro, North Carolina. William returned to Georgia after the war and died at Milledgeville after a lengthy illness on 9 July 1900.

Nichols, James H. Enlisted in Company A on 4 July 1861 at Camp McDonald; 1 August–31 October 1861, absent without leave; January and February 1864, "acting assistant quartermaster since August 1, 1863," September and October 1864, absent on horse detail since 21 September 1864 by order Gen. Lee; elected second lieutenant on 20 June 1861; promoted to captain 9 August 1862; paroled Greensboro, North Carolina, 1 May 1865.

Puckett, William B. C. Enlisted as captain/major on 11 June 1864 at Camp McDonald; Company C and Field and Staff; age 39 per 31 August 1864 muster; 1 October 1864 muster showed absent in Spotsylvania County, VA, after blankets and overcoats by order Gen. Lee; elected captain 11 June 1861, promoted to major September 1862; 30 November 1864; Inspection report of Young's cavalry brigade, 1st cavalry division, commanded by Col. J. F. Waring, showed "absent in GA commanding detail dismounted men" by order Gen. Young 25 November 1864; 31 December 1864, showed on detail in Georgia with Gen. Young. Gen. Lee 25 November 1864; 30 November 1864, Inspection report of Young's cavalry brigade, lst cavalry division, commanded by Col J. F. Waring, showed "absent in GA commanding detail dismounted men" by order Gen. Young 25 November 1864; 31 December 1864; showed on detail in Georgia with Gen. Young by order of Gen. Lee 25 November 1864.

Rich, William Wofford. Enlisted as captain in Company B, later lieutenant colonel at Camp McDonald; elected captain; age 38 per 31 August 1861 muster; promoted to lieutenant colonel of legion; date of appointment 15 August 1863, date of confirmation; 16 February 1864 to take rank; 9 July 1862; date of cc; 25 August 1863; delivered Gen. R. E. Lee; October 1864, last muster showed on sick leave since 4 October 1864; resigned 27 January 1865 "physical disability." Note: file contains several letters regarding promotion, history of company, and resignation.

Sams, Calhoun. Born in Beaufort District, South Carolina, on 12 January 1838 to Dr. Lewis Reeve Sams, Jr., and Sarah Givens Graham. Dr. Sams graduated from the South Carolina Medical College in 1861. He married Mary Ann Seabrook and two children were produced. He served as assistant surgeon at Camp Winder Hospital, Richmond, VA, in November 1862 and at Camp Winder itself in some as-yet-unknown capacity from 15 May to 12 June 1862. He was promoted to surgeon on 16 April 1864. Dr. Sams served variously with the Phillips Georgia Legion Cavalry Battalion, Battery Dantzler, First South Carolina Cavalry, Second North Carolina Cavalry, and Stuart Hospital at Richmond, VA. He was relieved from duty with the Phillips Georgia Legion Cavalry battalion on 18 July 1864 and served with Battery Dantzler to the end of the war. He left a diary describing his experiences with the First South Carolina Cavalry, which is dated from 19 October 1863 to 30 November 1863. Dr. Sams relocated to Texas after the war and died in November 1908 in Taylor, Texas.

Stevens, Jacob R. Enlisted as private/captain in Company B on 1 January 1864 at Floyd County, Georgia; 4 May 1864, commissioned/appointed F and S AQM; October 1864, last muster showed present as AQM; paroled at Greensboro, NC, 1 May 1865; first listing as captain.

Thomas, Wesley W. Enlisted as captain/major in Company F on 16 May 1862, place not stated; elected Captain 16 May 1862; paroled Greensboro, NC, 1 May 1865; Special Order (number illegible, perhaps 101) 17 January 1865-DNV-subject-"court martial"; succeeded Lieutenant Colonel W. W. Rich as cavalry battalion commander and surrendered cavalry battalion at Greensboro, NC, 1 May 1865.

Wells, F. J. Surgeon; appears on list of miscellaneous and field officers of the cavalry; no further information.

Willcoxon, John Butler. Born in Newnan, Hancock County, Georgia, in 1823; admitted to Bar in 1848, judge of inferior court Coweta County; elected captain of company D, Coweta Rangers, trained at Camp McDonald; became major of cavalry when the Phillips Georgia Legion was formed; taken sick in South Carolina; married to Mary West 1850 and produced four children; Mary West died in 1857, and in 1861 Willcoxon remarried Mary H. Cleveland and produced two children.

Willcoxon, Levi J. Born on 15 March 1835 in Coweta County, Georgia, to Levi Willcoxon and wife, Lennah; Dr. Willcoxon received his medical degree from the University of Pennsylvania. He was married to Fannie L. Turpin on 4 May 1858. They had seven children. Dr. Willcoxon served with the Phillips Georgia Legion cavalry beginning on 19 July 1861 and continuing through October of the same year. Records do not indicate whether he served with the infantry or cavalry battalion. He died in Alabama on 2 July 1891.

Wofford, John W. Enlisted as private/adjutant on 28 February 1862 at Cassville, Georgia; Field and Staff; 1 December 1862 elected second lieutenant, promoted lieutenant and adjutant.

Non-Commissioned Officers/Enlisted

Braselton, Cicero A. Enlisted as private in Company C on 2 or 7 August 1861 at Camp McDonald; age 23 per 31 August 1861 muster; February 1864, courier for brig. commissary since October 1863; April 1864, present; 31 August 1864, clerk for brig. commissary since March 1863, last muster card showed present; paroled Greensboro, NC, 1 May 1865.

Burris, William D. Enlisted in Company B on 2 August 1861 in Cobb County, Georgia; Field and Staff, Reg't Bugler/Ordnance Sgt.: no record of when promotion took place for February 1864, shows bugler and muster for October 1864; shows ordnance sgt; paroled Greensboro, NC, 1 May 1865.

Chamblee, Enoch (also as Chamlee). Enlisted in Company C as private on 6 March 1862 in Cherokee County; February 1864, on horse furlough since 4 February 1864; 31 August 1864, muster showed wagoner for brig. comm. since 20 May 1864; October 1864, on detail for a horse by order of Gen. Lee since 19 September 1864.

Chastain, G. B. Enlisted in Company C as private 2 July 1861 at Camp McDonald; age 25 per 31 August 1861 muster; February 1864, on duty for brig. commissary since 31 August 1863; 31 August 1864 muster showed beef herder since 18 September 1863; paroled Greensboro, NC, 1 May 1865.

Chastain, James. Enlisted in Company C as private 22 June 1861 at Camp McDonald; age 31 per 31 August 1861 muster; February 1864, wagon master for brig. comm. since 1 August 1863; October 1864 last muster showed present; paroled Greensboro, NC, 1 May 1865.

Chastain, Joshua. Enlisted in Company C as private on 1 March 1862 at Cherokee County; 31 August 1864, last muster showed brig. provost guard since 20 April 1864; October 1864 on detail for a horse by order of Gen. Lee since 19 September 1864.

Fitts, John G. Enlisted in Company C as private on 25 March 1862 in Cherokee County, 1 January 1864, in hands of enemy since 15 December 1863; February 1864 at infirmary camp; 31 August 1864, guard for brig. commissary 20 July 1864; October 1864 last muster showed present; paroled Greensboro, NC, 1 May 1865.

Mainus, George W. (Manis, Manus). Enlisted in Company D as private/bugler on 11 or 20 June 1861 at Camp McDonald; age 29 per 30 August 1861 muster; 28 February 1863, showed on detached service by order of War Department; 11 April 1864, on detail in Georgia to procure a horse since 3 February 1864; April 1864, detailed in gov. shop by ordr sect'y of war, Athens, GA, 7 March 1864, S. O. No. 55; 11 October 1864, last muster showed detailed in Athens, GA, by order sect'y of war, S. O. 55; Special Order: No 26018, 1116162, Adj. and Inspec. Gen. Off., "Detailed," Special Order No. 55.29, 7 March 1864, Adj. and Inspec. Gen Off., "Detailed for Duty"; letter in file dated 11 October 1862 from Columbus Huges for Cooke and Brothers Rifle Factory requesting that Private Mainus be detailed to work in their factory for 60 to 90 days.

Nowell, Reuben. Enlisted in Company B 4 March 1864 as private on March 1862 at Cassville, GA; 30 November 1862 muster roll showed "Transferred to this company 21 August 1862," October 1863 on detached service at hospital; 1 November–31 December 1863 employed as nurse at Kingston Hospital; August 1864, last muster showed present; no further record.

Pearson, William (Pierson). Enlisted in Company F on 14 May 1862 in Newnan, GA; October 1864 muster showed detached as provost guard of Army N. VA under Major Bridgeport; October 1864 last muster showed absent sick at hospital; appeared on list of men employed as clerks and guards in Provost Marshall's office, Weldon, NC, dated 22 February 1865. "Laborer for field service-light duty" by order Major Gen. W. Hampton.

Sewell, J. E. Enlisted in Company E as private, Company E, cavalry or infantry; no enlistment information; appeared on a list of medical officers, hospital stewards, detailed attendants and patients in General Hospital No. 11, Charlotte, NC, May 1865; listed as patient-paroled at Charlotte, NC, May 1865.

Seymore, G. W. Enlisted in Company E as corporal on 12 May 1862 at Macon, GA; October 1864 on detached service with brigade ordnance train since 2, 12, or 14 August 1864; paroled Greensboro, NC, 1 May 1865.

Seymore, H. H. Enlisted in Company E as private on 12 May 1862 at Macon, GA; 29 February 1864, muster stated at recruiting camp, left 4 February 1864; October 1864 last muster showed detailed with Brigade QM Dept. since 21 or 24 September 1864; paroled Greensboro, NC, 1 May 1865.

Sligh, James (also Sleigh and Sligh, James A.). Enlisted as private in Company B on March 1862 at Cass County (also 1 March 1862 Bartow County); 1

May 1863 to 23 March 1864. employed as nurse at hospital at Orange Court House; April 1864 on detail since 30 April 1864 for horse; October 1864 last muster showed on detached service by order of Gen. Lee since 2 September 1864.

Smith, S. P. Enlisted in Company E as private on 12 May 1862 at Macon, GA; October 1864 with brigade ordnance train since 26 December 1863; paroled Greensboro, NC, 1 May 1865.

Tailbird, Marion B. Enlisted in Company A as private on 25 September 1861 at Milledgeville, GA; (Company A and G;); July August 1864 and September/October 1864, "on extra duty in medical department"; enlistment papers in file; file contains letter dated 30 November 1864 from J. M. Coxe, assistant surgeon, recommending that Tailbird be appointed hospital steward; appointment approved by J. H. Nichols, no date; no further record.

Wofford, John M. Enlisted as private/adjutant in Company B on 28 February 1862 at Cassville, GA; F and S; 1 December 1862 elected second lieutenant 1 February 1863; promoted lieutenant and adjutant.

Casualties, other losses for the Phillips Georgia cavalry battalion from available records. Company G/A was formed predominantly from Cobb, Hall, and Baldwin Counties.

Company G/A

Total Enrollment:	131
Death/Disease/Accident:	11
Discharge/Disability:	14
Captured:	11
WIA:	14
Exchanged:	2
AWOL:	6
Imprisoned/Point Lookout:	5
Imprisoned/Old Capital Prison:	1
Imprisoned/Hart's Island:	1
Imprisoned/Fort Delaware:	4
Transferred to Artillery:	1
Detached Service:	5
Horse Detail:	23
Extra Duty:	6

Paroled at Greensboro, NC: 37
Dismounted Cavalry: 23
POW: 5
Paroled/DeCamp Gen. Hosp,
   David's Island, NY Harbor: 1
Paroled Talladega: 1
Paroled/Appomattox: 3
Deserted/Oath then went
   north of the Ohio River: 1
Galvanized Yankee: 2

Note: any one individual may appear in several categories; e.g., he might have been captured, sent to prison, and exchanged.

PHILLIPS GEORGIA LEGION

Cavalry Battalion

Company A

The DuBignon Cavalry or Governor's Horse Guards

Andrews, James R. Enlisted as private on 4 July 1861 at Camp McDonald, chief bugler; paroled at Greensboro, NC, 1 May 1865, died 30 December 1930, buried in Fortville Cemetery.

Armstrong, William. Enlisted as private on 1 March 1862 at Gainsville, GA; with the dismounted cavalry under Major Farley July August 1864; paroled Greensboro, NC, 1 May 1865.

Baker, John W. Enlisted as private on 4 July 1861 at Camp McDonald; 1 April 1864, muster rolls show absent at infirmary camp since 1 March 1863 by order of Gen. J. E. B. Stuart; with the dismounted cavalry under Major Farley July August 1864; September/October rolls show absent wounded since 22 October 1864; no further record.

Bales, Isaac. Enlisted as private on 25 September 1861 at Gainesville, GA; on extra duty as blacksmith July August 1864; absent on horse detail by order Gen. Lee; since 21 September 1864; (Note: there was a large group of dismounted A.N.V. cavalrymen who returned to Georgia under command of Gen P. M. B. Young; most of this group remained south for the rest of the war) no further record.

Bales, James. Enlisted as private on 25 September 1861 at Gainesville, GA; Shown with dismounted cavalry under Major Farley on July/Aug 1864 rolls, listed at hospital since 25 October 1864 on September/October roll, paroled Greensboro, NC, 1 May 1865.

Barker, Martin V. Enlisted as private on 25 September 1861 at Gainsville, GA; born 1835 in Georgia to Alsey B. and Elizabeth Barker, paroled Greensboro, NC, 1 May 1865.

Beall, James V. Enlisted at Camp McDonald, fifth sergeant, first sergeant; absent, home on furlough January February 1864 since 18 February 1864; absent, wounded September/October 1864 since 27 October 1864; admitted to Jackson Hospital at Richmond, VA, 30 October 1864, furloughed 60 days on 24 November 1864; appears on a list of passports issued from Jackson

Hospital for the week ending 26 November 1864, destination: Albany, GA; no further record.

Beaman, Frank A. Enlisted as private on 10 October 1861; no further record.

Beecher, George B. Enlisted 4 July 1864in Georgia; Third Lieutenant, First Lieutenant

promoted to First Lieutenant 2 August 1863, resigned as First Lieutenant 4 January 1864, buried at Memory Hill Cemetery at Milledgeville.

Best, John S. Enlisted as private 4 July 1861 at Camp McDonald, corporal; absent on horse detail in Georgia to procure a remount horse by order of Gen. R. E. Lee 1 April; absent wounded since 27 October 1864, September/October 1864; appeared on POW roll, card states captured at Gettysburg 3 July 1863 and paroled at DeCamp General Hospital, David's Island, New York Harbor, 24 August 1863; admitted to Jackson Hospital at Richmond on 30 October 1864, returned to duty (admitted for gun shot wound to the left hand); no further record.

Bonner, James O. Enlisted as private on 4 July 1861 at Camp McDonald, sergeant; with dismounted cavalry under Major Farley July August 1864; absent wounded since 27 October 1864, September/October 1864; age 14 in Baldwin County census, son of Oliver P. Bonner, paroled Greensboro, NC, 1 May 1865.

Bonner, William. Enlisted as private on 6 April 1864 at Hamilton's Crossing, VA; with dismounted cavalry under Major Farley July August 1864; "hands of enemy" September/October 1864 on 27 October 1864; captured 27 October 1864 at battle of Williamsburg Road, sent to Point Lookout, MD, and transferred for exchange; admitted to Jackson Hospital at Richmond on 16 February 1865 for pneumonia; died 23 February 1865.

Britton, John C. Enlisted as private on September 1861 at Gainesville, GA; May 1862 on detached service; 30 April 1863 transferred to Chestatee Artillery.

Brown, Perrin, W. Enlisted as private 4 July 1861 at Camp McDonald, sergeant; absent on wounded furlough since 5 July 1863 (absent through April 1864, showed present on July and August 1864 muster; 22 August 1864, admitted to Confederate Hospital at Petersburg; September and October 1864 muster showed him as absent wounded since 27 October 1864, brother of R. R. Brown, born 6 May 1839 to David P. and Lucetta Brown, died 1912 and buried at Memory Hill Cemetery at Milledgeville, GA, paroled at Greensboro, NC, 1 May 1865.

Brown, Robert Richard. Enlisted as private on 1 March 1862 at Milledgeville;

November and December 1862, WIA (left hip) 3 August 1863 near Brandy
Station, VA, November/December 1863 roll shows him on wounded
furlough since 1 August 1863, still absent as of October 1864 but returns at
some point because he surrenders with the company at Greensboro, NC, at
war's end; born 29 October 1843 in Baldwin County to David P. and Lucetta
Brown, brother of Perrin Brown, died 1915 and buried at Memory Hill
Cemetery at Milledgeville, GA, paroled Greensboro, NC, 1 May 1865.

Butts, James, Simmons. Enlisted as 1st sergeant at Camp McDonald on 4 July
1861, born 13 September 1834, died 12 December 1861, buried at
Butts/Thomas Cemetery in Baldwin County, GA, likely that he was a victim
of the many diseases that swept the legion in western Virginia;
August/September 1861present, no further record.

Byers, William L. Enlisted as private on 1 March 1862 at Gainesville, GA
(Company A and G); with dismounted cavalry under Major Farley July
August 1864; extra duty as wagoner September/October 1864, paroled
Greensboro, NC, 1 May 1865.

Carleton, Wesley A. Enlisted in legion infantry Co. A, transferred to cavalry Co.
A between November 1861 and September 1862, Enlisted as private on 26
June 1861 at Camp McDonald; hospitalized at CSA General Hospital at
Charlottesville, VA, on 7 March–10 May 1863 and 10 August–11 1863;
paroled Greensboro, NC, 1 May 1865.

Carter, E.,. Enlisted as private; POW roll, paroled at Talladega; no further
information.

Couch, David T. Enlisted as private on 25 September 1861 at Gainesville, GA;
promoted to second lieutenant; 14 January 1864; paroled Greensboro, NC, 1
May 1865.

Couch, William D. Enlisted as private A. G. C., 1 March 1862 at Gainesville,
GA; January February 1864, absent on home in Georgia to procure a
remount by order of Gen. R. E. Lee July August 1864; absent in hands of the
enemy, captured 4 May 1864; captured Spotsylvania Courthouse 12 May
1864; sent to Point Lookout, MD; transferred to Elmira, NY, 8 August 1864;
died November 1864 of pneumonia; buried Grave No. 906 at Woodlawn
Cemetery, born 12 January 1829 in Hall County to Terry and Agnes Barnett
Couch.

Cox, Robert B. Enlisted 4 July 1861 as corporal at Camp McDonald; August to
31 October 1861, absent; sick; discharged 26 January 1862; no further
details or record.

Dance, Leander W. Enlisted 4 July 1861 as private at Camp McDonald; November/December 1863, on extra duty as forager for the battalion; detailed 1 March 1863; January February1864, absent sick at hospital since 15 February 1864 (at Jackson Hospital); admitted to Gen. Hospital No. 9 in Richmond on 11 February 1864; sent to Jackson Hospital on 12 February 1864 for syphilis; returned to duty 1 March 1864; July August 1864, on detached service at recruiting camp for horses since 11 August 1864; no further record.

Daniel, James R. Enlisted 1 July 1861 at Camp McDonald; July August 1864, with dismounted cavalry under Major Farley; paroled Greensboro, NC, 1 May 1865.

David, J. W. Enlisted 1 May 1864 at Macon, GA; July August 1864 detached service at recruiting camp for horses; September/October 1864, same as above, no further record.

Davis, John. Enlisted 1 May 1862 at Milledgeville, GA; September/October 1864, absent in hands of enemy since 27 October 1864 but no Federal POW records; Oath of Allegiance and released 26 June 1865; place of residence, Baldwin County, GA; complexion, light; hair, brown; eyes, gray; height 5' 8 1/2".

Davis, William R. Enlisted 28 August 1861 at Milledgeville, GA; April 1862– June 1862, on sick furlough; discharged 14 November 1862; no further details or records.

DeBerry, Henry. Enlisted 4 July 1861 as private at Camp McDonald; present on 31 October 1861; no further records.

DeGraffenreid, Edwin F. Enlisted as private at Camp McDonald; 17 April 1862, discharged for disability; no further detail or records.

Denson, William A. Enlisted as private; died 11 March 1863 of diarrhea; born 12 June 1836; leaves wife and two children; wife, Naomi E. Denson, filed claim 15 June 1864 in Twiggs County.

Dickson, J. A. Enlisted on 1 May 1864 as private at Milledgeville, GA; 1864 GA Militia Census shows him residing in Wilkinson County, age 16 years, 7 months, paroled Greensboro, NC, 1 May 1865.

Dixon, John W. Enlisted on 1 March 1863 as private at Gainesville, GA, hospitalized at Charlottesville, VA, 19 February 1863–11 March 1863 of debilitas; captured 1 August 1863 at Brandy Station; first sent to Old Capitol Prison, Washington, D.C.; sent to Baltimore on 23 August 1863 and then to Point Lookout; exchanged 16 March 1863.

Dowdy, John C. Enlisted 25 September 1861 at Gainesville, GA; January February1864, absent on horse detail in Georgia since 4 February 1861; April 1 1864, absent on horse detail to go to Georgia to procure fresh horse by order of Gen. R. E. Lee; July August 1864, with dismounted cavalry under Major Farley; paroled Greensboro, NC, 1 May 1865.

DuBignon, Charles Joseph Poulain, Jr. Enlisted as captain, resigned 9 August 1862 due to deafness rendering him wholly incapable of performing duties, age 54, born 4 January 1809 at Jekyl Island, died 13 September 1875 and buried at Memory Hills Cemetery at Milledgeville, GA,
1 August–31 October 1864, absent.

DuBignon, Charles, Jr; No enlistment record but shown as discharged for disability 14 October 1861 at Green Sulphur Springs, VA, later joined 26 GA Battalion as a 2nd lt., died of meningitis at Dalton, GA, 11 February 1864, born to Captain Charles and Anne Grantland DuBignon, buried at Memory Hill Cemetery in Milledgeville, GA.

DuBignon, Samuel. Enlisted 11 June 1861 as 1st lt., resigned 20 July 1861.

Dyer, Bluford L. Enlisted as private on 25 September 1861 at Gainesville, GA, born in 1832 in Georgia to Bluford E. and Elizabeth Clark Dyer, died in Montana in 1907, no further record.

Dyer, Elisha. Enlisted as private on 25 September 1861 at Gainesville, GA; discharged 17 April 1862 for disability; no further record.

Earnest, Burwell. Enlisted as private on 4 July 1861 at Camp McDonald; admitted General Hospital No. 21 for diarrhea, 25 October 1861 returned to duty; 30 October 1862 admitted to Hosp. 18 in Richmond for typhoid fever; 12 November 1862 furloughed for 30 days; 20 March 1863 discharged for disability "pthisis pulmonalis" by surgeon's certificate; born Abbeville, SC; farmer; 45 years old in 1863; 6' tall, light complexion, blue eyes, brown hair, born 1818 in Tennessee to James and Mary Curl Earnest, died 1923 in Fayette County, AL, disability resulted from injury received from fall from his horse, right lung diseased; surgeon's certificate noted that his general health was bad; "his recovery is distant and uncertain."

Echols, Fayette J. Enlisted May 1862 as private at Hardeeville, SC; hospital card showed admitted 18 November 1862 to General Hospital Charlottesville, VA, for pneumonia; discharged 3 March 1863 for phthisis; 27 at discharge; 5' 10 1/2" tall, dark complexion, dark hair, occupation, farmer, born 4 September 1835 in Hancock County to Peter and Virginia A. Echols, brother of William Echols.

Echols, William B. Enlisted as private on 4 July 1861 at Camp McDonald; September/October 1864, on horse detail since 3 September 1864, born in Hancock County to Peter and Virginia Echols, brother of Fayette Echols, paroled Greensboro, NC, 1 May 1865.

Elliott, Daniel Stewart Enlisted as private; discharged 29 September 1861 "pulmonary disease with repeated hemorrhages," letter signed by Charles G. DuBignon dated 30 October 1861 provided these details; age 35, 6' 2", light complexion, gray eyes, dark hair, planter, born in Liberty County, GA, to U.S. Senator John Elliott and wife, died in hospital in Marietta, GA 3 August 1862 and buried at Roswell Presbyterian Church Cemetery.

Ennis, Charles William. Enlisted 17 April 1864 at Chesterfield, VA, shown sick at hospital on 23 October 1864, POW card, captured at Tallens Bridge, SC; received Hart's Island 10 April 1865; released 15 June 1865, born to Pleasant and Eveline Ennis, 5' 9" tall with grey eyes and light hair, died 25 February 1904 and buried at Memory Hill Cemetery at Milledgeville, GA, place of residence, Baldwin County, GA.

Ennis, George M. Enlisted on 12 May 1862 as private at Camp Pritchard, SC (or 1 May 1862 at Milledgeville, GA); died 25 February 1862 at Charlottesville General Hospital of "Cong. Of Lungs," born in Baldwin County, GA; age 25 at time, of death; 5' 8", buried at University of Virginia Confederate Cemetery of Charlottesville, VA, florid complexion, gray eyes, dark hair; farmer by occupation.

Fields, Henry F. Enlisted as private 1 March 1862 Milledgeville, GA; wounded, gunshot wound thigh and leg; admitted to General Hospital No. 9 Richmond 20 July 1863; transferred to Chimborazo Hosp. No. 4 21 July 1863; returned to duty 3 August 1862; March/April 1864, absent on furlough of indulgence since 1 March 1864, age 18 in 1860 Baldwin County Census, born to William and Mary E. Fields, paroled Greensboro, NC, 1 May 1865.

Fricks, Henry F. Enlisted as private on 25 September 1861 at Gainesville, GA; no further records.

Fuller, J. F. Enlisted as private, paroled Appomattox 9 April 1865.

Gibson, Adam J. Enlisted as private on 1 March 1864; July August 1864, with dismounted cavalry under Major Farley; 31 October 1864, absent on horse detail since 21 September 1864, born 5 February 1842 in Baldwin County to James and Patience Gibson, died 22 August 1912, paroled Greensboro, NC, 1 May 1865.

Green, Thomas F. Enlisted as private either on 1 June 1861 or 1 July 1861 (both listed); September/October 1864, on horse detail since 22 September 1864, born in Baldwin County to Dr. Thomas F. and Adaline Green, died 1874, buried at Memory Hill Cemetery at Milledgeville, GA, paroled Greensboro, NC, 1 May 1865.

Gregory, James T. Enlisted as private at Camp McDonald; July August 1864; with dismounted cavalry under Major Farley, age 17 in 1860 Baldwin County Census, paroled Greensboro, NC, 1 May 1865.

Hall, Bowling (Bolen) C. Enlisted as private; July August 1864, with dismounted cavalry under Major Farley, born 1842 in Baldwin County to John W. and Nancy Sayers Hall, brother of James M., John W., and Thomas J. Hall, paroled Greensboro, NC, 1 May 1865.

Hall, James M. Enlisted on 4 July 1861 at Camp McDonald; 2 August to 31 October 1861, sick at Lynchburg, VA, "left begin there 25 September 1861 and is now there," 28 October 1861, surgeon wrote "incapable of performing duties because of youth and debility," 31 August 1862 to 30 November 1862, sick in hospital; 30 November 1862 to 31 December 1862, "Left sick near Winchester, Virginia, November 1, 1862 and not heard of since"; January February 1863, sick at hospital; September/October 1864 at hospital; March/April 1864, sick; May/June 1864, at hospital: July August 1864, at hospital; no further record. Note: although cards for 1864 showed him in the hospital, there is another card that showed he died 15 April 1863; card is entitled "J. M. Hall appears in Register of Officers and Soldiers of the Army of the Confederate States who were killed in battle, or who died of wounds." Born 1837 to John W. and Nancy Sayers, brother of Bolen, John W., and Thomas J. Hall.

Hall, John Wesley. Enlisted as private on 28 February 1863 at Milledgeville, born 13 November 1844 in Baldwin County to John W. and Nancy Sayer, died in 1928, brother of Bolen, James M., and Thomas J. Hall, paroled at Greensboro, NC, 1 May 1865.

Hall, Rabun M. Enlisted as private on 1 July 1861 at Camp McDonald; WIA at Gettysburg, furloughed 8 July 1863; March/April 1864, absent on wounding furloughed since 8 July 1863; July August 1864 with dismounted cavalry under Major Farley; paroled Greensboro, NC, 1 May 1865.

Hall, Thomas Hartley. Enlisted as corporal on 4 July 1861 at Camp McDonald; 1 August to 31 October 1861, absent on detached service; discharged 17 December 1861, age 23 in 1860 Baldwin County Census, became a Doctor after the war, no further record.

Hall, Thomas Jefferson. Enlisted 25 August 1862 at Macon, on horse detail 28 March 1864, shown "with dismounted cavalry under Major Farley" on July August 1864 roll, September/October 1864 roll states "absent on horse detail since 21 September, 1864, by order of Gen. Lee." (Note: there was a large group that remained south for the rest of the war.) No further record, born 1831 to John W. and Nancy Sayers Hall, brother of Bolen, James M., and John W. Hall, buried at Montpelier Methodist Church Cemetery, no date of death indicated.

Hanigan, T. Captured at Gettysburg, 3 July 1863; sent to Fort Delaware, 12 July 1863, no further record.

Harris, Iverson L. Enlisted as sergeant 4 July 1861 at Camp McDonald, appointed asst. surgeon 17 April 1862 (effective 24 February 1862), resigned 1 August 1862, associate justice Georgia Supreme Court 1865–1875, born 7 January 1805, died 12 March 1876 and buried at Memory Hill Cemetery at Milledgeville, GA.

Hayes, J. B. Enlisted as private; captured at Westminster, 30 June 1863, received at Fort Delaware, 12 July 1863; no further record.

Haygood, Thomas S. Enlisted 4 July 1861 at Camp McDonald, died 25 January 1863 at Culpeper Court House, VA, age 19, in 1860 Baldwin County Census, son of Archibald and Elizabeth Hagood (also listed as Hayfood).

Holland, Elisha Enlisted 5 July 1861 as private at Camp McDonald; January February 1864, absent on horse detail since 4 February 1864; 1 April, detailed to go to Georgia to procure a fresh horse by order of Gen. R. E. Lee; July August 1864, AWOL since 26 June 1864; no further record.

Holland, Marion Reuben. Enlisted on 24 November 1863 as private at Cherokee; January February 1864, absent on horse detail since 4 February 1864; 1 April, detailed to procure fresh horse by order of Gen. R. E. Lee; September/October 1864, on horse detail since 2 September 1864 by order of Gen. Lee; appeared on bounty pay roll card for $50, 1 July 1863; (Note: there was a large group of dismounted A.N.V. cavalrymen who returned to Georgia under command of Gen. P. M. B. Young, most of the group remained south for the rest of the war.) no further record.

Holt, W. J. No enlistment record, Holt had enlisted in Co. B, 21st Georgia Infantry in June 1861, became a 2nd Lt. in 1863 and resigned 26 July 1864 to join the legion cavalry, paroled at Greensboro, NC, 1 May 1865.

Honeycut (Hunnicut), Charles P. Enlisted on 4 July 1861 at Camp McDonald; August/October 1861, absent sick 21 April 1862, died of disease in SC; no further record.

Howard, J. H. Enlisted as private on 4 March 1862 at Eatonton; July August 1864, absent, "Has just been assigned to the company and has not yet reported," September/October 1864, absent, "Wounded and at hospital since September 29, 1864"; no further record.

Hubbard, J. D. (no company designation). Sgt. major; paroled at Greensboro, NC, 1 May 1865, possible late war enlistee or transfer from another command.

Hudson, Henry D. Enlisted as private on 4 July 1861 at Camp McDonald, age 22 in 1861 Baldwin County Census, paroled Greensboro, NC, 1 May 1865.

Humphries, Elisha J. Enlisted as sergeant on 4 July 1861 at Camp McDonald; March/April 1864, absent on horse detail since August 1864; July August 1864, with the dismounted cavalry under Major Farley; September/October 1864, absent wounded since 27 October 1864; paroled Greensboro, NC, 1 May 1865. (Note: appeared to have served in Company G in 1862; he is listed in company A in 1861, 1863, 1864, and 1865.), born 1834 to Thomas and Cynthia McCord Humphries, died 28 October 1911, and buried at Humphries Family Cemetery in Baldwin County, GA.

Jones, Joseph T. Enlisted as private on 4 July 1861 at Camp McDonald; July August 1864, with dismounted cavalry under Major Farley; September/October 1864, absent, on horse detail since 21 September 1864 by order of Gen. Lee; paroled Greensboro, NC, 1 May 1865. (Note: no card showed Company G; two hospital cards showed Company B in June 1864, and a receipt for clothing showed Company H in August 1863. All other cards showed Company A.) Returned north before war's end. (Note: there was a large group of dismounted A.N.V. cavalrymen who returned to Georgia under command of Gen. P. M. B. Young.)

Jones, Joseph W. Enlisted as private/corporal on 1 May 1862 at Milledgeville, GA; January February1864, absent on horse detail in Georgia since 4 February 1864; 1 April 1864, absent on detail to go to Georgia to procure a remount horse by order of Gen. R. E. Lee; July August 1864, with the dismounted cavalry under Major Farley; September/October 1864, absent on horse detail since 21 September 1864 by order of Gen. R. E. Lee. (Note: there was a large group of dismounted A.N.V. cavalrymen who returned to Georgia under command of Gen. P. M. B. Young, most of this group remained south for the rest of the war.) No further record.

Kenan, Thomas Holmes. Enlisted as second lieutenant on 4 July 1861 at Camp

McDonald; elected second lieutenant 20 July 1864, date of appointment 2 August 1861; resigned 2 January 1862, vacancy filled by Geo. B. Beecher, born 1842 in Georgia to Augustus H. and Henrietta Alston Kenan, no further details or records.

Lamar, Richard Nichols. No enlistment record, entry states, "Aug 1 to Sept 2 (year illegible)—discharged in Georgia by Governor Brown." Another record shows, "Richard Lamar-Private Co. A Phoenix Regiment, paid for 12 days February 17, 1863 to February 28, 1863." The 63rd Georgia Infantry was known as the Phoenix Regt. and there is a record of a Richard N. Lamar serving with this unit from 1863 to 1865; there is also a Richard Lamar age 15 in the 1860 Baldwin County Census. It is possible that this Richard Lamar joined Co. A of the legion cavalry in 1862, was discharged, and later enlisted in the 63 Georgia, born 19 January 1845, died 31 July 1909 and buried at Memory Hill Cemetery in Milledgeville, GA.

Lawrence, John H. Enlisted as private on 23 September 1861 at Lynchburg, VA; from November/December 1863 to September/October 1864, all cards indicated absent-on-sick leave since 1 October (some say 10th) 1863, born 4 March 1841 to Harriet E. Lawrence, died 1926, no further record.

Lednum, W. H. Enlisted as private on 1 May 1864 at Macon, GA; July August and September/October 1864 indicated sick at hospital since 20 June 1864.

Lester, Lucius L. Enlisted as private on 1 May 1862 at Milledgeville, GA; Last muster card September/October 1864 showed present, son of William and Sarah Lester, died 29 December 1923 in Chilton County, AL.

Leverett, D. N. (also listed as Levitt, Levett, Levrett). Enlisted as private at Camp Pritchard, SC; September/October 1863, taken prisoner at Gettysburg; muster cards for May/June and July August 1864 indicated absent "paroled prisoner"; prisoner of war card indicated captured 3 July 1864 at Gettysburg; arrived at Fort Delaware 22 October 1863; forwarded to Point Lookout, MD, no date; paroled and sent to Aiken's Landing, VA, for exchange on August 1864; admitted to Jackson's Hospital at Richmond at Richmond on 23 September 1864 for chronic diarrhea; died 5 October 1864.

Love, Andrew P. Captain, no enlistment information; title card also indicates service in 22nd Al Inf., 4th Batt'n Al. Cav., Jeff Davis Legion, Miss. Cav.; POW card indicated captured at Petersburg on 27 October 1864 captured at Petersburg on 27 October 1864; first sent to Old Capitol Prison in D.C. on 27 October 1864; transferred to Fort Delaware 16 December 1864; Oath of Allegiance and released 16 June 1865; place of residence, Pike, AL;

complexion dark, eyes black, 5' 9".

Mapp, William T. Enlisted as private on 4 July 1861 at Camp McDonald; promoted 2 January 1862 to second lieutenant; promoted 9 August 1862 to second lieutenant; promoted first lieutenant 14 June 1864; wounded 13 September 1863, "v.s. flesh I. thigh," 30 day furlough on 23 September 1863; residence listed as Milledgeville, GA; 1 April 1864, absent on horse duty by order Gen. Lee; September/October 1864, absent on horse detail since 21 September 1864 by order Gen. Lee. (Note: there was a large group of dismounted cavalrymen who returned to Georgia under command of Gen. P. M. B. Young, returned north before war's end.) Paroled Greensboro, NC, 1 May 1865.

Martin, Joab. Enlisted as private 1 March 1862 at Gainesville, GA; July August 1864 with dismounted cavalry under Major Farley; (Note: April 1862 regimental return indicated Company G; all others Company A.) Born 16 January 1837 in Alabama to Green and Elizabeth Martin, died 18 October 1916 in Hall County, GA.

McCrary, George W. (also listed as McCreary). Enlisted as private on 31 October 1861 at Gainesville, GA; 1 August to 31 October 1861 showed present; register of payments to discharged soldiers indicated discharged 15 February 1862; age 24 in 1860 Union County Census, son of James and Barhubee McCrary; no further record.

McCutcheon, Henry. Enlisted 21 September 1861 in Atlanta; October 1861 last muster card showed present; disability discharge 5 September 1862; discharge cert. showed born in Virginia; attorney by occupation, 54 years old at discharge, 5' 7", gray eyes, gray hair, and florid complexion, regimental returns for April, May, and June 1862 all indicate "absent without leave."

McCutcheon, James. Enlisted as private on 21 September 1861 at Gainesville, GA; register of payments to discharged soldiers indicated discharged 22 July 1862 due to chronic rheumatism. Born in Virginia.

McDowell, John W. Enlisted as private on 4 July 1861 at Camp McDonald; 1 August to October 1861 "absent sick"; Register of payments to discharged soldiers indicated date of discharge, 13 November 1862, age 40 in 1860, Baldwin County Census, no further record.

McGee, William K. Enlisted as private on 25 September 1861 at Gainesville, GA; register of payments to discharged soldiers indicated date of discharge, 1 March 1862 age 28 in 1860 Union County Census, no further record.

Miller, Oliver. Enlisted as private 1 March 1862 at Gainesville, GA; muster rolls for November/December 1863 through July August 1864 all indicate on sick furlough since 1 September 1863; muster roll card for September/October 1864 indicated "absent without leave since Jan. 1 1864"; no further record.

Moran, James Barnes. Enlisted as private on 1 May 1862 at Milledgeville, GA; July August 1864 with dismounted cavalry under Major Farley; September/October 1864, on horse detail since 21 September 1864 by order Gen. Lee; captured 12 April 1865 "in the field" near Raleigh, NC; paroled and released 22 April 1865; oath not to bear arms until exchanged. (Note: there was a large group of dismounted A.N.V. cavalrymen who returned to Georgia under command of Gen. P. M. B. Young); returned north before war's end and was captured near Raleigh, NC, 12 April 1865, born 16 June 1865 in Georgia to John B. and Jane Colter Moran, died 6 August 1894 and buried at Black Springs Baptist Church Cemetery in Baldwin County.

Nelms, Joseph T. Enlisted as private on 25 September 1861 at Gainesville, GA; 1 August to 31 October 1861, absent sick; April 1862, at home sick (Company G); May 1862, sick furlough (company G); June 1862, discharge for disability June 28 1862 (company G); Register of payments to discharged soldiers indicated discharge date of 14 November 1862; no further record.

Nelson, John A. Enlisted as private on 4 July 1861 at Camp McDonald; regimental return for May 1862 showed discharged for disability on 21 May 1862 at Camp Pritchard (Company G).

Newell, Tomlinson Fort. Enlisted as private; August/September (year?), discharged in Georgia by Governor Brown, he later became lt/capt. of Company G 45th Georgia Infantry and had left foot shot off at Gettysburg 3 July 1863; born 31 January 1838 to Isaac and Barmelia Newell, died 1912 and buried at Memory Hill Cemetery at Milledgeville, GA; no further record.

Nichols, James H. Enlisted 4 July 1861 as 2nd lt. at Camp McDonald, age 25, in 1860 County Census, promoted 1st lt. 20 July 1861, promoted to captain 9 August 1862, AWOL August/October 1861, January February 1864 roll states acting asst. quartermaster since 1 August 1863, September/October 1864 roll stated absent on horse detail since 21 September 1864 by order of Gen. Lee. (Note: there was a large group of dismounted A.N.V. cavalrymen who returned to Georgia under command of Gen. P. M. B. Young, returned north before war's end). Paroled at Greensboro, NC, 1 May 1865, buried at Memory Hill Cemetery in Milledgeville, GA.

Nolan, Benjamin F. Enlisted 1 May 1862 at Camp Pritchard, SC; POW card;

153

captured Gettysburg on 3 July 1863; arrived at Fort Delaware 12 July 1863; forwarded to Point Lookout, MD, 13 October 1863, age 28 in 1860 Baldwin County Census, son of Anthony and Lucinda Nolan, known to have survived the war because he is found in postwar censuses for Baldwin County, died there in 1895.

O'Neal, J. Surrendered at Appomattox 5 April 1865; no other information.

Orme, John Adams. Enlisted 1 March 1864 as private at Macon, GA; July August 1864, with dismounted cavalry under Major Farley; September/October 1864, absent on horse detail; paroled Greensboro, NC, 1 May 1865.

Orme, John Enlisted as private on 1 March 1864 at Macon, GA; April 1864, absent, recruit on route to the command with horse detail, shown "with dismounted cavalry under Major Farley" on July August 1864, born 1846 in GA to Richard M. and Abby Adams Orme, died 1870, paroled at Greensboro, NC, 1 May 1865

Osbern, J. Surrendered at Appomattox 9 April 1865; no further information.

Porter, Gideon. Enlisted as private 25 September 1861 at Gainesville, January February 1864 rolls showed absent on horse detail in Georgia since 4 February 1864, April 1864 roll listed him still on horse detail, September/October 1864 roll stated absent on horse detail since 21 September 1864 by order Gen. Lee (Note: there was a large group of dismounted A.N.V. cavalrymen under command of Gen. P. M. B. Young, most of this group remained south for the rest of the war), no further record, age 15 in 1860 Hall County Census, son of James M. and Juda Porter.

Prosser, Charles E. Enlisted as private on 2 August 1861 at Cobb County; born 4 January 1845 to William and Elizabeth Johnson Prosser, brother of Reuben and Thomas A. Prosser, died 21 August 1909.

Prosser, James A. Enlisted as private on 1 March 1862 at Milledgeville, GA: January February1864 horse detail in Georgia since 4 February 1864; 1 April 1864, detailed to go to Georgia to procure fresh horse by order of Gen Lee, born 21 July 1843 at Baldwin County to Thomas and Rachel Prosser, brother of Thomas Prosser, died 11 March 1931 and buried at Memory Hill Cemetery in Milledgeville, GA, paroled Greensboro, NC, 1 May 1865.

Prosser, Reuben A. (also R. A.). Enlisted as private on 1 May 1862, age 25, at Milledgeville, GA; 1860 Washington County Census, January February 1864 roll showed absent on horse detail in Georgia since 4 February 1864; 1 April 1864, detailed to go to Georgia to procure fresh horse by order of Gen.

Lee; September/October 1864, on horse detail since 12 September 1864 (Note: there was a large group of dismounted A.N.V. cavalrymen who returned to Georgia under command of Gen. P. M. B. Young, returned north before war's end), paroled Greensboro, NC, 1 May 1865, born 1835 in Baldwin County to William and Elizabeth Johnson Prosser, brother of Charles E. and Thomas A. Prosser.

Prosser, Thomas Enlisted as private on 1 May 1862 at Milledgeville, GA; 1 April 1864, detailed to go to Georgia to procure fresh horse by order of Gen. Lee; July August 1864 with dismounted cavalry under Major Farley; September/October 1864, on horse detail since 2 September 1864; paroled Greensboro, NC, 1 May 1865, born 14 January 1836 in Baldwin County to Thomas and Rachel Prosser, brother of James Prosser, died 16 April 1902 and buried at Memory Hill Cemetery at Milledgeville, GA.

Prosser, Thomas A. Enlisted as private (Farrier) on 4 July 1861 at Camp McDonald, January February 1864 roll showed him "home on sick furlough–debility," born in 1832 to William and Elizabeth Prosser, brother of Charles and Reuben A. Prosser, died 1868, no further record.

Pugh, Jasper Littleton. Enlisted 4 July 1861 at Camp McDonald, died from disease at Lynchburg, VA, 14 October 1861, buried Lynchburg City Cemetery, born 1834 in Georgia to Thomas J. and Martha Arnold Pugh, brother of John Newton Pugh.

Pugh, John Newton. Enlisted as private on 4 July 1861 at Camp McDonald, born 1837 in GA to Thomas J. and Martha Arnold Pugh, brother of Littleton Pugh, died 1865 and buried at Pugh Family Cemetery in Baldwin County, GA, paroled Greensboro, NC, 1 May 1865.

Renfroe, William P. Enlisted as private on 4 July 1861 at Camp McDonald, last card August 1 to 31 October 1861 showed "absent by transfer October 30 1861," no further information.

Roberts, John W. Enlisted as private on 4 July 1861 at Camp McDonald; last card September/October 1864 showed present for extra duty in commissary department; no further record but 1910 pension application stated he was furloughed home 24 November 1864 due to the amputation of his big toe and could not return to the army because of Sherman's presence in the Carolinas, born 2 August 1842, died 28 November 1928, buried at Memory Hill Cemetery at Milledgeville, GA.

Robinson, E. Enlisted as private on 11 April 1864 at Hamilton's Crossing; July August 1864 with dismounted cavalry under Major Farley;

September/October 1864, horse detail since 9 February 1864; no further record.

Robinson, George M. (also George W.). Enlisted as private on 21 August 1861 at Camp McDonald; last card showed absent with leave; no further detail.

Robinson, John W. Enlisted as private on 1 March 1862 at Gainesville, GA; detailed as wagoner 1 September 1863; January February1864, absent on horse detail since 4 February 1864; September/October 1864, last card indicated "on extra duty as wagoner," paroled Greensboro, NC, 1 May 1865.

Robinson, Jolly Enlisted as private on 25 September 1863 at Gainesville, GA; July August 1864, absent without leave since 6 June 1864; listed on registers of "Deserters from Rebel Army," received at Chattanooga 10 August 1864, deserted at Fredericksburg 30 April 1864; showed received 1 September 1864 at Military Prison, Louisville; captured Hall County, GA, sent from the Department of the Cumberland "to be released north of the Ohio River," oath and released 4 September 1864 on condition that he would remain north of the Ohio River; light complexion, dark hair, hazel eyes 5' 9"; (Note: odd that Union records showed he deserted on 30 April 1864 but CSA records showed him missing since 6 June 1864.)

Robinson, Thomas C. Enlisted as private on 1 March 1862 at Gainesville, GA; November/December 1863, on extra duty or daily duty as wagoner, detailed 1 November 1863; January February1864, absent on furlough since 28 February 1864; 1 April 1864, detailed to go to Georgia to procure fresh horses by order Gen. Lee; July August 1864, at recruit camp for horses since 26 August 1864; September/October 1864, last card showed at recruit camp for horses since 26 August 1864; no further record.

Robinson, William E. Enlisted as private on 20 February 1863 at Gainesville, GA; wounded 12 June 1864 at Trevillian Station and admitted to Charlottesville, VA, General Hospital 14 June 1864 for "Vulu. Sclo.," transferee to convalescent camp 18 June 1864; September/October 1864, last card showed absent on wounded furlough since 12 June 1864; born in Georgia 1845 to William and Francis Robinson, no further record.

Russell, Joel B. Enlisted as private on 4 July 1861 at Camp McDonald; July August 1864, recruit camp since 26 August 1864 for horses, born 22 February 1835 in Baldwin County to James G. and Sarah Boswell Russell, paroled Greensboro, NC, 1 May 1865.

Sherlock, James H. Enlisted as private (farrier) on 4 July 1861; card for May 1862 showed "on detached service," discharged 21 July 1862, no details provided, born 1833 in New Jersey, no further record.

Smith, Dionecious (Dionyssius) Mead. Enlisted as private on 4 July 1861 at Camp McDonald; July August 1864, sick at hospital since 23 August 1864; September/October 1864 (last card), showed absent on sick furlough since 6 September 1864; April 4 1865, granted extension of furlough for 30 days by reason of chronic diarrhea, born 25 January 1842 in Baldwin County to L. L. and Martha Smith, died 23 June 1917 and buried at Memory Hill Cemetery in Milledgeville, GA, no further record.

Smith, James W. Enlisted as private on 1 March 1862 at Gainesville, GA; July August 1864, on furlough of indulgence since 5 August 1864; paroled Greensboro, NC, 1 May 1865; (Note: April 1862 card showed company G, all other cards showed company A.)

Smith, Tillman D. Enlisted as private 1 May 1862 at Milledgeville, GA; July August 1864, with dismounted cavalry under Major Farley; September/October 1864, on horse detail since 2 September 1864, born 1834 in South Carolina to William and Dedama Smith, died 5 January 1914 and buried at Memory Hill Cemetery, Milledgeville, GA, paroled Greensboro, NC, 1 May 1865.

Smith, William J. Enlisted 4 July 1861 at Camp McDonald; July August 1864, with dismounted cavalry under Major Farley; September/October 1864, absent, wounded 27 October 1864, born 1839 in Baldwin County to Levin J. and Matilda P. Smith, no information on wounding; paroled Greensboro, NC, 1 May 1865.

Stafford, Gilbert (also John Gilbert Stafford). Enlisted as private on 21 September 1861 at Milledgeville, GA; May 1862 (Company G) detailed as teamster, died 27 May 1863 Buckingham County, VA; no information on cause of death, born 1839 in GA to Malcolm and Martha Stafford.

Stembridge, John H. Enlisted as private on 4 July 1861 at Camp McDonald; discharged 19 September 1861 (no information about reasons), no further detail, born in Baldwin County in 1829 to William and Nancy Lewis Stembridge, buried at Memory Hill Cemetery at Milledgeville, GA

Stokes, J. Enlisted as private on 23 May 1864 at Macon, GA; July August 1864 and September/October 1864 showed "absent without leave since 6 June 1864," hospital registers showed admitted to General Hospital No. 9 at Richmond on 26 June 1864; no further record.

Tailbird, Marion B. Enlisted as private on 25 September 1861 at Milledgeville, GA; (Company A and G); July August 1864 and September/October 1864, on extra duty in medical department; enlistment papers in file; filed contains letter dated 30 November 1864 from J. M. Coxe, assistant surgeon, recommending that Tailbird be appointed hospital steward; appointment approved by J. H. Nichols, born 1829 in South Carolina to William H. Talberd, buried at Memory Hill Cemetery at Milledgeville, GA as M. B. Tailbird, M.D., no death date, no further record.

Terry, John H. Enlisted as private on 1 May 1862 at Milledgeville, GA; last card September/October 1864, on horse detail since 2 September 1864, born 1829 to William W. and Elenor D. Terry, no further record.

Trulove, Elijah (galvanized Yankee). Enlisted as private on 1 March 1862 at Gainesville, GA; November/December. 1863 through September/October 1864 "in hands of enemy," captured 1 August 1863; prisoner of war cards indicated captured at Brandy Station 1 August 1863; arrived at Baltimore 23 August 1863 and sent to Point Lookout Prison; joined U.S. Service 14 October 1864, and released 15 October 1864, age 18 in 1860 Hall County Census.

Turner, James Jarrett. Enlisted as private on 25 September 1861 at Gainesville, GA; (Company A and G); "Appears as a signature to an Oath of Allegiance to the United States subscribed and sworn to at Chattanooga, Tenn., the day and year set opposite the several names," dated 5 March 1864; showed place of residence as White Co., GA, fair complexion, light hair, gray eyes, 5' 10", born 1845 in Georgia to Henry and Celia Daniel Turner.

Walker, T. J. Enlisted as private, no enlistment information; one card April 1862 showed absent on sick leave; no further record.

Watson, Henry W. (also listed as Henry C.). Enlisted as private on 12 March 1864 at Atlanta, GA; (Company A and G); July August 1864, with dismounted cavalry under Major Farley; POW cards indicated captured 8 March 1865 in Richmond County, NC; arrived New Berne, NC, on 30 March 1865 and transferred to Point Lookout; Oath of Allegiance and released 22 June 1865 at Point Lookout; resident of Hall County, GA; fair complexion, light brown hair, blue eyes, 5' 7 3/4". (Note: second POW card showed captured 6 April 1865 probably in error.). Born to Hampton F. and Hannah Malden Watson.

Weld, William Henry Enlisted as private on 1 July 1864 in Decatur, GA; July August 1864 and September/October 1864, sick at hospital since 27 July 1864; appeared on receipt for clothing at the General Hospital at Kittrell Springs on 10 September 1864; no further record; buried at Weeks Family

Cemetery, Moncks Comer, SC; born 26 December 1844, died 3 March 1865 at Weeks Plantation, born 27 December 1844 to Calvin S. and Sarah A. Weld.

White, George C. Enlisted as private (Company A and G) on 1 March 1862 at Gainesville, GA: last muster card January February1864 showed present; appeared on register of "Prisoners received and disposed of by the Provost Marshall General, Army of the Potomac"; showed Rebel Deserter received on 3 August 1864, sent to Washington, D.C. on 12 March 1864; appeared on register of "Oaths and Deserters, Provost Marshall General, Washington, D.C.," indicated sent north to Philadelphia, age 21 in 1860 Dawson County Census.

White, Oliver Thomas. Enlisted as private (company A and G), probably late war enlistee, born October 1845 to Benjamin A. and Jane DeClancy White, buried at Memory Hill Cemetery, Milledgeville, GA. Paroled Greensboro, NC, 1 May 1865.

Wise, Henry A. Enlisted as private/corporal; November/December 1863; on extra duty as wagon master; detailed 1 August 1863, July August 1864 through September/October 1864, on extra duty as wagon master, born 1830 in GA in Lake County, FL, per 1909 pension application from his widow, Winnie Wise; no further record.

Casualties, other losses for the Phillips Georgia Legion cavalry battalion from available records. Company H/B was formed predominantly from Cobb and Bartow (Cass) counties.

Company H/B

Total Enrollment:	160
Death/Disease/Accident:	11
Discharge/Disease/Accident:	12
Reenlisted:	1
Deserted:	1
KIA:	1
WIA:	6
Resigned/Substitute:	3
Exchanged:	2
Conscript:	3
Surrender/Appomattox:	1
AWOL:	14

Imprisoned/Point Lookout:	9
Imprisoned/Old Capitol Prison:	5
Imprisoned/Fort Delaware:	6
Imprisoned City Point:	1
Imprisoned Louisville, Kentucky:	2
Imprisoned Rock Island:	1
Imprisoned Fort Monroe:	1
Imprisoned Camp Douglas:	1
Discharged/Remain North of Ohio River:	2
Transferred Out:	2
Transferred In:	3
Detached Service:	53
Horse Detail:	38
Extra Duty:	4
Paroled at Greensboro:	23
Paroled Hartwell, Georgia:	5
Paroled Augusta, Georgia:	4
Paroled Albany, Georgia:	1
Paroled Fort Delaware:	2
Paroled Anderson, South Carolina:	1
Paroled Elsewhere/Unknown:	2

PHILLIPS GEORGIA LEGION
Cavalry Battalion

Company B
The Johnson Rangers

Alexander, Isaac W. Enlisted as private on 1 March 1862 at Cassville, Georgia; discharged 3 October 1863 at Staunton, VA, for chronic bronchitis with incipient phthisis; born in Calhoun, AL; age 25 on 10 March 1863; florid complexion, black hair, black eyes, 5' 11"; carpenter.

Anderson, John C. Enlisted as private on 27 February 1862 at Marietta, Georgia; Company B and H.

Baker, Isaac (Baker, J.). Enlisted as private on 22 February 1862 at Cassville, GA; last muster for October 1864 showed in hands of enemy; captured 28, 29 February 1864 at Rapidan River, VA; sent to Fort Delaware from Old Capitol Prison, D.C.; arrived Fort Delaware 17 June 1864; exchanged and paroled 30 October 1864.

Barnwell, Posey. Enlisted as private on 11 June 1861 at Camp McDonald; age 30 per 31 August 1861 muster; October 1864 showed on detached service by order of Gen. Lee since 2 September 1864.

Barron, Benjamin. Enlisted as private on 11 June 1861 at Camp McDonald; last muster showed detached service by order of Gen. Lee since 2 September 1864.

Bass, Thomas (Bass, T. J.). Enlisted as private on 25 February 1862 at Marietta, GA; October 1864 last muster showed on detached service by order of Gen. Lee since 2 September 1864.

Bates, J. C. Enlisted as private in August 1863; 31 December 1863 to 30 April 1864 listed as "absent without leave"; card noted Special Order No. 26218, 4 November 1863 "furlough."

Bellinger, Robert A. Enlisted as private on 20 March 1862 at Marietta, GA; October 1864 last muster showed on detached service by order of Gen. Lee since 2 September 1864.

Best, Hezekiah. Enlisted as private, later sergeant, on 26 June 1861 in Cobb County, GA; age 23 per 31 August 1861 muster; 18 September 1861, transferred to Capt. Rich's Cavalry, Co. B; May 1862, last muster card showed absent on sick furlough.

Best, Robert. Enlisted as sergeant on 11 June 1861 at Camp McDonald; age 19 per 31 August 1861 muster; October 1864 last muster showed on detached service by order of Gen. Lee since 2 September 1864.

Bowles, Leroy. Enlisted as private on 8 January 1862 at Knoxville, Tennessee; 30 September 1864, last muster card showed absent without leave since 12 October 1863.

Bowles, Leroy. Enlisted as private on 8 January 1862 at Knoxville, Tennessee; 30 September 1864, last muster showed absent without leave since 12 October 1862.

Box, James M. Enlisted as private on 1 March 1862 at Cassville, Georgia; one muster card for 22 March 1862 does not state present or absent.

Box, Thomas. Enlisted as private on February 1862 in Cass County, Georgia; 30 September 1864, last muster card showed present.

Branson, S. S. Enlisted as private on 2 February 1864 in Cass County, GA; October 1864 last muster showed "at hospital"; 22 June to 4 July 1864, Jackson Hospital (Febris Int.); 11 August 1864, admitted to General Hospital No. 7, Raleigh, NC, "sick."

Brown, James J. Enlisted as private on 4 March 1862 at Cassville, GA; last muster card showed present; February 1864, no additional information.

Burris, William D. Enlisted on 2 August 1861 in Cobb County, GA; Field and Staff, Reg't bugler/ordnance sgt.; no record of when promotion took place for February 1864, shows bugler and muster for October 1864; shows ordnance sgt.; paroled Greensboro, NC, on 1 May 1865.

Calder, Nathaniel M. (N. M.). Enlisted as private on 27 February 1862 at Marietta, GA; one card muster showed present; S.O. 35/1, 4 April 1863, Dept. and Army of NV "leave of absence," showed him as N. M. Calder Capt., ACS, PL.

Carlton, R. G. Enlisted as private; one POW card showed paroled at Augusta, GA on 19 May 1865.

Carlton, Wesley A. (also listed as W. H. Carlton). Enlisted as private on 26 June 1861 at Camp McDonald; age 23 per 31 August 1861 muster; 31 August 1861 must shows Company A, Rifle Battalion, 31 October 1861 muster shows Company A, Infantry Battalion; 2 September 1862 muster shows Company B, Cavalry; paroled Greensboro, NC, 1 May 1865.

Carney, Waddy T. Ent. as private on 11 June 1861 at Camp McDonald; age 24 per 31 August 1861 muster; 31 August 1864 reported absent without leave since 8 May 1864; 30 September 1864, reported in hands of enemy since 12 May 1864; POW records indicate captured at North Anna 23 May 1864; sent to Point Lookout, MD; died of scurvy at Point Lookout 26 April 1865; buried grave number 1567, hospital number 5841.

Carpenter, Thomas H. Enlisted as private on 11 June 1861 at Camp McDonald; age 16 per 30 August 1861 muster; 30 April 1864 muster reports reported absent; provost guard at Hanover Junction; 31 August 1864, last muster showed present; POW records reported captured and paroled at Hartwell, GA, 19 May 1865.

Carswell, Hudson W. Enlisted as 3rd Corp., later corp on 11 June 1861 at Camp McDonald; age 18 per 31 August 1861 muster; October 1864 last muster showed absent; detached by order of Gen. Lee 21 September to get horse.

Carter, James. M. Enlisted as private on 11 June 1861 at Camp McDonald; age 23 per 3 August 1861 muster; died 26 October, 4 November, or 5 November 1862 of "Haemoptysis [also shown as "Feb.typ."] at General Hospital Camp Winder in Richmond; (Most records show 4 November 1862); claim made by father, A. D. Carter; claim shows no wife or children.

Carter, Justa, H. Enlisted as private on 11 June 1861 at Camp McDonald; Company B and H; age 17 per 3 August 1861 muster; October 1864 last muster showed absent-by order of Gen. Lee 21 September to get horse.

Christian, James, W. Enlisted as private on 3 August 1861 in Cass County, October 1864 last muster showed absent-detached by order of Gen. Lee 21 September to get horse; paroled Greensboro, NC, 1 May 1865.

Cobb, George S. Enlisted as private, later corporal on 11 June 1861 at Camp McDonald; (Company B and H); age 19 per 31 August 1861 muster; October 1864 last muster showed detached by order of Gen. Lee 21 September to get horse; POW records showed captured and paroled at Hartwell, Georgia on 19 May 1865.

Cobb, John H. Enlisted as private, later corporal on 11 June 1861 at Camp McDonald; age 20 per 31 August 1861 muster; December 1863 muster showed 1 corporal; 30 April 1864 muster showed sgt.; wounded 30 April 1864, admitted to Jackson Hospital for V. S. neck; transferred to General Hospital Camp Winder 28 June 1864; September 1864 last muster showed present; paroled Greensboro, NC, 1 May 1865.

Conyers, Christopher B. (also middle initial C). Enlisted as private on 2 August 1861 at Camp McDonald; age 28 per 31 August 1861 muster; 29 November 1861, Capt. Rich requests discharge for disability of left arm from old wound; born in Coweta County, GA; 5' 10", dark complexion, dark hair, gray eyes; no further record.

Conyers, William J. Enlisted as private on 11 June 1861 at Camp McDonald; (Company B and H); age 21 per 31 August 1861 muster; 31 October 1861 last muster showed present; no further record.

Cooper, Adam J. Enlisted as private on 4 March 1862 at Cassville, Georgia, (Company B and H), 30 April 1864; absent on detail for horse; 30 September 1864, absent-detached service by order of Gen. Lee, 20 September; October 1864 last muster showed detached service by order of Gen. Lee, 21 September.

Cross, Alfred. Enlisted as private on 4 March 1862 at Cassville, Georgia; (Company B and H); one card dated 22 March 1862 showed rejected by army surgeon 17 March 1862 at Atlanta.

Crow, Asa C. Enlisted as private/wagoner on 11 June 1862 at Martinsburg, VA; (Company B and H); February 1864, muster reported absent on detail to procure fresh horses; left camp 4 February 1864; October 1864 last muster showed AWOL since 12 April 1864; POW card showed paroled Augusta, GA, 20 May 1865.

Crow, John F. Enlisted as private on 11 June 1861 at Camp McDonald; (Company B and H); 3 August 1861, sick furlough; 1 September 1861, wounded in left arm by accidental shot in Georgia; 31 October 1861, absent, furlough, wounded by accidental pistol shot; no further record.

Day, Alfred C. Enlisted as private on 21 August 1861 at Cobb County, 30 April 1864, absent at hospital since 5 April 1864; 30 October 1864, last muster showed detached at hospital by order of Gen. Lee; hospital records showed 25 March 1864 during unfitness for field service, is detached for hospital or other light duty; attached to Jackson Hospital 4 April 1864, approved 25 March 1864 Gen. Lee; employed as nurse and wardmaster.

Day, Joseph S. Enlisted as private on 11 June 1861 at Camp McDonald, age 19 per 31 August 1861 muster; discharged for disability 12 November or 17 November 1862 for Epilepsia; born Cassville, GA, 5' 10", dark complexion, blue eyes, light hair, student.

Day, William S. Enlisted as private on 11 June 1861 at Camp McDonald; age 17, per 31 August 1861 muster; December 1863, reported in hands of enemy; captured at Hedgesville 25 July 1863, October 1864 last muster showed absent-in hands of enemy since July 1863; appeared on roll of POWs received and disposed of at Fort Mifflin, PA; "Captured by our cavalry while returning from picket" 23 July 1863, Martinsburg, VA; received at Fort Mifflin 21 July 1863 and transferred to Fort Delaware 1863;

Oath of Allegiance and released 15 June 1865; residence Cass County, light complexion, light hair, blue eyes, 5' 8".

Devereau, Joseph W. (also Deaveneau, Devineau, Devane). Enlisted as private on 4 March 1862 in Cassville, GA; February 1864 at division headquarters, blacksmith, left camp 20 November 1863; October 1864 last muster showed detached service by order of Gen. Lee 21 September; paroled at Albany, Georgia, 24 May 1865.

Dobbs, Jasper. Enlisted as private on 11 June 1861 at Camp McDonald; age 23 per 23 August 1861 muster; October 1864 last muster showed detached service by order of Gen. Lee 21 September; paroled Greensboro, NC, 1 May 1865.

Dodgen, Alfred N. Enlisted as private on 11 June 1861 at Camp McDonald; age 26 per 3 August 1861 muster; October 1864 last muster showed detached service by order of Gen. Lee 21 September; paroled Greensboro, NC, 1 May 1865; brother-in-law of Captain John Fielding Milhollin.

Dodgen, John Calvin. Enlisted as private on 15 January 1864 in Cobb County; October 1864 last muster showed detached service by order of Gen. Lee 21 September; paroled Greensboro, NC, 1 May 1865; brother-in-law of Captain John Fielding Milhollin.

Dodgen, William M. Enlisted as private on 11 June 1861 at Camp McDonald; age 21 per 31 August 1861 muster; February 1864 muster reported on detached service to procure fresh horses for cavalry, left camp 4 February; October 1864, last muster showed on detached service after fresh horses by order of Gen. Lee; brother-in-law of Captain John Fielding Milhollin.

Drake, James G. Enlisted as private on March 1862 in Cass County (also listed as S110162 at Camp Pritchard, SC; December 1863 muster reported "in hands of enemy—captured at recruiting camp December 10"; 30 September 1864 last muster reported in hands of enemy since November 1863; appeared on list of POW confined in military prison at Wheeling, Virginia; age 31, 5' 10", fair complexion, hazel/gray eyes, dark hair, farmer, residence, Bartow, GA; sent to Camp Chase 31 December 1863; received at Camp Chase 1 January 1864; POW records for Camp Chase reported arrested Craig County, Virginia on 15 December 1863; received at Camp Chase on 1 June 1864 and transferred to Fort Delaware 14 March 1864; paroled Fort Delaware, February, 1865 and exchanged 7 March 1865.

Drake, S. C. Enlisted as private on March 1862 at Cass County (also shown as Camp Pritchard, SC 10 May 1862); October 1864 last muster showed "absent at hospital"; 6 October 1864, admitted to Jackson Hospital (General Hospital No. 9) at Richmond for chronic diarrhea; returned to duty 13 October 1864; 12 December 1864, admitted to General Hospital No. 13 at Raleigh, NC; 12 December 1864, furloughed for 60 days.

Drake, Thomas G. Enlisted as private/wagoner/teamster on 1 March 1862 at Cassville, GA; October 1864 last muster reported on detached service by order of Gen. Lee since 2 September 1864.

Dykes, Francis. Enlisted as private on 11 June 1861 at Camp McDonald; age 20 per 31 August 1861 muster; October 1864 last muster reports on detached service by order of Gen. Lee since 21 September 1864; residence Pine Log, GA.

Dykes, John. Enlisted as private on April 1862 at Cass County (also shown as Bartow County 1 May 1862); October 1864 last muster showed on detached service by order of Gen. Lee since 2 September 1864.

Edmonston, James (also Edmondson, Edmanston). Enlisted as private on 27 February 1864 at Marietta, GA; February 1864, on detail to procure fresh horse-left camp 4 February 1864; April 1864 on detail to procure fresh horse; 30 September 1864, muster showed absent-detached service infirmary camp since 28 August 1864; October 1864 muster showed present no further record.

Elrod, J. H. Enlisted March 1862 at Cass County (also showed Camp Pritchard, SC, 10 May 1862); February 1864, on detail to procure fresh horses since 20 February 1864; 31 August 1864, showed in hospital since 20 June 1864; wounded; 20 June 1864, admitted to Jackson Hospital in Richmond for VS right side; October 1864 last muster showed "at hospital."

Fagons, Wilmot. Enlisted as private; one card; paroled Greensboro.

Falvey, Michael (also Falvery and Farley). Enlisted as private on 4 July 1863 at Martinsburg, VA; a substitute; December 1863 muster showed "in hands of enemy—captured Brandy Station" 1 August 1863; on roll of prisoners committed to Old Capitol Prison, D.C., between 1 August and 15 August 1863; sent to Point Lookout, MD; arrived 23 August 1863; 11 April 1864; admitted to camp hospital; died 18 April 1864 of diarrhea.

Franklin, Augustus, M. Enlisted as private on 11 June 1861 at Camp McDonald; promoted to first lieutenant; age 41 per 31 August 1861 muster; resigned due to ill health; accepted 10 July 1862.

Fullilove, John L. Enlisted as 1st sgt./later sgt. on 11 June 1861 at Camp McDonald; age 23 per 31 August 1861 muster; October 1864 last muster showed detached service under Gen. Lee since 21 September 1864; paroled Greensboro, NC, 1 May 1865.

Gaines, Albert B. (also A. A. Gaines). Enlisted as private on 28 February 1862 at Cassville, GA; 15 July 1863, admitted to CSA hospital at Farmville for Debilitas-returned to duty 12 August 1863; another card showed (A. B. Gaines); deceased 8 July 1863 at Boonsborough, MD; no further record.

Gladden,George H. Enlisted as private on 11 June 1861 at Camp McDonald; age 21 per 31 August 1861 muster; 31 October 1861, present-wounded-wounded in action 28 October 1861; 30 September 1864 muster reports absent with leave since 12 June 1864; October 1864 last muster reported absent without leave since 12 June 1864; POW records show he was captured at Cass County and sent to Louisville, KY, 14 June 1864; discharged on oath 26 June 1864 by Capt. S. Jones "to remain north of the Ohio River during the war"; oath 22 June 1864 showed place of residence Cass County, 6', light complexion, dark hair, blue eyes; oath 20 June 1864 showed dark complexion.

Gladden, John A. Enlisted as private/corporal on 11 June 1861 at Camp Mcdonald; age 22 per 31 August 1861 muster; February 1864 muster showed absent on detail for fresh horses; left camp 4 February 1864; 31 August 1864 muster showed at infirmary camp since 3 February 1864; 30 September 1864 muster reports on detached service at infirmary camp since 18 March 1864; October 1864 last muster reported at infirmary camp since May 1864; no further record.

Goodwin, Charles, L. Enlisted as Sgt. Major on 11 June 1861 at Camp McDonald; age 18 per 31 August 1861 muster; 8 July 1861 appointed sgt. major of battalion; October 1864 last muster reported in Georgia after fresh horse by order of Gen. Lee.

Grady, John M. Enlisted as private on 11 June 1861 at Camp McDonald; age 22 per 31 August 1861 muster; December 1863 muster reported "in hands of enemy—captured at Hedgesville" 25 July 1863; 29 July 1863 received at Fort Mifflin, PA; sent to Fort Delaware 17 November 1863; POW records show captured at Martinsburg 23 July 1863 by 12 PA Cavalry; paroled Fort Delaware 28 September 1864; 7 October 1864 admitted Jackson Hospital in Richmond for scurvy; 14 October 1864 furloughed for 30 days; no further record.

Griffin, Gerald. Enlisted as private on May 1862 at Cass County, GA (also listed as Camp Pritchard, SC 10 May 1862); February 1864 muster showed on detail to procure fresh horse; 31 August 1864 muster reported in hands of enemy since May 1864; POW records indicate captured in King County, Virginia; 16 May 1864; and sent to Old Capitol Prison in D.C.; paroled at Fort Delaware, 1865.

Hall, J. Thomas (also J. F.). Enlisted as private on 27 February 1862 at Marietta, GA; 4 April 1862, discharged for disability; no further record.

Hannah, John H. (also J. P. and J. H.). Enlisted as private on 1 March 1862 at Cassville, GA (also shows Camp Pritchard, SC, 10 May 1862); 11 May 1863 appeared on receipt roll for commutation of rations for a detachment of the cavalry; February 1864 muster showed at infirmary camp; left 16 February 1864; April 1864, on detail for horse since 30 April 1864; October 1864 muster reported on detached service by order of Gen. Lee 2 September 1864, contained card that showed John "P" Hannah died 28 February 1863 at Culpeper Court House, VA; no cause listed.

Harden, W. H. Enlisted as private; one card regimental return showed enlisted 26 May 1862 at Camp Pritchard, SC.

Hargis, Richard R. Enlisted as private on January 1862 (also showed 1 March 1862) at Cass County,GA; February 1864 muster reported on detail for horse; left camp 4 February 1864; October 1864 last muster showed detached by order of Gen. Lee 2 September 1864.

Hargis, William H. Enlisted as private on 11 June 1861 at Camp McDonald; age 21 per 31 August 1861 muster; 19 February 1863, admitted to Charlottesville Hospital for gonorrhea; hospital muster showed deserted 15 March 1863"; went off with lt. of the company; said to have been furloughed from regiment; February 1864 on detail for horse; left camp 4 February 1864; October 1864, last muster showed detached service by order of Gen. Lee.

Harris, Charles. Enlisted as private on 2 August 1861 in Cobb County; age 19 per 31 August 1861 muster; 30 April 1864 on detail for horse since 5 April 1864; 30 September 1864, AWOL since 18 June 1864; October 1864 last muster showed absent on sick leave; appeared on register of rebel deserters and refugees; captured Locust Grove, VA; sent to Point Lookout and transferred to Fort Monroe; received at Fort Monroe, VA, 31 March 1864; 4 April 1864 oath and released, sent to New York; residence Macon, GA, blue eyes, dark hair, light complexion.

Heggie, I. N. (also J. N.). Enlisted as private on May 1861 in Cobb County (also showed May 1862 Cobb and October 1862, VA); February 1864 absent, courier at HDQ brigade; 30 April 1864 at brigade HDQ since November

1863; 31 August 1864 on detached service; 30 September 1864 detached
service Albemarle County, VA, by order of Gen. Young; October 1864 last
muster showed present.

Henderson, E. T. (Ezekial Thomas). Enlisted as private at Cassville, Georgia; 12
November 1863, admitted to Jackson Hospital; morning report showed
thrown from horse 11 November 1863; February 1864 on detached service at
Essex County, VA, left 28 February 1864; 30 April 1864 on detail for horse
since 30 April 1864; October 1864 last muster showed detached service by
order of Gen. Lee 2 September 1864.

Henderson, John R. Enlisted as private on 17 March 1862 at Cassville, GA (also
showed 17 March 1862 Bartow County); 10 March 1863 discharge for
disability at Staunton, VA, for Phthisis Pulmonalis; born Bartow County, 26
years old, 6' 5", fair complexion, blue eyes, dark hair; farmer.

Hicks, William J. Enlisted as private at Camp McDonald; age 34 per 31 August
1861 muster; 6 November 1861 discharged for disability "affection of the
eyes"; "unfit for duty in consequence of weak eyes—disease seems
incurable"; discharged at Camp Dickinson, VA; entitled to transportation for
himself, his horse, and baggage from Camp Dickinson to Big Shanty, GA;
born Pike County, 6', black hair, dark complexion, black eyes, farmer.

Honed, Berry B. (also D. B.). Enlisted as private on 11 June 1861 at Camp
McDonald, age 25 per 31 August 1861 muster; 17 October 1861 appointed
wagoner; 31 August 1864 muster showed AWOL since May 1864; 30
September 1864, muster showed deserted in May 1864; October 1864 last
muster showed prisoner May 1864; POW records indicated captured at
Milford Station 22 May 1864; sent to Point Lookout, MD, and exchanged 11
March 1865.

Huggins, W. H. (also W. N.). Enlisted as private on March 1862 or May 1862 at
Cass County; 30 April 1864 muster showed "in hands of enemy" since 29
February 1864, Ely's Ford; POW records report captured at Rapidan River
29 February 1864; received at Old Capitol Prison, D.C., and transferred to
Fort Delaware; arrived June 1864; no further record.

Ingram, Joseph J. Enlisted as private on 11 June 1861 at Camp McDonald; age
34 per 31 August 1861 muster; 2 September 1862 last muster showed
present; 11 May 1863, appeared on receipt roll for commutation of rations
for a detachment of the cavalry; no further record.

James. B.J. Enlisted as private on July 1864 in South Carolina; October 1864,
last muster showed on detached service by order Gen. Lee since 2 September

1864.

James. B. L. Enlisted as private on 9 July 1864 in Virginia; 31 August 1864, last muster showed present; admitted to Jackson Hospital on 22 August 1864 with Rubeola; returned to duty 29 August 1864; paroled Greensboro, NC, 1 May 1865.

Jones, B. W. Enlisted as private on March or May 1862 in Cass County (also listed as 10 May 1862 Camp Pritchard, SC); October 1864 last muster showed on detached service by order of Gen. Lee since 2 September 1864.

Jones, Rutherford P. Enlisted as private on 11 June 1861 at Camp McDonald; age 23 per 31 August 1861 muster; 11 May 1863 appears on receipt roll for commutation of rations for a detachment of cavalry; October 1864 last muster showed present.

Kenney, James R. (also Kenney). Enlisted as private at Camp McDonald; age 26 per 31 August 1861 muster; 30 April 1864 muster showed on detached service by order Gen. Lee since 9 February 1864; POW records showed captured 5 November 1864 Cass County; received at Louisville 22 November 1864 and sent to Camp Douglas; arrived Camp DougJas 26 November 1864; oath and discharged 17 June 1865; residence Cass County, fair complexion, dark hair, 5' 10".

Killian, Daniel B. Enlisted as private on 11 June 1861; Camp McDonald; age 21 per 31 August 1861 muster; died 1 November 1862 at Berkeley County, VA; no cause listed.

Knight, James A. (also James J.). Enlisted as private on 27 February 1862 at Marietta, GA; absent infirmary camp; left camp 23 February 1864; 4/3Q/ 4; on detail for horse since 30 April 1864; 30 September 1864 muster reports detailed as nurse in Richmond hospital on 30 August 1864 by order of Gen. Lee; returned to duty 19 October 1864; October 1864 showed present; paroled Greensboro, NC, 1 May 1865.

Lane, John P. Enlisted as private on 27 February 1862 at Marietta, Georgia; discharged for disability 12 December 1862; born in Wilkes County, GA; age 24, 5' 3", light complexion, blue eyes, farmer.

Latimer, George T. Enlisted as bugler on 11 June 1861 at Camp McDonald; age 18 per 31 August 1861 Muster; 30 April 1864, muster showed on horse detail since 30 April 1864; October 1864, last muster; detached service by order of Gen. Lee since 2 September 1864.

Latimer, Robert C. Enlisted as 4th sergeant, later 1st lt. On 11 June 1861 at Camp McDonald; ago 23 per 31 August 1861 muster; 11 October 1863;

promoted 2nd lt.; 1 February 1863, promoted 1st lt ; 30 November 1864, inspection report showed on leave; paroled Greensboro, NC, 1 May 1865.

Leake, John S. Enlisted as private on 4 March 1862 at Cassville, GA; 30 April 1864, muster reports on horse detail since 5 April 1864; October 1864, last muster showed present.

Leake, Thomas W. Enlisted as private on 4 March 1862 at Cassville, GA; February 1864, on horse detail to procure fresh horse, left camp 4 February 1864; 30 April 1864, on detail for horse since 30 April 1864; October 1864 last muster showed on detached service by order of Gen. Lee.

Lewis, F. J. Enlisted as private; one card; register of general hospital at Petersburg showed admitted 8 September 1863 for vulnus sclopeticum left leg; furloughed 20 days on 15 September 1863; no further record.

Light, William P. (also W. T.). Enlisted as private on April 1862 at Cass County (also showed 1 May 1862 at Bartow County); December 1863, muster showed absent on furlough of indulgence 24 days; February 1864, detached at Hanover Junction, left camp 12 February 1864; 30 April 1864, absent, provost guard Hanover Junction since 29 February 1864; October 1864 last muster showed on detached service by order of Gen. Lee since 2 September 1864.

Linn, James F. Enlisted as private/corporal on 11 June 1861 at Camp McDonald; age 19 as of 31 August 1861 muster; 11 May 1863, appeared on receipt roll for commutation of rations for a detachment of the cavalry; 30 April 1864 muster reported horse detail since 5 April 1864; October 1864 last muster showed at hospital sick since 10 August 1864; hospital register for Hospital No. 3 at Goldsboro, NC, reported discharged 22 August 1864, "to return to duty and ordered to report at or near Atlanta."

Long, James A. Enlisted as private on 11 June 1861; age 21 per 31 August 1861 muster; 31 October 1861 showed absent "sick."

Lovingood, William J. Enlisted as private on 11 June 1861 at Camp McDonald; age 26 per 31 August 1861 muster; February 1864 reported on detail for fresh horse, left camp 4 February 1861; October 1864 last muster sowed AWOL since 4 April 1864; no further record.

Lowe, O. W. (Oliver). Enlisted as private on April 1862 at Cass County (also 10 May 1862 at Camp Pritchard, SC); 11 May 1863, appeared on receipt roll for commutation of rations for a detachment of the cavalry; 30 April 1864, last muster reported on detached service by order of Gen. Lee since 2 September 1864; 5 March 1865, paroled, HDQ of the post, Cheraw, SC.

Lowe, William J. Enlisted as private on 1 March 1862 at Cassville; October 1864, last muster showed on detached service by order of Gen. Lee since 2 September 1864; POW reported captured at Hartwell 18 May 1865; paroled, date and place not given.

Martin, Green (also Greene). Enlisted as private on November 1862 at Cass County; conscript; February 1864, detailed for fresh horse since 4 February 1864; 31 August 1864, AWOL since 20 June 1864; October 1864 last muster showed AWOL since 11 June 1864.

Martin, William A. Enlisted as private; no other enlistment information, enlisted as conscript; February 1864, on detail for fresh horse since 4 February 1864; 27 October 1864, admitted to Pettigrew General Hospital No. 13 at Raleigh, NC; returned to duty 9 November 1864.

Martin, William S. Enlisted as private; one POW card showed captured at Hartwell, GA; paroled.

McConnell, Eli V. H. Enlisted as corporal, later 2nd lt. on 11 June 1861 at Camp McDonald; age 18 per 31 August 1861 muster; 7 April 1863, promoted; 11 October 1864, promoted to 2nd lt; 14 May 1864, wooded; VS to right shoulder; admitted to General Hospital No. 4 for VS right knee (other card showed right thigh); died of wounds 6 September 1864 or 25 September 1864, vulvus sclopeticum, General Hospital No. 4. Note: one hospital card showed E. V. McConnell age 32.

McElreath, John T. Enlisted as private on 1 March 1862 at Cassville, GA; October 1864 last muster showed detached service by order of Gen. Lee since 2 September 1864; paroled Greensboro, NC, 1 May 1865.

McMurry, Albert G. Enlisted as private on 11 June 1861 at Camp McDonald; age 19 per 31 August 1861 muster; 11 September 1861, last muster showed "transferred"; no further record.

McNinch, William W. (also William M. McNich). Enlisted as private on 11 June 1861 at Camp McDonald; age 20 per 31 August 1861 muster; February 1864 showed detailed to procure fresh horse since 4 February 1864; 30 April 1864 showed on detail for horse since 30 April 1864; 30 August 1864 muster showed in hospital at Richmond wounded; 17 August 1864, admitted to Jackson Hospital at Richmond, VS left shoulder; 29 August 1864, furloughed for 30 days, left hospital 31 September 1864, destination Chester, SC; October 1864 last muster showed AWOL since 6 October 1864.

McNinch, David. Enlisted as private on March 1862 at Cass County (also 10 May 1862 at Camp Pritchard, SC); paroled Greensboro, NC, on 1 May 1865.

McReynolds, John G. Enl, as private on 11 June 1861 at Camp McDonald; age 17 per 31 August 1861 muster; June, 1862, regimental return showed transferred from Col. Phillips INC. staff; February 1864, detailed to procure fresh horse, left camp on 4 February 1864; 30 April 1864, muster showed in hands of enemy since 29 March 1864; POW records showed captured in Stafford County, Virginia on 17 March 1864; sent to Old Capitol Prison, D.C., on 22 March 1864, transferred to Fort Delaware 17 June 1864; arrived at Fort Delaware; paroled February 1865.

Milhollen, John F. (also Millhollan). Enlisted as 2nd lt., later captain on 11 June 1861 at Camp McDonald; age 29 per 31 August 1861 muster; elected 2nd lt. 11 June 1861; promoted September 1862 to Captain; killed in action 11 October 1863 (had orders for promotion to major in uniform pocket when killed).

Miller, J. A. Enlisted as private; one card, surrender at Appomattox 9 April 1865.

Murphey, J. B. F. (also Murphy, B. F.). Enlisted as private in March 1862 at Cobb County; 30 September 1864 on furlough, sick since 24 August 1864; 19 August 1864 admitted to General Hospital No. 9 Richmond for diarrhea; 22 August 1864 sent to Jackson Hospital; 28 August 1864 furloughed 30 days, still in hospital 31 September 1864, destination: Williamston, SC; 6 March 1865, admitted to General Hospital No. 11 Charlotte, NC, with debilitas; returned to duty 24 March 1865.

Murphey, Jeff J. Enlisted as private on May 1862 at Cass County (also 10 May 1862 at Camp Pritchard, SC); February 1864, absent, detailed to go after horse, Buckingham County, ten days, left 20 February 1864; October 1864 last muster showed on detached service since 9 February 1864.

Murphey, Louis. Enlisted as private on May 1862 at Cobb County; February 1864, absent, provost guard, Fredericksburg 25 January 1864; no further record.

Murphey, T. L. Enlisted as private on March 1862 at Cobb County; April 1864, on detail for horse detail since 30 April 1864; October 1864 last muster showed on detached service by order of Gen. Lee since 2 September 1864.

Nowell, Reuben. Enlisted as private 4 March 1862 at Cassville, Georgia; 30 November 1862 muster roll showed "transferred to this company" 21 August 1862; October 1863 on detached service at hospital; 1 November 1863–31 December 1863 employed as nurse at Kingston Hospital; August 1864, last muster showed present; no further record.

Patton, William B. Enlisted as sergeant on 11 June 1861 at Camp McDonald; age 19 per 31 August 1861 muster; February 1864, at infirmary camp, Nelson County, VA—left 16 January 1864; 30 April 1864, horse detail since 30 April 1864; October 1864 last muster showed present.

Phillips R. S. Enlisted as private; one card showed paroled Greensboro, NC, 1 May 1865.

Pitts, James C. (also John C.). Enlisted as private on 11 June 1861 at Camp McDonald; age 31 per 31 August 1861 muster; 11 September 1861 or 15 September 1861 discharged (no cause); November 1863, reenlisted in same company at Decatur, GA; 31 August 1864, deserted in May 1864; no further record.

Powell, Thomas. Enlisted as farrier on 11 June 1861; age 49 per 31 August 1861 muster; 21 December 1861, discharged for disability, "accidental injury to left wrist"; born in Laurens District, SC, 5' 8", sandy hair, hazel eyes; fair complexion, trader by occupation.

Rhodes, Enoch, A. Enlisted as private on 11 June 1861; age 30 per 31 August 1861 muster; May 1862 showed "on detached service"; 11 May 1863, appeared on receipt for commutation of rations for a detachment of the cavalry; no further record.

Rich, James W. Enlisted as private on 28 February 1862 at Cassville, GA (also 28 February 1862 at Bartow County); 30 April 1864 muster showed on furlough since 21 April 1864; October 1864 last muster showed on detached service by order of Gen. Lee since 2 September 1864.

Rich, William Wofford. Enlisted as captain, later lieutenant colonel, at Camp McDonald; elected captain; age 38 per 31 August 1861 muster; promoted to lieutenant colonel of legion; date of appointment: 15 August 1863, date of confirmation: 16 February 1864; to take rank: 9 July 1862; date of cc: 25 August 1863; delivered Gen. R. E. Lee; October 1864 last muster showed on sick leave since 4 October 1864; resigned 27 January 1865 "physical disability." Note: file contained several letters regarding promotion, history of company and resignation.

Roach, A. J. Enlisted as private in May 1863 in Virginia; October 1864 last muster showed AWOL since 12 June 1864.

Scott, Green M. Enlisted as private on 4 March 1862 at Cassville, GA, October 1864 showed present.

Serf, T. H. Enlisted as private; one card captured Anderson, SC, paroled.

Sewell, Columbus T. (C. T.). Enlisted as private on 28 April 1862 at Marietta,

GA; 28 November 1862, transferred to cavalry (also showed 1 November 1862); April 1864, on detail for horse since 30 April 1864; October 1864 last muster reported on detached service by order of Gen. Lee since 2 September 1864.

Sewell, Isaac (also I. A.). Enlisted as private on 28 April 1862 at Marietta, GA (also showed March and May 1862); 28 November 1862, transferred to cavalry (also showed 1 November 1862); 30 April 1864, on detail for horse since 5 April 1864; October 1864 last muster reported on detached service by order of Gen. Lee since 2 September 1864; 24 February 1865, admitted to General Hospital No. 11 at Charlotte, NC, for Icterus (Jaundice); 14 March 1865, returned to duty; 20 April 1865, admitted to hospital for Febris Typhoides; no further record.

Shaw, Joseph P. (also Joe and J. P.). Enlisted as private on March, 1864 at Cass County, GA; October 1864 last muster showed on detached service by order of Gen. Lee since 9 February 1864; paroled Greensboro, NC, 1 May 1865.

Sheets, J. Thomas (also Shades, Sheats, and T. J. Sheets). Enlisted as private on 15 February 1862 at Marietta, GA; 30 April 1864, on detail for horse since 5 April 1864; October 1864 last muster showed on detached service by order of Gen. Lee since 2 September 1864; POW card showed paroled at Albany, GA.

Shiman, Thomas. Enlisted as private; card showed June 1862 on extra duty as teamster.

Simms. Thomas S. Enlisted as private in December 1862 in Virginia (also 9 February 1862 Culpeper C. H.); 28 December 1863 attached to Jackson Hospital as carpenter; August, 1864, muster showed "in hospital at Richmond" since 10 January 1864; September 1864 detailed in hospital at Richmond; 26 October 1864, returned to duty; October 1864 last muster showed present; POW records showed captured Bennettsville, SC, 6 or 8 March 1865; sent to Point Lookout, MD, and released 8 June 1865.

Sims, Nathan, G. (also Simms; also N. J.). Enlisted as private/corporal on 11 June 1861 at Camp McDonald (also 4 May 1862 at Camp Pritchard, SC); age 41 per 31 August 1861 muster; 9 March 1863 discharged for disability, chronic bronchitis; POW records, captured Burkeville 6 April 1865, sent to Point Lookout, MD, oath 19 June 1865; residence Polk County, GA, fair complexion, light brown hair, blue eyes, 5' 7" or 5' 10", farmer, born in Franklin County. Note: Nathan is listed as a member of Company D until capture. POW card showed Company B. Since he was discharged for disability in 1863, he may have reenlisted in Company B prior to his capture in April 1865.

Sligh, James (also Sleigh and Sligh, James A.). Enlisted as private in March 1862 at Cass County (also 1 March 1862 Bartow County); 1 May 1863 to 23 March 1864, employed as nurse at hospital at Orange Court House; April 1864 on detail since 30 April 1864 for horse; October 1864 last muster showed on detached service by order of Gen. Lee since 2 September 1864.

Smith, A. H. Enlisted as private on March 1864 at Cass County; October 1864 last muster showed present.

Smith, D. W. Enlisted as private; one card showed paroled at Greensboro, NC, on 1 May 1865.

Stevens, Jacob R. Enlisted as private/captain on 1 January 1864 at Floyd County, GA; 4 May 1864, commissioned/appointed F and S AQM; October 1864 last muster showed present as AQM; paroled at Greensboro, NC, 1 May 1865; first listing as captain.

Stowe, Polk. Enlisted as private on 4 February 1864 in Virginia; 24 August 1864, wounded at Reams Station; admitted to Way Hospital No. 1 at Weldon, NC; died 25 August 1864 Vulnus Sclopet.

Swift, Thomas H. Enlisted as private on 11 June 1864 at Camp McDonald; age 21 per 31 August 1861 muster; October 1864 last muster showed on detached service by order of Gen. Lee since 2 September 1864.

Talbert, Levi, J. Enlisted as private on April 1862 at Cass County (also 20 May 1862 Bartow County); June 1862 muster indicated extra duty as blacksmith; on horse detail since 30 April 1864; October 1864 last muster reported AWOL since 7 August 1864; POW records showed captured Cherokee County, GA; on roll of deserters, received at Louisville, 24 June 1864; oath and discharged 26 June 1864, to remain north of the Ohio River during the war; residence Cherokee, GA, light complexion, dark hair, gray/hazel eyes, 5' 9".

Thompson, J. B. Enlisted as private on 1 March 1862 at Bartow County, GA; February 1864, on 24 day furlough, left 2 February 1864; 30 April 1864, present; October 1864 last muster showed on detached service by order of Gen. Lee since 9 February 1864.

Thompson, Rufus M. Enlisted as private on 28 February 1862 at Cassville, GA; died 16 April 1863 at Buckingham County, VA, no cause listed.

Tuck, William J. Enlisted as private on March 1862 in Cass County (also 10 May 1862 at Camp Pritchard, SC); 11 May 1863 appeared on receipt for commutation of rations for a detachment of the cavalry; 30 April 1864 on detail for horse since 30 April 1864; October 1864 last muster reported detached service by Gen. Lee since 2 September 1864.

Tumlin, Isaac. Enlisted as private on 11 June 1861 at Camp McDonald; age 18 per 31 August 1861 muster; 30 April 1864 on detail for horse; October 1864 last muster reported on detached service by order of Gen. Lee since 2 September 1864.

Turner, A. M. Enlisted as private on 1 August 1862 in Cobb County; 10 June 1864, admitted to Jackson Hospital for diphtheria, returned to duty 27 August 1864; October 1864 last muster reported on detached service by order of Gen. Lee since 2 September 1864.

Turner, Columbus M. Enlisted as private on 11 June 1861 at Camp McDonald; age 18 per 31 August 1861 muster; February 1864, detached to go after fresh horse, left 4 February 1861; October 1864 last muster reported on detached service by order of Gen. Lee since 2 September 1864.

Turner, James Polk. Enlisted as private in June or August 1863 in Cass County; 30 April 1864, on detail for horse since 5 April 1864; October 1864 last muster showed on detached service by order of Gen. Lee since 2 September 1864.

Turner, W. Dallas. Enlisted as private on January/February 1864; 30 April 1864, on detail for horse; paroled Greensboro, NC, 1 May 1865.

Vaughan, H. H. Enlisted as private on 4 March 1862 at Cassville, GA: May 1862, regimental return reported discharge for disability at Camp Pritchard, South Carolina on 5 May 1862, no information as to cause.

Waldrop, Edward P. (Waidroup). Enlisted as private on 11 June 1861 at Camp McDonald; age 21 per 31 August 1861 muster; 11 May 1863 appeared on receipt roll for commutation of rations for a detachment of the cavalry; 30 April 1864, absent at infirmary camp since 23 February 1864; October 1864 last muster showed present.

Warwick, Jeff (T. J.). Enlisted as private on March 1862 at Cass County, GA; August 1863, detailed at QM Dept. at Orange Court House; no record of return; paroled Greensboro, NC, 1 May 1865.

Warwick, William A. Enl.as private on 11 June 1861 at Camp McDonald; age 24 per 31 August 1861 muster; 30 September 1864 muster reported on detached service by order of Gen. Lee 20 September 1864; paroled Greensboro, NC, 1 May 1865.

Waters, John R. (Walters, J. R. and Watters). Enlisted as private on 11 June

1861 at Camp McDonald; age 22 per 31 August 1861 muster; 11 May 1863 appeared on receipt roll for commutation of rations for a detachment of cavalry; POW card reports captured at Boonsborough, MD, on 8 July 1863; arrived at Baltimore 20 August 1863, transferred to Point Lookout, MD, arrived 21 August 1863; 24 October 1863, admitted to Hammond General Hospital for diarrhea; 1 November 1863, sent to General Hospital, remarks: Small Pox Hospital; died 12 January 1865, chronic dysentery; number and locality of grave-795-POW Grave Yards Hospital No. 5716.

Watts, Fletcher S. Enlisted as private/teamster on 31 June 1861 at Camp McDonald; age 17 per 31 August 1861 muster; 30 April 1864, on detail for horse since 30 April 1864; October 1864 last muster showed on detached service per Gen. Lee since 2 September 1864.

Watts. Wilson (also Watts, W. W. W.). Enlisted as private on 11 June 1861 at Camp McDonald; age 20 per 31 August 1861 muster; 30 April 1864, on detail for horse since 30 April 1864; October 1864 last muster showed AWOL since 7 August 1864.

Wells, Jasper. Enlisted as private on 10 March1862 at Cassville, GA; died 6 September 1862, Richmond, no cause; black eyes, brown hair; dark complexion; age 22; 5' 7 1/2", born Habersham County, GA; teamster by occupation; claim filed by Samuel Wells.

Wells, W. A. Enlisted as private; no enlistment information, conscript; one card, 31 August 1864, muster showed present.

Wells, William J. Enlisted as private/conscript; February 1864, on detached service to procure fresh horse since 4 February 1864; October 1864 last muster showed on detached service by order of Gen. Lee since 2 September 1864; POW card showed paroled Augusta, GA, 18 May 1865.

White, Robert P. Enlisted as private on 11 June 1861 at Camp McDonald; age 32 per 31 August 1861 muster; October 1861, appointed wagoner; October 1864 last muster showed on detached service by order of Gen. Lee since 2 September 1864.

Whitfield, Henry. Enlisted as private on 23 April 1864 at Cass County; paroled Augusta, GA, 18 May 1865.

Wilkes, Thomas T. Enlisted 11 June 1861 as 3rd lt./captain at Camp McDonald; age 22 per 31 August 1861 muster; 11 June 1861 elected 3rd lt.; 9 July 1862 promoted 2nd lt.; 1 August 1862, promoted 1st lt.; 11 October 1863, promoted to captain; POW records showed captured at Hartwell, GA, 18 May 1865; paroled.

Williams, J. A. F. Enlisted as private/substitute on December 1863; 1st muster in file showed absent; 30 August 1864, last muster showed AWOL, left camp 15 or 21 June 1863.

Wilson, John H. Enlisted as private on August 1863 at Cass County; 30 April 1864, on horse detail since 5 April 1864; October 1864 last muster showed AWOL since 12 June 1864; POW records showed captured 17 May 1864 in Tilton, GA; sent to Louisville and then to Rock Island, arrived 6 June 1864; Oath at Rock Island Barracks 18 October 1864; place of residence, Murray County, GA, dark complexion, light hair, hazel eyes, 5' 5", age 19; released 18 October 1864.

Wilson, John R. Enlisted as private on 1 September 1862 in Georgia; POW records showed capture at Burkeville 6 April 1865, sent to City Point and forwarded to Point Lookout, MD; oath and released 22 June 1865 place of residence Greene County, GA, dark complexion, brown hair, gray eyes, 5' 5".

Wofford, A. P. Enlisted as private at Cassville, GA, on 4 March 1862; February, detailed to go to Georgia for fresh horse since 4 February 1864; October 1864 last muster showed on detached service by order of Gen. Lee since 2 September 1864.

Wofford, Benjamin F. Enlisted 11 June 1861 at Camp McDonald; age 18 per 31 August 1861 muster; February 1864, absent on detail to procure fresh horse for cavalry, left 4 February 1861; October 1864 last muster showed on detached service by order of Gen. Lee since 2 September 1864; 1 November 8 1864, appointed 2nd lt., appointed 5 December 1864, confirmed 5 December 1864, to take rank November 1864, accepted 19 December 1864, under act approved 16 April 1862 for valor and skill.

Wofford, Charles N. Enlisted as private on 4 March 1862 at Cassville, Georgia on 22 March 1862 muster; note on card reports "rejected by army surgeon" 17 March 1862 at Atlanta, December 1863 muster report reports present; February 1864, on horse detail since 4 February 1864; 30 September 1864 muster reports AWOL since 7 August 1864; October 1864 last muster showed absent "sick."

Wofford, John W. Enlisted as private/adjutant on 28 February 1862 at Cassville, GA; F and S; 1 December 1862 elected 2nd lt.; 1 February 1863, promoted lt.and adjutant.

Wright, Miller A. Enlisted as private on 1 June 1861 at Camp McDonald; age 20 per 31 August 1861 muster; discharged 28 October 1861; 31 October 1861, last muster reports absent "sick." "Appears as a signature to a Receipt Roll for commutation for a detachment of the Cavalry connected with Phillips Georgia Legion detailed under orders from Hdqrs. Army of Northern Virginia dated March 29, 1863, to procure horses in Georgia for the dismounted men of the Legion. The commutation being for April 9, 1863, when they left their command in Virginia, to June 10, 1863, the detachment being ordered to return to their command through the country and on horse-back."

Roll dated Atlanta, GA
May 11, 1863.

Casualties, other losses for the Phillips Georgia Legion cavalry battalion from available records. Company I/C was formed predominantly from Cherokee County.

Company I/C

Total Enrollment:	214
Death/disease/accident:	21
Discharge/disability:	18
Deserted:	3
Captured:	24
KIA:	5
WIA:	6
Exchanged:	9
AWOL:	33
Imprisoned/Point Lookout, MD:	7
Imprisoned/Old Capitol Prison, D.C.:	4
Imprisoned/Hart's Island, NY:	1
Imprisoned/Fort Delaware, DE:	8
Imprisoned/Camp Douglas, IL:	4
Imprisoned/Johnson's Island, OH:	1
Imprisoned/Elmira, NY:	2
Imprisoned/Fortress Monroe, VA:	2
Transferred Out:	5

Transferred In:	3
Detached Service/Extra Duty:	13
Horse Detail/Furlough:	99
Paroled Augusta, GA:	1
Paroled/Hartwell, GA:	1
Paroled/Fort Delaware, DE:	1
Paroled/Unknown/Unclear:	5
Paroled/Greensboro, NC:	62
Took oath and released (location, circumstances unclear):	5
Resigned (Officer):	1
POW:	10
Courts Martial:	3

Note: Any one individual may appear in several categories; e.g., he may have been captured, sent to prison, and exchanged.

PHILLIPS GEORGIA LEGION
Cavalry Battalion

Company C
The Cherokee Dragoons

Alexander, D. A. Enlisted as private on 4 January 1861 at Marietta, GA; discharged 20 March 1863, "Valvular disease of the heart"; fair complexion, gray eyes, dark hair, 5' 11", age 42, blacksmith.

Alexander, Doctor. Enlisted as private on 25 February 1862 at Cherokee County; discharged 13 April 1863 for disability; born Walton County, GA, age 40, fair complexion, blue eyes, light hair, 5' 10", farmer.

Alla, James. Enlisted as private; (This may be James Alley listed in Company C, infantry battalion.) One card showed captured 14 September 1862 Boonesboro; sent to Fort Delaware and exchanged 11 October 1862.

Allen, A. H. Enlisted as private; one card, killed 8 July 1863 at Boonsboro, born in Georgia, claim filed by Arubella Allen on 5 February 1864.

Allen, William K. (also W. R.). Enlisted as private on 26 August 1861 at Camp McDonald; February 1864, on horse furlough since 4 February 1864; 30 September 1864 showed present; no further record.

Bagby, A. William. Enlisted as private on 11 September 1861 at Lynchburg, VA; January 1864, at hospital; October 1864 AWOL since 11 October 1863.

Bagby, John R. Enlisted as private on 11 September 1861 at Lynchburg, VA; February 1864, on horse furlough since 2 February 1864; April 1864, on horse furlough since 6 April 1864; October 1864 on detail 19 September 1864 for a horse by order of Gen. Lee.

Bagby, Thomas M. Enlisted as private on 16 May 1863 at Hardeeville, SC; (also Camp Pritchard, SC); February 1864, on horse furlough since 4 February 1864; October 1864 AWOL since 6 August 1864 (also shown as July 1864).

Bailey, James M. (also Baily, also John M.). Enlisted as private on 13 March 1862 at Cherokee County, Georgia; paroled Greensboro.

Bailey, R. W. (Baily, W.). Enlisted as Sergeant on 22 June 1861 at Camp McDonald (also 2 August 1861 at Cobb County); age 29 per 31 August 1861 muster; killed Boonsboro, MD, 8 July 1863; born South Carolina.

Barrett, W. W. Enlisted as private; admitted to General Hospital No. 9 on 12 March 1865 transferred to Jackson Hospital, Richmond; admitted to Jackson Hospital 13 March 1863 for chronic diarrhea; POW records: captured 3

April 1865 at Richmond, transferred to Point Lookout 2 May 1865; admitted to U.S.A. General Hospital, Point Lookout 3 May 1865 for chronic diarrhea; oath and released 26 June 1865.

Bates, Russell, J. Enlisted as private on 2 or 7 August 1861 at Cobb County; age 25 per 3 August 1861 muster; discharged 31 October 1861; suffered hernia last 14 years; born in Cherokee County,GA; 6', fair complexion, blue eyes, sandy hair, farmer; (must have reenlisted); January 1864, muster showed AWOL since 20 July 1863; October 1864 last muster showed AWOL since 25 November 1863.

Beck, Samuel H. Enlisted as private on 2 August 1861 at Camp McDonald; February 1864 on horse furlough since 4 February 1864; October 1864 on detail 19 September 1864 for a horse by order of Gen. Lee.

Bennett, E. C. Enlisted as private on 14 February 1862 at Cherokee County; January 1864, last muster card showed detailed by secretary of war as tanner since October 1862.

Benson, N. H. Enlisted as private on 2 August 1861 at Camp McDonald; age 27 per 31 August 1861 muster; discharged 29 September 1861; no further information.

Boston, Henry, F. Enlisted as private/corporal on 22 June 1861 at Camp Mcdonald; age 22 per 31 August 1861 muster; paroled Greensboro, NC, on 1 May 1865.

Boston, M. J. (J. M.). Enlisted as private on 11, 13, or 15 March 1862 at Roswell, GA; November 1863, transferred from Cobb's Legion (Roswell Troopers) Cavalry battalion to Phillips Legion; October 1864 last muster card showed on detail for horse by order of Gen. Lee since 19 September 1864.

Bozeman, James W. Enlisted as private on 1 March 1862 at Cherokee County; February 1864, AWOL since 13 March 1863; 30 April 1864, present; October 1864 AWOL since 4 May 1864.

Brannon, George W. Enlisted as private on 2 or 7 August 1861 at Camp McDonald; age 19 per 31 August 1861 muster; died 6 or 17 December 1862 at Ladies Relief Hospital, Lynchburg, VA, of diarrhea; born in Georgia.

Braselton, Cicero A. Enlisted as private on 2 or 7 August 1861 at Camp McDonald; age 23 per 31 August 1861 muster; February 1864, courier for brig. commissary since October 1863; April 1864, present; 31 August 1864, clerk for brig. commissary since August 1863; October 1864 last muster card showed present; paroled Greensboro, NC, 1 May 1865.

Brassellton, Robert M. (Braselton). Enlisted as private on 28 April 1862 at Marietta; 16 October 1862, transferred to cavalry; April 1864, horse furlough; August 1864, on furlough since 8 August 1864, without leave since 9 August 1864; October 1864 AWOL since 9 August 1864; appeared on roll of prisoners of war arriving at Louisville during six days ended 31 October 1864, captured Cherokee County 9 February 1864, also listed as Chadwick County; send to Camp Douglas 29 October 1864, arrived 11 November 1864; oath and released 17 June 1865; place of residence, Marietta, Cobb County, dark complexion, black hair, gray eyes, 5' 8".

Brooks, B. W. Enlisted as private on 24 April 1864 at Atlanta, GA; died 10/4 1861; no further information.

Brooks, E. B. Enlisted as private on 1 August 1862 at Cherokee County; October 1864 absent, on detail 19 September 1864 for a horse by order of Gen. Lee.

Brooks, N. H. Enlisted as 1st sergeant/sergeant on 21 August 1861 at Camp McDonald; age 20 per 31 August 1861 muster; October 1864, absent on detail 19 September 1864 for a horse by order of Gen. Lee; paroled Greensboro 1 May 1865; (No record of date of promotion but he was listed as 1st sergeant in October 1864, but listed as sergeant at parole.)

Brooks, Robert. Enlisted as private on 11 June or 22 June 1861 at Camp McDonald; age 21 as 3 August 1861 muster; October 1864, in Georgia after fresh horse by order of Gen. Lee; paroled Greensboro, NC, on 1 May 1865.

Brooks, William. Enlisted as private on 24 July or 2 August 1861 at Camp McDonald; age 22 per 31 August 1861 muster; paroled Greensboro, NC, 1 May 1865.

Brown, A. M. Enlisted 12 September 1864 at Cherokee County; October 1864, AWOL since 15 August 1864; paroled Augusta, Georgia 25 May 1865.

Brown, James J. Enlisted as private on 12 December 1864 at Cherokee County; October 1864 AWOL since 15 August 1864; paroled at Augusta, GA, 25 May 1865.

Brown, R. M. Enlisted as private; captured Kirk County, VA, 15 December 1863; paroled Fort Delaware 14 September 1864; 22 September 1864, admitted to Jackson Hospital;VS right arm, M. B. (Minnie ball); last card showed furloughed 26 September 1864 for 30 days.

Brown, Samuel W. Enlisted as private on 1 March 1862 at Cherokee County; October 1864 last muster card showed present.

Brown, Thomas K. Enlisted as private on 26 June 1861 at Camp McDonald; age

33 per 31 August 1861 muster; October 1864 muster showed "in hands of enemy" since 11 June 1864; captured at Louisa Court House on 11 June 1864; arrived Fortress Monroe 20 June 1864; transferred to Elmira Prison, NY, 25 July 1864; died at Elmira 13 March 1865 of Variola; locality of grave No. 2408.

Burton, Ransom C. Enlisted as private on 2 August 1861 at Cobb County or 11 September 1861 at Lynchburg; 1 January 1864, on detail for horse; 30 April 1864 on horse furlough since 4 June 1864; October 1864 on detail for horse by order of Gen. Lee since 19 September 1864; paroled Greensboro, NC, 1 May 1865; Receipt roll for commutation of rations, 17 April 1863, Atlanta.

Cantrell, John, C. (also Cantrel). Enlisted as private on 22 July or 2 August 1861 at Camp McDonald; age 18 per 31 August 1861 muster; 12 November 1863 transferred to Cobb's Legion.

Catching, F. E. Enlisted as private; admitted Jackson Hospital, Richmond 14 August 1864 "FebruaryInt."; 11 September 1864, furloughed 30 days; destination Hatchers Crossing, GA.

Chambers, James T. Enlisted as private on 25 February 1862 in Cherokee County; February 1864, on horse furlough since 4 February 1864; 30 April 1864, AWOL since 16 April 1864; October 1864 last muster showed present; paroled Greensboro, NC, 1 May 1865.

Chambers, William M. Enlisted as private on 25 February 1862 in Cherokee County; 1 January 1864, "in hands of enemy" 15 December 1863; October 1864 last muster showed in hands of enemy since 15 December 1863; no POW record; 10 March 1865, admitted to Receiving and Wayside Hospital or G. H. No. 9, Richmond, disposition: "Camp Lee" 11 March 1865; receipt roll for commutation of rations 11 May 1863, Atlanta.

Chamblee, Enoch (also shown as Chamlee). Enlisted as private on 6 March 1862 in Cherokee County; February 1864, on horse furlough since 4 February 1864; 31 August 1864, muster showed wagoner for brig. comm. since 20 May 1864; October 1864 on detail for a horse by order of Gen. Lee since 19 September 1864

Chastain, Asbury. Enlisted as private on 22 June 1861 at Camp McDonald; age 25 per 31 August 1861 muster; February 1864, on horse furlough since 4 February 1864; 30 August 1864, on furlough since 7 June 1864; October 1864, AWOL since 5 September 1864.

Chastain, G. B. Enlisted as private 2 July 1861 at Camp McDonald; age 25 per 31 August 1861 muster; February 1864, on duty for brig. commissary since 1

185

August 1863; 31 August 1864 muster showed beef herder since 18 September 1863; paroled Greensboro, NC, 1 May 1865.

Chastain, James. Enlisted as private on 22 June 1861 at Camp McDonald; age 31 per 31 August 1861 muster; February 1864, wagon master for brig. comm. since 1 August 1863; October 1864 last muster showed present; paroled Greensboro, NC, 1 May 1865.

Chastain, Joshua. Enlisted as private on 1 March 1862 at Cherokee County; 31 August 1864, last muster showed brig. provost guard since 20 April 1864; October 1864 on detail for a horse by order of Gen. Lee since 19 September 1864.

Cole, Francis. Enlisted as private on 22 June 1861 at Camp McDonald; age 23 per 31 August 1861 muster; October 1864 on detail for a horse by order of Gen. Lee 19 September 1864.

Couch, William D. Co. A, G, and C (see Company A Roster).

Cowan, James M. Enlisted as private on 1 March 1862 at Cherokee County; 1 January 1864, absent on furlough for 24 days since 1 January 1864; 30 April 1864, on horse detail since 4 June 1864; October 1864 on detail 19 September 1864 for a horse by order of Gen. Lee.

Delaney, Thomas N. (T. N.). Enlisted as private on 22 June 1861 at Camp McDonald; age 20 per 31 August 1861 muster; February 1864, on horse furlough since 24 February 1864; 31 August 1864 at recruitint camp since 20 June 1864; October 1864 on detail for horse by order of Gen. Lee since 19 September 1864 admitted to General Hospital Charlottesville for 1 December 1863; returned to duty 19 December 1863, receipt roll for commutation of rations, 8 May 1863 to 8 July 1863, Atlanta.

Delaney, William G. Enlisted as private on 25 September 1862 in Milton County; October 1864 on detail for horses since 19 September 1864.

Delaney, W. N. Enlisted as private 25 February 1862 at Cherokee County; died in hospital in Gordonsville, VA, 11 June 1863 of "Febris Typhoides"; claim presented by W. A. Walton, Atty, 11 April 1864 on behalf of widow Mary M. Delaney; John Delaney born at Spartanburg, SC.

Dobbs, John P. Enlisted as private on 1 March or 9 March 1862 in Cherokee County; October 1864 showed present; Court Martial, GO 69-5/Dept. of NV, Gen Lee 7 December 1864; paroled Greensboro, NC, 1 May 1865.

Dobbs, Oliver S. (Dowbs). Enlisted as private on 6 August 1863 at Cherokee County; January 1864, on detail for horse since 9 November 1863; October 1864 last muster showed AWOL 11 October 1863; POW records indicated captured Cherokee County, GA, 27 September 1864, sent to Nashville and then to Louisville, arrived 28 October 1864; transferred to Camp Douglas, arrived 11 November 1864; discharged 13 June 1865.

Dobbs, Wiley P. (William P.) Enlisted as private on 28 June 1863 in Cherokee County County; February 1864, at infirmary camp; 30 April 1864, on horse furlough since 4 June 1864; October 1864 last muster card showed present; paroled Greensboro, NC, 1 May 1865.

Donald, A. F. Enlisted as private on 29 September 1862 in Milton County; February 1864, on horse furlough since 4 February 1864; October 1864 last muster card showed present; paroled Greensboro, NC, 1 May 1865.

Donald, Lewis D. (L. D.). Enlisted as private on 22 June 1862 at Camp McDonald; age 29; February 1864, on horse furlough since 4 February 1864; 31 August 1864, at hospital since 10 July 1864; October 1864, on sick furlough since 15 September 1864 for 60 days; paroled Greensboro, NC, 1 May 1865. Note: record contained certificate of disability dated 28 March 1864: "Unfit for field service because of fracture of upper end of radius and the of the scapula and owing to improper adjust. of bones has resulted in atrophy of and perm. of elbow joint. Injury was caused by the falling off of the roof of a house and occurred while in the line of duty. Examination of surgeon December 1864, permanently disabled to perform duty of soldier on account of his having had an arm fractured by the falling of Injury occurred while in the regular line of duty. Recommend he report to enrolling officer in GA (copy enclosed)."

Donald, M. M. (also N. M.). Enlisted as private on 22 June 1861 at Camp McDonald, age 24 per 31 August 1861 muster; June 1862, regiment return showed absent on sick furlough. No further record.

Dunn, William G. Enlisted as private on 11 June or 18 June 1863 in Cherokee County; February 1864, on horse furlough since 4 February 1864; October 1864 on detail for horses by order of Gen. Lee since 19 September 1864; admitted Jackson Hospital 29 November 1863; returned to duty 11 January 1864; paroled Greensboro, NC, 1 May 1865.

Dyer, Joel H. Enlisted as private on 25 February 1862 in Cherokee County; October 1864 last muster card showed present; admitted General Hospital No. 19 on 14 October 1862; 3 December 1862, 30-day furlough approved; paroled Greensboro, NC, 1 May 1865.

Emerson, Henry C. Enlisted as private on 1 July 1861 at Camp McDonald; age 18 per 31 August 1861 muster; 1 November 1861, last muster card showed present.

Evans, Amos M. Enlisted as private on 13 January 1864 in Cherokee County; October 1864 on horse detail since 19 September 1864 by order of Gen. Lee; paroled Greensboro, NC, 1 May 1865.

Evans, Phillip J. Enlisted on 11 June 1861 at Camp McDonald; age 45 per 31 August 1861 muster; elected 2nd lt. on 1 June 1861; promoted 1st lt. on September 1862; 31 August 1861, at home on sick furlough; October 1864 last muster showed resignation accepted by the President 13 October 1864; POW records indicate captured in Cherokee County 26 September 1864; sent to Louisville, arrived 26 September 1864; sent to Johnson's Island, arrived 11 November 1864; paroled and transferred to City Point, VA, for exchange 24 February 1865; residence, Atlanta; letter of resignation dated 18 September 1864 and addressed to Secretary of War Seddon in file; resigned on account of expiration of term of service and over age 48 on 12 January 1864.

Ezzard, Thomas W. Enlisted as private on 15 April 1863 at Cherokee County; 30 April 1864, on horse furlough since 4 June 1864; October 1864 last muster card showed AWOL since 20 August 1864.

Finch, John T. Enlisted as private on 4 April 1863 at Cedartown, GA; August 1864, last muster showed AWOL since 19 September 1863; POW records showed captured Marietta, GA, on 30 October 1864; sent to Louisville, arrived 22 November 1864; sent to Camp Douglas, arrived 26 November 1864; oath and discharged 17 June 1865; residence, Polk County, GA; dark complexion, black hair, gray eyes, 5' 10"; remarks: cartersville, GA. Note: POW records showed Company C but all other cards showed Company O, Infantry.

Fitts, John G. Enlisted as private on 25 March 1862 in Cherokee County, 1 January 1864, in hands of enemy since 15 December 1863; February 1864, at infirmary camp; 31 August 1864, guard for brig. commissary 20 July 1864; October 1864 last muster showed present; paroled Greensboro, NC, 1 May 1865.

Foster, Knight S. Enlisted as corporal on 22 June 1861 at Camp McDonald; age 23 per 31 August 1861 muster; 1 November 1861, absent sick; 30 April 1864, infirmary camp since 11 February 1864; 31 August 1864, present; October 1864 on detail for horses since 9 February 1864 by order of Gen. Lee.

Foster, R. T. (Robert). Enlisted as 4th sergeant/farrier; age 22 per 31 August

1861 muster; transferred to Co. G, Cobb's Legion Cavalry by S. O. 29/6, Dept. and Army of N. VA, 29 January 1863.

Fowler, E. B. (Eddie B.). Enlisted as private on 27 June 1861 at Camp McDonald; age 32 per 31 August 1861 muster; February 1864, on horse furlough since 4 February 1864; 31 August 1864, at infirmary camp since 20 June 1864; 30 September 1864, at General Hospital Lynchburg since August 1864; born in Union District, SC, 5' 10", fair complexion, blue eyes, brown hair, merchant. Note: record contains card showing "discharged for disability" on 8 October 1862, must have recovered and returned to service.

Fowler, J. B. Enlisted as private on 21 or 26 September 1862 in Virginia; February 1864, at infirmary camp; 30 April 1864, died April 1864; no cause shown, no hospital record.

Fowler, Lacy W. Enlisted as private on 26 September 1862 in Virginia; 11 April 1864, on detail for horse, returned before muster; October 1864 detail for horse by order of Gen. Lee since 19 September 1864; court martial, G.O. No. 69/5, Dept. of NV, 7 December 1864 (no information); paroled Greensboro, NC, 1 May 1865.

Fowler, N. A. Enlisted as private on 10 May 1862 at Camp Pritchard, SC; February 1864, on horse furlough since 4 February 1864; October 1864 on detail for horse by order of Gen. Lee since 19 September 1864; paroled Greensboro, NC, 1 May 1865.

Fowler, T. M. Enlisted as 2nd corporal/sergeant on 22 June 1861 at Camp McDonald; age 23 per 31 August 1861 muster; 3 December 1863, admitted to General Hospital at Charlottesville for pneumonia; returned to duty 8 January 1864; February 1864, on horse furlough since 4 February 1864; 31 August 1864, killed in action 16 August 1864 (also showed killed 10 August and 16 August). Note: no information on promotions but 1 November 1861 muster showed private and 1 January 1864 muster showed 2nd corporal.

Freeman, Benjamin F. Enlisted as 3rd lieutenant and later, 1st lieutenant on 22 June 1861 at Camp McDonald; age 35 per 31 August 1861 muster; February 1864, at infirmary camp; 30 April 1864, muster showed present; October 1864 last muster showed present; Promotion information: 2 August 1861, elected 3rd lieutenant, promoted 2nd lieutenant; 4 October 1864, promoted 1st lieutenant; paroled Greensboro, NC, 1 May 1865.

Freeman, John W. Enlisted as private/sergeant on 22 June 1861 at Camp McDonald; age 25 per 31 August 1861 muster; 1 January 1861, on detail for horse, returned since muster; 30 April 1864, on horse furlough since 4 June

1864; October 1864 detail for horse by order of Gen. Lee since 19 September 1864; paroled Greensboro, NC, 1 May 1865 (listed as private).

Freeman, Thomas J. (Thomas L.). Enlisted as private on 15 June 1863 in Cherokee County; 1 January 1864, on detail for horse since 9 November 1863; February 1864, AWOL since 1 January 1864; October 1864 on detail for horse since 19 September 1864.

Futrell, Joseph. Enlisted as private on 1 March 1862 at Cherokee County; 31 August 1864, last muster card indicated "died from gunshot accident"; no further information.

Futrell, William A. Enlisted as private on 27 June 1861 at Camp McDonald; age 25 per 31 August 1861 muster; February 1864, at infirmary camp; October 1864 last muster showed present.

Gault, James T. (G. T.). Enlisted as private on 16 July 1861 at Camp McDonald; age 29 per 31 August 1861 muster; 30 April 1864, on horse furlough since 4 June 1864; October 1864 on detail for horse by order of Gen. Lee since 19 September 1864; paroled Greensboro, NC, 1 May 1865.

Gray, James F. Enlisted as private on 1 March 1862 or 11 March 1862 at Cherokee County; February 1864, on horse furlough since 4 February 1864; October 1864 on detail for horse since 19 September 1864.

Gresham, Hezekiah. Enlisted as private on 27 May in Cherokee County in Milton or 27 July 1863 in Marietta; February 1864, on horse furlough since 4 February 1864; October 1864 on detail for horse by order of Gen. Lee since 19 September 1864; paroled Greensboro, NC, 1 May 1865.

Grimes, James C. Enlisted as private on 25 February 1863 or 5 July 1863 at Cherokee County; 1 January 1864, on detail for horse since 9 November 1863; October 1864 AWOL since 16 April 1864; no further record.

Grogan, G. W. Enlisted as private on 27 December 1863 in Virginia; February 1864, on horse detail since 4 February 1864; 30 April 1864, AWOL since 16 April 1864; 31 August 1864, last muster showed died at home on horse furlough, 1864.

Gross, F. M. Enlisted as private; no enlistment information; POW card showed captured at Gettysburg 3 July 1863 and arrived at Fort Delaware on 12 July 1863; showed discharged 26 August (year not listed).

Haley, D. L. (Halley). Enlisted as private on 24 July 1861 at Camp McDonald; age 25 per 31 August 1861 muster; February 1864, on horse furlough since 4 February 1864; October 1864 last muster showed in hands of enemy since 4 May 1864; POW records: captured Spotsylvania 12 May 1864, sent to Belle

Plain, VA, 17 May 1864, transferred to Point Lookout and then to Elmira, NY, arrived 12 August 1864; oath and released 16 June 1865; place of residence, Marietta, GA; fair complexion, light hair, blue eyes.

Haley, Joel C. (J. C.). Enlisted as private on 15 April or 16 May 1862 at Hardeeville or 10 May 1862 at Camp Pritchard, SC; 1 January 1864, muster showed AWOL since 11 November 1863; February 1864, muster showed AWOL since 1 January 1864; October, deserted November 1863.

Hancock, John C. Enlisted as private on 18 March 1862 at Camp Pritchard, SC; age 18 per 31 August 1861 muster; died General Hospital No. 1 Lynchburg, VA, 17 January 1863 "Phthisis Pulmonalis"; claim filed by father; Robert Hancock stated that he left neither wife nor child, black eyes, dark hair, sallow complexion, 5' 8".

Hancock, Joseph, N. (G.W.). Enlisted as private on 22 June 1861 at Camp McDonald; age 22 per 3 August 1861 muster; October 1864 last muster showed present; paroled Greensboro, NC, 1 May 1865.

Hardin, Eli C. (Harden). Enlisted on 11 June 1861 as 1st lieutenant/captain at Camp McDonald; February 1864, absent on sick furlough since 27 December 1863; 26 June 1864, admitted to Jackson Hospital for "Debilitas"; 27 June 1864, sent to Winder Hospital; 3 July 1864, admitted General Hospital No. 4 in Richmond, chronic diarrhea and general debility; furloughed 21 July 1864, no further record. Note: no promotion information, 6 November 1861 muster showed 1st lieutenant and 1 January 1864 muster showed captain.

Hardin, William C. Enlisted as private on 16 or 20 June 1863 at Cherokee County; February 1864, on horse furlough since 4 February 1862; October 1864 on detail for horse since 19 September 1864, paroled Greensboro, NC, 1 May 1865. Note: last card showed transferred to Smith's Legion by S. O. 166/27181862; must have transferred back.

Harris, James T. Enlisted as private on 14 March 1862 in Cherokee County; February 1864, on furlough since 18 February 1864; October 1864 at hospital, Columbia, SC, since 11 August 1864; hospital Charlottesville, VA, showed adm. 19 February 1863 for "Debilitas"; deserted (from hospital) 9 March 1863, returned and reentered hospital (no hospital records for August of 1864).

Harris, Wm. D. Enlisted as private 2 June 1861 at Camp McDonald; age 42 per 31 August 1861 muster; 31 August 1864, last muster showed discharged by expiration of service on 25 July 1864; discharge certificate showed discharged for being over 45 years of age; born in Wilkes County, 5' 11", dark complexion, blue eyes, dark hair, farmer.

Hawkins, John L. Enlisted as private on 13 or 19 March 1862 at Cherokee County; February 1864, at infirmary camp; 30 April 1864, on horse furlough since 4 June 1864; October 1864 on detail for horse since 19 September 1864. Note: showed transferred to Co. G, Cavalry of Cobb's Georgia Legion, S. O. 29/6, Dept. and Army of N. VA (transferred back).

Hawkins, William W. Enlisted as corporal on 22 July 1861 at Camp McDonald; age 26 per 31 August 1861 muster; 1 January 1864, on detail for horse, returned since muster; February 1864, on horse furlough since 4 February 1864; 30 April 1864, AWOL since 16 April 1864; October 1864 at recruiting camp by order of Captain Church since 1 July 1864.

Haynes, James. Enlisted as private on 21 or 26 June 1861 at Camp McDonald; age 19 per 31 August 1861 muster; 1 January 1864, on horse detail since 9 November 1863; October 1864 on detail for horse by order of Gen. Lee since 19 September 1864.

Haynes, Richard L. (R. L.). Enlisted as private on 1 or 16 July 1861 at Camp McDonald; age 16 per 31 August 1861 muster; February 1864, at infirmary camp; 30 April 1864, on furlough since 30 March 1864; 31 August 1864, at hospital since 7 August 1864; October 1864 AWOL since 9 August 1864.

Haynes, Robert. Enlisted as private on 22 June 1861 at Camp McDonald; age 18 per 31 August 1861 muster; died 28 November 1861 at Peterstown, VA (death date also shown as 1 December 1861); claim presented by father, Harper Haynes, on 23 May 1864.

Haynes, Z. J. Enlisted as private on 16 September 1863 at Atlanta; February 1864, on horse furlough since 4 February 1861; October 1864 on sick furlough since 10 September 1864, furloughed for 60 days.

Haynie, James, (Hawley, J. S. and Haney, J. S.). Enlisted as private on 22 June 1861 at Camp McDonald; age 31 per 31 August 1861 muster; 1 November 1861, absent sick; 1 January 1864, on detail for horse, returned since muster; 30 April 1864, on detail for horse since 4 June 1864; October 1864 last muster card showed present; paroled Greensboro 1 June 1865.

Hensley, F. M. Enlisted as private on 4 or 14 March 1862 at Cherokee County; February 1864, on horse furlough since 4 February 1864; captured 30 May 1864 at Milford Station and sent to Point Lookout; paroled and transferred to Aikens Landing, VA, on 14 March 1865 for exchange; 17 March 1865, admitted to Jackson Hospital for "Gelatio," furloughed on 24 March 1865 for 60 days.

Hood, Clayton. Enlisted as private on 1 November 1861 at Northwest, VA; 1 January 1864, muster showed at hospital, wounded since 10 July 1863; 30 August 1864, muster showed died at hospital in 1863 from wounds received 8 July 1863.

Hood, Robert. Enlisted as private on 1 November 1861 at Northwest, VA; October 1864 last muster showed in hands of enemy since 4 May 1864; POW records showed captured at Spotsylvania C. H. on 12 May 1864, arrived at Belle Plain, VA, on 17 May 1864 and sent to Point Lookout; 14 March 1865, paroled at Point Lookout and transferred to Aikens Landing for exchange; exchanged 15 March 1865.

Howell, A. L. Enlisted as private on 1 March 1863 at Cherokee County; February 1864, on furlough since 2 February 1864; 30 April 1864, muster showed at hospital since 4 April 1864; October 1864 on detail for horse since 19 September 1864 by order of Gen. Lee; admitted to Jackson Hospital in Richmond on 4 April 1864 for Rubeola, furloughed on 30 April 1864 for 30 days; no further record.

Howell, Charles (C. L.). Enlisted as private on 2 August 1861 or 11 September 1861 at Lynchburg, VA; 1 November 1861, muster showed absent sick; February 1864, on furlough since 12 February 1864; October 1864 on horse detail by order of Gen. Lee since 19 September 1864; admitted to Jackson Hospital, Richmond, on 28 May 1864 for VL left hip, M.B. (Minnie ball); no further record.

Howell, John D. Enlisted as private on 25 February 1862 at Cherokee County; October 1864 last muster showed in hands of enemy since 15 December 1863; POW records showed arrested in Craig County, VA, on 21 December 1863; received at Camp Chase on 1 January 1864 from Wheeling, VA; 14 March 1864, transferred to Fort Delaware, oath and released at Fort Delaware on 7 June 1865; description from oath: 5' 6", light complexion, auburn hair, gray eyes, farmer.

Jameson, James M. (Jamison). Enlisted 15 January or 27 January 1864 in Cherokee County (also shown as 25 February 1864 Milton County); 31 August 1864, muster showed at hospital since 12 August 1864; October 1864 last muster showed admitted to Jackson Hospital, Richmond on 18 August 1864 for "Rubeola"; Company C and L (Company L is on title card but does not appear elsewhere); returned to duty 7 September 1864.

Johnson, F. M. Enlisted as private on 25 or 27 July 1863 at Marietta (also

showed 25 February 1863); 31 August 1864, muster showed wagoner for
brig. HDQ since 30 July 1864; paroled Greensboro, NC, 1 May 1865.

Johnson, George, R. Enlisted as private on 14 March 1862 at Cherokee County;
1 January 1864, muster showed in hands of enemy since 13 December 1864;
arrested by U.S. troops in Craig County, VA; appears on list of prisoners
confined in military prison at Wheeling Virginia on 31 December 1863; sent
to Camp Chase 31 December 1863; POW records show: age 23, fair
complexion, gray eyes, brown hair, farmer, resident Cherokee County; 10
March 1865, admitted to General Hospital No. 9 in Richmond; 11 March
1865; sent to Camp Lee; no further record.

Jones, S. A. Enlisted as private; one card, appears on "Roll of Prisoners of War
captured by U.S. Forces under Bvt. Brig. S. B. Brown and paroled at
Hartwell, Georgia, and Anderson and Greenville, South Carolina"; showed
captured 23 May 1865 at Greenville, SC.

Kemp, Henry M. (H. M.). Enlisted as private on 25 or 28 February 1863 in
Cherokee County (also showed 27 July 1863); February 1864, on horse
furlough since 4 February 1864; October 1864 on detail for horse by order of
Gen. Lee since 19 September 1864; paroled Greensboro, NC, 1 May 1865.

Kemp, J. H. Enlisted as private on 11 January 1864 in Cherokee County;
October 1864 last muster showed on detail for horse by order of Gen. Lee
since 19 September 1864; paroled Greensboro, NC, 1 May 1865.

Kemp, W. D. G. Enlisted as private on 4 March 1864 in Cobb County; 31
August 1864, muster showed at hospital since 12 August 1864; 30
September 1864, muster showed at Jackson Hospital, Richmond since 27
July 1864; October 1864 last muster card showed sick at General Hospital
since 1 September 1864 admitted to Jackson Hospital 13 August 1864 for
"Debilitas"; transferred to Charlottesville on 23 August 1864; returned to
duty 19 September 1864; admitted to Charlottesville Hospital on 19
September 1864; admitted to Confederate States Hospital at Petersburg on 2
September 1864; died 24 September 1864, "February Int."

Knox, James. Enlisted as private; one card dated 11 September 1861 showed
enlisted 2 August 1861 at Cobb County.

Land, William H. Enlisted as private on 28 April 1862 at Marietta, GA
(Company M); elected 2nd lieutenant; 29 January 1863, was sent before a
board and found "incompetent," "reduced to ranks"; 12 February 1863,
transferred to cavalry battalion; on horse furlough since 4 February 1864;
October 1864 on detail for horse by order of Gen. Lee since 19 September

1864.

Latham, A. J. Enlisted as private on 24 February, 25 February, or 1 March (year not listed), Cherokee County; no records prior to 1864; 1 January 1864, muster showed at hospital; February 1864, muster showed absent, on sick furlough since 20 November 1863; 31 August 1864, muster showed division ambulance driver since 15 April 1864; October 1864 last muster card showed present; paroled Greensboro, NC, 1 May 1865.

Latham, Samuel W. Enlisted as private on 1 or 2 August 1861 at Camp McDonald, age 22 per 31 August 1861 muster; 1 November 1861, muster showed absent sick; February 1864, on furlough since 18 February 1864; killed by RR accident 27 February 1864.

Latimer, D. F. (Lattimer). Enlisted as private on 12 or 25 April 1863 in Cherokee County; February 1864, on horse furlough since 4 February 1864; 31 August 1864, muster showed at hospital since 10 August 1864; died 24 August 1864 at General Hospital No. 8, Raleigh, NC, "Febris. Remittins."

Latimer, H. R. (also R. H.). Enlisted as private/sergeant on 16 May 1862 at Hardeeville, SC (also 10 May 1862 at Camp Pritchard, SC); 1 January 1864, on detail for horse returned 11 June 1864; 30 September 1864, muster (listed as 4th sergeant); 10 August 1864; muster showed died at General Hospital Gordonsville, VA, 7 August 1864; register of officers and soldiers killed in battle or died of disease 29 July 1864 at General Hospital at Gordonsville.

Latimer, James R. Enlisted as private on 11 June 1861 at Camp McDonald; age 26 per 31 August 1861 muster; discharged 8 December 1863 for disability; age 28 at discharge, 6', fair complexion, blue eyes, light hair, farmer.

Latimer, John R. Enlisted as private on 25 February (year not listed) in Cherokee County; February 1864, on horse furlough since 4 February 1864; October 1864 last muster showed on horse detail since 19 September 1864; paroled Greensboro, NC, 1 May 1865.

Little, James, J. (G. G.). Enlisted as private on 26 June or 2 August 1861 at Camp McDonald; age 18 per 31 August 1861 muster; 1 January 1864, muster showed on detail for horse since 9 November 1863; 30 April 1864, on horse furlough since 4 June 1864; October 1864 on horse detail by order of Gen. Lee since 19 September 1865.

Long. John A. Enlisted as private on 6 July 1863 at Cherokee County; February 1864, on horse furlough since 24 January 1864; October 1864 on detail for horse by order of Gen. Lee since 19 September 1864; paroled Greensboro, NC, 1 May 1865.

Going Back the Way They Came

Lowe, Alfred. Enlisted as private on 25 February 1862 in Cherokee County; 1 January 1864, muster showed AWOL since 10 October 1863; October 1864 last muster card showed deserted since 13 September 1863; receipt of commutation of rations, 11 May 1863, Atlanta.

Lummas, Ellison. Enlisted as private on 4 March 1862 at Cherokee County; February 1864, on horse furlough since 4 February 1864; 30 April 1864, muster showed died March, 1864; 31 August 1864, muster showed died at home on horse furlough, April 1864.

Mansell, P. A. Enlisted as private on 25 February 1862 in Cherokee County; February 1864, muster showed at infirmary camp; October 1864 on horse detail since 19 September 1864 by order of Gen. Lee; paroled Greensboro, NC, 1 May 1865.

Mansell, W. T. Enlisted as private; paroled Greensboro, NC, 1 May 1865; no other information.

McAfee, D. R. Enlisted as private on 22 July 1861 at Camp McDonald; age 23 per 31 August 1861 muster; 1 November 1861, last muster card showed absent sick.

McCollum, Benjamin F. Enlisted as private on 6 August 1863 at Richmond, Virginia; 30 April 1864, on furlough since 25 April 1864; 31 August 1864, on furlough since 24 July 1864; October 1864 AWOL since 16 August 1864.

McCollum, Robert A. Enlisted as private on 25 February 1864; 31 August 1861, muster showed at hospital since 12 June 1864; 30 September 1864, at home on furlough, wounded, since 11 June 1864; October 1864 last muster card showed AWOL since 16 August 1864.

McConnell, Eli J. Enlisted as private on 16 July or 2 August 1861 at Camp McDonald; 1 January 1864, on detail for horse, returned since muster; 30 April 1864, on horse furlough since 4 June 1864; October 1864 last muster card showed present.

McConnell, H. G. Enlisted as private on 17 July or 2 August 1861 at Camp McDonald; 1 November 1861, last muster showed present; appeared on register of payments to discharged soldiers; discharged 7 July 1862.

McConnell, John M. Enlisted as private/sergeant on 6 August or 25 September 1862 in Cherokee County; 1 January 1864, on detail for horse, returned since muster; 30 April 1864, on horse furlough since 4 June 1864, paroled at Greensboro, NC, 1 May 1865.

McConnell, Joshua. Enlisted as private on 2 August 1861 at Cobb County or 11 September 1861 at Lynchburg, VA; June 1862, regimental return showed

196

discharged for disability on 17 June 1862.

McConnell, William D. R. Enlisted as private/2nd lieutenant on 7 August 1861 at Camp McDonald; age 20 per 31 August 1861 muster; 30 April 1864, absent, in charge of horse detail since 30 April 1864; elected 3rd lieutenant 1 December 1862; promoted 4 October 1864 to 2nd lieutenant; paroled Greensboro, NC, 1 May 1865.

McCraw, James B. (McGraw, J. B.). Enlisted as private on 1 February or 25 February 1862 in Cherokee County; 1 January 1864, on detail for horse, returned since muster; February 1864, on furlough since 18 February 1864; October 1864, last muster card showed on horse detail since 19 September 1864 by order of Gen. Lee; paroled Greensboro, NC, 1 May 1865.

McNairen, L. H. (McNairn). Enlisted 25 September 1861 in Milton County; October 1864 last muster card showed present; paroled Greensboro, NC, 1 May 1865.

Merritt, G. W. (Merrett). Enlisted as private on 25 February 1862 in Cherokee County; February 1864, on horse furlough since 4 February 1861; October 1864 last muster card showed on horse detail since 19 September 1864.

Merritt, James A. (Merrett). Enlisted as private on 1 or 4 October 1863 in Atlanta; February 1864, on horse furlough since 4 February 1864; October 1864 on horse detail since 19 September 1864 by order of Gen. Lee.

Merritt, Levi T. (Merrett, Miner L. T., and Thomas). Enlisted 10 or 16 May 1862 at Camp Pritchard, SC; 29 January 1863, transferred to Co. G, Cobb's Cavalry Georgia Legion by S. O.; February 1864, on horse since 4 February 1864; October 1864 on horse detail by order of Gen. Lee since 19 September 1864; captured Cherokee County 28 September 1864; sent to Nashville and forwarded to Camp Douglas, arrived 11 November 1864; admitted to prison hospital 20 March 1865; died 2 April 1865 of pneumonia; buried Block 3, Chicago City Cemetery.

Mitchell, Thomas P. Enlisted as private on 27 July 1863 at Marietta, GA; 1 January 1864, muster showed AWOL; October 1864 last muster card showed deserted 17 June 1863.

Morris, John S. Enlisted as private on 2 August 1861 at Lynchburg, VA (also showed as 11 September 1861); 30 April 1864, on horse furlough since 4 June 1864; October 1864 last muster card showed present; paroled Greensboro, NC, 1 May 1865.

Morris, M. G. Enlisted as private on 2 August 1861 at Cobb County (also 11 or 13 September 1861 at Lynchburg, VA; discharged 31 October 1861, kidney affliction, "unfit for duty for 40 days"; age 31 at discharge, 5' 10", fair complexion, hazel or blue eyes, black hair, farmer.

Morris, Newton M. Enlisted as private/sergeant on 10 July 1861, 7th GA infantry, Co. H. 13 August 1862, "Transferred"; 1 January 1864, muster showed present; February 1864, courier for Gen. Hampton since 10 October 1862; October 1864 last muster card showed present; paroled Greensboro, NC, 1 May 1865.

Mullins, F. M. (Mullens). Enlisted as private on 21 January 1862 in South Carolina; February 1862, at infirmary camp; 30 April 1864, at infirmary camp since September 1863; 31 August 1864, at infirmary camp since November 1863; 30 September 1864, at recruiting camp Lynchburg since 18 September 1863 by order Captain H.; October 1864 last muster card showed at recruiting camp Lynchburg since September 1863.

Mullins, James C. Enlisted at age 21 per 3 August 1861 muster; 1 January 1864, on detail for horse since 4 November 1863; February 1864, AWOL since 1 January 1864; 30 April 1864, muster showed present; October 1864 on horse detail by order of Gen. Lee since 19 September 1864.

Newton, E. B. Enlisted as private on 15 April 1863 in Cherokee County; 1864; muster showed AWOL since 10 October 1863; October 1864 last muster card showed AWOL since 14 October 1863.

Nichols, David. Enlisted as private, no enlistment date, enlisted in Cherokee County; 31 August 1864; muster showed at hospital since 10 July 1864; October 1864 last muster card showed on detail for horse by order of Gen. Lee since 19 September 1864; paroled Greensboro, NC, 1 May 1865.

Nix, Charles. Enlisted as private on 2 August 1861 in Cobb County (also 11 September 1861 at Lynchburg); on horse furlough since 4 June 1864; 31 August 1864, muster showed courier for Gen. Butler; October 1864 last muster card showed present; paroled Greensboro, NC, 1 May 1865.

Nix, M. Enlisted as private; one card showed enlister 2 August 1861 in Cobb County.

Nix, William Enlisted as private on 11 September 1861 in Lynchburg, VA; 1 November 1861, last muster card showed present.

Nox, J. S. (Nix). Enlisted as private on 11 September 1861 at Lynchburg, VA; 1 November 1861, last muster showed present.

Oaks, William. Enlisted as private on 23 January 1864 or 22 February 1864 in Cherokee County; October 1864 last muster card showed present; 11 April 1864, admitted to Jackson Hospital for "Rubeola," returned to duty 9 April

1864; 12 July 1864; admitted to General Hospital No. 13 Richmond for "Dysentaria" Disposition: castle Thunder 16 July 1864.

Paden, M. S. Enlisted as private on 11 June 1861; age 33 per 3 August 1861 muster; 3 August 1861, last muster card showed discharged by the Gov. of Georgia.

Palmer, James A. (Palmer, J. L.). Enlisted as private on 7 August 1861 at Camp McDonald; age 24 per 31 August 1861 muster; discharged 31 October 1861, unfit for duty for 30 days, "Pain in the breast and diseased veins of the leg for the last 3 years"; born Walton County, GA, age 24 at date of discharge, 5' 8", dark complexion, hazel eyes, black hair, blacksmith.

Perkins, Moses. Enlisted as private on 2 or 7 August 1861 at Camp McDonald; POW records: captured Brandy Station and sent to Old Capitol Prison between 1 and 15 August 1863; sent to Point Lookout arrived 23 August 1863; paroled at Point Lookout and transferred to Aikins Landing,VA, 24 February 1865for exchange; paroled Greensboro, NC, 1 May 1865.

Petree, C. H. Enlisted as private on 25 July 1862 at Cherokee County; October 1864 on horse detail by order of Gen. Lee since 19 September 1864; paroled at Greensboro, NC, 1 May 1865.

Petree, L, H. Enlisted as private on 25 February 1862; 1 January 1864, muster showed on detail for horse since 9 November 1863; February 1864, AWOL since 11 January 1864; October 1864 AWOL since 1 January 1864.

Popham, A. J. Enlisted as private on 31 August 1862 or 31 August 1863 at Camp McDonald; 30 April 1864, on horse furlough since 4 June 1864; October 1864 last muster card showed present; hospitalized at Jackson Hospital, Richmond on 16 June 1864 for syphilis, returned to duty 13 October 1864; paroled Greensboro, NC, 1 May 1865.

Puckett, William B. C. Enlisted as captain/major on 11 June 1864 at Camp McDonald; Company C and Field and Staff; age 39 per 31 August 1864 muster; 11 October 1864; muster showed absent in Spotsylvania County, VA, after blankets and overcoats by order Gen. Lee; elected captain 11 June 1861, promoted to major September 1862; 30 November 1864, inspection report of Young's cavalry brigade, 1st cavalry division commanded by Col. J. F. Waring showed "absent in Georgia commanding dismounted men" by order Gen. Young 25 November 1864; 31 December 1864, showed on detail in Georgia with Gen. Young, Gen. Leo 25 November 1864; 30 November 1864, inspection report of Young's cavalry brigade, 1st cavalry division, commanded by Col. J. G. Waring, showed "absent in Georgia commanding detail dismounted men" by order Gen. Young 25 November 1864; 31 December 1864, showed on detail in Georgia with Gen. Young by order of Gen. Lee 25 November 1864.

Reaves, Benjamin W. (Revis, Reeves). Enlisted as private on 13 March 1864 in Milton, Cherokee County; October 1864 last muster card showed on horse detail by order of Gen. Lee since 19 September 1864.

Richardson, Thomas C. (T. W., W. F., William Thomas). Enlisted as private on 15, 18, or 28 June 1862 in Cherokee County; February 1864, muster showed in hands of enemy since 13 September 1863; 30 April 1864, absent, paroled prisoner; 31 August 1864, muster showed present; paroled Greensboro, NC, 1 May 1865; POW records: captured near Madison C. H., VA, sent to Old Capitol Prison, arrived 15 September 1863; transferred to Point Lookout on 26 September 1863; exchanged 17 March 1864.

Roberts, Agustus M. (A. M.). Enlisted as private/corporal on 1 March 1862 in Cherokee County; February 1864, on horse furlough since 4 February 1864; 30 September 1864, last muster card showed on detail since 19 September 1864 for horse by order Gen. Lee; POW records: captured 1 October 1862 at Emmitsburg, paroled and sent from Fort Delaware to Fortress Monroe, Virginia, for exchange on 15 December 1862.

Rogers, Henry H. Enlisted as private on 25 February 1862 in Cherokee County; 11 August 1864, muster showed absent, wagoner for brig. commissary since January 1863; October 1864 last muster card showed present.

Rudacille, James E. Enlisted as private on 1 March 1862 in Cherokee County; 1 January 1864, muster showed on detail for horse, returned since muster; October 1864 last muster card showed on horse detail by order of Gen. Lee since 19 September 1864.

Rumph, John, G. (Rump). Enlisted as private on 10 May 1862 at Camp Pritchard, South Carolina; February 1864, muster showed on horse furlough since 4 February 1864; October 1864 last muster card showed on horse detail by order of Gen. Lee since 19 September 1864.

Rusk, James, E. Enlisted as private on 1 July 1861 at Camp McDonald; age 39 per 31 August 1861 muster; 20 September 1864, discharged, no additional information.

Rusk, James M. Enlisted as private on 1 January 1863 in Cherokee County; October 1864 last muster card showed on horse detail since 19 September 1864.

Rusk, William D. Enlisted as private on 25 February or 25 July (no year listed);

1 January 1864, muster showed present; killed in action 11 June 1864; no additional information.

Russom, J. P. Enlisted as private on 25 February 1862 in Cherokee County; 1 January 1864, muster showed AWOL, returned since muster; 30 April 1864, on horse furlough since 4 June 1864; October 1864 last muster card showed present; paroled Greensboro, NC, 1 May 1865.

Russom, William A. Enlisted as private on 19 March (no year) in Cherokee County; 1 January 1864, muster showed AWOL-returned since muster; 30 April 1864, on horse furlough since 4 June 1864; October 1864 last muster card showed on wounded furlough since 29 June 1864.

Sergeant, E. B. Enlisted as private on 25 July 1863 in Cherokee County; 30 April 1864, on horse furlough since 4 June 1864; October 1864 on detail for horse by order of Gen. Lee since 19 September 1864.

Saye, William M. Enlisted as private on 25 February 1862 in Cherokee County; 30 April 1864, muster showed on horse furlough since 4 June 1864; October 1864 last muster card showed deserted since 1 July 1864.

Scott, Andrew J. Enlisted as private on 2 August 1861 at Camp McDonald; age 21 per 31 August 1861 muster; February 1864, on horse furlough since 4 February 1864; October 1864 last muster card showed on horse detail by order of Gen. Lee since 19 September 1864; paroled Greensboro, NC, 1 May 1865.

Scott, John A. (J. A.). Enlisted as private on 14 June 1861 in Georgia; 30 April 1864, muster showed on horse furlough since 4 June 1864; descriptive list in file: born in Franklin County, Georgia, age 25, gray eyes, black hair, dark complexion, 5' 10", farmer; 17 September 1862, killed at Sharpsburg.

Shamlee, G. W. (Chamblee, Chamley, George, W.). Enlisted 2 August 1861 at Camp McDonald; age 21 per 31 August 1861 muster; 20 September 1861, discharged for disability, hernia; born Cherokee County; fair complexion, hazel eyes, light auburn hair, 6' 1", farmer.

Smithwick, George W. Enlisted as private on 25 February 1862 in Cherokee County; died 13 or 15 August or 1864 at General Hospital No. 7, Raleigh, NC, "February Remittens."

Smithwick, John W. Enlisted as private on 1 August 1861 at Camp McDonald; age 20 per 31 August 1861 muster; February 1864, on horse furlough since 4 February 1864; died 11 or 14 August or 1864 at General Hospital No. 7, Raleigh, NC, no cause listed.

Smithwick, S. S. Enlisted as private (bugler); April 1864, on horse furlough since 4 June 1864; October 1864 last muster card showed on horse detail by order of Gen. Lee since 19 September 1864; paroled Greensboro, NC, 1 May 1865.

Smithwick, S. W. Enlisted as private (no year listed); October 1864 last muster card showed on detail for horse by order of Gen. Lee since 19 September 1864.

Stevenson, Alex. Enlisted as private on 25 February 1862 in Cherokee County; 30 April 1864, muster showed on furlough since 26 April 1864; October 1864 last muster card showed Wilson Hospital since 31 August 1864; furloughed 60 days 20 October 1864.

Tate, John E. Enlisted as private on 25 or 26 September 1863 in Virginia; 1 January 1864, muster showed detail for horse, returned since muster; October 1864 last muster card showed present; paroled Greensboro, NC, 1 May 1865.

Terrell, Henry C. (Terrill). Enlisted as private on 10 April 1863 at Buck County, VA; October 1864 last muster card showed present; paroled Greensboro, NC, 1 May 1865.

Terrell, James A. (G. N.). Enlisted as private/corporal on 11 June 1861 at Camp McDonald; age 23 per 31 August 1861 muster; 30 April 1864, on horse furlough since 4 June 1864; October 1864 last muster card showed on detail for horse by order of Gen. Lee since 19 September 1864; paroled Greensboro, NC, 1 May 1865.

Terrell, John D. (J. D.). Enlisted as private on 25 February 1862 in Cherokee County; 30 September 1864, at Lynchburg recruiting camp since 1 September 1864; October 1864 last muster card showed present.

Terrell, Timothy. Enlisted as private on 25 February 1862 in Cherokee County; February 1864, furlough since 18 February 1864; October 1864 last muster card showed on detail for horse by order of Gen. Lee since 19 September 1864.

Terrell, William L. Enlisted as private on 11 June 1861 at Camp McDonald; age 26 per 31 August 1861 muster; died 19 October 1861, near Cotton Hill, VA, at a private home; mother, Easter Terrell filed claim 15 August 1862; age 27 at death, light hair, blue eyes, fair complexion, 6' 3", had neither wife nor children.

Tippen, James W. (J. W. and. G. W.). Enlisted as private on 22 June 1861 at Camp McDonald; October, last muster card showed present; POW records: captured in front of Petersburg and forwarded to City Point, Virginia on 5

February 1865, arrived 9 February 1865; also showed captured at Gettysburg on 3 July 1863 and paroled at Point Lookout on 18 February 1865.

Tripp, J. H. Enlisted as private on 25 February 1863 in Cherokee County; February, on horse furlough since 4 February 1864; October 1864 last muster showed on horse detail since 19 September 1864; paroled Greensboro 1 May 1865.

Tripp, John K. Enlisted as private on 25 February 1863 in Cherokee County; February 1864, on horse furlough since 4 February 1864; October 1864 last muster card showed on horse detail by order of Gen. Lee since 19 September 1864; paroled Greensboro, NC, 1 May 1865.

Tripp, J. P. Enlisted as private on 1 November 1863 in Cherokee County; 31 August 1864, AWOL since 10 July 1864; October 1864 last muster card showed present.

Tripp, R. H. Enlisted as private on 22 June 1861 at Camp McDonald; age 27 per 31 August 1861 muster; 17 June 1863, discharged for disability.

Tripp, William M. Enlisted as private; 1 January 1864, on detail for horse, returned since muster; October 1864 last muster card showed on horse detail by order of Gen. Lee sine 19 September 1864; paroled Greensboro, NC, 1 May 1865.

Turner, G. C. (infantry or cavalry); one card showed captured Gettysburg 3 July 1863, received at Fort Delaware on 7 or 12 July 1863.

Underwood, J. W. Enlisted as private on 11 June 1861 at Camp McDonald; age 21 per 31 August 1861 muster; February 1864, on horse furlough since 4 February 1864; October 1864 last muster card showed on detail for horse by order of Gen. Lee since 19 September 1864.

Underwood, William B. Enlisted as private on 21 January 1862; October 1864 last muster showed in hands of enemy since 27 February 1864; POW records: captured Rapidan River 29 February 1864-sent to Old Capitol Prison on 3 February 1864, transferred to Fort Delaware, arrived 17 June 1864; paroled Fort Delaware 10 March, 11 March, or 12 March 1865; captured and paroled at Andersonville, 3 May 1865.

Wallace, James. M. (Wallis, J. M.). Enlisted as private on 24 February 1862 in Cherokee County; 31 August 1864, on furlough since June 1864; October 1864 last muster card showed AWOL since 5 August 1864.

Westbrooks, John W. Enlisted as private on 7 August 1861 at Camp McDonald; age 20 per 31 August 1861 muster; 1 November 1861, last muster card showed present.

White, William. Enlisted as private on 15 February, 15 March, or 18 March 1864 in Cherokee County; 30 April 1864, absent, never reported; October 1864, last muster card showed AWOL.

Whitten, William J. Enlisted as private on 8 February 1862 in Cherokee County; February 1864, in infirmary camp; 30 April 1864, on horse furlough; 31 August 1864, AWOL since 10 July 1864; October 1864 last musket card showed AWOL since 6 August 1864.

Wise, Henry G. Enlisted as private on 3 February or 3/3 (year not listed) in Cherokee County; October 1864 last muster card showed on detail for horse by order of Gen. Lee since 19 September 1864.

Wood, Bowen G. Enlisted as private on 14 or 18 March 1863 in Cherokee County; February 1864, on horse furlough since 4 February 1864; 30 April 1864, on detail for horse since 4 June 1864; 30 September 1864, detail as shoemaker, Orange C. H., VA, by order of Gen. Stuart 23 April 1864; October 1864 last muster card showed present; admitted to Pettigrew General Hospital No. 13, Raleigh, NC, on 24 March 1865 for bronchitis; appeared on a list of rebel prisoners of war who were in hospital at Raleigh, NC, 13 April 1865 when the city was captured; residence, Cherokee, Georgia, Post Office: Hickory Flat.

Wood, J. A. Enlisted as private; October 1864, last muster card showed on detail for horse by order of Gen. Lee since 19 September 1864; paroled Greensboro, NC, 1 May 1865.

Wood, Jacob G. Enlisted as private/corporal on 2 August 1861 at Camp McDonald; age 22 per 31 August 1861 muster; 1 January 1864, absent with leave for horses, returned since muster; 30 April 1864, on furlough since 28 April 1864, October 1864 last muster card shows present; court martialed, G. O. 69-5 Dept. of N. VA, 7 December 1864, disobedience of orders, findings: guilty; sentence: "And the court does therefore sentence him, Corp. Jacob Wood of Co. C of the Phillips Legion of Georgia Cavalry to be reduced to the ranks, and to hard labor for the period of two calendar months and to be kept under guard for said time."

Wood, J. J. Enlisted as private on 10 March1864; October 1864, last muster showed AWOL since 6 August 1864.

Worley, E. J. (Worley, E. Z.). Enlisted as private on 16 April 1863 in Cherokee County; 1 January 1864, AWOL since November, 1864; October 1864 AWOL since 1 November 1863.

Worley, James P. Enlisted as private; 13 March 1863, died in Rockingham

County, VA; claim presented by Wm. Worley 5 May 1863.

Worley, John W. Enlisted as private 24 February 1862 in Cherokee County; February 1864, on horse furlough since 4 February 1864; October 1864 last muster card showed AWOL since 6 August 1864.

Yamrick, M. M. (Yarcimick, Yarmmick). Enlisted as private; POW records: captured Gettysburg 2 or 3 July 1863; arrived Fort Delaware 7 or 12 July 1863; arrived Point Lookout 22 October 1863; exchanged 18 February 1865.

Casualties, other losses for the Phillips Georgia Legion cavalry battalion from available records. Company K/D was formed predominantly from Coweta, Carroll, and Bibb counties.

Company K/D

Total Enrollment:	204
Death/disease/accident:	11
Discharge/disability:	9
Captured:	25
KIA:	2
WIA:	5
MWIA:	1
Exchanged:	4
AWOL:	16
Imprisoned/Point Lookout, MD:	8
Imprisoned/Old Capitol Prison, D.C.:	5
Imprisoned/Hart's Island, NY:	1
Imprisoned/Fort Delaware, DE:	12
Imprisoned/Elmira, NY:	2
Imprisoned/Fortress Monroe, VA:	1
Imprisoned/Camp Chase, OH:	6
Transferred Out:	5
Transferred In:	5
Transferred to C. S. A. Navy:	3
Detached Service/Extra Duty:	21
Horse Detail/Furlough:	77
Paroled/Greensboro, NC:	55

Resigned (Officer):	3
POW:	11
Courts Martial:	1
Reenlisted:	1
Surrendered/Appomattox:	1
Paroled/Fortress Monroe, VA:	2
Paroled/Point Lookout, MD:	2
Paroled/Farmville, VA:	1
Paroled/Fort McHenry/MD:	1
Paroled/Old Capitol Prison, D.C.:	2

Note: any one individual may appear in several categories; e.g., he may have been captured, sent to prison, and exchanged.

PHILLIPS GEORGIA LEGION
Cavalry Battalion

Company D
The Coweta Rangers

Abrahams, John W. Enlisted as corporal/1st lieutenant in 1861 at Camp
McDonald; age 25 per 31 August 1861 muster; promoted to 2nd lieutenant 2
December 1862; 31 August 1864, muster showed wounded at Riddles Shop
17 August 1864; October 1864 last muster showed absent/wounded at
hospital in Richmond since 17 August 1864; hospital records: admitted to
General Hospital No. 4 in Richmond on 16 August 1864 for V.S. through
lower portion left thigh and hemorrhage; furloughed, 24 August 1864;
November 1864, inspection report stated absent wounded, leave by med.
exam. board.
Allen, Julius. Enlisted as private/sergeant on 11 June or 2 August 1861 at Camp
McDonald; 22 per 31 August 1861 muster; October 1864 last muster showed
AWOL since 7 August 1864.
Allen, N. G. Enlisted as private on 27 or 28 February 1862 at Newnan, GA;
April 1864, absent at infirmary camp since 13 January 1864 by order Gen.
Lee; 11 October 1864, muster showed absent infirmary corps Elk Creek, NC,
4 January 1864; October 1864 last muster showed absent on detached
service (infirmary corps), Lynchburg since 4 February 1864.
Allen, S. G. Enlisted as private on 12 September 1861, 11 January 1862 or 11
May 1862 at Newnan, GA; April 1864 muster showed courier at corps, HDQ
since October 1863 by order of Gen. Stuart; 31 August 1864, muster showed
present; October 1864 last muster card showed present.
Armor, W. G. (Armer). Enlisted as private on 15 May 1862 at Newnan, GA;
April 1864, last muster showed present; transferred to Navy by S. O. 118/10,
Dept. and Army of N. Va. dated 30 April 1864.
Arnold, Hugh, M. Enlisted as private on 22 September 1861 at Newnan, GA; No
further record.
Bailey, Robert (Baily). Enlisted as private on 12 or 20 September 1861 or 12
September 1862 in Newnan, GA; October 1864 last muster showed absent,
on detail to procure a remount horse since 2 September 1864; paroled
Greensboro, NC, 1 May 1865.
Barron, Joseph, A. Enlisted as private/sergeant on 2 August 1861 in Cobb

County; age 30 per 31 August 1861 muster; February 1864, absent on furlough since 21 February 1864; 1 April 1864, muster showed present; October 1864 last muster showed present; paroled Greensboro, NC, 1 May 1865; (no promotion information but 31 August 1864 muster showed private and 11 October 1864 showed 4th sergeant.)

Beavers, Ephraim W. (Ephugh, W.). Enlisted as private on 11 June 1861 at Camp McDonald or 2 August 1861 at Cobb County; age 25 per 31 August 1861 muster; 11 April 1864, muster showed absent, on detail to procure a fresh horse since 31 February 1864; 31 August 1864, muster showed AWOL since 12 July 1864; October 1864 last muster showed absent on detached service with Major Beggs since 15 September 1864; POW records: captured Williamsburg 19 September 1862 and paroled at Fort Monroe on 12 September 1862.

Beavers. F. M. (M.F.). Enlisted as private on 27 or 28 February 1862 at Newnan, GA; February 1864, on detail to procure fresh horse since 31 February 1864; 31 August 1864, present; October 1864 on detail to procure a remount horse since 2 September 1864; paroled Greensboro, NC, 1 May 1865.

Beavers, John A. Enlisted as sergeant on 11 June 1861 or 2 August 1861 at Camp McDonald; age 29 per 31 August 1861 muster; April 1864, on detail to procure a fresh horse by order of Gen. Lee; 31 August 1864, present; October 1864 absent to procure a remount horse to Georgia since 2 September 1864 by order Gen. Lee.

Beavers, Joseph S. Enlisted as private on 28 February 1862 at Newnan, GA; 11 April 1864, last muster card showed died in hands of enemy in February; (Note: POW records indicate he was alive and exchanged in February, 1865; see below); POW records: captured at Gettysburg on 3 July 1863; arrived at Fort Delaware on 7 or 12 July 1863 and then forwarded to Point Lookout; arrived at Point Lookout 22 October 1863; exchanged and paroled at Point Lookout 18 February 1865.

Bense, J. S. Enlisted as private in Company D; in either cavalry or infantry; one card in fileshowed surrendered at Appomattox 9 April 1865.

Berry, Joel W. Enlisted as private/corporal on 11 June 1861 at Camp McDonald; age 21 per 3 August 1861; 28 February 1863, muster showed absent on furlough, surgeon's certificate; 30 August 1864, last muster showed AWOL since 1 August 1863.

Bevis, Levi J. (Beavis). Enlisted as private on 27 or 28 February 1862 in

Newnan, GA; 11 April 1864, muster showed on detail to GA to procure a fresh horse since 31 February 1864; October 1864 last muster showed on detail for remount horse since 2 September 1864 by order of Gen. Lee; paroled Greensboro, NC, 1 May 1865.

Bleckley, Logan E. (Bleckly). Enlisted as private on 2 August 1861 at Camp McDonald; age 34 per 31 August 1861 muster; 31 October 1861, last muster card showed absent on detached service; discharged 23 April 1862; also showed discharged 31 December 1861 by S. 0. 252, AGO 61, par. 14, no reason listed.

Bohanan, A. C. Enlisted as private on 12 or 20 September 1861 in Newnan, GA; 28 February 1863, last muster card showed present.

Box, C. W. Enlisted as private on 25 March 1862 at Hardeeville, SC; October 1864 last muster showed on detail for remount horse since 2 September 1864 by order Gen. Lee.

Boyd, And. J. (Boyed, A. J.). Enlisted as private on 26 April 1862 at LaGrange, GA; April 1864, muster showed on furlough of indulgence since 22 April 1864; October 1864 last muster card showed absent, in hands of the enemy since 11 June 1864; POW records: captured 11 June 1864 at Louisa C. H.; sent to Fortress Monroe, transferred to Point Lookout on 20 June 1864; paroled and exchanged at Point Lookout on 18 February 1865.

Bradfield, James W. Enlisted as private on 27 or 28 February 1862 in Newnan, GA; October 1864 on detail to procure a remount horse since 2 September 1864.

Bradfield, John R. Enlisted as private on 11 June 1861 or 2 August 1861 at Camp McDonald; age 20 per 31 August muster; 31 October 1861, absent on detached service; February 1864, on furlough since 21 February 1864; 11 April 1864, at brigade infirmary camp since 22 February 1864; October 1864 last muster card showed present; paroled Greensboro, NC, 1 May 1865.

Bradfield, R. P. Enlisted as private on 10 or 11 May1862 at Newnan, GA; October 1864 last muster showed present; paroled Greensboro, NC, 1 May 1865.

Branson, J. J. Cavalry or infantry, one card in file, showed captured Mine Run 4 May 1864; arrived at Elmira, NY 17 August 1864 from Point Lookout; transferred for exchange. 11 October 1864.

Brooks, A. W. Enlisted as private on 27 or 28 February 1862; at brigade infirmary camp since 20 December 1863; October 1864 last muster showed on detail for remount horse since 2 September 1864 by order Gen. Lee.

Brown, A. J. Enlisted 27 or 28 February 1862 at Newnan, GA; 11 April 1864, muster showed on detail to Georgia to procure a fresh horse since 31 February 1864; October 1864 last muster card showed "died at Lynchburg from wounds" 31 July 1864; admitted to Charlottesville Hospital on 13 June 1864, "Vulu. Sclopet. Scalp"; died at hospital of gunshot wound on 3 July 1864; widow listed as Nancy Brown.

Brown, Andrew B. Enlisted as private on 11 June 1861 or 21 August 1861 at Camp McDonald; age 43 per 31 August 1861 muster; 31 October 1861 muster showed on detached service; 1 April 1864, last muster card showed on detail to Georgia to procure a fresh horse since 31 February 1864; discharged 22 July 1864 for being over 45 years of age at discharge, light complexion, blue eyes, light hair, farmer, born in Morgan County, GA.

Brown, C. B. (Christopher). Enlisted as private on 27 February 1862 at Newnan, GA; Certificate of disability for discharge in file, dated 23 October 1862, "During the last two months, said soldier has been unfit for duty sixty days"; age listed as 29, 6', fair complexion, gray eyes, brown hair, farmer; reenlisted same company May 1864 at Camp Randolph; October 1864, absent, gone to Georgia for remount horse by order Gen. Lee 2 September 1864; paroled Greensboro, NC, 1 May 1865.

Brown, J. L. Enlisted as private on 1 or 12 September 1863 at Newnan, GA; October 1864 last muster showed on detail for remount horse since 2 September 1864 by order Gen. Lee; paroled Greensboro, NC, 1 May 1865.

Brown, P. J. (J. P., Peter). Enlisted as private on 8 March 1861 in I (Ramsey's) GA Inf., regiment disbanded 8 March 1862; reenlisted 10 May or 3 June 1862 in Co. K, PL, Newnan, GA; 28 February 1863, last muster card showed present.

Buchanan, Hugh (Buchanon, Buckhanan). Enlisted as second lieutenant/captain on 11 June 1861 at Camp McDonald; age 37 per 31 August 1861 muster, elected second lieutenant 11 June 1861; promoted First Lieutenant 9 July 1863; promoted Captain 26 August 1864; 31 August 1864 muster showed "absent wounded at Louisa C. H."; October 1864 last muster, absent wounded since 1 June 1864; report of the examining board in General Hospital No. 4 at Richmond for furlough showed date of injury 1 June 1864, "V. S. through the left lung much debilitated" given 60 day furlough, destination, Newnan, GA.

Burham, W. W. (also contains cards for Burhan, T. J.). Enlisted as private on 4 March 1862 in Newnan, GA; discharged 14 January 1863 for ulcer on left leg; October 1864 last muster card showed absent on surgeon's certificate since 7 May 1863, "Reported regularly"; information from certificate of disability for T. J. Burnham; born in Coweta County, GA, age 36 at discharge, 5' 8 1/2", dark complexion, gray eyes, dark hair, farmer. Note: muster cards show W. W. Burnham; discharge register and certificate showed T. J. Burnham (also Thomas J.) Carmichael, William D. Enlisted as private/comm. sergeant on 11 June 1861 at Camp McDonald; age 21 per 31 August 1861 muster; April 1864, muster showed absent on sick furlough Newnan, GA, since 2 July 1863; 3 August 1864, muster showed present; October 1864 last muster showed present.

Carpenter, Robert T. Enlisted as private on 27 February 1862 at Newnan, GA; one muster card dated 28 February 1863 showed present.

Carpenter, Sterling H. Enlisted as private on 11 June 1861 at Camp McDonald; age 21 per 31 August 1861 muster; October 1864 last muster card shows in hands of enemy since 18 December 1863; prisoner of war records: captured 15 December 1863 in Craig County, VA; received at Camp Chase, OH, January 1864 from Wheeling, VA; 5' 8", 24 years old, gray eyes, brown hair and fair complexion; transferred to Fort Delaware 14 March 1864, arrived 17 March 1864; paroled February 1865; exchanged 7 March 1865; died 9 March 1865 in Varina, VA.

Carter, Charles W. Enlisted as private on 10 May 1862 at Newnan, GA; 11 April 1864, muster showed on detail to Georgia to procure fresh horse 31 February 1864; April 1864, muster showed present; October 1864 last muster showed on detail for remount horse since 2 September 1864 by order of Gen. Lee; paroled Greensboro, NC, 1 May 1865.

Carter, C. R. G. Enlisted as private on 14 September 1863 at Newnan, GA; October 1864 last muster showed present; prisoner of war records: captured at Stoney Creek (state not listed) on 1 December 1864; arrived City Point, VA, on 5 December 1864 and transferred to Point Lookout, MD; oath and released 9 June 1865.

Carter, Reuben. Enlisted as private on 11 June 1861 at Camp McDonald in Company B infantry, D and K, cavalry; age 24 or 34 in December 1863; October 1864 last muster showed in hands of enemy since 18 December 1863; POW records: captured 15 December 1863 Craig County, VA, received at Camp Chase on 1 January 1864, transferred to Fort Delaware and arrived 17 March 1864; released 14 June 1865; description per POW records: 5' 10", fair complexion, brown hair, hazel eyes; shows residence as

Coweta, GA, farmer by occupation.

Carter, Welcome P. Enlisted as private on 10 or 15 May 1862 at Newnan, GA; April 1864, muster showed on detail to GA to procure a horse; October 1864 last muster showed on detail for remount horse since 2 September 1864 by order Gen. Lee; paroled Greensboro, NC, 1 May 1865.

Chatham, T. J. Enlisted as private, cavalry or infantry; POW records only; 3 July 1863, captured at Gettysburg, arrived Fort Delaware 12 July 1863; transferred to Point Lookout, MD, arrived 22 October 1863; died December 1863 at Point Lookout, no additional information.

Christian, Isaac W. (also J. W.). Enlisted as private/first lieutenant on 21 August 1861 at Camp McDonald; promoted to First Lieutenant of Company F on 16 May 1862; appointed AQM 25 June 1863; date of resignation, death, transfer, or promotion showed "declined" (some requisition forms in 1863 were signed by him as lt and A. A. Q. M); resigned on 10 January 1865 (resignation letter in file but too faint to read); October 1864 last muster card showed present.

Clemmons, J. M. Enlisted as Sergeant, Company E; cavalry or infantry; one card showed surrendered at Appomattox 4/9 1865.

Clinkscales, A. L. Enlisted as First Lieutenant, company E and N; elected First Lieutenant 12 May 1862, resigned 10/151862 for health reasons; no enlistment information; letter of resignation in file; letter from Acting Assistant Surgeon in file stating that Clinkscales would be unfit for duty for some time; suffering from jaundice in October 1862, previous suffering from attacks of "bilious and typhoid fever."

Cook, Perkins T. Enlisted as private on 27 February 1862 at Newnan, GA; October 1864 last muster card showed on detail 4 February 1864 in the infirmary camp corps, Lynchburg, VA, by order of General Stewart.

Couch, Henderson, (B. H.). Enlisted as private on 6 June 1863 at Newnan, GA; April 1864, last muster card showed on detail to Georgia to procure a horse by order Gen. Lee; no further record.

Cowan, J. W. (Cowen, Cowin). Enlisted as private on 12 May 1862 at Macon, GA; 29 February 1864–at recruiting camp since 4 February 1864; October 1864 last muster stated present; paroled Greensboro, NC, 1 May 1865.

Crocker, Evans. Enlisted as private on 5/12 or 6 August 1864, company E and N; October 1864 last muster showed sick at hospital Raleigh since 24 October 1864.

Cummings, Rockwood (Cammings, R., Cummins, Lockwood, Cummins, R.).

Enlisted 27 February 1862 in Newnan, GA; 11 April 1864, muster showed on detail to Georgia to procure a fresh horse since 31 February 1864; April 1864, muster showed AWOL since 19 April 1864 Palmetto Campbell County; 31 August 1864, muster showed AWOL; October 1864 last muster showed on detail for a remount horse since 2 September 1864 by order Gen. Lee; Prisoner of War Records: captured 13 February 1865 at Orangeburg, SC; arrived Newbern, NC, and sent to Point Lookout, MD, on 3 April 1865; oath and released 6 June 1865; admitted to U.S.A. Post Hospital, Savannah, GA, on 23 June 1865; returned to duty 28 June 1865.

Davis, David M. Enlisted as private on 13 April 1862 or 10 May 1862 in Newnan, GA; 11 April 1864, muster showed on detail to Georgia to procure a fresh horse since 31 February 1864; April 1864, muster showed present; October 1864 last muster showed on detail for remount horse since 2 September 1864 by order Gen. Lee.

Davis, E. Enlisted as private, cavalry, or infantry; one regimental return for June 1862 showed absent sick.

Davis, G. M. Enlisted as First Lieutenant on 12 May 1862 at Macon, GA; 12 May 1862, elected Third Lieutenant; 10/11862, promoted to Second Lieutenant 9/22 1863, promoted First Lieutenant, October 1864; last muster stated present.

Davis, L. C. Enlisted as private on 4 June 1864 at Newnan, GA; October 1864 last muster showed on detail for remount horse since 2 September 1864 by order Gen. Lee; age 17 per April 1864 muster; paroled Greensboro, NC, 1 May 1865.

Deracken, E. (Derackin, Elon). Enlisted as private on 12 May 1862 in Macon, GA; October 1864 last muster showed on horse detail since 2 September 1864 by order Gen. Lee.

Dial, Henry T. Enlisted as private on 27 December 1862 at Newnan, GA; April 1864, on detail to Georgia to procure a horse 5 April 1864; October 1864 last muster showed present.

Dickson, Thomas G. (Dixon/Dixson). Enlisted as private on 1 or 10 May 1862 at Newnan, GA; April 1864, on detail to Georgia to procure a fresh horse since 31 February 1864; October 1864 last muster showed on detail for remount horse since 2 September 1864 by order Gen. Lee.

Dixon, N. S. (Dickson, N. L.). Enlisted as corporal on 12 May 1862 at Macon, GA; October 1864 last muster stated captured 6 February 1864; POW records: 6 February 1864, captured Rapidan River and sent to Old Capitol

Prison, D.C.; 15 June 1864, sent to Fort Delaware, arrived 17 June 1864; no additional information.

Dunlap, S. S. Enlisted as captain, Company E on 12 May 1862, place not listed; 12 May 1862, elected captain; hospital records: wounded 3 July 1863, "V. S. forearm (flesh)"; furloughed for 30 days on 20 July 1863 from General Hospital No. 10, Richmond; resigned 31 August 1863; letter of resignation in file, resigned due to general health and stiff arm from "severe wound"; he also has a substitute (no named) already serving in Captain Smith's company, Evan's regiment, Cobb's Brigade.

Dykes, Daniel. Enlisted as private on 12 May 1862 at Macon, GA; 11 April 1864, absent on detail for horse 4 February 1864, by order Gen. Lee; 1 September 1864, left Beaver Dam Station 15 August 1864 disable, horse; October 1864 last muster showed on horse detail 2 September 1864 by order Gen. Lee; 259 information card, Daniel Dykes, Co. E, Phillips Legion, "arrested as deserter," see personal papers "C. C. Buchanan, Co. G, 4 Georgia Cav," reference card, manuscript no. 3188 "Deserter" 17 September 1863, Macon, GA (no reference to desertion on muster cards, but no cards for 1863 in file.)

Dyson, John. Enlisted as private in Company D; only record in file is a claim for a horse killed at the Battle of Williamsburg on 9 September 1862; no additional information.

Eubanks, J. H. Enlisted as private on 25 March 1862; reg. return for April 1862 shows enlisted 25 March 1862; no further information.

Eubanks, John W. Enlisted as private on 15 April 1862 at Newnan, GA; age 17 at enlistment; died 22 or 24 October 1862, typhoid fever, Richmond, VA; letter in file stated he was a farmer, light complexion, light eyes, and light hair.

Fambro, Edward A. (Fambrough). Enlisted as private on 1 October 1861 at Newnan, GA; killed in battle on 26 December 1863; left no wife or child, claim filed by widowed mother, Susan Fabrough. A letter from John Swan of Company D stated that Fambro was killed by a local citizen on Christmas night when he demanded supper at the man's house and was refused. Fambro went after the man intending to strike him on the head with his pistol but was relieved of his weapon and then shot.

Fambro, George (Fambrough, G. R. G.). Enlisted as private at Newnan, GA; 11 April 1864, muster showed "assigned to this company by orders of Gen. Lee from Co. F, 16 Georgia Battalion"; April 1864, on detail to Georgia to procure a horse since 5 April 1864; Special Order: 150/10, 28 June 1864, adjutant and inspector general's office, "Return to Comd.," Co. F, 16 Georgia Batt'n.

Fleming, William E. Enlisted as private on 21 August 1861 at Camp McDonald; age 20 per 31 August 1861 muster; October 1864 last muster showed on detail with Major Williams (Quartermaster) Dept. since 10 December 1864; paroled Greensboro, NC, 1 May 1865.

Frey, John W. Enlisted as private on 13 April 1862 at Newnan, GA; died 5 August 1863 in Augusta County, VA; no additional information.

Gentry, William J. Enlisted as private on 3 or 4 March 1862 at Newnan, GA; 11 April 1864, last muster card showed present; paroled Greensboro, NC, 1 May 1865.

Gerrold, William H. Enlisted as private on 12 or 20 September 1861 at Newnan, GA; April 1864, on detail to Georgia to procure a horse since 5 April 1864; October 1864 last muster showed on detail for remount horse since 2 September 1864 by order Gen. Lee.

Gibson, Joel W. T. Enlisted as private on 20 June 1861 at Camp McDonald; age 18, per 31 August 1861 muster; 31 October 1861, last muster card showed absent sick.

Gibson, Samuel. Enlisted as private on 20 June 1861 at Camp McDonald; age 27 per 31 August 1861 muster; 31 October 1861, last muster card showed absent sick.

Graham, L. W. Enlisted as private in Company D; cavalry or infantry; one card in file showed paroled at Farmville, Virginia between 11 and 27 April 1865.

Grimes, Frederick. Enlisted as private on 27 February 1862 at Newnan, GA; 11 April 1864, on detail to Georgia to procure a fresh horse since 31 February 1864; October 1864 last muster showed present; paroled Greensboro, NC, 1 May 1865.

Grimes, Harverd (Harbert). Enlisted as private on 3 or 4 March 1862 at Newnan, GA; October 1864 last muster showed on detail for remount horse since 2 September 1864 by order Gen. Lee; paroled Greensboro, NC, 1 May 1865.

Grimes, Travis. Enlisted as private on 26 March 1863 at Camp Randolph; 11 April 1864, on detail to Georgia to procure a fresh horse since 31 February 1864; October 1864 last muster showed on detail for remount horse since 2 September 1864 by order Gen. Lee; paroled Greensboro, NC, 1 May 1865.

Hackney, R. G. (Hackeney). Enlisted as private on 1 or 31 July 1863 at Newnan, GA; April 1864, on detail in Georgia to procure a fresh horse since 31

February 1864; October 1864 last muster card showed present; paroled Greensboro, NC, 1 May 1865.

Hackny, Thomas B. (Hackney). Enlisted as private on 11 or 20 June 1861 at Camp McDonald; age 30 per 31 August 1861 muster; 31 October 1861, absent on detached service; 25 February 1863, last muster card showed present.

Hackny, William (Hackney). Enlisted as private on 11 June 1861 at Newnan, GA; age 31 per 31 August 1861 muster; 31 August 1861, absent sick; 11 September 1861, muster showed absent with leave; 31 October 1861, absent sick; died 8 November 1861 at Newnan, GA, "leaving neither wife nor child," claim made by father, Richard M. Hackney; statement by Captain Long stated that William was age 32 at his death, by occupation a mechanic, 5' 11", dark complexion and dark eyes; cause of death not listed.

Ham, J. G. Enlisted as private on 20 February 1863 at Newnan, GA; October 1864 last muster card stated surgeons certificate, wounded since 7 July 1863; not reported in three months.

Hammack, James W. Enlisted as private in Company D, cavalry or infantry; no enlistment information; first appeared on a register of medical director's office, Richmond, VA; 8 May 1863 "assigned to temporary duty at G. H. No. 9. Subsistence and quarters will be furnished them at the hospital until further notice." POW record showed captured at Amelia Court House 6 April 1865; sent to Point Lookout, MD, from City Point, VA, arrived 14 April 1865; oath and released 28 June 1865; oath stated place of residence Polk County, GA, complexion dark, hair dark brown, eyes hazel, 5' 10".

Hammond, C. M. Enlisted as private on 11 June 1861 at Camp McDonald, age 22 per 31 August 1861 muster; April 1864, absent on detail in GA to procure a fresh horse; 31 August 1864, AWOL in Coweta County, GA, since 12 May 1864; October 1864 last muster card stated AWOL since 12 June 1864, "In service as Lieut. with Georgia Reserves."

Hammond, E. F. Enlisted as private on 4 March 1862 at Newnan, GA; one card 28 February 1863 muster showed present (may be same as Elijah Q. Hammond but different enlistment dates.)

Hammond, Elijah, Q. Enlisted as private on 11 June 1861; February 1864, on furlough since 21 February 1864; April 1864, on detail to Georgia to procure a horse; October 1864 last muster showed AWOL since 7 August 1864.

HA.N.V.ey, James E. (Harvey, J.C.). Enlisted as private on 11 June 1861 at Camp McDonald; age 21 per 31 August 1861 muster; April 1864, on detail in GA to procure a horse since 31 February 1864; October 1864 last muster card showed absent on horse detail since 9 February 1864.

HA.N.V.ey, Sherwood P. Enlisted as private on 27 July 862 at Newnan, GA; one muster card dated 28 February 1863 showed present; Special Order: No. 202/11, Adjutant and Inspector General's Office, 2 August 1863 "Transfer to Co. A, 12 Bn, GA Art'y."

Hardegree, John T. Enlisted as private on 27 February 1864 at Newnan, GA; 11 April 1864, on detail to Georgia to procure a fresh horse since 23 February 1864; October 1864 last muster showed present, wagoner for Phillips Legion since 20 October 1863; paroled Greensboro, NC, 1 May 1865.

Harris, C. J. Enlisted as private on 12 March 1864 at Newnan, GA; October 1864 last muster showed on detail for remount horse since 2 September 1864 by order Gen. Lee.

Hearndon, Preston, A. (Herndon). Enlisted as private/1st sergeant on 11 or 20 June 1861 at Camp McDonald; age 23 per 31 August 1861 muster; 11 April 1864, on detail to procure a fresh horse since 31 February 1864; October 1864 last muster showed absent on horse detail at Lynchburg, VA, since 2 September 1864 by order Gen. Lee; paroled Greensboro, NC, 1 May 1865.

Henderson, James N. Enlisted as private in 1862 in Newnan, GA; October 1864 last muster showed on detail for remount horse since 2 September 1864.

Hendricks, J. W. (Hendrix). Enlisted as private on 12 March 1864 at Newnan, GA; age 17 per April 1864 muster; October 1864 last muster stated on detail for remount since 2 September 1864 by order Gen. Lee; admitted to CSA G. H. No. 11, Charlotte, NC, on 6 February 1865 for scabies; paroled at the hospital 7 May 1865.

Herring, H. E. Enlisted as private on 20 April 1862 at LaGrange, GA; 1 January 1864, first muster card showed assigned since muster, transferred from infantry; 11 April 1864, on detail to Georgia to procure a fresh horse since 31 February 1864; October 1864 last muster card showed on detached service by order Gen. Lee since 2 September 1864.

Herring, William. Enlisted as private on 16 December 1862 at Newnan, GA; October 1864 last muster showed on detail with Major Walton since 28 March 1864; paroled Greensboro, NC, 1 May 1865.

Hicks, James A. Enlisted as private on 27 August 1862 at Newnan, GA; February 1864, muster stated in the hands of the enemy since 2 July 1863; 11 April 1864, muster stated on furlough since 23 March 1864; October 1864 last muster card showed on detail for remount horse since 2 September

1864; POW records: captured 8 July 1863 at Funktown; 17 August 1863, admitted to U.S.A. G. H. at Frederick, MD, for G. S. F. (gunshot flesh), wound right thigh; paroled at Fort McHenry, MD, in August and sent to Point Lookout, MD, on 2 August 1863; 27 November 1863, transferred to Hammond G. H., Point Lookout, MD, on 21 August 1863; 17 March 1864, sent to Major Mulford for exchange; POW records showed age 40 at time of capture.

Higgins, B. C. Enlisted as private in Company D, cavalry or infantry; one card showed admitted to Jackson Hospital, Richmond, VA, on 18 August 1864; returned to duty 9 February 1864; no additional information; (appears to be the same soldier below, both were admitted to the hospital on 18 August 1864 and both returned to duty on 9 February 1864).

Higgins, Griffin. Enlisted as private/farrier on 12 September 1861 at Newnan, GA; age not listed; October 1864 last muster card showed present; 18 August 1864, admitted to Jackson Hospital, Richmond, VA, for debilitas, ret. to duty 9 February 1864.

Hodges, John R. Enlisted as private on 11 June 1861 at Camp McDonald; age 24 per 31 August 1861 muster; 28 February 1863, last muster card showed present.

Hodges, Phillips S. (Seth). Enlisted as private on 20 September 1861 at Newnan, GA; October 1864 last muster showed in hands of enemy since 9 July 1863 (date must be in error); POW records: 24 May 1863, captured at Warrenton, VA, sent to Fairfax Court House and transferred to Old Capitol Prison, Washington, D.C.; 10 June 1863, paroled at Old Capitol Prison; no additional record.

Hood, Joseph W. Enlisted as private on 13 April or 10 May 1862 at Newnan, GA; October 1864 last muster card showed on detail for remount horse since 2 September 1864.

Houston, William. Enlisted as private on 27 February 1862 at Newnan, GA; 11 April 1864, on detail to Georgia to procure a fresh horse since 31 February 1864; October 1864 last muster card showed on detail for remount horse since 2 September 1864; paroled Greensboro, NC, 1 May 1865.

Howell, G. W. Enlisted as private, cavalry or infantry, company K, one card, regimental return dated June 1862 showed absent sick.

Hubbard, John R. Enlisted as private on 20 June 1861 at Camp McDonald; age 18 per 31 August 1861 muster; 13 October 1861, died at White Sulpher Springs; no additional information.

Hubbard, Joseph. Enlisted as private/sergeant on 2 September 1861 at Newnan, GA; age not listed; April 1864, on detail to Georgia to procure a horse; October 1864 absent to procure a remount horse to Georgia since 2 September 1864 by order Gen. Lee; (31 October 1861 muster showed him as private, 28 February 1863 muster showed him as 4th corp., and 11 October 1864 showed him as 3rd sgt.)

Hughs, J. D. Enlisted as private on 7 May 1862 at Newnan, GA; 1 January 1864, muster stated "assigned to this company by order of Gen. Lee"; April 1864, on detail to Georgia to procure a fresh horse since 5 April 1864; Special Order No. 150/10, 28 June 1864, Adjutant and Inspector General's Office "Return to Comd., Co. F, 16 GA Bn."

Hunter, John A. Enlisted as private on 28 or 29 July 1862 in Newnan, GA; 11 April 1864, absent on sick furlough since 15 March 1863; 31 August 1864, muster showed present; October 1864 last muster showed assigned to light duty with Major Walton since 19 October 1864; hospital record showed hospitalized at Charlotteville, VA, on 12 January 1863, sent to Small Pox Hospital 16 January 1863 and "back to house February 28 1863 nurse"; furloughed for five days 14 March 1863; paroled at Greensboro, NC, 1 May 1865.

Hunter, Richard L. Enlisted as private on 27 February 1862 at Newnan, GA; April 1864, on detail to procure a horse; October 1864 on detail for remount horse since 2 September 1864.

Jackson, A. J. Enlisted as private on 15 March 1864 at Newnan, GA; age 17 per April 1864 muster; October 1864 last muster card stated present; paroled Greensboro, NC, 1 May 1865.

Jackson, Thomas J. Enlisted as private/corporal on 11 June 1861 at Camp McDonald; age 21 per 31 August 1861 muster; 31 October 1861, muster stated on detached service; 11 April 1864, muster stated at Brigade Infirmary Camp since 20 December 1863; October 1864 last muster stated present; paroled Greensboro, NC, 1 May 1865; (28 February 1863 muster showed Jackson as private, next muster dated 1 January 1864 showed 3rd corporal).

Jacobs, George, R. Enlisted as private on 3/3 or 4 March 1862 at Newnan, GA; 11 April 1864, on detail to GA to procure a fresh horse since 31 February 1864; October 1864 gone to GA for remount horse by order Gen. Lee since 2 September 1864; paroled Greensboro, NC, 1 May 1865.

Jacobs, James T. Enlisted as private on 10 March 1862 at Newnan, GA; April 1864, on detail to GA to procure a horse; October 1864 last muster showed on detail for remount horse since 2 September 1864 by order Gen. Lee.

Johnson, James C. Enlisted as private on 10 May 1862 at Newnan, GA; 11 April 1864, on detail to Georgia to procure a fresh horse since 31 February 1864; October 1864 last muster card showed present; paroled Greensboro, NC, 1 May 1865.

Johnson, L. A. Enlisted as private on 13 April 1862 at Newnan, GA; October 1864 last muster stated in hands of enemy since 29 February 1864; POW records: captured 29 February 1864 at Rapidan River, VA; sent to Old Capitol Prison in Washington, D.C. and then on to Fort Delaware, DE, arrived at Fort Delaware 17 June 1864; no additional information.

Johnson, William. Enlisted as private on 1 August 1862 at Newnan, GA; February 1864, muster stated regimental teamster since 31 February 1864; October 1864 last muster card showed on detail as teamster for Capt. Lumpkin since 15 September 1864; paroled Greensboro, NC, 1 May 1865.

Johnson, William P. Enlisted as private on 10 March 1862 at Newnan, GA; 11 April 1864, muster stated on detail with Major Walton as ambulance driver since 20 July 1864.

Kennedy, William S. Enlisted as private/corporal on 11 or 20 June 1861 at Camp McDonald; age 22 per 31 August 1861 muster; 11 April 1864 muster stated on detail to Georgia to procure a fresh horse since 31 February 1864; October 1864 last muster showed on detail for remount horse since 2 September 1864 by order Gen. Lee; paroled Greensboro, NC, 1 May 1865; (31 August 1864 muster showed him as 2nd corporal, 11 October 1864 muster showed him as private).

Lands, Patrick (P. B., B. P., Bevin, P.). Enlisted as private on 20 September 1861 at Newnan, GA; 31 October 1861, muster stated absent sick; June 1862, muster showed absent sick, died 24 May 1862, "left neither wife nor child"; claim filed by mother, Elizabeth C. Land.

Lavender, George E. Enlisted as private on 9 March 1862 or 27 February 1863 at Newnan, GA; October 1864 last muster showed present; paroled Greensboro, NC, 5/1/1865.

Leigh, Meriwether S. Enlisted as private on 11 or 20 June 1861 at Camp McDonald; age 18 per 31 August 1861 muster; 11 April 1864, muster stated on detail to Georgia to procure a fresh horse since 31 February 1864, last muster showed present although he had already been transferred; Special Order; No. 177/30, 28 July 1864, Adjutant and Inspector General's Office, Transferred Co. A, 12 GA Bn. Lt. Arty.

Lester, Thomas (Thomas D., T. M.) Enlisted as private on 27 February 1862 at Newnan, GA; 11 April 1864, on detail to GA to procure a fresh horse since 31 February 1864; April 1864, absent on sick furlough at Newnan, GA; 31 August 1864, AWOL since 12 July 1864; last muster showed present.

Lewis, Thomas W. Rank and enlistment information not shown; cavalry or infantry; one card, appeared on list of prisoners confined to military prison at Wheeling, VA; also notes sent to Camp Chase 31 December 1863; arrested 15 December 1863; Craig County, VA; age 22, 6' 1", dark complexion, dark hair, hazel eyes, farmer by occupation.

Long, Robert L. Y. Enlisted as captain on 11 or 20 June 1861 at Camp McDonald; age 36 per 31 August 1861 muster; 30 March 1864, tendered resignation, wife sick with consumption (in contrast to the age on the 31 August 1861 muster, Long stated he was over 45 years of age and has been a physician for the last 23 years); resignation effective 26 April 1864, S. O. 97; information cards indicate two court martial records: I. G. O. No. 90 HQ Dept. Northern VA, 25 September 1863; 2, Special Order 13/93 – 17/10 1863, Adjutant and Inspector General's Office.

Long, William L. Enlisted as private at Camp McDonald; age 20 per 31 August 1861 muster; 1 January 1864, muster stated AWOL since 24 October 1863; 11 April 1864, muster stated on detail to Georgia to procure a fresh horse since 31 February 1864; October 1864, last muster stated on detail for remount horse since 2 September 1864 by order Gen. Lee.

Lynch, Elijah, O. (Linch, E. O.). Enlisted as private on 11 or 20 June 1861 at Camp McDonald; age 25 per 31 August 1861 muster; 11 April 1864, last muster showed present; Special Order No. 1125 August, 5 February 1864, Adjutant and Inspector General's Office "Transferred to C. S. Navy."

Mainus, George W. (Manis, Manus). Enlisted as private/bugler on 11 or 20 June 1861 at Camp McDonald; age 29 per 31 August 1861 muster; 28 February 1863, showed on detached service by order of War Department; 11 April 1864, on detail in Georgia to procure a horse since 31 February 1864; April 1864, on detail in Georgia to procure a horse 31 February 1864; April 1864, detailed in Gov. Shop by order Secretary of War, Athens, GA, 7 March 1864, S. O. No. 55; 11 October 1864, last muster detailed in Athens, GA, by order Secretary War, S.O. 55; Special Order No. 260/8, 6 November 1862, Adj. and Inspec. Gen. Off, "Detailed"; Special Order No.55/29, 7 March 1864, Adj. and Inspec. Gen. Off. "Detailed for Duty"; letter in file dated 11 October 1862 from Columbus Hughes for Cooke and Brothers Rifles Factory requesting that Private Mainus be detailed to work in their factory for 60 to 90 days.

Martin, John N. (Morten, Morton). Enlisted as Corporal on 20 June 1861 at Camp McDonald; age 29 per 31 August 1861 muster; 31 October 1861, last muster card showed absent sick; no additional information.

Meachum, C. W. Enlisted as private on 1 May 1863 at Newnan, GA; October 1864 last muster showed in hands of enemy since 18 December 1863; no additional information.

Meachum, James M. Enlisted as private on 21 September 1861; April 1864, on detail to procure a horse by order Gen. Lee; October 1864, last muster showed on detail for remount horse since 2 September 1864 by order Gen. Lee.

Meadows, O. W. (W. O., Medows). Enlisted as private on 14 March 1861; April 1864, muster stated "Recruit 17 years of age," 31 August 1864 absent on sick furlough; 11 October 1864, on sick furlough since 25 July and extended 20 September; not heard from since; October 1864 last muster card showed AWOL since 20 September 1864; paroled Greensboro, NC, 1 May 1865.

Medaris, Fletcher. Enlisted as private on 11 or 20 June 1861 at Camp McDonald; age 40 per 31 August 1861 muster; 30 August 1861 muster showed Farrier and Blacksmith; April 1864, last muster showed present: Special Order No. 168/8, 19 July 1863, Dept. and Army of N. VA, R. E. Lee "served out term of Enlisted 45 years of age dischgd"; discharge papers stated 45 years of age at discharge, dark complexion, dark eyes, dark gray hair, 5' 11", blacksmith by occupation and born in Coweta County, GA.

Meriwether, Joseph R. (Merrewether). Enlisted as private on 11 or 20 June 1861 at Camp McDonald; age 24 per 31 August 1861 muster; 11 April 1864, on detail to procure a fresh horse since 23 February 1864; October 1864 last muster card showed on detail with Major Walton since 5 June 1864; paroled Greensboro 1 May 1865.

Meriwether, W. D. Enlisted as private on 20 February 1863 at Newnan, GA; 11 April 1864, on detail to procure a fresh horse since 31 February 1864, last muster card showed on detail for remount horse since 2 September 1864 by order Gen. Lee.

Merrill, James B. (Merrell). Enlisted as private on 6 July 1861 at Camp McDonald; age 17 per 31 August 1861 muster; 31 October 1861, last muster showed absent sick; April 1862, regimental return showed AWOL; May 1862 regimental return showed AWOL; June 1862, showed absent with leave from Gen. Pemberton.

Merritt, James D. Enlisted as private in Company D; cavalry or infantry, POW records: 23 May 1864, captured at Mt. Carmel Church, sent to Point Lookout, MD, on 30 May 1864, transferred to Elmira on 23 July 1864; appeared on a Roll or Prisoners of War at Elmira, NY, desirous to take the Oath of Allegiance to the United States, 30 September 1864. Remarks: "Was desirous to take the Oath of Allegiance to the United States, 30 September 1864. Was conscripted July 20 1863. He determined to desert at the first opportunity as he had opposed the war and loved the old Union. He voluntarily surrendered to the 1st Michigan Cavalry at Mt. Carmel Church, Caroline County, VA." Oath and released 17 May 1865.

Millirons, R. M. Enlisted as private on 14 March 1864 at Newnan, GA; 17 years of age per April 1864 muster; October 1864 last muster showed on horse detail since 12 September 1864; paroled Greensboro, NC, 1 May 1865.

Mitchum, Charles W. Enlisted as private in Company D; no enlistment information; POW records: arrested Craig County, VA, on 14 December 1863, sent to Camp Chase, OH, forwarded to Fort Delaware, DE, on 14 March 1864; oath and released 15 June 1865 by G. O. 109; age 18 at arrest, dark complexion, dark eyes, dark hair, 5' 10", farmer by occupation; resident of Merriweather County, GA (per arrest record). Note: record of oath described him light hair light complexion, and gray eyes, 5' 7".

Moore, Beverly F. Enlisted 20 June 1861 at Camp McDonald; age 28 per 31 August 1861 muster; elected 2nd lieutenant on 16 June 1862; May 1862, regimental return showed AWOL; June 1862, regimental return showed absent with leave from Gen. Pemberton; 18 December 1862, died of disease near Culpeper Court House, VA; claim presented by father, William W. Moore.

Moore, B. J. Enlisted as private on 7 February 1864 at Newnan, GA; 11 October 1864, muster showed on sick furlough; October 1864 last muster card showed AWOL since 6 October 1864.

Moore, Joseph (J. S.) No enlistment information; 31 August 1864, muster showed at sick at hospital (Richmond); Hosp. records state admitted to Jackson Hospital, Richmond, 23 August 1864, for "Febris Remt"; paroled Greensboro, NC, 1 May 1865.

Moore, Thomas J. Enlisted as private on 17 or 27 December 1862 at Newnan, GA; February 1864 on furlough 30 days since 12 February 1864, transferred to Navy; Special Order No. 113/4, Dept. of Army of N. VA, R. E. Lee, 25

April 1864, "trans. Navy," Special Order No. 1125 August, Adj. and Inspec. Gen Office, 21 May 1864, "Transferred."

Moore, William J. Enlisted as private on 11 or 20 June 1861 at Camp McDonald, company F, D, K, P; age 18 per 31 August 1861 muster; October 1864 last muster card stated present; paroled Greensboro, NC, 1 May 1865.

Neely, D. C. Enlisted as private on 27 February 1862 in Newnan, GA; April 1864, on detail to Georgia to procure a horse by order Gen. Lee; October 1864 last muster stated on detail for remount horse since 2 September 1864 by order Gen. Lee; paroled Greensboro, NC, 1 May 1865.

Neely, N. D. Enlisted as private in Company K; cavalry or infantry; reg. return for June 1862 showed absent sick; no further information.

Nimmons, William B. Enlisted as bugler on 27 or 28 February 1862 at Newnan, GA; 11 April 1864, on detail to Georgia to procure a fresh horse since 23 February 1864; October 1864 last muster showed sick at Jackson Hospital for dysentaria, return to duty 30 September 1864; 11 October 1864, admitted to Jackson Hospital for dysentaria, return to duty 11 November 1864.

Nunn, William W. (Noun). Enlisted as private on 11 or 20 June 1861 at Camp McDonald; age 28 per 31 August 1861 muster; October 1864 last muster card stated in hands of the enemy since 18 December 1863; died 27 June 1865 at U.S. Post Hospital in Savannah, GA, "Diarrhea Ch"; POW records: arrested 15 December 1863 in Craig County, VA, sent to Camp Chase, forwarded to Fort Delaware 14 March 1864; oath and released 7 June 1865; POW card showed age at arrest as 30, light complexion, light hair, blue eyes, 5' 7", place of residence Coweta, GA, and farmer by occupation; oath record showed dark complexion, brown hair, gray eyes, 5' 11".

Owens, Ruben. Enlisted as private on 27 February or 4 March 1862 at Newnan, GA; admitted to Jackson Hospital, Richmond, on 21 April 1864 for rubeola, returned to duty 14 June 1864; October 1864 last muster card showed present; paroled Greensboro, NC, 1 May 1865.

Parks, John J. Enlisted as private on 27 February 1862 at Newnan, GA; October 1864 last muster card stated in hospital at Liberty, VA, since 21 June 1864; hospital records: 1 July 1864, admitted to General Hospital Petersburg, VA, for chronic diarrhea.

Parks, Thomas B. (Parkes). Enlisted as private on 26 or 29 July 1862 at Newnan, GA; 11 April 1864, on detail to Georgia to procure a horse since 31 February 1864; October 1864 last muster showed on detail for remount horse since 2 September 1864 by order of Gen. Lee; paroled Greensboro, NC, 1 May

1865.

Pearce, John W. (Pierce). Enlisted as 3rd lieutenant/2nd lieutenant on 20 June 1861 at Camp McDonald; age 36 per 31 August 1861 muster; elected 2nd lieutenant 1 July 1861; resigned 11 November 1862 "unfit for military service," "disease of the spine."

Pearson, F. Enlisted as private in Company K; cavalry or infantry; regimental return showed enlisted 10 May 1862 in Newnan, GA; no other information.

Perkins, John A. (Pirkens, Purkins). Enlisted as private 30 July 1861 at Newnan, GA, in 7 Georgia Infantry, Co. A; enlisted 4 March 1862 as private in Phillips Legion cavalry, f p. D; 11 April 1864, on detail to Georgia to procure a fresh horse since 31 February 1864; October 1864 last muster stated on detail for remount horse since 9 February 1864 by order Gen. Lee; paroled Greensboro, NC, 1 May 1865.

Perkins, R. B. (Pirkens, Purkins). Enlisted as private (age 25) on 31 May 1861 in 7 Georgia Infantry, Co. A; 14 January 1863, transferred to Phillips Legion cavalry by exchange; October 1864 last muster showed on detail for remount horse since 2 September 1864 by order Gen. Lee.

Perry, James P. (Joseph H.). Enlisted as private in Company D on 27 February 1862 at Newnan, GA; October 1864 last muster card stated in hands of enemy since 18 December 1863; POW records: 15 December 1863, arrested in Craig County, VA, sent to Camp Chase, OH, and then forwarded to Fort Delaware on 14 March 1864; oath and released 7 June 1865; oath records list residence as Coweta County, GA, sallow complexion, brown hair, hazel eyes, 5' 5", farmer by occupation, age 18 at time of arrest; (Camp Chase POW records describe him as 5' 7", blue eyes, dark hair, light complexion).

Perry, W. C. Enlisted as private on 13, 24, or 25 July 1864 at Newnan, GA; October 1864 last muster card showed in the hospital sick since 29 September 1864; 6 February 1865, admitted to CSA Hospital No. 11 at Charlotte, NC, and "sent to other hospitals" on 22 February 1864; no additional information.

Perry, William H. Enlisted as private on 11 or 20 June 1861 at Camp McDonald; age 19 per 31 August 1861 muster; October 1864 last muster reported in hands of enemy since 4 January 1864; POW records: captured 29 February 1864 at the Rapidan River; sent to Old Capitol Prison in D.C. and transferred to Fort Delaware on 17 June 1864; no additional information.

Perry, William O. Enlisted as private/corporal on 6 June 1863 at Newnan, GA; April 1864, last muster stated present; paroled Greensboro, NC, 1 May 1865;

(31 August 1864 muster showed rank of private, 1 October 1864 muster showed rank of 4th corporal.)

Persons, A. J. Enlisted as private on 27 February 1862 in Newnan, GA; 11 April 1864, on detail to Georgia to procure a fresh horse since 31 February 1864; October 1864 last muster showed on detail for remount horse since 2 September 1864 by order Gen. Lee.

Persons, Henry T. (Henry J.). No enlistment information; 24 May 1863, arrested in Warrenton, VA, charges "Rebel Soldier"; sent to Old Capitol Prison in D.C. on 28 May 1863; 10 June 1863, paroled at Old Capitol Prison.

Petty, J. M. T. (Pettey). Enlisted as private on 4 March 1862 at Newnan, GA; April 1864, detached corps hdqrs. as wagoner 30 November 1863 by order Gen. Stuart; October 1864 last muster stated on detail with Stuart's horse artillery as teamster.

Pullen, Sebastian, C. Enlisted as private on 11 June 1861 at Camp McDonald; age 21 per 31 August 1861 muster; 11 April 1864; on detail to Georgia to procure a fresh horse since 31 February 1864; October 1864 last muster stated on detail for remount horse since 2 September 1864 by order Gen. Lee; paroled Greensboro, NC, 1 May 1865.

Pullen, S. H. Enlisted as private on 27 December 1862 in Newnan, GA; 31 August 1864 muster showed AWOL since 8 August 1864; October 1864 last muster showed present; paroled Greensboro, NC, 1 May 1865.

Rainey, Ethelred (Rainy, Rany, also filed as C. Rainy). Enlisted as private on 20 June 1861 at Camp McDonald; age 41 per 31 August 1861 muster; 29 October 1862, discharged for disability, Staunton, VA, no reason provided; born in Jackson County, VA, fair complexion, gray eyes, dark hair, a painter by occupation.

Ramsey, J. A. Enlisted as private on 11 August 1864, cavalry or infantry; 11 August 1864, admitted to Jackson Hospital, Richmond; appeared on list of passports issued from Jackson Hospital, 31 August 1864, destination, Jonesborough, GA.

Ransom, J. J. (Ranson). Enlisted as private on May 1861 or 15 June 1861 at LaGrange, GA; October 1864 last muster card stated in the hands of the enemy since 4 May 1864; POW record indicated captured 4 May 1864 at Mine Run, VA; sent to Point Lookout, MD, and transferred to Elmira, NY, 15 August 1864.

Ransom, William J. Enlisted as 1 sergeant/2 lieutenant on 11 or 20 June 1861 at Camp McDonald; age 33 per 31 August 1861 muster; promoted to 2nd lieutenant 25 April 1864; October 1864 last muster stated present.

Roberts, W. H. Enlisted as private on 12 or 20 September 1861 at Newnan, GA; October 1864 last muster stated present.

Robertson, J. R. Enlisted as private, no enlistment information; cavalry or infantry; hospital Records: 13 October 1862, 30 day furlough, hospital No. 8, Richmond, VA; 10 July 1864, admitted to Jackson Hospital for rubeola, furloughed 18 August 1864 for 30 days; no additional information.

Robinson, A. J. (Andrew, Robison). Enlisted as private on 1 March 1862 at Newnan, GA; Special Order: No. 309/3, Dept. and Army N. VA, Lee, 16 December 1863, "Transferred to Co. B, 4 GA Infantry in exchange for Henry Heming," transfer to take effect 1 January 1864.

Robinson, George M. (George W.). Enlisted as private on 2 or 9 August 1861 at Camp McDonald; age 26 per 31 August 1861 muster; 31 October 1861, last muster showed present; May 1862, regimental return stated absent with leave.

Robinson, James T. Enlisted as private on 4 March 1862 at Newnan, GA; October 1864 last muster card stated in hands of enemy since 29 February 1864; POW records: captured 29 February 1864, captured at Rapidan River, forwarded to Old Capitol Prison in D.C. then sent to Fort Delaware 15 June 1864; died 6 January 1865 at Fort Delaware of chronic diarrhea; location grave, Jersey Shore.

Robinson, J. H. (Robison). Enlisted as private on 15 April 1862 at Newnan, GA; April 1864, on detail in Georgia to procure a horse by order Gen. Lee; October 1864 last muster card stated present; paroled Greensboro, NC, 1 May 1865.

Robinson, R. Enlisted as private in Company K; cavalry or infantry; one card, regimental return dated June 1862, showed with leave from Gen. Pemberton.

Roland, James T. (Rolland, Rowland). Enlisted as private on 17, 22, or 27 December 1862 at Newnan, GA; 31 August 1864, on detached service by order Gen. Stewart; October 1864 last muster showed present; paroled Greensboro, NC, 1 May 1865.

Russell, J. W. H. Enlisted as private on 27 February 1862 at Newnan, GA; April 1864, on detail in Georgia to procure a horse; October 1864 last muster showed on detail for remount horse since 2 September 1864 by order Gen. Lee.

Saxon, Thomas W. (T. W.). Enlisted as private on 27 February 1862 at Newnan, GA; October 1864 last muster stated on detail with pontoon train A.N.V.

since 1 July 1863 by order Gen. Lee.

Scott, R. Enlisted as private in Company D; cavalry or infantry; no enlistment information; 25 July 1864, admitted to Jackson Hospital, Richmond, for "Diarrhea ac"; furloughed 5 August 1864 for 30 days; no additional information.

Scroggins, Glenn O. Enlisted as private on 11 or 21 June 1861 at Camp McDonald; age 21 per 31 August 1861 muster; 11 April 1864, on detail to go to Georgia to procure a fresh horse since 31 February 1864; October 1864 last muster showed on detail for remount horse since 2 September 1864 by order Gen. Lee.

Sewell, C. P. Enlisted as private on 14 September 1863 at Newnan, GA; 1 January 1864, muster stated "Recruit enlisted under 18 years of age"; October 1864 last muster stated present; paroled Greensboro, NC, 1 May 1865.

Sewell, James M. (J. M.). Enlisted as private on 27 January 1863 at Newnan, GA; died 7 September 1863 of typhoid fever, General Hospital, Hanover Academy, VA; claim made by father, Francis Sewell, on 1 November 7 1863 stated that James left neither wife nor child.

Sewell, J. N. Enlisted as private on 12 or 20 September 1861 at Newnan, GA; April 1864, muster showed on detail in Georgia to procure a horse; October 1864 last muster card showed present; paroled Greensboro, NC, 1 May 1865.

Sewell, John R. Enlisted as private on 14 February, 14 March, or 14 April 1862 at Newnan, GA; October 1864 , last muster card stated absent wounded since 13 September 1863 (no reporting), shot through lung and disabled September 1863.

Sewell, Levi F. Enlisted as private on 11 June or 30 July 1861 at Camp McDonald in Company D; age 21 per 31 August 1861 muster; October 1864 last muster card showed present.

Sewell, Thomas W. Enlisted as private on 16 March or 15 April 1862 at Newnan, GA; October 1864 last muster card stated in hands of enemy since 18 December 1863; POW records: arrested Craig County, VA, 15 December 1863; sent to Camp Chase, OH, 1 January 1864, transferred to Ford Delaware 14 March 1864; oath and released 16 June 1865; place of residenct, Campbell County, GA, 6', dark complexion, dark hair, gray eyes.

Simms, W. H. Enlisted as private on 27 February 1862 in Newnan, GA; died 26 November 1862 typhoid fever, General Hospital No. 25, Richmond, VA.

Sims, M. W. T. Enlisted as private on 27 February 1862 at Newnan, GA; 1

January 1864, muster stated transferred from artillery; 11 April 1864, on detail to Georgia to procure a fresh horse since 31 February 1864; October 1864 muster stated gone home to Georgia for remount horse by order Gen. Lee 2 September 1864; paroled Greensboro, NC, 1 May 1865.

Sims, Nathan G. (N. J.). Enlisted as private/corporal, Company B and D (see company B roster).

Smith, Ira E. C. W. Enlisted as private on 10 July or 21 August 1861 at Camp McDonald; age 21 per 31 August 1861 muster; 31 October 1861 muster showed absent sick; register of payments to discharged soldiers showed discharged 11 March1862; reenlisted 15 May or 15 September 1862; 31 August 1864, muster stated AWOL since 9 January 1864; October 1864 last muster stated AWOL since 12 June 1864, in service as lieutenant in Georgia reserves.

Smith, W. L. Enlisted as private on 9 July 1864 at Atlanta; October 1864 last muster stated on detail for remount horse since 2 September 1864 by order Gen. Lee; paroled Greenboro, NC, 1 May 1865.

Springer, R. H. Enlisted as private in Company K; cavalry or infantry; one card, regimental return dated May 1862 showed enlisted at Newnan, GA, on 10 May 1862.

Steed, John T. Enlisted as private on 27 February 1862 at Newnan, GA; October 1864 last muster card stated on detail for remount horse since 2 September 1864.

Story, Edward M. (Storey). Enlisted as first lieutenant on 11 or 20 June 1861 at Camp McDonald; age 26 per 31 August 1861 muster; elected second lieutenant 11 June 1861; elected first lieutenant on 1 July 1861; 9 July 1863, KIA Funktown, MD.

Story, W. F. (Storey). Enlisted as private on 12 March 1864 at Newnan, GA; October 1864 last muster stated on detail for remount horse since 2 September 1864 by order Gen. Lee; paroled Greensboro, NC, 1 May 1865.

Summer, James H. Enlisted as private on 27 February 1864 at Newnan, GA; February 1864, on detail to Georgia to procure a horse since 31 February 1864; October 1864 last muster stated on detail for remount horse since 2 September 1864 by order Gen. Lee; paroled Greensboro, 1 May 1865.

Summers, William (W. F.). Enlisted as private on 25 July 1861 at Camp McDonald; 31 August 1861 muster showed present in Company B, Rifle Battalion; 31 October 1861, muster showed present in Company D, Cavalry Battalion; 14 April 1864, on detail in Georgia to procure a fresh horse since

31 February 1864; October 1864 last muster showed present; paroled Greensboro, NC, 1 May 1865.

Swan, J. T. Enlisted as private at Conyers, GA: October 1864 last muster card showed prisoner in hands of enemy since May 1864, POW records: captured 29 February 1864 at Rapidan River, sent to Old Capital Prison, D.C. and transferred to Fort Delaware, arrived on 17 June 1864; transferred to City Point for exchange.

Talbot, James R. Enlisted as private on 1 March 1862 at Newnan, GA; 28 February 1863, only muster card in file showed present.

Taylor, S. J. Enlisted as private at Conyers, GA; 31 August 1864, muster showed absent sick at hospital in Columbia, SC, 30 September 1864, muster showed AWOL about six weeks in July and August 1864; October 1864 last muster showed present.

Thomas, James W. Enlisted 11 or 20 June 1861 at Camp McDonald; age 18 per 31 August 1861 muster; October 1864 last muster card stated in hands of enemy since 2 July 1863; captured 3 July 1863 at Gettysburg, sent to For Delaware, paroled Greensboro, NC, 1 May 1865 (must have returned to regiment before surrender).

Thomas, Wesley, W. Enlisted as captain/major on 16 May 1862, place not stated; elected Captain 16 May 1862; paroled Greensboro, NC, 1 May 1865; Special Order (number no legible, perhaps 101), 17 January 1865, DNV, subject, "court martial."

Thomas, William. Enlisted as private on 12 February or 12 July 1864 at Newnan, GA; October 1864 last muster stated on detail to procure fresth horse since 2 September 1864; paroled Greensboro 11 May 1865.

Thomasson, A. J. Enlisted as private on 9 or 12 May 1864 at Atlanta; October 1864 last muster showed absent on horse detail since 2 September 1864.

Thompson, Ivy F. Enlisted as private/sergeant on 14 June 1861 at Cobb County; age 23 per 31 August 1861 muster; August 1864, last muster showed prisoner of war; POW records; captured 3 December 1863 near Knoxville, TN, sent to Louisville, KY, and then to Rock Island, Barracks, IL, on 31 December 1863; oath and released at Rock Island on 21 June 1863; description per oath; fair complexion, light hair, 5' 6", age 28, resident Vanwert, Polk, GA.

Thurmond, Charles (Thurman). Enlisted as private on 11 April 1864 in Newnan, GA; October 1864 last muster showed present; paroled Greensboro, NC, 1 May 1865.

Thornton, Kinchen D. Enlisted as corporal/blacksmith on 10 April or 10 May 1862 at Newnan, GA; 28 February 1863 muster showed promoted to first corporal; April 1864, on detail to Georgia to procure horse by order of Gen. Lee; October 1864; last muster card stated absent to procure a remount horse since 2 September 1864 by order Gen. Lee; paroled Greensboro, NC, 1 May 1865.

Tinny, George W. (Tenney). Enlisted as private on 21 September 1861 at Newnan, GA; October 1864 last muster card showed in hands of enemy since 18 December 1863, no POW records.

Tomlinson, William J. Enlisted as private on 11 or 20 June 1861 at Camp McDonald; age 30 per 31 August 1861 muster; February 1864 muster stated "unloading cars at Milford Station" since 30 November 1863, October 1864 on detail with Major Walton at Stony Creek since 30 November 1863.

Trammel, Elisha (E. S.). Enlisted as private on 2 August 1861 at Camp McDonald; age 21 per 3 August 1861 muster; 28 February 1863; last muster card showed present.

Treadwell, Isaac. Enlisted as private 15 May 1862 at Conyers, GA; February 1864, last muster showed died in hospital at Richmond 11 February 1864; hospital records: admitted to General Hospital Howard's Grove in Richmond on 1 February 1864, died 11 February 1864 of "variola conft."

Vineyard, J. H. (Vinyard). Enlisted as private on 15 May 1862 at Newnan, GA; 11 April 1864, muster showed on detail to buy horse in Georgia since 4 February 1864; October 1864 last muster showed on horse detail since 2 September 1864.

Vineyard, Samuel, F. (Vinyard). Enlisted as private on 15 May 1862 at Newnan, GA; April 1864, muster showed absent on detail to buy a horse since 5 April 1864; 31 August 1864, muster showed AWOL since 9 June 1864; October 1864 last muster showed "AWOL since or deserted" 12 June 1864; appeared on list of deserters from the Rebel Army; received 25 September 1864; discharged 26 September 1864; "Oath and to remain north of Ohio River"; description from bath, 5' 7", hazel eyes, light complexion, dark hair, residence, Coweta Co., GA.

Waits, Thomas. Enlisted as private on 18 July 1864 in Newnan, GA; October 1864 last muster showed present.

Waldon, W. H. (Walldon). Enlisted as private on 13 or 15 April 1862 at Newnan, GA; October 1864 last muster card showed absent wounded since 29 November 1863, "not reporting" no information on wounding.

Waldrop, L. L. Enlisted as private on 15 May 1862 at Conyers, GA; April 1864,
muster showed absent at brigade infirmary camp since 4 January 1864; 31
August 1864, muster showed absent on sick furlough in Newton County,
GA; October 1864 last muster showed absent, detailed with ordnance store
for Young's Brigade with Major Paxton.

Ward, Wiley. Enlisted as second bugler on 20 June 1861 at Camp McDonald
age 42 per 31 August 1861 muster; 31 October 1861, last muster showed
absent sick.

Warland, W. H. Enlisted as private in Company K; cavalry or infantry;
regimental return dated May 1862, showed enlisted 10 May 1862 in
Newnan, GA.

Warren, George W. Enlisted as private at Conyers, GA; February 1864 muster
showed teamster for Major Goodwyn since 22 November 1863; 31 August
1864, muster showed on detached duty with division quartermaster, October
1864 last muster showed absent on sick furlough, paroled Greensboro, NC, 1
May 1865.

Watson, Ampry. Enlisted as private on 10 May 1863 at Newnan, GA; 11 April
1864 on detail to Georgia to procure a fresh horse since 31 February 1864;
October 1864; last muster card showed present; paroled Greensboro, NC, 1
May 1865.

Watson, James D. Enlisted as private on 11 or 20 June 1861 at Camp
McDonald; age 36 per 31 August 1861 muster; 11 April 1864, muster stated
on detail to Georgia to procure a fresh horse since 31 February 1864; muster
states AWOL since 19 April 1864, last muster stated AWOL since 25 April
1864.

Watts, A. Y. Enlisted as private in Company D; cavalry or infantry; no
enlistment information; POW card stated captured at Columbia, SC, 18
February 1865, and sent to Hart's Island, NY; oath and released 6 June 1865;
description per oath: dark complexion, dark hair, blue eyes, 5' 9", residence
Coosahatchie, GA.

Whatley, S. L. Enlisted as private at Newnan, GA; October 1864 last muster
card showed absent sick since 6 September 1864, "reporting by surgeon
certificate," admitted to Jackson Hospital, Richmond, 16 August 1864 for
dysenteria, furloughed 30 days on 9 September 1864.

Whatly, John T. (Whatley, J. T.). Enlisted as private on 27, 28, or 29 July 1862
at Newnan, GA; October 1864 last muster stated on detail for remount horse
since 2 September 1864 by order Gen. Lee.

Whitfield, J. T. Rank not listed; Company D, 11 April 1864, only muster card showed present.

Whitfield, M. S. Enlisted as private on 26 April 1861 at LaGrange, GA; October 1864 last muster showed on detail for remount horse since 2 September 1864 by order Gen. Lee.

Willcoxin, William. Enlisted as private/sergeant on 11 or 20 June 1861 at Camp McDonald; age 18 per 31 August 1861 muster; 11 April 1864, on detail to procure a fresh horse since 31 February 1864; October 1864 last muster stated detailed with the infirmary corps since 15 June 1864; paroled Greensboro, NC, 1 May 1865.

Willingham, A. Enlisted as private on 27 February 1864 at Newnan, GA; 11 October 1864, muster stated sick furlough since 13 September 1864 by board surgeons; October 1864 last muster card stated AWOL since 13 October 1864; paroled Greensboro, NC, 1 May 1865.

Wortham, Frank. Enlisted as private on 20 September 1861 at Newnan, GA; 31 October 1861; only muster card showed absent sick.

Wortham, Joseph C. Enlisted as private on 11 June 1861 at Camp McDonald; age 28 per 31 August 1861 muster; captured at Williamsburg September 1862 and paroled at Fort Monroe, VA, 12 September 1862; 28 February 1863, last muster showed present; Special Order: No. 228/10, Dept. and Army N. VA, Lee 21 September 1863 "Transf. Co. B, 4 GA Vols."

Wortham, Zack. Enlisted as private on 6, 13, or 26 1862 at Newnan, GA (also showed 10 May 1862 Newnan, GA); April 1864, muster stated on detail to procure a horse since 3 April 1862; October 1864 last muster card stated on detail for remount horse since 2 September 1864.

Casualties, other losses for the Phillips Georgia Legion cavalry battalion from available records. Company N/E was formed predominantly from Bibb County.

Company N/E

Total Enrollment:	108
Death/Disease/Accident:	4
Discharge/Disability:	5
Captured:	20
Discharged/Elected Civil Office:	1
KIA:	5

WIA:	9
MWIA:	1
Exchanged:	7
AWOL :	8
Deserted:	2
Conscripts:	8
Imprisoned/Fort McHenry, MD:	1
Imprisoned/Point Lookout, MD:	11
Imprisoned/Old Capitol Prison, D.C.:	4
Imprisoned/Hart's Island, NY:	1
Imprisoned/Fort Delaware, DE:	9
Imprisoned/Camp Chase, OH:	1
Detached Service/Extra Duty:	22
Horse Detail/Furlough:	44
Paroled/Greensboro, NC:	35
Paroled/Charlotte, NC:	1
Paroled/Newton, NC:	3
Paroled/Unknown:	1
Resigned/Officer:	2
POW:	8
Surrendered Appomattox:	2

Note: any one individual may appear in several categories; e. g., he may have been captured, sent to prison, and exchanged.

PHILLIPS GEORGIA LEGION
Cavalry Battalion

Company E
The Bibb Cavalry

Abney, W. N. Enlisted as private in Macon, GA, on 12 May 1862; October 1864 last muster showed on horse detail by order Gen. Lee; paroled Greensboro, NC, 1 May 1865.

Anderson, T. W. Enlisted as private in Macon, GA, on 12 May 1862; October 1864 last muster stated on detached service with brigade ordnance department 1 April 1863; paroled Greensboro, NC, 1 May 1865.

Avant, J. W. Enlisted as 1st sergeant/3rd lieutenant in Macon, GA, on 12 May 1862; 29 February 1864, muster stated absent on detail, left 21 February 1864; October 1864 last muster showed present; appeared on register containing a list of officers who were promoted for valor and skill, date 1 February 1864, for what position recommended: Jr. 2nd lieutenant, by whom recommended: 1st lieutenant G. M. Davis; register of appointments: date of appointment 3 February 1864, date of confirmation 26 May 1864, To take rank 19 February 1864, date of acceptance: 16 April 1864 (copy of letter recommending appointment is enclosed); admitted to Hospital No. 4 in Richmond, VA, 26 June 1864 for "V. Inc. R. Knee," date of injury 24 June 1864; furloughed on 12 July 1864 for 30 days.

Avant, R. C. (R. E.). Enlisted as private in Macon, GA, on 12 May 1862; October 1864 last muster showed sick at hospital Richmond since 14 October 1864; furloughed for 30 days 24 October 1864.

Barfield, A. A. (Barfield, Barefield). Enlisted as private on 12 May 1862 at Macon, GA (also showed 11 April 1864, Macon); October 1864 last muster showed absent at hospital Richmond 22 August 1864; admitted to Jackson Hospital 23 August 1864 for "Dia. Chr." returned to duty 11 October 1864; admitted to Jackson Hospital 24 October 1864 for "Dia. Chr." returned to duty 23 November 1864; appeared on a list of soldiers found with records of the 10th Michigan Cavalry, not dated (It is believed that the men on this list were paroled at Newton, NC, about 9 April 1865).

Barfield, G. W. (Barefield). Enlisted as sergeant on 12 May 1862 at Macon, GA; 11 May 1864, muster stated captured 1 August 1863 Culpeper Co., VA; POW records: captured 1 August 1863 at Brandy Station; arrived at Point

Lookout, MD, on 23 August 1863, paroled and sent to City Point, VA, for exchange 27 April 1864; Hospital Records: admitted to Chimborazo Hosp. No. 3 in Richmond on 11 April 1864 for diarrhea; furloughed 12 May 1864 for 60 days; October, last muster showed on furlough 6 August 1864; paroled Greensboro, NC, 1 May 1865.

Barfield, J. C. 11 October 1864, only muster card in file stated sent to hospital Richmond 22 August 1864.

Bazemore, J. C. (J. E., Bazemore, John T.). Enlisted as private on 12 May 1862 at Macon, GA; 29 February 1864, last muster stated at recruiting camp, left 25 January 1864; October 1864 last muster stated absent, wounded at hospital 11 June 1864; hospital records: admitted to Gen. Hosp. at Charlottesville, VA, on 13 June 1864 for "Vulu. Sclo. left thigh"; furloughed 22 June 1864; (file also contains a hospital card for a John T. Bazemore died 4 September 1862 of typhoid fever.)

Bond, J. H. Enlisted as private on 12 May 1862 at Macon, GA; 29 February 1864, muster stated absent sick at hospital, left 11 October 1863; 11 May 1864, muster stated on detached service to Georgia by order of medical board 8 June 1863; October 1864 last muster stated detailed by med. board at Macon, GA, 11 June 1864; hospital records for Floyd House and Ocmulgee Hospitals, Macon, GA: 11 April 1864, "Detail."

Bryan, William (Bryant). Enlisted as private on 16 September 1863 at Macon, GA; October 1864 last muster showed on horse detail 2 September 1864 by order Gen. Lee; paroled Greensboro, NC, 1 May 1865.

Bryant, A. J. Enlisted as private in Company N; regimental return for May 1862 showed "left in Macon, Georgia sick"; no enlistment or other information.

Bryant, J. L. Enlisted as private on 11 April 1864 at Macon, GA (Company E, N, and A); October 1864 last muster showed captured 26 October 1864; POW records: captured 27 October 1864 near Petersburg; arrived at Point Lookout, MD, 31 October 1864; oath and released 5 June 1865.

Burkner, H. J. (H. H.). Enlisted as private on 12 May 1862 at Macon, GA; October 1864 last muster showed on horse detail 2 September 1864 by order Gen. Lee; paroled Greensboro, NC, 1 May 1865.

Burns, W. P. (Burnes). Enlisted as private on 12 May 1862 at Macon, GA; October 1864 last muster stated "captured 1 August 1863 Culpeper Co"; POW records: captured 1 August 1863 at Brandy Station; arrived at Point Lookout, MD, 23 August 1863, oath and released 23 June 1865 (died before he was physically released); died 25 June 1865 at Point Lookout, MD;

record of death and interment: died of Scorbutus; Hospital Number 6903; location of grave: Pris. of War Grave Yard; information from oath: dark complexion, dark hair, black eyes, 5' 8 1/2", resident of Twiggs County, GA.

Chance, George. Enlisted as corporal, cavalry or infantry; POW card stated captured at Gettysburg 3 July 1863; arrived Fort Delaware, July 1863; remarks: "Pt. Loo," no other information.

Chapman, L. O. (O.). Enlisted as private on 14 February 1864 in Macon, GA; 1 February 1864, last muster showed on detail for horse, left 14 February 1864; paroled Greensboro, NC, 1 May 1865.

Chapman, S. O. (S. B.). Enlisted as private on 16 January or 1 February 1864 at Macon, GA; 11 April 1864, on detail for horse by order Gen. Lee; October 1864, last muster showed horse detail since 2 September 1864 by order Gen. Lee.

Edwards, T. W. Enlisted as private on 1 June 1863 at Corinth, MS; 11 April 1864, detailed at recruiting camp 4 February 1864 by order Col. Rich; October 1864 last muster card showed on horse detail since 2 September 1864 by order Gen. Lee.

Ellis, J. E. Enlisted as private/sergeant on 12 May 1862 at Macon, GA; 11 April 1864, absent on detail for horse; left 4 February 1864 by order Gen. Lee; 11 October 1864, absent on detail for horse, left 2 September 1864; sent home on horse detail; received an appointment as deputy clerk; papers forwarded and approved by commanding officer; was reported absent without leave; October 1864 last muster showed horse detail since 2 September 1864; paroled Greensboro, NC, 1 May 1865. Note: 11 April 1864 muster showed private, 11 October 1864 muster showed 3rd sergeant.

Elrod, E. H. No enlistment information, only hospital records; Company E; appeared on list of passports issued from Jackson Hospital, Richmond for week ending 22 August 1864, date: 18 August 1864, destination: Williamson, SC.

Evans, J. W. (J. E.). Enlisted as private on 5 April 1864 at Macon, GA; October 1864 last muster showed absent on horse detail since 2 September 1864 by order Gen. Lee; appeared on list of soldiers found with records of the 1 Od' Michigan Cavalry, list not dated, "It is believed the men on this list were paroled at Newton, North Carolina" about 19 April 1865.

Evans, T. J. Enlisted as private on 12 May 1862 at Macon, GA; October 1864 last muster showed captured 28 February 1864; POW records: captured 29 February 1864 Rapidan River, 1 March 1864, forwarded to Old Capitol

Prison, D.C.; transferred to Fort Delaware 15 June 1864; arrived 17 June 1864.

Failes, S. S. (Fails). Enlisted as private on 12 May or 24 July 1862 at Macon, GA; 1 September 1864, sent to Lynchburg, VA, with condemned horses 28 August 1864; October 1864 last muster showed present.

Felts, F. M. (Fels). Enlisted as private on 24 or 29 December 1863 at Macon, GA; 14 January 1864, muster showed absent, conscript 24 December, furlough of indulgence, rejoined the command a the expiration of his furlough 22 January 1864; October 1864 last muster showed on horse detail since 2 September 1864 by order Gen. Lee; paroled Greensboro, NC, 1 May 1865.

Franklin, J. E. No enlistment information, only POW records, cavalry or infantry; captured 3 July 1863 at Cashtown; received at Fort Delaware 12 July 1863, transferred to Point Lookout, MD; arrived at Point Lookout 22 October 1863; exchanged 18 September 1864.

Garthwright, S. W. Enlisted as private, Company E, cavalry or infantry; no information, only reference card, see Samuel W. Garthwright, 10 Batt'n VA H'y Arty.

Gilbert, E. C. Enlisted as corporal/sergeant, Company E, on 12 May 1862 at Macon, GA; October 1864 last muster showed present; paroled Greensboro, NC, 1 May 1865. Note: 11 April 1864 muster showed 3rd corporal; 1 May to 1 September 1864 muster showed 1st sergeant.

Green, W. Enlisted as private, Company E, cavalry or infantry; one card showed surrendered at Appomattox 9 April 1865.

Gustin, G. W. (Gastin). Enlisted as private on 26 February 1864 at Macon, GA; 11 April 1864, detail for horse in Georgia since 25 February 1864 by order of Major Harris, conscript officer; October 1864 last muster showed on horse detail since 2 September 1864 by order Gen. Lee; paroled Greensboro, NC, 1 May 1865.

Hall, M. M. Enlisted as private on 12 May 1862 in Macon, GA; POW records: captured Hanover 30 June 1863, confined at Fort McHenry, MD, sent to Fort Delaware, arrived 6 July 1863; 30 July 1863, sent to City Point for exchange; October 1864 last muster card showed "Detailed Signal Corps" 13 April 1864. (Note: record contains several letters regarding claim for his horse, killed on 30 June 1863 at Hanover).

Harris, C. Enlisted as private on 12 May 1862 at Macon, GA; 11 October 1864, muster showed captured by the enemy, "accepted a parole to remain in their lines"; October 1864 last muster showed captured 28 November 1863; POW records: 28 November 1863, captured at Mine Run, VA, committed to Old Capitol Prison, D.C. 5 December 1863; 4 February 1864, arrived Point Lookout, MD; 30 March 1864, released 11 April 1864, forwarded to New York.

Harris, P. A. Enlisted as corporal, Company E, cavalry or infantry; no enlistment information; "Appeared on a register of sick and wounded Confederates in the hospitals in and about Gettysburg, Pennsylvania, after the battle of July 1, 2, and 3, 1863"; complaint: G. S. left arm; POW records showed transferred to provost marshal, (no date).

Hawkins, N. E. Enlisted as private on 12 May 1862 at Macon, GA; 11 April 1864, muster showed absent, sick at hospital, Macon, GA, (wounded) left arm 1 August 1863; 11 October 1864, on detached service in Georgia by medical board, lost use of hand; October 1864 last muster showed detailed by medical board, Macon, GA, 11 May 1864; January to June 1864, "Appears on a roll of non-commissioned officers and privates employed on extra duty at Macon, Georgia"; nature of duty: arresting deserters; remarks: wounded; term of service: 1 January 1864 to 5 February 1864.

Holder, J. F. Enlisted as private on 12 May 1862; 11 October 1864, muster stated "Sent to hospital" 23 June 1863. "Never has been heard from since. Reported absent without leave." October 1864 last muster card showed absent without leave (was in hospital; see below); hospital records: 12 May 1864, admitted to Ocmulgee Hospital, Macon, GA, for Phthisis Pul.; November 1864, returned to duty.

Holleman, L. B. (Holliman). Enlisted as private on 12 May 1862 at Macon, GA; December 1863, absent, wounded at hospital; wounded last of October 1863; October 1864 last muster stated detailed to medical board, Macon, GA, 16 July 1864; Special Order: 167/47 Adj. and Inspec. Gen. Office "Detailed" 16 July 1864.

Howell, W. E. Enlisted as private on 12 May 1864 at Macon, GA (also showed 8 September and 20 September 1863, Rapidan, VA); 5 September 1864, muster showed sick at hospital 24 August 1864; October 1864 last muster card showed on sick furlough 20 October 1864 sent to CSA Hospital at Farmville, VA, returned to duty 18 May 1864; admitted Jackson Hospital 1 July 1864, rubeola; returned to duty 29 July 1864; admitted Wayside Hospital or General Hospital, Richmond, sent to Jackson Hospital 8 February 1864 for chronic diarrhea, furloughed 28 August 1864 30 days;

destination: Deacon's Station, GA.

Hughes, E. W. (Hughs). Enlisted as private on 14 February 1864 at Macon, GA;
April 1864, muster showed detail for horse in Georgia 14 February 1864 by
order of Major Harris commanding conscripts; 11 October 1864, muster
stated was assigned to the company 16 February 1864, has never been
reported, is absent without leave; October 1864 last muster showed absent
without leave since 14 February 1864.

Humphries, C. Enlisted as private on 11 April 1864 at Macon, GA; 1 September
1864, muster showed AWOL since 11 August 1864; 11 October 1864,
muster stated "Received detailed papers from the Bureau of Conscription.
Were forwarded to General Lee and disapproved by him. Left the command
August 11 1864"; October 1864 last muster showed absent without leave
since 11 August 1864.

Hunter, A. F. Enlisted as second lieutenant/captain on 12 May 1862 at Macon,
GA; elected second lieutenant 12 May 1862; promoted first lieutenant 1
October 1862; promoted captain 22 September 1863; October 1864; last
muster showed AWOL since 1 July 1864; 31 October 1864, inspection
report read; "Absent without leave med. Ex. board disease consumption.
Recommend that he be retired." Hospital records: admitted General Hospital
No. 4, Richmond on 25 April 1864 for asthma and phthisis. Recommended
for 60 day furlough 28 April 1864, approved 29 April 1864; admitted to
Ocmulgee Hospital, Macon, on 24 October 1864 for asthma, 25 October
1864; transferred; showed residence; Bibb County, GA; remarks: Vineville.

Jackson, P. W. Enlisted as private; no enlistment information; Company N;
regimental return dated June 1862 stated "absent sick"; admitted to Jackson
Hospital in Richmond on 17 February 1863 for "Debility"; discharged 28
February 1863; (certificate of discharge in file but writing is faint, most
information is illegible).

Johnson, B. (Johnston). Enlisted as private on 13, 15, or 16 February 1864 in
Macon, GA; 1 April 1864, detail for horse in Georgia, 15 February 1864 by
order Major Harris commanding conscripts; 1 September 1864, muster stated
wounded at Stony Creek Station 9 June 1864; 21 or 26 July 1864, died
General Hospital No. 8, Raleigh, NC, "Vul. Sclop."

Johnson, J. K. (Johnston). Enlisted as corporal on 12 May 1862 at Macon, GA;
11 April 1864, muster showed on detail to Georgia for horse since 4
February 1864; 1 September 1864, muster showed absent, wounded and sent
to Richmond 16 August 1864; October 1864 last muster showed furloughed

from hospital 16 August 1864; hospital records: admitted to Floyd House 26 October 1864 "V. S. left forearm ball entering at wrist joint and passing between the radius and ulna fracturing the former bone and making its exit near elbow joint and severely impairing use of arm and wrist"; paroled Greensboro, 1 May 1865.

Jones, J. J. (Johns). Enlisted as private on 12 May 1862 at Macon, GA; 1 September 1864, muster stated, "Sent with condemned horses to Lynchburg August 18 1864"; 11 October 1864, last muster stated present; POW cards stated captured "in field," no date; oath in file, stated captured at Raleigh, NC, on 12 April 1865, oath dated 22 April 1865.

Jourdan, Thomas (Jordan). Enlisted as private on 12 May 1862 at Macon, GA; 14 January 1864, muster showed AWOL, "been absent eight months left May 8 1863"; 29 February 1864, muster showed "under arrest since January 1 1864"; 11 April 1864, muster showed present; October 1864 AWOL since 18 June 1864; appeared on report of prisoners captured by the 1st brigade, 2nd cavalry division, during the month of April 1865. Report dated Hdqrs. 1st brig. 2nd cav. div. Macon, GA, 30 April 1865.

Kenyon, J. L. (John). Enlisted as sergeant on 12 May 1862 at Macon, GA; 29 February 1864, muster showed absent sick at hospital, left 24 November 1863; 11 April 1864, muster showed sick at hospital at Richmond; 1 September 1864, muster showed present; October 1864 last muster showed furlough of indulgence 20 October 1864; paroled Greensboro, NC, 1 May 1865; Descriptive list in file dated 24 January 1864; age 28, gray eyes, dark hair, dark complexion, born Albany, NY, occupation livery.

Kilpatrick, John T. (J. T.). Enlisted as private/sergeant on 12 May 1862 at Macon, GA; 1 April 1864, muster showed absent on detail for horse in Georgia 4 February 1864 by order Gen. Lee; October 1864 last muster showed horse detail 2 September 1864; POW records: captured 17 February 1865 Columbia, SC, received at Hart's Island, NY, 10 April 1865, released 14 June 1865 G. O. 109, 6 June 1865; oath dated 15 June 1865 stated residence Chatham County, GA; dark complexion, dark hair, dark eyes, 5' 10".

Kindrick, M. M. (Kendrick). Enlisted as private on 12 May 1862 at Macon, GA; 11 April 1864, muster showed absent on detail for horse in Georgia 4 February 1864 by order Gen. Lee; October 1864 last muster showed on horse detail 2 September 1864 by order Gen. Lee.

King, George W. Enlisted as private on 12 May 1862; October 1864 last muster

showed captured Martinsburg, VA, 19 July 1863; POW records: arrested
Berkeley County, VA, 19 July 1863; received at Camp Chase 30 July 1863,
transferred to Fort Delaware 29 February 1864; died at Fort Delaware 3 or 4
March 1865 "Erysipelos"; localtity of grave Jersey Shore; no effects;
description from POW card dated 24 July 1863: age 28, dark complexion,
blue eyes, dark hair, 5' 10".

King, H. J. Enlisted as private on 21 October 1861 at Macon, GA; admitted to
General Hospital, Charlottesville, VA, 19 February 1863 "Debilitas (Phthisis
Pulmon.)"; furloughed 28 April 1863; discharged 29 April 1863 for Phthisis;
description from discharge: born Wilkinson County, GA, age 21, light
complexion, blue eyes, auburn hair, 5' 6", farmer by occupation.

Lamar, G. A. Enlisted as private on 1 March or 3 February 1864 in Macon, GA;
11 April 1864, absent on detail for horse in Georgia 12 March 1864 by order
of Major Harris commanding conscripts; October 1864 last muster showed
present; paroled Greensboro, NC, 1 May 1865.

Lamar, H. G. Enlisted as private at Macon, GA; 11 April 1864, absent on detail
for horse in Georgia 12 March 1864 by order of Major Harris commanding
conscripts; 11 October 1864, muster showed absent sick, send to hospital at
Richmond 25 July 1864; October 1864 last muster showed present; hospital
records showed admitted to Stuart Hospital at Richmond on 3 July 1864 for
"Dysenteria acuta," furloughed 20 July 1864.

Miller, Thomas J. (T. J.). Enlisted as private on 12 May 1862 at Macon, GA; 14
January 1864, muster stated has been absent on detail for horses left 5
November 1863; 29 February 1864, muster stated at recruiting camp left 4
February 1864; October 1864 last muster showed "horse detailed September
2 1864"; paroled Greensboro, NC, 1 May 1865.

Mills, Alex. Enlisted as private on 12 May 1862 at Macon, GA; 11 April 1864,
on detail for horse in Georgia 4 February 1864 by order Gen. Lee; October
1864 last muster stated "Horse detailed 2 September 1864 by order Gen.
Lee." Paroled Greensboro, NC, 1 May 1865.

Mills, J. M. Enlisted as private on 12 May 1862 at Macon, GA; 11 April 1864,
muster showed detail for horse in Georgia 4 February 1864 by order Gen.
Lee; October 1864 last muster showed present.

Murphy, B. Enlisted as private, Company E, cavalry or infantry, no enlistment
information; captured 3 July 1863 Gettysburg, received at Fort Delaware,
DE, 12 July 1863.

Nelson, F. C. Enlisted as private, Company E; October 1864 last muster showed

captured 1 August 1863 in Culpeper County; POW records: captured 1
August 1863 Brandy Station, rec'd Point Lookout, MD, 23 August 1863;
exchanged 24 February 1865; paroled Greensboro, NC, 1 May 1865.

Overby, James L. Enlisted as private on 12 May 1862 at Macon, GA; 11 April
1864, detailed for horse in Georgia 4 February 1864 by order Gen. Lee;
October 1864 last muster showed absent sick at hospital 7 August 1864;
hospital records: admitted to Ocmulgee Hospital, Macon, GA, 23 August
1864 "Paralysis"; furloughed 5 September 1864; admitted to Ocmulgee
Hospital, Macon, GA, 11 February 1864 "Paralysis"; deserted November
1864; residence listed as Pulaski County, GA.

Patterson, H. H. Enlisted as private on 12 May 1862 at Macon, GA; 29 February
1864, muster showed at recruiting camp, left 23 February 1864; October
1864 last muster showed horse detail 2 September 1864 by order Gen. Lee;
paroled Greensboro, NC, 1 May 1865.

Powell, S. T. (S. V.). Enlisted as private on 12 May 1862 at Macon, GA;
October 1864 last muster showed captured 1 August 1863 Culpeper County;
POW records: captured 1 August 1863 Brandy Station; received at Point
Lookout, MD, 23 August 1863; exchanged 24 February 1865.

Ray, Joseph. Enlisted as private 1 May 1862 at Macon, GA, or 25 May 1862 at
Camp Wilcox; 1 April 1862, muster stated "Captured by enemy July 9 1863.
Since been paroled and furloughed and the elected to civil office of his
country." 5 September 1864, muster stated discharged by Gen. Lee. Elected
to civil office 3 January 1864 (file contains card for Joseph H. Ray showing
he was killed 8 July 1863 Boonsborough, MD); hospital records: admitted to
U.S.A. General Hospital Frederick, MD, 15 July 1863; wounded in right
lung, bullet entered through his back (detailed medical record of treatment in
file); age is listed as 30 in 1863.

Reed, B. F. Enlisted as private on 12 May 1862 at Macon, GA; October 1864
last muster showed horse detail 2 September 1864 by order Gen. Lee;
paroled Greensboro, NC, 1 May 1865.

Sanders, Jeff (Landers, Jefferson, J. F. and J. J.). Enlisted as private on 12 May
1862 at Macon, GA; October 1864 last muster showed captured 28 February
1864; POW records: captured Gen. Hosp, not dated; confederate hospital
records: admitted to Jackson Hospital Richmond 7 March 1864, "resec. L.
Shoul. Joint and Arms"; appeared on a register of Floyd House and
Ocmulgee Hospitals, Macon dated 30 January 1865; disease: "VS left arm
resection of 7 inches upper humerus."

Tarver, B. M. Enlisted as private on 15 February 1864 at Macon, GA; October 1864 last muster showed on horse detail since 2 September 1864; paroled Greensboro, NC, 1 May 1865.

Tarver, W. B. Enlisted as private on 15 February 1864 at Macon, GA; October 1864 last muster showed on horse detail 2 September 1864 by order Gen. Lee; paroled Greensboro, NC, 1 May 1865.

Taylor, James. Enlisted as private on 15 February 1864 at Macon, GA; 11 April 1864, on detail for horse in Georgia since 18 February 1864 by order of Major Harris commanding conscripts; October 1864 last muster showed on horse detail by order Gen. Lee; paroled Greenboro, NC, 1 May 1865.

Tease, J. W. Enlisted as private on 12 May 1862 at Macon, GA; 29 February 1864, last muster showed captured 5 July 1863; POW records: captured 5 July 1863 near Cashtown (also showed Gettysburg); sent to hospital at Chester, PA, transferred to Hammond Gen. Hospital at Point Lookout, MD, and arrived 4 October 1863; transferred to general hospital 30 April 1864; appeared on a register of enlisted men, rebel deserters, and refugees detained at camp, distribution awaiting orders "dated March 3 1864," forwarded to Philadelphia, 5 May 1864.

Tharp, Alexander. Enlisted as private on 6 August 1864 at Macon, GA; October 1864 last muster showed on horse detail 2 September 1864 by order Gen. Lee.

Voluntine, W. N. (Valentine). Enlisted as private on 12 May 1862 at Macon, GA; 29 February 1864 muster showed on recruiting service, left 25 February 1864; October 1864 last muster showed horse detail 2 September 1864 by order Gen. Lee; paroled Greensboro, NC, 1 May 1865.

Walker, D. K. Enlisted as private on 12 May 1862 at Macon, GA; 11 April 1864, detail for horse in Georgia 4 February 1864 by order Gen. Lee; October 1864 last muster showed horse detail 2 September 1864 by order Gen. Lee; hospital records: admitted to General Hospital Charlottesville 9 August 1863 "Vulu. Sclo." furloughed 30 August 1863; remarks: "Left in fact 28."

Walker, G. D. Enlisted as private on 12 May 1862 at Macon, GA; 29 February 1864, at recruiting camp, left 10 December 1864 (63); October 1864 last muster showed horse detail 2 September 1864 by order Gen. Lee; paroled Greensboro, NC, 1 May 1865.

Walker, J. L. Enlisted as private on 12 May 1862 at Macon, GA; 11 April 1864, on detail for horse in Georgia 4 February 1864 by order Gen. Lee; October

1864 last muster showed present; paroled Greensborp, NC, 1 May 1865.

Wiggins, W. A. Enlisted as private on 15 February 1864 at Macon, GA; 11 April 1864, detail for horse in Georgia 15 February 1864 by order Major Harris commanding conscripts; October 1864 last muster showed on horse detail 2 September 1864 by order Gen. Lee.

Williams, H. L. Enlisted as sergeant on 12 May 1862; killed 10 May 1864; no information; remarks: "J. L. Walker, Co. E, Phillips Legion (L. R.)"

Williams, H. M. Enlisted as private on 12 May 1862 at Macon, GA; October 1864 last muster showed present.

Wood, A. O. (O. A.). Enlisted as private on 9 March 1864 at Macon, GA; 11 April 1864, muster showed detailed for horse in Georgia by order of Major Harris commanding conscripts; killed 12 June 1864 at Trevillian Station; remarks: "Do not know (LR)."

Woodall, F. Enlisted as private on 12 May 1862 at Macon, GA; one muster card dated 14 January 1864 showed AWOL, left 1 November 3 1863.

Wyche, John W. Enlisted as private on 12 May 1862 at Macon, GA: October 1864 last muster showed detailed division headquarters since 20 August 1864; paroled Greensboro, NC, 1 May 1865.

Wynn, R. W. (Winn, Wynne). Enlisted as private on 12 May 1862 at Macon, GA; 11 April 1864, muster showed detail for horse in Georgia since 4 February 1864 by order Gen. Lee; 1 September 1864, muster showed sick at hospital Richmond 1 July 1864; October 1864 last muster showed present; paroled Greensboro, NC, 1 May 1865.

Wyse, Joe (J. W., Wise). Enlisted as private on 12 May 1862 at Macon, GA; 29 February 1864, on detail at Port Royal since 8 February 1864; 1 September 1864, muster showed sick furlough, left 20 July 1864, 60 days; October 1864 last muster showed present; hospital records: appeared on a register containing a record of cases examined by the board of surgeons," acute diarrhea of 5 weeks standing. Succeeding obstinate constipation. Also a recent attack of continued fever. Furlough 60 days."

Casualties, other losses for the Phillips Georgia Legion cavalry battalion from available records. Company P/F was formed predominantly from Coweta, Newton, and Carroll counties;

Company P/F

Total Enrollment:	105
Death/Disease/Accident:	9
Discharged/Disability:	2
Captured:	11
WIA:	1
Exchanged:	5
AWOL:	12
Deserted:	2
Imprisoned/Point Lookout, MD:	6
Imprisoned/Old Capitol Prison, D.C.:	1
Imprisoned/Fort Delaware, DE:	5
Imprisoned/Camp Chase, OH:	2
Imprisoned/Louisville, KY:	1
Imprisoned/Camp Douglas, IL:	1
Oath and to Remain North of the Ohio River:	1
POW:	8
Galvanized Yankees:	1
Courts Martial:	1
Detached Service/Extra Duty:	10
Horse Detail/Furlough:	43
Paroled/Greensboro, NC:	35
Paroled/Charlotte, NC:	1

Note: Any one individual may appear in several categories; e.g., he may have been captured, sent to prison and exchanged.

PHILLIPS GEORGIA LEGION
Cavalry Battalion

Company F

Arnold, W. M. Enlisted as private on 25 July 1861 at Montgomery, AL; April 1864, absent on detail to buy a horse in Georgia; October, last muster showed absent on horse detail since 2 September 1864.

Banks, T. M. Enlisted as private on 14 February 1863 at Newnan, GA; December 1863, muster showed left on detail to buy horse 3 November 1863 and returned 9 January 1864; 31 August 1864; muster showed AWOL in Heard County, Georgia; October 1864 last muster showed AWOL since 7 August 1864.

Bentley, W. D. C. (Bently, W. B. C.). Enlisted as private on 15 May 1862. at Conyers, GA; December 1863, muster showed left on detail to buy a horse 3 November 1863 and returned 9 January 1864; April 1864, absent on detail to procure a fresh horse; October 1864 absent on horse detail since 2 September 1864; paroled Greensboro, NC, 1 May 1865.

Carter, J. R. Enlisted as private on 15 May 1862 at Newnan, GA; last muster showed present.

Carter, M. S. Enlisted as private on 16 April 1864 at Chesterfield, VA; October 1864 last muster showed present.

Carter, W. W. Enlisted as private on 15 June 1862 at Augusta, GA; 11 April 1864, absent on detail in Georgia to buy horse since 4 February 1864; April 1864, muster showed AWOL; 31 August 1864, muster showed present; 30 September 1864 muster showed AWOL for about two months from 11 June 1864; October 1864 last muster showed present; 12 February 1864, admitted to General Hospital DA.N.V.ille, VA, for "Icterus," returned to duty 17 February 1865.

Cavender, A. J. Enlisted as private on 15 May 1862 at Newnan, GA; October, last muster showed present.

Cavender, J. E. Enlisted as private on 15 May 1862 at Newnan, GA; October, last muster showed present.

Cavender, J. W. Enlisted as sergeant on 15 May 1862 at Newnan, GA; October 1864 last muster showed present; 1 September 1864, admitted to General Hospital Farmville, VA, for "Vul. Cont. below knee"; 26 September 1864, returned to duty; paroled Greensboro, NC, 1 May 1865.

Chambers, A. J. Enlisted as private on 1 May 1862 at Newnan, GA; October 1864 last muster showed present; paroled Greensboro, NC, 1 May 1865.

Chambers, James. Enlisted as private, Company F; "Statement of Service" "does not appear on muster roles" (perhaps confused with A. J. Chambers) 24 June 1864, was paid for services rendered during the months of January and February 1864.

Chandler, Hope W. Enlisted as private on 15 May 1862 at Newnan, GA; "Statement of Service," "does not appear on muster rolls"; 10 December 1862, died at Gordonville, VA, of "Febris Typhoides"; claim filed by Amanda J. Chandler.

Christian, Isaac W. See Company D and K (DKFP).

Christian, J. F. Enlisted as private on 3 August 1862 at Calhoun, GA: April 1864, muster showed absent on detail to procure a fresh horse; October 1864 last muster showed absent on horse detail since 9 February 1864; paroled Greensboro, NC, 1 May 1865.

Christian, J. H. Enlisted as private on 17 December 1863 at Decatur, GA; April 1864, muster showed absent in Georgia on detail to buy horse since 4 February 1864; 31 August 1864, absent sick at hospital in Columbia, SC; 30 September 1864, muster showed present but noted: AWOL about six weeks in July and August 1864; October 1864 last muster showed present.

Christian, J. M. Enlisted as Sergeant on 15 May 1864 at Conyers, GA; October 1864 last muster showed present; paroled Greensboro, NC, 1 May 1865.

Christian, T. H. P. Enlisted as private on 19 April 1864 at Chesterfield, VA; October 1864 last muster showed present; paroled Greensboro, NC, 1 May 1865.

Christian, W. H. Enlisted as private on 15 May 1862 at Conyers, GA; April 1864, muster showed absent on detail in Georgia to buy horse since 4 February 1864; 29 September 1864, muster showed "absent sick in Newton Co., Georgia, since 4 August 1864. Now very low with chronic diarrhea"; October 1864 last muster showed absent sick.

Crawford, H. F. Enlisted as private on 23 September 1864 at Newnan, GA; October 1864 last muster showed present.

Crawford, W. D. (William). Enlisted as Sergeant on 15 May 1862 at Newnan, GA; February 1864, muster showed sick at hospital at Richmond, VA, 1 February 1864; 1 April 1864, muster showed absent at his home in Carroll Co., GA, on sick furlough. Granted a sick furlough from hospital in Richmond about 20 March 1864; 31 August 1864, muster showed absent on sick furlough in Carroll, Co., GA; October 1864 last muster showed present; hospital records: admitted to Small Pox Hospital 21 February 1864 for "Variola," furloughed 60 days 24 March 1864; admitted to DA.N.V.ille General Hospital on 12 December 1864 for "V. S. in left foot," furloughed 16 January 1865 for 60 days.

Dale, R. F. Enlisted as private in Company F, cavalry or infantry; POW records: captured at Fairfield on 3 July 1863, arrived at Fort Delaware July 12 1863, transferred to Point Lookout and arrived 22 October 1863; exchanged 18 February 1865.

Duncan, J. R. Enlisted as private on 15 May 1862 at Newnan, GA; October 1864 last muster showed on horse detail since 2 September 1864; paroled Greensboro, NC, 5/1 1865.

Duncan, M. T. (M. S., T. M.). Enlisted as private on 15 May 1862 at Newnan, GA; October 1864 last muster showed in hands of enemy since 17 December 1863; POW records: captured 15 December 1863 Craig Co., VA, arrived at Camp Chase on 1 January 1864 and transferred to Fort Delaware. Arrived at Fort Delaware 17 March 1864. Transferred to Point Lookout and arrived 31 October 1864. Exchanged 31 October 1864; description per POW records; 5' 9", age 24, (2nd card showed 34), gray eyes, light hair, light complexion, farmer by occupation.

Farmer, F. M. Enlisted as private on 15 May 1862 at Newnan, GA; April 1864, absent on detail in Georgia to buy a fresh horse; October 1864 last muster showed present; paroled Greensboro, NC, 1 May 1865.

Fanner, J. A. Enlisted as private on 15 May 1862 at Conyers, GA; October 1864 last muster showed present; paroled Greensboro, NC, 1 May 1865.

Gill, H. M. Enlisted as private on 15 May 1862 at Newnan, GA; 30 September 1864, muster showed absent in Coweta, GA, on 60 day sick furlough since 9 February 1864; October 1864 last muster showed on sick furlough; paroled Greensboro, NC, 1 May 1865.

Gray, J. T. Enlisted as private on 15 May 1862 at Newnan, GA; 30 September 1864 (dated October 1864), muster showed absent on recruit furlough of 30 days until 10 February 1864. Since then AWOL; October 1864 last muster showed AWOL since 10 February 1864; paroled Greensboro, NC, 1 May 1865.

Gray, Samuel. Enlisted as private on 15 May 1862 at Newnan, GA; February 1864, AWOL since 9 January 1864; 11 April 1864, muster showed present; October 1864 last muster showed absent at horse infirmary camp near

Stoney Creek Depot; paroled Greensboro, NC, 1 May 1865.

Haisten, J. M. Enlisted as private on 3, 4, or 15 March 1862 at Newnan, GA; February 1864, muster showed absent at infirmary camp for horses since 26 January 1864; October 1864 last musters showed absent on horse detail since 2 September 1864.

Haisten, T. S. (Harsten). Enlisted as private on 15 May 1862 at Newnan, GA; April 1864, absent on detail in Georgia to buy a fresh horse; 31 August 1864, absent on sick furlough in Coweta Co., GA; 30 September 1864 (dated 10 August 1864), muster showed absent on sick furlough of 30 days until 27 September 1864. Since then AWOL; October 1864 last muster showed present; Hospital Records showed admitted to Jackson Hospital 19 August 1864 for "Diarrhoea Ch." furloughed for 30 days on 28 August 1864.

Hammond, C. M. (See Company D, D and F). Harvey, James E. (See Company D, D and F).

Hesterly, E. L. Enlisted as private in Company F, cavalry or infantry; title card only, notation stated "filed with Cobb's Legion GA."

Hill, B. P. Enlisted as private on 15 May 1862 at Newnan, GA; December 1863, muster showed absent wounded," wounded near Boonsboro Gap 9 August 1863. Hand amputated in Newton Co., GA; other muster cards show wounding on 9 July 1863; October 1864 last muster showed absent wounded, hand amputated.

Hill, T. W. Enlisted as private on 15 May 1862 at Newnan, GA; April 1864, absent on detail in Georgia to buy a fresh horse since 4 February 1864; October 1864 last muster showed absent on detail at receiving depot for div. quartermaster.

Hollingsworth, J. H. Enlisted as private on 15 May 1862 at Conyers, Georgia; April 1864, on detail to procure a fresh horse; October 1864 last muster showed on horse detail since 2 September 1864.

Hollingsworth, William R. Enlisted as private on 15 May 1862 at Conyers, GA; April 1864, muster showed absent on detail in Georgia to buy a fresh horse; October 1864 last muster showed absent on horse detail since 2 September 1864; POW records: captured: 17 October 1864 at DeKalb County, GA, sent to Louisville and transferred to Camp Douglas, IL. Arrived Camp Douglas 11 November 1864; discharged 12 June 1865; description per POW records: 5' 8", blue eyes, complexion, residence Conyers, GA.

Holloway, P. M. (Halloway). Enlisted as private/corporal on 15 May 1862 at Newnan, GA, 14 April 1864, muster showed teamster in Stewarts Horse

Artillery since 2 December 1863; 31 August 1864, muster showed present; October 1864 last muster showed absent teamster with Harts Battery; paroled Greensboro, NC, 1 May 1865.

Houseworth, J. M. (Housworth). Enlisted as private on 15 May 1862 at Conyers, GA; October 1864 last muster showed absent on horse detail since 2 September 1864.

Houston, J. C. (Housten). Enlisted as private on 15 May 1862 at Newnan, GA; February 1864, last muster showed "deserted from another company from another company and sent off under arrest February 6 1864."

Houston, N. B. (M. B.). Enlisted as private on 15 May 1862 at Newnan, GA; October 1864 last muster showed present; POW records: captured 1 December 1864 at Stoney Creek and sent to Point Lookout, arrived 5 December 1864; exchanged 17 January 1865.

Houston, O. R. Enlisted as private on 24 February 1862 at Newnan, GA; February 1864, absent on sick furlough since 10/1 1863; April 1864, absent on detail in GA to procure a fresh horse; 30 September 1864, muster showed absent sick in Carroll Co., GA since 12 June 1864; October 1864 muster showed AWOL since 20 September 1864.

Hubbard, J. L. Enlisted as private on 15 May 1862 in Newnan, GA; October 1864 last muster showed in hands of enemy since May 1864; POW records: captured on 21 May 1864 at Milford Station, arrived at Point Lookout on 30 May 1864; died 19 January 1865 from "Chronic Diarrhoea"; Grave No. 831, Prisoner of War Graveyard; Hospital No. 6375.

Huckeba, J. B. (Huckaba, Juckabe). Enlisted as private on 9 January 1864 at Newnan, GA; April 1864, absent on detail to Georgia to buy a horse; October 1864, last muster showed present; paroled Greensboro, NC, 1 May 1865.

Huffman, Henry (Hoffman). Enlisted as private on 14 February 1862 at Newnan, GA; 30 September 1864, muster showed absent in Carroll County, GA, since 31 August 1864 on 60 day sick furlough; October 1864 last muster showed on sick furlough; paroled Greensboro, NC, 1 May 1865; hospital records showed admitted to Jackson Hospital on 13 August 1864 for "Dia. Chron"; returned to duty 18 August 1864.

Hunt, W. H. Enlisted as private on 15 May 1862 at Conyers, GA; February 1864, teamster for General Young since 9 January 1864; October 1864 last muster showed absent teamster at brigade headquarters.

Jenkins, Thomas W. Enlisted as private, Company F, cavalry or infantry; one card, POW card showed captured at Gettysburg 3 July 1863 and sent to Fort Delaware, arrived 12 July 1863; remarks: "Joined U.S. 3d Md. Cav. By S. O. S. War."

Kidd, J. M. Enlisted as private on 15 May 1862 at Newnan, GA; October 1864 last muster showed present; paroled Greensboro, NC, 1 May 1865.

King, C. W. Enlisted as private on 15 May 1862 at Newnan, GA; October 1864 absent on horse detail since 2 September 1864.

King, E. C. Enlisted as private, Company P; one card, regimental return dated June 1862, stated absent on sick furlough.

King, W. G. Enlisted as private on 2 October 1863 at Newnan, GA; 11 April 1864, absent on detail in Georgia to buy fresh horse since 4 February 1864; 30 September 1864, last muster showed he died 31 July 1864, "His widow Mrs. King on Carroll Co., Georgia, is entitled to receive arrearages of pay of the deceased as his legal representative." Book containing the consolidated report of sick and wounded in the hospitals of North Carolina, dated August 1864 showed he died 8 February 1864 of "February cont." General Hospital No. 8 Raleigh.

Kucaba, D. Enlisted as private, Company F; one card showed paroled Greensboro, NC, 1 May 1865.

Lavender, George, E. (See Company D, DKF).

Malone, T. J. (J. T.). Enlisted as private on 23 December 1863 at Decatur, GA; 11 April 1864, muster showed on detail to Georgia to purchase a horse since 4 February 1864; 30 September 1864, muster showed absent sick since 15 August 1864, now on sick furlough in Georgia; hospital records: admitted to Pettigrew Hospital No. 13 at Raleigh, NC, for "Febris. Cont." furloughed on 12 September 1864 for 60 days, showed residence Greene, GA.

Laney, J. H. (James). Enlisted as private on 12 May 1862 at Macon, GA; 11 October 1864, muster stated "sent to Lynchburg with condemned horse August 17 1864"; October 1864 last muster showed present.

Lee, Jesse E. Enlisted as private on 12 May 1862 at Macon, GA; 29 February 1864, with ambulance corps since 4 February 1864; 1 September 1864, muster showed present; 11 October 1864, last muster showed killed 11 October 1864; Mrs. Jane Lee Longstreet, Pulaski County, GA (LR; living relative.)

Lowe, J. W. Enlisted as sergeant on 12 May 1862 at Macon, GA; 1 September 1864, muster stated left at Beaver Dam Station with disabled horse 15 August 1864; October 1864 last muster showed horse detail 2 September

1864; paroled Greensboro, NC, 1 May 1865.

Lowe, T. J. Enlisted as private on 6 January 1864 at Macon, GA; 1 September 1864, muster stated left at Beaver Dam Station 15 August 1864; 11 October 1864, last muster stated, "Was on duty in Culpeper County, Virginia. Was killed by the enemy September 19 1864. Have learned the facts since the Roll was made out. (L. R.) John N. Cowan, Co. E, Phillips Legion."

Lumsden, B. D. Enlisted as private on 12 May 1862 at Macon, GA; 1 February 1864, muster stated absent without leave, "been absent since October 1863"; 11 April 1864, muster showed detached from company 8 August 1863 by order Gen. Lee; Special Order 94/12, Dept. and Army No. VA/Lee, "Disch. from service" dated 5 April 1864.

Lumsden, J. F. Enlisted as private, no enlistment information; admitted to General Hospital, Charlottesville, VA, 25 July 1863 for "February Typhoides," returned to duty 21 August 1863; Special Order 276 AGO 63 Part 12 "Discharged November 20, 1863."

Mathews, J. F. Enlisted as private on 12 May 1862 at Macon, GA; 14 January 1864, muster stated in hand of enemy, captured 1 August 1863; October 1864, last muster showed captured 1 August 1863 Culpeper County; POW records: captured Brandy Station, VA, 1 August 1863; arrived at Point Lookout 13 August 1863; exchanged 18 February 1865.

Mathews, J. N. Enlisted as private on 12 May 1862 in Macon, GA; 29 February 1864, muster stated AWOL since 4 November 1863; 11 April 1864, muster stated "Detailed for horse in GA November 4 1863 and has since been elected civil office of his country." 5 September 1864, last muster showed discharged by order Gen. Lee January 1864; Special Order 1117 May, Dept. and Army of N. VA, R. E. Lee, 27 April 1864, "Appointed Sheriff Crofford Co—discharged the service."

McLane, W. A. Enlisted as second lieutenant on 12 May 1862 at Macon, GA; elected second lieutenant 1 December 1862; promoted first lieutenant 22 September 1863; October 1864; last muster stated absent sick at hospital Macon, GA, left 1 November 1863; hospital records: admitted Gen.Hosp. No. 4 Richmond, 20 November 1863 "Phthisis Pulmonatis," furloughed 60 days on 28 November 1863; inspection report dated 31 October 1864 "In hospital Macon, Georgia since November 1863, recommended that he be retired." Inspection report dated 31 December 1864, "In hospital Macon, Georgia."

McCollum, J. W. Enlisted as private on 25 May 1862 at Conyers, GA; 11 April

1864, muster showed on sick furlough at home in Georgia, furlough granted at hospital in Richmond; October 1864 last muster showed absent sick in Newton Co., GA; hospital records: 12 March 1864, admitted to Jackson Hospital for "fistula in ano." Furloughed for 60 days on 19 March 1864.

McCoy, D. E. Enlisted as corporal on 15 May 1862 in Newnan, GA; October 1864 last muster showed prisoner in hands of enemy since May 1864; POW records: captured 21 May 1864 at Milford Station. Arrived at Point Lookout on 30 May 1864. Exchanged 11 November 1864; paroled Greensboro, NC, 1 May 1865.

McDonald, H. H. Enlisted as private on 15 May 1862 at Conyers, GA; October 1864 last muster showed absent on horse detail since 2 September 1864; paroled at Greensboro, NC, 1 May 1865.

Merk, J. E. Enlisted as private on 15 May 1862 at Newnan, GA; 11 April 1864, sick at hospital at Richmond since 6 February 1864; April 1864, muster showed present; October 1864 last muster showed present on horse detail since 2 September 1864; hospital records: admitted to Jackson Hospital on 27 February 1864 for abscess foot; admitted to Jackson Hospital on 20 March 1864 for ulcer right foot; returned to duty 7 April 1864.

Merrill, J. B. Enlisted place not stated; elected 2nd lieutenant 16 May 1862; April 1864, muster showed on detached duty at brigade infirmary since 20 December 1863; October 1864 last muster showed absent in command of detachment in Georgia to procure fresh horses; paroled Charlotte, NC, 3 May 1865.

Merrill, John L. Enlisted as private on 11 January 1862 at Hardeville, SC; April 1864, muster showed absent since April 5 to procure a fresh horse; October 1864 absent on horse detail since 2 September 1864.

Millians, Alexander. Enlisted as private on 4 March 1862 at Newnan, GA; October, last muster showed absent prisoner in hands of enemy since 17 December 1863; POW records: captured Craig Co., VA, on 15 December 1863, sent to Camp Chase 31 December 1863 and transferred to Fort Delaware, date not given; died at Fort Delaware 26 June 1864 "Typhoid Mal. Fever"; description from POW records: 6' 1/2", age 24, dark complexion, blue eyes, brown hair, farmer by occupation.

Millians, William (Millines). Enlisted as private on 15 May 1862 at Newnan, GA; October 1864 last muster showed absent on horse detail since 2 September 1864; paroled Greensboro, NC, 1 May 1865.

Millirons, R. M. (Millians). (See Company D and K, DKP).

Moore, Beverly (B. F.). See Company D, DKFP).

Moore, G. A. Enlisted as private on 6 or 7 January 1864 at Newnan, GA; April 1864, muster showed absent on detail in Georgia to buy a fresh horse; 30 September 1864, muster showed absent sick since July 12; recently permitted to go to Carroll Co., GA, on sick furlough; October 1864 last muster card showed absent on sick furlough.

Moore, Thomas. Enlisted as private on 15 May 1862 at Newnan, GA; October 1864 last muster showed absent on horse detail since 2 September 1864; paroled Greensboro, NC, 1 May 1865.

Moore, William J. See Company D (DKFP).

Morris, Joseph C. (J. C.). Enlisted as private on 15 June 1862 at Hardeeville, SC; 11 April 1864, muster showed sent to hospital in Richmond 20 December 1863, "now at home in Georgia on sick furlough out. Now AWOL"; April 1864, muster showed present; October 1864 last muster showed absent sick at hospital in Richmond; hospital records: 22 December 1862, admitted to Jackson Hospital for "vaccine poison"; furloughed 30 December 1863 for 30 days; 29 October 1864, admitted to Jackson Hospital for "consumption" (also showed "phthsis. pul"); returned to duty November 1864; paroled Greensboro, NC, 1 May 1865.

Oglesby, J. M. (Oglesbey). Enlisted 15 May 1862 (place not stated); jr. lieutenant, Company F; 4 March 1863, elected jr. 2nd lieutenant; February 1864, last muster showed died in Newton, Co., GA, 20 January 1864 of pneumonia.

Pace, J. W. Enlisted as private on 15 May 1862 at Newnan, GA; October 1864 last muster showed present; paroled Greensboro, NC, 1 May 1865.

Pace, J. H. H. Enlisted as private on 19 May 1863 at Newnan, GA; April 1864, muster showed absent on detail to procure a fresh horse; October 1864 last muster showed AWOL in Coweta Co., GA, since 12 June 1864; paroled Greensboro, NC, 1 May 1865; hospital records: admitted to Chimborazo Hospital on 20 July 1863 for shell wound foot flesh, transferred to General Hospital Camp Winder in Richmond 29 August 1863 for "vul. Sclo." returned to duty 6 October 1863.

Parker, James R. Enlisted as private, Company F; one card showed died 20 November 1862 of "Chr. Diarrhoea" in Richmond, VA.

Pate, J. M. En. as Corporal on 15 May 1862 in Newnan, GA; October 1864 muster showed present; hospital records: admitted to DA.N.V.ille General Hospital on 12 December 1864 for V.S. in left thumb, furloughed on 15

December 1864 for 60 days.

Pearson, William M. (Pierson). Enlisted as private on 14 May 1862 at Newnan, GA; 30 September 1864, muster showed detailed as provost guard of Army N. VA under Major Bridgeport; October 1864 last muster showed absent sick at hospital; appeared on list of men employed as clerks, and guards in provost marshal's office, Weldon, NC, dated 22 February 1865, "Laborer fit for field service, light duty" by order Major Gen. W. Hampton.

Penn, M. C. Enlisted as private on 15 May 1862 at Conyers, GA; October 1864 last muster showed present.

Robison, J. H. (Robinson, J. M.). Enlisted as private/corporal on 15 May 1862 at Newnan, GA; April 1864, last muster showed "prisoner in hands of enemy—died 3 February 1864"; (3 February 1864 may be when they learned of his death since POW records showed that he died 4 November 1863); POW records: captured Brandy Station, VA, 11 August 1864, arrived Point Lookout 23 August 1863; died 4 November 1863.

Roop, J. K. Enlisted as 1st sergeant on 15 May 1862 at Newnan, GA; October 1864 last muster showed absent on horse detail since 2 September 1864.

Roop, R. H. Enlisted as private on 20 April (year and place not stated), died 14 February 1864 at Richmond, VA, from smallpox.

Roop, W. W. Enlisted as bugler/corporal on 15 May 1862 at Newnan, GA; 11 April 1864, muster showed absent on sick furlough at his home in Carroll Co., GA, since 26 March 1864, furlough granted from hospital from Orange C. H., VA; April 1864, muster showed absent on sick furlough; October 1864 absent on horse detail since 2 September 1864; paroled Greensboro, NC, 1 May 1865.

Sewell, A. F. Enlisted as private, Company F; one card, paroled Greensboro, NC, 1 May 1865.

Simms, A. F. Enlisted as private on 15 May 1862 at Conyers, GA; April 1864, muster showed absent on detail to buy a horse since 5 April 1864; 31 August 1864; muster showed absent sick at hospital in Raleigh since 15 August 1864; October 1864 last muster showed absent sick at hospital; "Diarrhoea Acuta," returned to duty 9 September 1864.

Simrill, A. F. Enlisted as private on 15 May 1862 at Newnan, GA; 30 September 1864, muster showed detailed as provost guard in Army of N. VA under Major Bridgeport; October 1864 last muster showed absent provost guard with Major Bridgeport for A.N.V.

Sims, J. N. Enlisted as private on 15 May 1862 at Conyers, GA; October 1864 last muster showed absent on horse detail since 9 February 1864.

Smallwood, J. H. Enlisted as private on 15 May 1862 at Newnan, GA; October 1864 last muster showed absent on horse detail since 2 September 1864; paroled Greensboro, NC, 1 May 1865.

Smith, E. M. Enlisted as private on 15 May 1862 at Newnan, GA; 11 April 1864, muster showed on detail in Georgia to buy horse since 4 February 1864; October 1864 last muster showed absent on horse detail since 2 September 1864; paroled Greensboro, NC, 1 May 1865.

Smith, Ira E. C. W. See Company D (D and F).

Smith, William A. Enlisted as private on 15 May 1862 at Newnan, GA; 11 April 1864, muster showed on detail in Georgia to buy horse since 4 February 1864; 30 September 1864 (dated 10 August 1864); muster showed absent since 20 September 1864 in Georgia to procure fresh horse by order of Gen. R. E. Lee and AWOL about five weeks in July and August 1864; October 1864 last musters showed absent on horse detail since 2 September 1864. 29 February 1864 Rapidan River, received at Old Capital Prison, D.C. 3 February 1864; sent to Fort Delaware and arrived 17 June 1864; paroled 28 September 1864.

Sewell, J. E. Enlisted as private, Company E, cavalry or infantry; no enlistment information; appeared on a list of medical officers, hospital stewards, detailed attendants and patients in General Hospital No. 11, Charlotte, NC, May 1865; listed as patient, paroled at Charlotte, NC, May 1865.

Seymore, G. W. Enlisted as corporal on 12 May 1862 at Macon, GA; October 1864 on detached service with brigade ordnance train since 2, 12, or 14 August 1864; paroled Greensboro, NC, 1 May 1865.

Seymore, H. H. Enlisted as private on 12 May 1862 at Macon, GA; 29 February 1864, muster stated at recruiting camp, left 4 February 1864; October 1864 last muster showed detailed with brigade QM dept. since 21 or 24 September 1864; paroled Greensboro, NC, 1 May 1865.

Seymore, R. H. Enlisted as private on 12 May 1862 at Macon, GA; October 1864 last muster showed present.

Shelverton, Norman. Enlisted as private on 12 May 1862 at Macon, GA; 1 September 1864, muster showed on detached service at recruiting camp since 4 February 1864; October 1864 last muster showed on horse detail since 2 September 1864 by order Gen. Lee.

Slappy, R. R. Enlisted as private on 15 or 16 February 1864 at Macon, GA; 11 April 1864, on detail for horse in Georgia since 14 February 1865 by order of Major Harris commanding conscripts; 11 October 1864, muster showed on sick furlough 60 days 17 August 1864; October 1864 last muster showed on horse detail since 2 September 1864 by order Gen. Lee; paroled Greensboro, NC, 1 May 1865.

Smith, John. Enlisted as private on 12 May 1862 at Macon, GA; October 1864 last muster showed on horse detail since 2 September 1864 by order Gen. Lee; paroled Greensboro, NC, 1 May 1865.

Smith, S. P. Enlisted as private on 12 May 1862 at Macon, GA; October 1864 with brigade ordnance train since 26 December 1863; paroled Greensboro, NC, 1 May 1865.

Stubbs, J. W. Enlisted as private on 4 February or 5 April 1864 at Macon, GA; October 1864 last muster showed absent sick at Hospital at Richmond since 26 August 1864; paroled Greensboro, NC, 1 May 1865; hospital records: 28 August 1864, admitted to Jackson Hospital for "Dia. Chron." returned to duty 30 September 1864; 28 November 1864, admitted to CSA General Hospital, Danville, VA, returned to duty 2 December.

Sykes, Isaac (Sikes). Enlisted as musician in Company E on 12 May 1862 at Macon, GA; 11 April 1864, muster stated "captured by enemy July 4, 1863 and paroled and furloughed March 18, 1864"; 1 September 1864, muster stated, "On detached service in Macon, Georgia, by order of medical Board since March 19, 1864"; October 1864 last muster stated absent, wounded at hospital Macon, GA, 19 March 1864; POW records: captured Cashtown 5 July 1863; sent to General Hospital Chester, PA, and transferred to Hammond General Hospital, arrived 4 October 1863; paroled at Hammond U.S.

Warren, William. Enlisted as private on 15 August 1862 at Charlotte, NC; February 1864, on furlough since 21 February 1864; 11 April 1864, muster showed on furlough at home in Alabama since 21 February 1864; April 1864, muster showed absent since sick in Randolph Co., AL; October 1864 last muster showed absent on horse detail since 2 September 1864.

Wiley, J. W. Enlisted as private on 15 May 1862 at Newnan, GA; 11 April 1864, muster showed on horse detail in Georgia since 4 February 1864; April 1864, on detached duty in QM dept. with Major Goodwin; 30 September 1864, muster showed on detached duty with div. QM; October, last muster showed present.

Wood, A. S. Enlisted as private, Company F; one card, paroled Greensboro, NC, 1 May 1865.

Wood, Beverly. Enlisted as private, Company P; "Not on rolls" but appeared on regimental return for June 1862 as "absent on sick furlough."

Wood, C. P. Enlisted as private on 15 September 1862 at Newnan, GA; October 1864 last muster showed present; paroled Greensboro, NC, 1 May 1865.

Wood, J. N. Enlisted as private on 15 May 1862 at Newnan, GA; April 1864, on detail to buy a horse in Georgia since 4 February 1864; October 1864 last muster showed detailed at recruiting camp; paroled Greensboro, NC, 1 May 1865.

Young, J. J. Enlisted as sergeant on 15 May 1862 at Newnan, GA; October 1864 last muster showed absent on horse detail since 2 September 1864.

APPENDIX I

COMPANY G

THE RICHMOND DRAGOONS

Composed of men from Richmond County and formerly Company K, the 11th cavalry company of Cobb's Georgia Legion cavalry battalion. This company was transferred by Confederate authorities as G Company to the Phillips Georgia Legion cavalry battalion in late 1864 under command of Captain Frances Edgeworth Eve. Company G remained with the Phillips Georgia Legion until the end of the war when it surrendered at Greensboro, NC. Records for Company G are incomplete. Various sources of Confederate soldier listings lumped companies together and may have duplicated and/or missed some names.

Abercrombie, C. Enlisted as private, Company G; paroled Greensboro, NC, 1 May 1865.

Bates, William. Enlisted as private, Company G, paroled Greensboro, NC, 1 May 1865.

Bennett, G. W. Enlisted as sergeant, Company G, cavalry or infantry; no enlistment information; captured at Smithfield, NC; no date of capture; copy of oath, 22 April 1865, Raleigh, NC.

Bowen, James. Enlisted as first lieutenant, Company G; elected first lieutenant, February 1863; resigned November 1863.

Bradbury, J. L. Enlisted as private in Company G; no further information.

Cato, John L. Enlisted as private, Company G; no enlistment information; one card; paroled at Greensboro, NC, 1 May 1865. Courier detached from his command and servicing at army headquarters.

Clanton, James L. Enlisted as second lieutenant/first lieutenant, Company G, elected second lieutenant February 1863; promoted first lieutenant on 24 November 1863; no enlistment information; roster dated 7 January 1865 showed promotion information.

Clark, J. T. Enlisted as private, Company G, paroled Greensboro, NC, 1 May 1865.

Echols, F. G. Enlisted as private, Company G; no further information.

Edwards, James. Enlisted as private, Company G, at Lynchburg, VA, on August

1861; 26 years of age at enlistment; letter dated 29 October 1861 and signed by Captain R. T. Cook stated he was shot through the wrist on the 28 October while on picket duty 19 October 1861 at Camp Dickenson by an accidental discharge of his gun, a Mississippi rifle; recommended discharge. (Letter in file from surgeon A. Connell is dated 19 October 1861 and also recommended discharge. Must have been wounded on the 18th instead of the 28th.) Discharge approved; 6' 2", dark complexion, dark hair and eyes, farmer; appeared on POW roll not dated. Captured Anderson, SC, 8 May 1865; "Paroled at Hartwell, Georgia, and Anderson and Greenville, South Carolina."

Ennis, G. M. Enlisted as private in Company G; no further information.

Eve, Frances Edgeworth. Enlisted as captain, Company G; roster dated 6 January 1865 showed elected captain February 1863; inspection report dated 31 December 1865 showed in Georgia with Gen. Young, by order of Gen. Lee; no further records or enlistment information.

Green, Byron B. Enlisted as private/sergeant in Company G; no further information.

Hammon, John. Probably enlisted in Captain F. E. Eve's Company G late in the war; killed on 11 February 1865 at Orangeburg, SC, near the railroad depot; he is buried in the cemetery of the Protestant Episcopal Church of the Redeemer.

Henderson, J. L. Enlisted as private in Company G; no further information.

Martin, J. C. Enlisted as private, Company G; one card, regimental return dated April 1862, showed enlisted 3 March 1862.

Matthews, James Enlisted as private, Company G; one card showed paroled Greensboro, NC, 1 May 1865.

O'Hare, Patrick Enlisted as private, Company G; no enlistment information; POW records showed captured 7 February 1865 at Columbia, SC; sent to Hart's Island, NY; arrived 10 April 1865; oath and released 6 June 1865; place of residence, Richmond, GA; fair complexion, light hair, gray eyes, 5' 7 1/2".

Thomas, James. Enlisted as corporal, Company 0; one card; paroled Greensboro, NC, 1 May 1865.

Walker, J. W. Enlisted as sergeant, Company G; one card-regimental return dated June, 1862 showed detached service-secretary to Col. Phillips.

West, J. K. Enlisted as private, Company G; one card, reg. return, May 1862 showed enlisted at Camp Pritchard, SC.

White, Augustus. Enlisted as second lieutenant, Company G; one card, elected second lieutenant February 1863; resigned per roster dated 7 January 1865 (date of resignation not listed).

Willis, Thomas J. Enlisted as private, Company G; paroled Greensboro, NC, 1 May 1865; "courier detached from his command and serving army headquarters."

Worley, James P. Enlisted as private in Company G; no further information.

APPENDIX II

THE LOVELIES

Companies H, I, and K of the Jeff Davis Legion were originally companies A, B, and C of Love's 4th Battalion, Alabama Cavalry. These three companies served in Alabama before going to Virginia in May 1864 when they joined the Phillips Georgia Legion cavalry battalion where they became cavalry companies A, B, C, and D. They served with the Phillips Georgia Legion under the command of Captain Andrew Pickens Love until the following November 1864 when they were reassigned to the Jeff Davis Legion. The men of the Phillips Georgia Legion cavalry battalion often referred to their Alabama comrades as the "Lovelies."

Company H

Barber, James. No further records.

Beard, Adolphus. No further records.

Bell, C (C. A. Bell). Enlisted 19 August 1863, Troy, AL, for three years; Hosp. Richmond June 1864 and August 1864 "acute dysentery," (born Barbout Co., AL, enlisted Clayton, AL, on 3 September 1863; paroled at Hillsboro, AL, 1865.

Bell, M. M. ("Monroe"). Paroled as member of 3rd Ala. Cav., 7 June 1865. Bell, W. N. No further records.

Bond, William M. ("Bill" Bonds, Bounds). Orderly sgt. enlisted 24 August 1863 in Troy, AL, for three years; present October 1864.

Boswell, Wilson (William Boswell, Baswell). Enlisted 21 August 1863, Troy, AL, for three years. A farrier; surrendered Greensboro, NC, 1 May 1865.

Boutwell, Holley. Enlisted 29 November 1863 at Troy, AL, for three years; present October 1864.

Bowden, Elisha L. Enlisted 29 September 1863 at Troy, AL, for three years; Hosp. Danville, VA, 51864 "acute dysentery."

Bowden, Lem. No further records.

Bowden, Sims. No further records.

Brabham, James G. (James B. Brabham). Enlisted 28 September 1863 for three years.; surrendered Greensboro, NC, 25 May 1865.

Brannon, Samuel A. No further records.

Brown, Henry C. Enlisted 24 August 1863 in Troy, AL, for three years; Hosp.

Charleston, SC, 31864 "icterus."

Brunson, Samuel A. Enlisted 20 October 1863 at Troy, AL, for three years; present October 1864.

Capps, Spencer W. Enlisted 30 September 1863 at Troy, AL, for the war; surrendered Greensboro 1 May 1865.

Carlisle, Daniel. Enlisted November 1863, Troy, AL, hosp. August 1864; paroled 2 June 1865 at Montgomery, AL.

Carmichael, George A. Enlisted 20 October 1863 at Troy, AL, for three years; present October 1864.

Carnley, Zedekiah (Ky, Kigh). Enlisted 1 August 1863 at Troy, AL, for three years. Hosp. Richmond; 61864; died hosp. Lynchburg, VA, 27 July 1864; married.

Carter, Creen T. Enlisted 24 August 1863 at Troy, AL; Hosp. Troy August 1864; present October 1864.

Carter, Grinnel. No further records.

Carter, John. No further records.

Carter, Seabom. Enlisted 25 August 1863 at Troy, AL, for three years; musician; Hosp. Montgomery, AL, August 1864; present October 1864.

Chesser, John W. Enlisted 31 August 1863 at Troy, AL, for three years; hospital August 1864; died at home.

Childs, Alfred S. Enlisted as cpl. at Troy, AL, for three years.

Cox, John W. Enlisted 18 October 1863 at Troy, AL, for three years; present October 1864.

Curry, Bud. No further records.

Darby, John R. (Darbey). Enlisted 22 December 1863 at Troy, AL, for three years; surrendered Greensboro, NC, 1 May 1865.

Dawson, James P. No further records.

Devane, J. T. Enlisted 24 August 1863 as lieutenant at Troy, AL, for three years; present October 1864.

Devant, Frank (Devine). Lieutenant; no further records.

Duncan, William J. ("Bill"). Enlisted 24 August 1863 as lieutenant on 24 August 1863 at Troy, AL, for three years; hosp 41864, Danville, VA, "retinitis"; hosp "diarrhea" June 1864 Weldon, VA, August 1864.

Geotes, Sam No further records.

Grantham, James F. (James T.). Enlisted 1863 at Troy, AL, for three years; to Co. H, 18th reg. AL, August 1864

Griffin, Hardy. Enlisted 1 September 1863 at Troy, AL, for three years; present

October 1864.

Griffin, Joe. No further records.

Griffin, R. D. Paroled June 1865 at Montgomery, AL.

Harlow, John. Enlisted 25 September 1863 at Troy, AL, for three years.

Henderson, G. A. ("Guss"). No further records.

Henderson, J. A. Enlisted 1 March 1864 at Troy, AL, for three years; present October 1864.

Henderson, J. H. Enlisted 1 March 1864 at Troy, AL; surrendered Greensboro, NC, 1 May 1865.

Henderson, J. M. ("Munrow"). Enlisted 4 November 1863 at Troy, AL, for three years; Hosp. Richmond, June 1864; present October 1864.

Herring, Stephen. Enlisted 12 January 1864 at Troy, AL, for three years; surrendered Greensboro, NC, 1 May 1865.

Hobdy, Ira. Enlisted 24 August 1863 at Troy, AL, for three years; detached dty QM sgt October 1863; present October 1864.

Hobdy, Jackson P. No further records.

Hobdy, John. Enlisted October 1864 at Troy, AL, for the war.

Horn, William E. G. Enlisted 21 October 1863 at Troy, AL, for three years.

Horn, Green (may be the same as above). No further records.

Jeter, Ransom. Enlisted 17 October 1863 at Troy, AL, for three years; surrendered Greensboro, NC, 1 May 1865.

Jeter, W. M. (W. M. Jester, Geter). Paroled Montgomery, AL, 1 May 1865.

Johnson, R. C. (Ruffin C. C. Johnson). Enlisted 17 September 1863 at Troy, AL, for three years; Hosp. Lynchburg, VA, 1 May 1864; died disease 14 May 1864.

Jones, J. A. No further records.

Keith, Wiley (W. C. Keith). Enlisted 24 August 1863 at Troy, AL, for three years; hosp. May 1864 Richmond; wounded furlough 31 August 1864; paroled Montgomery, AL, May 1865.

Kelly, Michael. Enlisted 24 August 1863 at Troy, AL, for three years; Hosp. Raleigh, NC, August 1864; surrendered Greensboro, NC, 1 May 1865.

Kendrick, J. F. (J. T. Kendrick). Enlisted 17 September 1863 at Troy, AL, for three years; captured August 1864 near Petersburg, VA; imprisoned City Point, Hosp. Charlotte, NC, February 1865 "parotitis"; surrendered Greensboro, NC, 1 May 1864.

King, Jack (Jackson H. King). Enlisted as sgt on 31 August 1863 at Troy, AL, for the war; surrendered Greensboro, NC, 1 May 1865.

Kirkland, Reuben R. (Rueben). Enlisted as lieutenant 24 August 1863; elected
 second lieutenant 51864; detached dty Lynchburg, VA, August 1864;
 paroled Montgomery, AL, April 1865; (lived at Union Springs, AL).
Kirksey, John E. Enlisted 5 January 1864 at Montgomery, AL, for three years;
 Hosp. Weldon, NC, August 1864.
Kirksey, William. Corporal; no further records.
Kirvin, Ichabod. No further records.
Kirvin, R. J. (R. H. Herring, may be the same as above). Enlisted 15 December
 1863 at Covington Co., AL, for three years Hosp. Richmond, October 1864;
 lived at Covington, AL.
Lee, Evan. Enlisted as Corporal 27 August 1863 at Troy, AL, for three years;
 Hosp. Weldon, NC, August 1864.
Love, Andrew Pickens. Enlisted 29 August 1864 as captain at Troy, AL, for
 three years; elected captain 24 August 1863; Hosp. Dinwiddie, VA,
 September 1864 "chronic diarrhea"; (Delegate to secession convention in
 1861; captured at Burgess Mill near Dinwiddie, VA, October 1864; a
 merchant from Pike Co., AL, at enlistment. Originally was captain of Co. I,
 22nd Ala. Inf, later captain of 4th Batt. Ala. Cavalry.)
Lucus, W. H. Corporal; no further records.
Lynn, Whit. Corporal; no further records.
McDonald-Corporal; no further records.
McDougold, John D. (McDougold, McDougal, probably same as above).
 Enlisted as corporal 30 September 1863 at Troy, AL, for the war; Hosp.
 Raleigh, NC, August 1864 "inguinal hernia"; lived in New Providence, Pike
 Co., AL; surrendered Greensboro, NC, 1 May 1865.
Mancil, James. No further records.
May, Alex ("Elick," A. S. May). Enlisted 30 September 1863 as sgt. at Troy,
 AL, for three years; Hosp. Raleigh, NC, July 1864, August 1864 "febris
 remitt bilious"; detached duty as fisherman August 1864; surrendered
 Greensboro, NC, 1 May 1865.
Mount, William P. ("Pickney"). Enlisted 3 October 1863 at Troy, AL, for three
 years; present October 1864.
Pilate, J. M. (Minor Pilate, Mirian Pilate). Enlisted 28 October 1863 at Troy,
 AL, for three years; present October 1864.
Reeves, William M. (William W. Reeves). Enlisted 3 August 1863 at Troy, AL,
 for three years; present October 1864.
Rice, William R. Enlisted 17 September 1863 as sgt maj at Troy, AL, for three

years; detached dty as acting sgt maj at post of Troy, AL; present October 1864; paroled Montgomery, AL, June 1865.

Richardson, Augustus. Enlisted 7 October 1863 at Troy, AL, for three years; hosp July 1864 at Richmond, "chronic diarrhea," Hosp. Petersburg, VA, August 1864; present October 1864.

Richburg, Sanders (S. J. Richbourg, A. J. Richburg). Enlisted as sgt 2 August 1863 at Troy, AL, for three years; surrendered Greensboro, NC, 1 May 1865.

Sanders, James N. (J. M. Saunders). Enlisted 25 August 1863 at Troy, AL, for three years; Hosp. Richmond, June 1864 and July 1864; present October 1864.

Smart, William E. Enlisted 6 September 1863 at Troy, AL, for the war; Hosp. Raleigh, NC, December 1864 "rubeola," hosp. January 1865 Raleigh, NC; surrendered Greensboro, NC, 1 May 1865.

Smith, Richard. Enlisted 24 August 1863 at Troy, AL, for three years; hosp VA, August 1864; present October 1864.

Stevens, Felix ("Feilicks"). Enlisted 31 August 1863 for three years; surrendered Greensboro, NC, 1 May 1865.

Stevens, James E. (Stephens). Enlisted 25 August 1863 at Troy, AL, for three years 25 August, Hosp. Charlotte, NC, February 1865 "icterus"; discharged 29 March 1865 surg. cert. "adhesions between the pleura and the walls of the chest and strong tendency to pthisis pulmonale"; Hosp. Charlotte, NC, April 1865 "typhoid fever."

Stevens, J. L. (James T. Stephens). Enlisted 1 September 1863 at Troy, AL, for three years; Hosp. Richmond, August 1864; present October 1864.

Stevens, Needham. Enlisted 31 August 1863 at Troy, AL, for three years.

Stevens, Samuel (Stephens). Enlisted 27 August 1863 at Troy, AL, for three years; Hosp. Troy, AL, August 1864; paroled Montgomery, AL May 1865.

Steward, William. No further records.

Stinson, James M. Enlisted as corporal 26 November 1863 at Troy, AL, for three years; Hosp. Petersburg, VA, August 1864; paroled Montgomery, AL, June 1865.

Taylor, Meridith D. Enlisted 31 August 1863 at Troy, AL, for three years; detached dty as commissary sgt at post of Troy, October 1863.

Taylor, M. S. (may be same as above). No further records.

Tedman, Samuel. No further records.

Thomas, W. E. No further records.

Thomas, W. M. (may be same as above). Enlisted 1 October 1863 at Troy, AL, for three years; Hosp. Richmond May 1864, June 1864, August 1864; paroled Montgomery, AL, 1 May 1865.

Vickers, Joel (J. W. Vickers). Enlisted 6 October 1863 at Troy, AL, for three years; present October 1864.

Wesley, B. M. Enlisted 1 September 1863 at Troy, AL, for three years; Hosp. Richmond, June 1864, July 1864; surrendered Greensboro, NC, 1 May 1865.

Wesley, Moses. No further records.

Williams, F. S. Enlisted 23 February 1864 at Troy, AL, for three years; surrendered Greensboro, NC, 1 May 1865.

Wilson, Edward (Edwin). Enlisted as corporal on 26 August 1863 at Troy, AL, for three years; Hosp. Richmond, August 1864 "chronic rheumatism," also September 1864; paroled Montgomery, AL, 1 May 1865.

Wilson, Fred. No further records.

Wilson, Jeff. No further records.

Wilsom Warren. Enlisted 2 August 1863 at Troy, AL, for three years; detached dty as wagoneer; Hosp. Augusta, GA.

Wilson, Z J. Enlisted 30 August 1863 at Troy, AL, for three years; Hosp. Richmond June 1864; detached dty July 1864 as wagoneer; present October 1864.

Company I

Andrews, Stephen A. Enlisted as corporal 8 September 1861 at Montgomery, AL, for three years; surrendered at Greensboro, NC, 1 May 1865.

Barnes, William. Enlisted as sergeant 8 September 1861 at Montgomery, AL, for three years.

Barr, John P. Enlisted as corporal 8 September 1861 at Montgomery, AL, for three years; surrendered Greensboro, NC, 1 May 1865.

Boxley, William. Enlisted 18 September 1863 at Montgomery, AL, for three years; wounded Trevillian's Station, VA, June 1864.

Baxter, James A. (James August Baxter). Enlisted 18 September 1863 at Montgomery, AL, for three years; surrendered Greensboro, NC, 1 May 1865; born 1846, Barbour Co., AL; enlisted 17 December 1863, Louisville, AL; living in 1907.

Beasley, James T. Enlisted Montgomery, AL, 18 September 1863 for three years; surrendered Greensboro, NC, 1 May 1865.

Bickerstaff, Warren R. (Biggerstaff). Enlisted as sergeant 18 September 1863 at

Montgomery, AL, for three years; Hosp. Richmond June 1864; surrendered Greensborn, NC, 1 May 1865.

Broach, Absalom L. Enlisted Montgomery, AL, 18 September 1863 for the war; surrendered Greensboro, NC, 1 May 1865.

Broach, William. Enlisted 18 September 1863 at Montgomery, AL, for three years; Hosp. Richmond June 1864; discharged surg cert 14 September 1864.

Bostick, Samuel G. (Bastick). Enlisted 18 September 1863 at Montgomery, AL, for three years; surrendered Greensboro, NC, 25 May 1865.

Bostick, William C. Enlisted 11 October 1863 at Montgomery, AL, for three years; Hosp. Richmond June 1864.

Burke, James A. Enlisted 18 September 1863 at Montgoery, AL, for three years; Hosp. Richmond June 1864; surrendered Greensboro, NC, 1 May 1865.

Burton, W. M. Enlisted 1 November 6 1863 at Eufala, AL, for the war; present August 1864.

Day, L. Paroled, Montgomery, AL, 1 May 1865.

Dorman, Alexander A. Enlisted as sergeant 18 September 1863 at Montgomery, AL, for three years; enlisted 3 April 1863 at Clayton, AL; paroled at Hillsboro, AL (NC?).

Dowling Elias G. (G. T. Dowling). Enlisted 18 September 1863 at Montgomery, AL, for the war; Hosp. Richmond, May, June 1864 "Confusion"; Hosp. July, August 1864 "Phthisis pulmonale."

Duke Ranson (B. Duke). Enlisted 18 September 1863 at Montgomery, AL, for three years; Hosp. Richmond 8 September 1864; surrendered Greensboro, NC, 1 May 1865.

Eidson, Wiley. Enlisted 16 September 1863 at Montgomery, AL, for three years; present August 1864.

Elliott, William. Enlisted 18 September 1863 at Montgomery, AL, for three years; KIA Staunton River Bridge, 18 May 1864.

Euford, John A. (Eaford, Eford). Enlisted 1 December 1863 at Montgomery, AL, for three years; Hosp. August 1864, Richmond.

Fielder, Alonzo D. Enlisted as lieutenant 18 September 1863 at Montgomery, AL, for the war; Hosp. Richmond June, July, August 1864, "Phthisis pulmonale," detached in command of Co. C, AL. Batt. Cav, August 1864; sent with dismounted men to Georgia with Gen. Young, 24 November 1864, paroled Montgomery, AL, May 1865.

FlouMay Thomas J. (P. J. FlouMay, P. E. Floynoy). Enlisted as bugler, age 17, Montgomery, AL, for three years; Hosp. Richmond June 1864 "irreducible inguinal hernia," discharged surg. cert. 5 July 1864; born Eufala, AL, a student at enlistment.

Gartner. James H. Enlisted 10 October 1863 at Montgomery, AL, for three years; Hosp. Richmond May 1864 "confusion."; surrendered Greensboro, NC, 1 May 1865.

Giles, Hugh. Enlisted 18 September 1863 Montgomery, AL, for three years; on sick furlough August 1864.

Gremillian, Jesse (Pinkney J.Gremillian). Enlisted 11 November 1863 at Montgomery, AL, for three years; present 8 September 1864.

Grubbs, James W. (James Walton Gribbs). Enlisted 18 September 1863 at Montgomery, AL, for the war; surrendered Greensboro, NC, 1 May 1865; (born 1846, Barbour, AL; enlisted 8 September 1863; paroled Hillsboro, NC, May 1865.)

Grubbs, Worthy J. Enlisted as lieutenant 18 September 1863 at Montgomery, AL, for the war; detached dty to Montgomery, AL, October 1863 with 30 men to procure horses; Hosp. Richmond, June 1864; retired 11 January 1865.

Holloway, J. D: (John D. Holloway). Enlisted 18 September 1863 Montgomery, AL, for three years; Hosp. Richmond, May 1864 "debilitas."

Hudson, Erwin (Irba). Enlisted 18 September 1863 at Montgomery, AL, for three years; died 24 June 1864.

Hurst, J. A. (James A. Hurst). Enlisted 10 February 1864 at Montgomery, AL, for three years; surrendered Greensboro, NC, 1 May 1865; (Enlisted 3 Sept 1863 at Clayton, AL; paroled Greensboro, NC.)

Jinks, W. (William Jenks). Enlisted 1 December 1863 at Montgomery, AL, for the war: Hosp. Richmond, Hosp. July 1864 "Chronic Rheumatism," Hosp. October 1865 Raleigh, NC, "chronic diarrhea,"; lived in Tuskegee, Macon Co, AL; surrendered Greensboro, NC, 1 May 1865.

Jones, James A. Enlisted 1 December 1863 at Montgomery, for three years; present 8 September 1864.

Lampley, Linton J. Enlisted 18 September 1863 at Montgomery, AL, for three years; Hosp. August 1864; surrendered Greensboro, NC, 1 May 1865.

Lane, Henry C. Enlisted as corporal on 10 October 1863 at Montgomery, AL, for three years; Hosp. August 1864; discharged 10 August 1864.

Lauftis, Nathan W. (Nathaniel W. Loftus). Enlisted 20 October 1863 at Montgomery, AL, for three years; wounded Trevillian's Station, VA, 11 June 1864; "Absent wounded, leg amputated (left thigh)" 30 September

1864.

Leak, William W. Enlisted 11 November 1864 at Montgomery, AL, for the war; Hosp. Richmond, May 1864; present 8 September 1864.

Lightner, Thomas S. Enlisted 18 September 1863 at Montgomery, AL, for the war; present August 1864.

McCall, Gilbert. Enlisted 18 September 1863 at Montgomery, AL, for the war; Hosp. Richmond, May, July, August 1864, "chronic diarrhea," transferred to 2nd div. 14 July 1864; surrendered Greensboro, NC, 1 May 1865.

McDonald, Daniel. Enlisted 10 October 1863 at Montgomery, AL, for three years; absent wounded 1 May 1864; wounded Staunton Bridge 18 May 1864; Hosp. Danville, VA, 11 June "injury to leg."

McGildrey, J. W. (John W. McGilvay, McGilver, McGiloray). Enlisted age 19, 1 February 1864 at Montgomery, AL, for three years; Hosp. Richmond, July 1864 "chronic diarrhea"; captured Salisbury 12 April 1865; imprisoned Nashville and Louisville, KY, then Camp Chase, OH; lived in Barbour Co, AL; paroled June 1865.

McKenzie, Bethune Beaton (Burton B. McKenzie). Enlisted as captain 18 September 1863; Hosp. Richmond June 1864, "diarrhea and debility"; Hosp. Richmond "remittent fever, relapsing fever," October 1864; surrendered Greensboro, NC, 1 May 1865; born 1837 near Louisville, Barbour Co., AL; enlisted as sergeant 7 April 1861 in Louisville Blues, Co. B, 7th Alabama infantry until September 1861; discharged Pensacola later to reenlist at Montgomery, AL, in 39th AL. Inf., Co. B until October 1862 when he was reassigned because of sickness; made captain in Love's 4th AL cavalry batt. before becoming officer of Jeff Davis Legion; lived in Louisville, AL.

McRae, Christopher M. Enlisted 18 September 1863 at Montgomery, AL, for three years; Hosp. 8 September 1864.

McRae, Daniel N. (N. D. McRae, D. W. McRay). Enlisted 1 February 1864 at Montgomery, AL, for three years; Hosp. Danville, VA, May 1864 "confusion,"; surrendered Greensboro, NC, 1 May 1865.

Matthies, Henry. Enlisted 1 February 1864 at Montgomery, AL, for three years; Hosp. Danville, VA May 1864 "confusion"; surrendered Greensboro, NC, 1 May 1865.

Matthews (William M. Matheis). Enlisted 18 September 1863 Montgomery, AL, for the war: "Absent Wounded, leg amputated."

Miller, W. B. Enlisted 18 September 1863 at Montgomery, AL, for three years; Hosp. Raleigh, NC, July 1864.

Moreman, Benjamin F. (Moman). Enlisted 1 February 1864 Montgomery, AL, for three years; surrendered Greensboro, NC, 1 May 1865.

Mosely, William B. Enlisted 18 September 1863 at Montgomery, AL, for three years; surrendered Greensboro, NC, May 1865.

Nicholls, Franklin M. (F. N. Nickolls, Nuckolls, Nuckoals). Enlisted as sergeant 1 November 1863 at Montgomery, AL, for the war; Hosp. Danville, VA, May 1864 "confusion"; wounded Sapony Church 27 June 1864; surrendered Greensboro, NC, 1 May 1865.

Ratton, W. 0. (Rotten). Enlisted 18 September 1863 at Montgomery, AL, for three years; surrendered Greensboro, NC, 1 May 1865.

Raley, John W. Enlisted 1 September 1863 at Montgomery, AL, for three years; present 8 September 1864.

Reavis, W. A. Hosp. Richmond June 1864.

Roberts, Henry. Enlisted 18 September 1863 at Montgomery, AL, for three years; Hosp. Richmond June 1865; surrendered Greensboro, NC, 1 May 1865.

Robinson, Moses (Roberson, Robertson). Enlisted as corporal 18 September 1863 at Montgomery, AL, for three years; surrendered Greensboro, NC, 1 May 1865.

Ryles, R. B. (Ryalls). Enlisted 18 September 1863 at Montgomery, AL, for three years; Hosp. Columbus, GA, September 1864; surrendered Greensboro, NC, 1 May 1865.

Sanders, A. (Andrew). Enlisted 18 September 1863 at Montgomery, AL, for three years; Hosp. Danville, VA, "rheumatism"; surrendered Greensboro, NC, 1 May 1865.

Sanders, Jacob. Enlisted 18 September 1863 Montgomery, AL, for three years; captured near Petersburg, VA, 27 October 1864; imprisoned City Point; from Pike Co., AL.

Slaughter, H. T. Enlisted as sergeant 13 September 1863 at Montgomery, AL, for three years; surrendered Greensboro, NC, 1 May 1865.

Smith, Seaborn J. Enlisted 18 September 1863 at Montgomery, AL, for three years; present 8 September 1864.

Smith, William. Enlisted 18 September 1863 at Montgomery, AL, for three years, present 8 September 1864.

Spivy, H. (Henry Spivey, H. C. Springs). Enlisted 1 November 1863 at Montgomery, AL, for the war; Hosp. Charlotte, NC, February 1865 "febris intermittens tertian"; surrendered Greensboro, NC, 1 May 1865.

Traut, Daniel K. Enlisted as corporal 18 September 1863 at Montgomery, AL, for three years; Hosp. October 1864.

Utsey, Govan (Utley). Enlisted 1 September 1863 at Montgomery, AL, for three years; surrendered Greensboro, NC, 1 May 1865.

Vinson, Nicholas W. (A. W. Vinson). Enlisted as lieutenant 18 September 1863 at Montgomery, AL, for three years; elected second lieutenant 18 September 1863; surrendered Greensboro, NC, 1 May 1865.

Warren James B. (James Burrus Warren). Enlisted 18 September 1863 at Montgomery AL, for three years; Hosp. Danville, VA, May 1864 "gonorrhea"; Hosp. Richmond, June 1864; absent furlough August 1864 "a lunatic" About 65 in 1907; enlisted in Clayton, Barbour Co, AL; in Jeff Davis Legion in Yancy's (Young's) Brg; paroled Hillsboro, NC.

Warren, Joel M. Enlisted 18 September 1863 at Montgomery, AL, for three years; absent wounded 8 September 1864; Hosp. Charlotte, NC, 15 May 1865 "gunshot wound."

Wheeler, J. T. Corporal Hospital Richmond; March 1864 "chronic diarrhea."

White, Joseph, M. Enlisted 18 September 1863 at Montgomery, AL, for three years; present 8 September 1864.

Wise, John Edward. No further records; born 1846 in Barbour Co., AL; enlisted 1 December 1863 Eufala, AL; paroled 20 May 1865.

Wright, R. J. Enlisted 18 September 1863 at Montgomery, AL, for three years; surrendered Greensboro, NC, 1 May 1865.

Wright, W. M. No further records.

Company K

Barnard, E. S. Enlisted 17 October 1863 at Eufaula, AL, for the war; detached dty city government shops; Eufala, AL.

Bates, Andrew. Enlisted 17 October 1863 at Eufaula, AL, for three years.

Bell, C. A. (Kirvin Bell). Enlisted 10 February 1864 at Montgomery, AL, for three years; Hosp. Richmond, June 1864 "rebeola".

Bray, W. H. Enlisted as lieutenant 17 October 1863 at Eufaula, AL, for three years; wounded Cold Harbor, VA, 16 August 1864; Hosp. Richmond, August 1864 "chronic diarrhea"; surrendered Greensboro, NC, 1 May 1865.

Brock, W. M. Lieutenant.

Buruss, Charles. Enlisted 29 October 1863 at Eufaula, AL, for the war; discharged by civil process 26 December 1864.

Burtin, J. T. (Burton, Burten). Enlisted 24 October 1863 at Eufaula, AL, for the war; Hosp. Richmond, June 1864.

Bush, D. A. Enlisted 17 October 1863 as a musician at Eufaula, AL; Hosp. Eufaula, AL, May 1864; surrendered Greensboro, NC, 1 May 1865.

Bush, J. J. Enlisted 9 December 1863 at Eufaula, AL, for the war; Hosp. Richmond, August 1864; lived in Eufaula, AL (surrendered Albany, GA, May 1865).

Bush, W. B. Hosp. Charlotte, NC; 28 February 1865 "Febris Int. Tertius."

Callaway, J. S. Enlisted as sergeant 17 October 1863 at Eufaula, AL, for the war; surrendered Greensboro, NC, 1 May 1865.

Carter, H. G. Enlisted 17 October 1863 at Eufaula, AL, for the war; Hosp. Richmond, June 1864, Hosp. Charlotte, NC, April 1865 "irritatious Spinalis."

Catchings, F. E. Enlisted 22 December 1863 at Eufaula, AL, for the war; Hosp. Richmond, August 1864.

Cherry, A. J. Enlisted 9 November 1863 at Eufaula, AL, for the war; Hosp. Richmond, June 1864.

Crawford, A. P. Enlisted 24 October 1863 at Eufaula, AL, for the war; present August 1864.

Drew, John H. Enlisted 1 November 7 1863 at Eufaula, AL, for the war; Hosp. Richmond, June 1864.

Dubose, J. P. Enlisted 17 October 1863 at Eufaula, AL, for the war; present August 1864.

Ferrer, Camillus (Farrar, Cornelius Ferris). Enlisted 12 December 1863 at Eufaula, AL, for the war; Hosp. Eufaula, AL, April 1864; captured 27 February 1865 at Lynch Creek, SC; imprisoned Point Lookout, MD; paroled June 1865; lived in Barbour,Co., AL.

Flowers, Wright. Enlisted 17 October 1863 at Eufaula, AL, for three years; surrendered Greensboro, NC, 1 May 1865.

Gannon, W. C. Enlisted 17 October 1863 at Eufaula, AL; surrendered Greensboro, NC, 1 May 1865.

Glenn, A. T. Enlisted 17 October 1863 at Eufaula, AL; surrendered Greensboro, NC, 1 May 1865.

Griffin, R. D. No further records (may belong to another Co, Jeff Davis Legion).

Howell, Turner. No further records; born 1831 in Georgia; enlisted 1863 at Eufaula, AL; paroled Eufaula, AL.

Jernigan, J. J. Enlisted 17 October 1863 at Eufaula, AL; surrendered

Greensboro, NC, 1 May 1865 (born 1835, Barbour County, AL; enlisted November 1863 in 4th Battalion Jeff Davis Legion and continued service four months then transferred to Kolb's Battery.

Kerns, Thomas J. Prisoner took oath at Fort Delaware, June 1865; lived in Mecklenburg, NC.

Lewis, J. J. (Louis). Enlisted 17 October 1863 at Eufaula, AL, for three years; surrendered Greensboro, NC, 1 May 1865.

Lewis, T. I. (T. J. Louis). Enlisted 17 October 1863 at Eufaula, AL; surrendered Greensboro, NC, 1 May 1865.

Locke, A. J. Enlisted as lieutenant 17 October 1863 at Eufaula, AL; record 1864 states "has never joined co since its origin"; reports from hosp. in Alabama medical board, February 1865, found him "phthisical diasthesis, hemorrhage from lungs, and inflammatory rheumatism."

McIntosh, John G. Enlisted as corporal 17 October 1863 at Eufaula, AL, for three years; surrendered Greensboro, NC, 1 May 1865.

McRaw, H. A. Enlisted as sergeant 1863 at Eufaula, AL, for the war; present 8 September 1864.

McRae, J. (McRay). Enlisted 19 October 1863 Eufaula, AL, for the war; Hosp. Eufaula, AL, April 1864; detached to light duty due to illness.

McSwain, J. C. Enlisted 28 October 1864 at Eufaula, AL, for the war; detached duty as overseer; detailed by sec. of war on farm.

Mandavill, W. H. Enlisted 10 December 1863 at Eufaula, AL, for the war; Hosp. Weldon, NC, August 1864; Hosp.8 September 1864 transferred to Co. B, Cobb's Legion, GA, 9 January 1865.

Marit, J. H. (Merritt, Marit). Enlisted 17 October 1863 at Eufaula, AL, for the war; KIA Trevillian's Station, VA, 11 June 1864.

Mitchenn, W. B. Enlisted 23 December 1863 at Eufaula, AL, for the war; present August 1864.

Moore, W. A. Enlisted 5 December 1863 at Eufaula, AL, for the war, present August 1864.

Mynard, G. C. Enlisted 12 December 1863 at Eufaula, AL, for the war; Hosp. Raleigh, NC, August 1864; present 8 September 1864.

Nawton, G. W. Enlisted 21 October 1863 at Eufaula, AL, for the war; wounded Trevillian's Station, VA 11 June 1864; ;discharged surg. cert. January 1865.

Nawton, James (Norton). Enlisted 21 October 1863 at Eufaula, AL, for the war; Hosp. Raleigh, NC, August 1864.

Nix, D. E. Enlisted 23 November 1863 at Eufaula, AL, for the war; Hosp.

Raleigh, NC, August 1864; surrendered Greensboro, NC, 1 May 1865.

Nix, T. E. Enlisted 1863 at Eufaula, AL, for the war; Hosp. Eufaula, AL, April 1864, August 1864.

O'Hara, Edward C. Enlisted 17 October 1863 at Eufaula, AL, for three years; surrendered Greensboro, NC, 1 May 1865.

Read, J. W. (Reed, Reid). Enlisted 28 October 1863 at Eufaula, AL, for the war; Hosp. Richmond, August 1864, 8 September 1864.

Reaves, C. C. Enlisted 17 October 1863 at Eufaula, AL, for the war; Hosp. Richmond, June 1864; Hosp. Richmond August 1864 "sick."

Reaves, D. S. Enlisted 12 October 1863 at Eufaula, AL, for the war; Hosp. Eufaula, AL.

Redman, C. D.(Redmon, C. B.). Enlisted 17 October 1863 at Eufaula, AL, for the war; Hosp. Richmond August 1864 "sick."

Requemon, J. A. (Roquemire). Enlisted 17 October 1863 at Eufaula, AL, for the war; wounded Trevillian's Station, VA 11 June 1864; "gunshot it ankle, leg amputated."

Richards, J. L. (James Lafayette Richards). Enlisted 1 December 1863 at Eufaula, AL, for the war; present 8 September 1864; (born 1845 Barbour Co., AL; enlisted fall of 1863 at Eufaula, AL, in 4th AL Cav., Co. C, and continued service until the close of the war; paroled at Albany, GA, 25 May 1865; died 1914.

Richards, T. D. (may be R. D. Richards). Enlisted 7 November 1863 at Eufaula, AL, for the war; present 8 September 1864.

Richards, Thomas W. Enlisted 18 September 1863 at Montgomery, AL, for three years; captured 11 June 1864 at Trevillian's Station, VA; imprisoned Point Lookout, MD; died in prison.

Richards, William H. Enlisted 11 November 1863 at Montgomery, AL, for three years; enlisted Montgomery, 1 March 1864 for three years; Hosp. Danville, VA, May 1864 "confusion"; died "rubeola" Hosp. Richmond 25 June 1864.

Richardson, J. W. Enlisted 19 October 1863 at Eufaula, AL, for the war; present 8 September 1864.

Roberts, G. A. (G. O. Roberts, G. H. Roberts). Enlisted as captain 17 October 1863 at Eufaula, AL, for three years; elected captain 17 October 1863, May 1864 "injury, severe contusion of the body and head from fall from horse; absent sick since June 1864"; Hosp. Richmond, August 1864; medical board 8 September 1864 "chronic cystitis"; retired 31 October 1864.

Rodgers, James. Enlisted 17 October 1863 at Eufaula, AL, for the war; Hosp.

Eufaula, AL, April 1864; Hosp. Richmond, August 1864 "febris intermittens" present 8 September 1864.

Rollings, G. W. Enlisted 17 October 1863 at Eufaula, AL, for three years; surrendered Greensboro, NC, 1 May 1865.

Russell, L. A. Enlisted 19 October 1863 at Eufaula, AL, for the war; wounded Trevillian's Station, VA, 11 June 1864, "gunshot wound rt thigh"; Hosp. Richmond, VA June 1864.

Ryan, L. A. Enlisted as sergeant 17 October 1863 at Eufaula, AL, for the war; present 8 September 1864.

Saulsbury, Frank. Enlisted 16 December 1863 at Eufaula, AL, for the war; Hosp. Eufaula, AL April 1864.

Seacy, B. (B. W. Searcy). Enlisted 17 October 1863 at Eufaula, AL, for the war; Hosp. Richmond, July 1864; present 8 September 1864.

Searcy, Britton. Enlisted 7 November 1863 at Eufaula, AL, for the war; Hosp. Richmond, July 1864 "morbii intern."

Seacy, Monroe (Searcy). Enlisted 14 October 1863 at Eufaula, AL, for the war; died 31 March 1864 at Montgomery, AL.

Shannon, Henry. Enlisted 17 October 1863 at Eufaula, AL, for the war; died Montgomery, AL 17 March 1864.

Shockley, W. D. Enlisted 6 November 1863 at Eufaula, AL, for the war; captured at Trevillian's Station, VA, 11 June 1864.

Sims, G. W. (Simes). Enlisted as lieutenant 17 October 1863; elected second lieutenant October 1863; absent sick May 1864; Hosp. Richmond, June 1864; Hosp. Charlottesville, VA, February 1865 "entiritis."

Sparrow, J. W. Enlisted 24 November 1863 at Eufaula, AL, for the war; Hosp. Macon, GA, April 1864; Hosp Eufaula, AL, May 1864.

Stokes, H. Z. Enlisted 25 October 1863 at Eufaula, AL, for the war; Hosp. Greensboro, NC, June 1864; Hosp. Weldon, NC, August 1864; paroled Macon, GA April 1865.

Stokes, J. D. Enlisted 1 November 9 1863 at Eufaula, AL; Hosp. Greensboro, NC, July 1864; Hosp. Weldon, NC, August 1864.

Streater, C. B. Enlisted 17 October 1863 at Eufaula, AL, for the war; Hosp. Eufaula, AL March 1864.

Streater, Thomas H. Enlisted 17 October 1863 at Eufaula, AL, for the war; surrendered Greensboro, NC, 1 May 1865.

Taylor, W. H. Enlisted 17 October 1863 at Eufaula, AL, for the war; Hosp. Richmond, June 1864, "acute dysentery"; hosp. August 1864; surrendered

Greensboro, NC, 1 May 1865.

Thomas, H. C. Enlisted 17 October 1863 at Eufaula, AL, for the war; died Abbeville, SC, 29 April 1864, "Representative unknown."

Thomas, J. E. Enlisted 26 December 1863 at Eufaula, AL, for the war; present 8 September 1864.

Thornton, Henry C. Enlisted 17 October 1863 at Eufaula, AL, for three years; Hosp. Petersburg, VA, August 1864; Hosp. Charlotte, NC, February 1865; "debilitas"; surrendered Greensboro, NC, 1 May 1865.

Watson, G. L. Enlisted 24 October 1863 at Eufaula, AL, for the war; Hosp. Eufaula, AL, 1864; captured Salisbury, NC, 12 April 1865; imprisoned Nashville, TN, Louisville, KY, and Camp Chase, OH; paroled June 1865.

Watson, John. Enlisted 1863 at Eufaula, AL; Hosp. Eufaula; AL; present August 1864.

Watson, M. M. Enlisted 24 October 1863 at Eufaula, AL, for the war; present 8 September 1864.

Whigham, S. A. Enlisted as Corporal 17 October 1863 at Eufaula, AL, for the war; surrendered Greensboro, NC, 1 May 1865.

White, Benjamin. Enlisted 9 November 1863 at Eufaula, AL, for the war; present 8 September 1864.

Wise, J. E. Enlisted 1 December 1863 at Eufaula, AL, for the war; present 8 September 1864.

Wise, L. L. Enlisted 27 October 1863 at Eufaula, AL, for the war; present 8 September 1864.

Wood, J. W. Enlisted as corporal 17 October 1863 at Eufaula, AL, for the war; wounded Trevillian's Station, VA, "gunshot wound rt hand."

Wood, W. D. Enlisted 17 October 1863 at Eufaula, AL, for the war: detached duty as adjutant April 1864; Hospital Richmond June 1864; surrendered Greensboro, NC, May 1865.

Source: Hopkins, Donald A. *The Little Jeff, The Jeff Davis Legion, Cavalry, Army of Northern Virginia* (Shippensburg, PA: White Mane Books, 1999); also see Hopkins, *Horsemen of the Jeff Davis Legion, The Expanded Roster of the Men and Officers of the Jeff Davis Legion, Cavalry* (Shippensburg, PA: White Mane Books, 1999).

*The Civil War era hospital in Charlotte, North Carolina, was the building that housed the North Carolina Military Institute with General Daniel Harvey Hill as the headmaster and was located at Morehead and South Boulevard;

see "The Hornet's Nest: An Historical Drama in Commemoration of Charlotte's Bicentennial, 1768–1968."

APPENDIX III

Private John Calvin Dodgen of Company B of the Phillips Georgia Legion Cavalry Battalion never dreamed he would be attending the premier of a classic Civil War motion picture that would become the top ranking movie of all time. Dodgen enlisted as a private in the legion on 15 January 1864 and fought in Company B under the command of his brother-in-law, Captain John Fielding Milhollin, surrendering at Greensboro on 1 May 1865. Many decades later, Dodgen received a front-row seat with three other Confederate veterans at the first presentation of the film version of Margaret Mitchell's masterpiece *Gone With the Wind* on 13 December 1939.

Ninety-three years old at the time of the premier of the film at Loew's Grand Theatre on Peachtree Street in Atlanta, Dodgen hobnobbed with the likes of Clark Gable, Vivian Leigh, Leslie Howard, and Lawrence Olivier. At this time, John Calvin Dodgen resided at the Soldiers Home four miles north of the Georgia state capital on Confederate Avenue in East Atlanta. This comfortable, two-story brick building had been established by the Georgia legislature in 1891 for the care of Civil War soldiers who, because of disabilities or infirmities of age, were not able to care for themselves. Before establishing his residence in Atlanta, Dodgen lived in Coffee County, Broxton, Georgia, with his great-nephew, J. H. Milhollin.

At least a few of the old veterans are believed to have fallen asleep before the movie ended.

(Photo of John Calvin here.)

BIBLIOGRAPHY

1. Primary Sources

Eleanor Brockenbrough Library, Museum of the Confederacy, Richmond VA.
   Moxley Sorrell diary, Longstreet's Staff.
Confederate Reminiscences and Letters 1861–1865. Volume 7.
   Ivy F. Thompson diary, Phillips Georgia Legion.
Duke University Library, Durham NC.
   William Shockley letters, 18th Georgia.
   Alexander Brown letters.
Emory University, Woodruff Library, Atlanta.
   Confederate miscellany.
   William Dobbins letters, Phillips Georgia Legion.
   Alexander H. Stephens letters.
Georgia Department of Archives and History.
   Wofford family genealogy file.
   James Lewis Barton diary, Phillips Georgia Legion.
   Pierce Manning Butler Young correspondence.
Georgia Historical Society Library, Special Collections: J. Fred Waring Papers,
   Collection no. 1275.
Hargrett Rare Book and Manuscript Library, University of Georgia, Athens GA.
   Etheldred Rainey diary, 25 November 1861.
The Historical Society of Pennsylvania, Philadelphia.
   General Thomas F. Drayton papers.
Kennesaw Mountain National Military Park.
   Phillips Georgia Legion company flag.
National Archives.
   Letters received by the Confederate Secretary of War 1861–1865, record
   group 10785.
New Hampshire Historical Society.
   John Bachelder papers.
North Carolina State Archives, Raleigh NC.
   Willaim Francis Shine, J. B. Clifton diary, Phillips Georgia Legion.

Private Collections

Buchanan, Hugh. Letters, 1862-1865. In private possession of Libby Buchanan. Newnan GA.

Dodgen, J., to Dear Sister, 21 December 1863, from Camp near Orange C. H. Virginia, Georgia Department of Archives & History, Morrow GA.

Harris, William. Letters, 1861-1865. Georgia Department of Archives & History, Morrow GA.

Housworth, J., to Mrs. Swan, 3 March 1864, from Hamilton's Crossing VA. Georgia Department of Archives & History, Morrow GA.

Humphries, E. Letters. In private possession of the Humphries family, Macon, Georgia.

Jones, Abraham. Letters, 1861-1864. In private possession of Mr.and Mrs. David Gandy, Atlanta.

Latimer, D., to Will, 25 September 1863, from Camp Phillips Legion. In private possession of Mr. and Mrs. David Gandy.

Mapp, W. T., to wife, n.d., in Georgia State Archives and History.

Milhollin, John F. Leave request signed by JEB Stuart, 29 September 1865. In private possession of Milhollin family, Susan Milhollin, Charlotte NC.

Mitchell, T. M. Diary. 1861-1865. In private possession of Robert Thomas, Chattanooga TN.

Nichols, James H. In private possession of Thomas Nichols, Milledgeville GA.

Rich, William Wofford. Letters. In private possession of Darryl Starnes, Mechanicsville VA.

Swan, John. Letters, 1861-1865. Collection number 0827 Swann Family Papers, Special Collection Library Wison Library UNC, Chapel Hill NC.

Smyrna Historical Society, Smyrna GA.
    "Personal Account Written by William Phillips."

Southern Confederacy, 12 January 1862, dispatch from Major John B. Willcoxon, commanding Phillips Georgia Cavalry Battalion, to Major General Lee, C. S. A., commanding Confederate State Forces in South Carolina and Georgia, 23 December 1861.

Southern Historical Collection, University of North Carolina Library.

John Alexander Barry papers, Phillips Georgia Legion.

Thomas J. Riddle, "Reminiscences of Floyd's Operations in West Virginia in 1861," 11 (1883) 92–98.

Rev. George G. Smith, "Autobiography," Phillips Georgia Legion, Southern Historical Collection, UNC Chapel Hill NC.

Rev. George G. Smith "Reminiscences," 1894. Phillips Georgia Legion.

Major General Henry Heth, "Causes of Lee's Defeat at Gettysburg," vol. 4: 157.
Major General Lafayette McLaws, "Gettysburg Revisited: The Opportunity Missed—The Planning for the 2nd Day." 68–69.
W. Youngblood, "Unwritten History of the Gettysburg Campaign," vol. 38: 315.
South Carolina Historical Society, Columbia SC.
T. C. Albergotti, "Memoir," Hampton's Legion.
South Caroliniana Library, University of South Carolina.
Joseph Kershaw papers.
United States Army Military History Institute, Carlisle Barracks, Pennsylvania.
John F. Milhollin correspondence.
University of North Carolina, Wilson Library.
Frederick J. Waring diary, 1864–1865.
Washington Library, Macon GA.
Charles A. Ells diary, 1862, Macon Light Artillery.

2. Newspapers
Atlanta Constitution
Atlanta Journal
Atlanta Southern Confederacy
Athens (GA) *Southern Banner*
Athens (GA) *Southern Watchman*
Augusta (GA) *Daily Chronicle & Sentinel*
Bartow (GA) *Herald*
Cassville (GA) *Pioneer*
Central Georgian
Charleston (SC) *Mercury*
Columbus (GA) *Daily Times*
Federal Union, Georgia.
Loudon Times, Virginia.
Marietta (GA) *Advocate*
New York Herald
Orangeburg Democrat, South Carolina.
Philadelphia Weekly Times
Philadelphia Weekly Press
Richmond (VA) *Sentinel*
Rome (GA) *Weekly Courier*
Savannah (GA) *Morning News*
Time and Democrat, Southern Recorder, Milledgville GA.

3. Official Publications

Georgia General Assembly, Acts and Resolutions, 1834–1877.

Army of Northern Virginia Special Order No. 104, 23 March 1863. M921, Roll 2.

Compiled Service Records of Confederate Soldiers Who Served in Organizations from the State of Georgia, War Department of Confederate Records, M266, Reels 592–600, Record Group 109, Phillips Georgia Legion.

Confederate Pension Records of Georgia, Georgia Department of Archives and History, Morrow GA.

Confederate Records of the State of Georgia 1860–1865, Atlanta: Bond, 1911.

Incoming Correspondence to Governor Joseph E. Brown, 1861. Call number 1564, Rare Book Collection University of North Carolina Library.

Governor's Letter Book, 1861–1865. Georgia Department of Archives and History, Morrow GA.

Muster Rolls and Lists of Confederate Troops Paroled in North Carolina, M1781-Reel 1, Cavalry Battalion, Phillips Legion. National Archives, Washington, DC and NC State Archives, Raleigh NC.

National Archives, Washington, DC. Compiled Service Records Showing Service of Military Units in Confederate Organizations, Confederate Service Records of Confederate Soldiers in Organizations from the State of Georgia, Reference File Relating to Confederate Medical Officers.

US Census Office. Seventh, Eighth, and Ninth Census Records, 1850–1870. National Archives, Washington DC.

The War of the Rebellion: A Compilation of the Official Records of the Union and Confederate Armies, ed. Robert N. Scott (Washington, DC: Government Printing Office: 1888). The Civil War CD-Rom, the War of the Rebellion, A Compilation of the Official Records of the Union and Confederate Armies, Guild Press of Indiana, Inc.

4. Other Printed Materials

Adams Troop File, Mississippi Department of Archives and History, Jackson MS.

Alexander, Edward P. "Assault on Fort Sanders." In *Battles and Leaders of the Civil War*, R. U. Johnston and C. C. Buell. New York, 1885-1887.

Ammen, D. "DuPont and the Port Royal Expedition." In *Battles and Leaders*, vol. 1. 671–91.

Anonymous. "Sharpshooting in Lee's Army." In *Confederate Veteran*, 3 (1895) 98.

Biddle J. "General Meade at Gettysburg." In *Annals of the War*. Edison NJ: Blue and Gray Press, 1966.

Chancellor, Sue. "Recollections of Chancellorsville." In *Confederate Veteran* (June 1921) 214.

Church, M. "The Hills of Habersham." In *Reminiscences of E. H. Sutton, 24th Georgia*. 13 December 1862.

Cooke, J. *Wearing of the Gray: Being Personal Portraits, Scenes and Adventures in the War*. Bloomington IN: P. V. Stern, 1959.

Couch, Darius. "The Chancellorsville Campaign." In *Battles and Leaders*, 154.

Coxe, J. "The Battle of Gettysburg." In *Confederate Veteran*, 21/9 (1913) reprint: 435.

Davis, (Major) George B., Leslie J. Perry, and Joseph W. Kirkley. *The Official Military Atlas of the Civil War*. New York: Barnes & Noble Books: 2003.

Dent, Stephen. "With Cobb's Brigade at Fredericksburg." In *Confederate Veteran* 22 (1914): 550–51.

Evans, J. "With Hampton's Scouts." In *Confederate Veteran* 12/32 (December 1924) 470.

"From Spotsylvania Court House to Andersonville." In *Georgia Historical Quarterly*, edited by E. M. Coulter. 41 (June 1957): 528–29.

Gaines, Lizzie. "We Begged to Hearts of Stone: The Wartime Journal of Cassville's Lizzie Gaines." In *Northwest Georgian* 20 (1988): 1–6.

Guide to Historic Bluffton, Bluffton Historical Preservation Society, Heyward House Historic Center, vol. 2, Bluffton SC 29910.

Hansel, Charles Paine, Diary of Charles Paine Hansel, Georgia Department of Archives and History, Civil War Miscellany, Morrow GA.

Happel, R. "The Chancellors at Chancellorsville," *The Virginia Magazine*. 71/3 (July 1863): 259–77.

Heth, Henry. "Memoirs of Henry Heath II." Edited by James L. Morrison. *Civil War History* 8 (September 1862): 300–26.

Johnson, Robert Underwood and Clarence Clough Buel. *Battles and Leaders of the Civil War*. New York: The Century Co., 1888.

Kavanaugh, Mrs. John. Pension application, Georgia State Archives and History, Morrow GA.

Law, Evander. "From the Wilderness to Cold Harbor." In *Battles and Leaders*, vol. 4. 118–44.

Longstreet, James. "The Campaign of Gettysburg." In *Philadelphia Weekly Times*, 3 November 1877.

____. "Lee in Pennsylvania," In *Annals of War*. Philadelphia: Times Publishing, 1879.

____. "Lee's Invasion of Pennsylvania." In *Battles and Leaders*, vol. 3, 244–51.

McLaws, Lafayette. "The Battle of Gettysburg," In *Philadelphia Weekly Press*, 21 April 1886.

Pleasonton, Alfred. "The Successes and Failures of Chancellorsville." In *Battles and Leaders*, vol. 3. 172.

Pope, John. "The Second Battle of Bull Run." In *Battles and Leaders*, vol. 2. 449–94.

Redd, B. F. "McLaws' Division at Chickamauga." In *Confederate Veteran* 21 (1913) 585–86.

Sanders, C. C. "Chancellorsville." In *Southern Historical Society Papers* (1921) 166–72.

Sparkman, J. Diary, US National Military Park, Manassas, VA.

Taliaferro, E. "Ordnance Return of Cobb's Brigade." 26 December 1862. Compiled SVC Records of E. Taliaferr, National Archives, Washington DC. RG 109, M331, Roll 24.

Wood, J. S. "Co. D, Reminiscences." Georgia Department of Archives & History, Morrow GA. Drawer 284, Box 4.

5. Books/Primary

Alexander, E. P. *Fighting for the Confederacy: Personal Recollections of General E. Porter Alexander*. Edited by Gary Gallagher. Chapel Hill: University of North Carolina Press, 1989.

Andrews, Eliza Frances. *Wartime Journal of a Georgia Girl*. Edited by Spencer King, Jr. Macon GA: Ardivan, 1960.

Andrews, W. A. *First Sergeant, Company M, Footprints of a Regiment*, Atlanta: Longstreet Press, 1992.

Blackford, W. W. *War Years with Jeb Stuart*. New York: Charles Scribner's Sons, 1945.

Brooks, Ulysses R. *Butler and His Cavalry in the War of Secession, 1861–1865*. Columbia SC: The State Company, 1909.

Crist, Lynda, L. and Mary S. Dix. *The Papers of Jefferson Davis*. Vol. 7. 1861. Baton Rouge LA: LSU Press, 1992.

Dickert, Augustus. *History of Kershaw's Brigade*. Newberry SC: Aull, 1899.

Duganne, A. J. H. *The Fighting Quakers*. New York: J. P. Robens, 1866.

Evans, Clement. *Confederate Military History.* Vol. 6. Atlanta: Confederate Publishing, 1889.

Folsom, J. M. *Heroes and Martyrs of Georgia: Georgia's Record in the Revolution of 1861.* Macon GA: Burke and Boykin, 1864.

Georgia Sharpshooter: The Civil Diary and Letters of William Rhadamanthus Montgomery. Edited by George Montgomery, Jr. Macon GA: Mercer University Press, 1997.

Longstreet, James. *From Manassas to Appomattox.* Philadelphia: Lippencott, 1896.

McClellan, H. *The Campaigns of Stuart's Cavalry.* Secaucus NY: Blue & Gray Press, 1993.

Myers, Robert Manson. *The Children of Pride.* New Haven and London: Yale University Press, 1972.

Owen, William Miller. *In Camp and Battle with the Washington Artillery of New Orleans.* Baton Rouge LA: LSU Press, 1885.

Ridley, Bromfield L. *Battles and Sketches of the Army of Tennessee.* Mexico MO: Missouri Printing & Publishing Co., 1906.

Sorrell, Moxley. *Recollections of a Confederate Staff Officer.* Jackson TN: McCowat-Mercer, 1958.

Von Borcke, Heros. *Memoirs of the Confederate War for Independence.* New York: Smith, 1938.

5. Books/Secondary

Alexander, Bevin. *Robert E. Lee's Civil War.* Holbrook MA: Adams Media Corporation, 1998.

Arnold, James R. *Chickamauga 1863: The River of Death.* Oxford, United Kingdom: Osprey Press, 1992.

Barrett, John G. *Sherman's March through the Carolinas.* Chapel Hill: University of North Carolina Press, 1956.

Black, Robert C. III. *The Railroads of the Confederacy.* Chapel Hill and London: University of North Carolina Press, 1998.

Boatner Mark M. III. *The Civil War Dictionary.* Revised Edition. New York: David McKay Company, 1988.

Bowers. J. *Chickamauga & Chattanooga: The Battles that Doomed the Confederacy.* New York: Harper Collins, 1994.

Bradley, M. *This Astounding Close: The Road to Bennett Place.* Chapel Hill and London: University of North Carolina Press, 2000.

_____. *Last Stand in the Carolinas.* Mason City IA: Savas Publishing Co., 1996.

Bragg, W. A. *Joe Brown's Army: The Confederate State Line*. Macon GA: Mercer University Press, 1987.

Bridges, Herb. *Gone With the Wind: The Three-Day Premiere in Atlanta*, Macon GA: Mercer University Press, 1999.

Bryan, T. *Confederate Georgia*. Athens: University of Georgia Press, 1953.

Butler and His Cavalry in the War of Secession 1861–1865. Edited by U. R. Brooks. Germantown TN: Guild Press, 1994.

Calkins, Chris. *The Battle of Saylor's Creek, April 6, 1865*. Farmville VA: The Farmville Herald, 1992.

_____. *From Petersburg to Appomattox*. Farmville VA: The Farmville Herald, 1983.

_____. *Lee's Retreat: A History and Field Guide*. Richmond VA: Page One History Publications, 2000.

_____. *Thirty-Six Hours before Appomattox*. Farmville VA: The Farmville Herald, 1980.

Catton, Bruce. *Bruce Catton's Civil War: Three Volumes in One*. New York: Fairfax, 1984.

Clayton, Charles Marlow. *Matt W. Ransom, Confederate General from North Carolina*, Jefferson NC and London: Mcfarland & Company, 1996.

Coddington, E. *The Gettysburg Campaign: A Study in Command*. Dayton: The Morningside Bookshop. Reprint, 1979.

Cohen, Stanley. *The Civil War in West Virginia*. Charleston WV: Pictorial Histories Publishing Company, 1976.

Cohen, S. *Historic Springs of the Virginias*. Charleston WV, June 1981, Pictorial Histories Pub. Co.

Crute, Joseph H. *Units of the Confederate States Army*, Midlothian VA: Derwent Books, 1987.

Cunningham, H. H. *Doctors in Gray: The Confederate Medical Service*. Baton Rouge LA: LSU Press, 1986.

Cunyus, Lucy. *History of Bartow County, Formerly Cass*. Easley SC: Southern Historical Press, 1976.

Davis, R. *The Georgia Black Book. Morbid, Macabre, & Sometimes Disgusting Records of Genealogical Value*. Easley SC: Southern Historical Press, 1982.

Deaderick, L. *Heart of the Valley: A History of Knoxville, Tennessee*. Knoxville TN: East Tennessee Historical Society, 1976.

Dowdey, Clifford and Louis Manarin. *The Wartime Papers of R. E. Lee*, New York: Bramhall House, 1961.

Eanes, Greg. *Black Day of the Army, April 6, 1865.* Burkeville VA: E & H. Publishing, 2001.

Foote, Shelby. *The Civil War: A Narrative.* 3 volumes. New York: Random House, 1963.

Fox, John J. III. *Red Clay to Richmond, Trail of the 35th Georgia Infantry Regiment, C.S.A.* Winchester VA: Angle Valley Press, 2004.

Freeman, Douglas-Southall. *Lee's Lieutenants.* 3 volumes. New York: Scribner's, 1944.

____. *R. E. Lee.* Volume 2. New York: Scribner's, 1934.

Furgurson, Ernest B. *Chancellorsville 1863: The Souls of the Brave.* New York: Knopf, 1992.

____. *Not War but Murder, Cold Harbor.* New York: Knopf, 2000.

Greeley, Horace. *The American Conflict: A History of the Great Rebellion in the United States of America, 1860–1865.* Hartford CT: O. D. Case and V. W. Sherwood, 1864.

Hahn, Steven. *The Roots of Southern Populism: Yeoman Farmers and the Transformation of the Georgia Up-Country.* New York: Oxford, 1983.

Hennessy, John J. *Return to Bull Run: The Campaign of Second Manassas.* New York: Simon & Schuster, 1993.

Hesseltine, William B. *Civil War Prisons: A Study in War Psychology.* New York: Unger, 1964.

Holland, L. M. *Pierce M. B. Young: The Warwick of the South,* Athens: University of Georgia Press, 1964.

Hopkins, Donald A. *The Little Jeff: The Jeff Davis Legion, Cavalry Army of Northern Virginia.* Shippensburg PA: Beidel Printing House, 1999.

____. *Horsemen of the Jeff Davis Legion.* Shippensburg PA: White Mane Books, 1999.

Jaynes, Gregory. *The Killing Ground: Wilderness to Cold Harbor.* Alexandria VA: Time-Life Books, 1986.

The Journal of a Milledgeville Girl, 1861–1867. Edited by J. Bonner. Athens: University of Georgia Press, 1978.

Kennett, L. *Marching through Georgia: The Story of Soldiers and Civilians during Sherman's Campaign.* New York: Harper Perennial, 1995.

Kohn, Richard H. *Eagle and Sword.* New York: The Free Press, 1975.

Korn, J. *The Fight for Chattanooga, Chickamauga to Missionary Ridge.* Alexandria VA: Time-Life Books, 1985.

Longacre, E. *The Cavalry at Gettysburg.* Lincoln and London: University of Nebraska Press, 1986.

_____. *Gentleman and Soldier: The Extraordinary Life of General Wade Hampton*. Nashville TN: Rutledge Hill Press, 2003.

_____. *Lee's Cavalrymen*. Mechanicsburg PA: Stackpole Books, 2002.

_____. *Lincoln's Cavalrymen*. Mechanicsburg PA: Stackpole Books, 2000.

Mahr, Theodore C. *The Battle of Cedar Creek, Showdown in the Shenandoah*. Lynchburg VA: H. E. Howard, Inc., 1992.

Mason, P. *The Plank Road Craze: A Chapter in the History of Michigan's Highways*. Detroit MI: Michigan Historical Center, Department of History, Arts and Libraries, Wayne State University, 1986.

Mims, Edwin. *Sidney Lanier*. Boston: Houghton-Mifflin, 1905.

Newell, Clayton R. *Lee vs. McClellan*. Washington D.C.: Regnery Publishing Co., 1996.

O'Reilly, Frank A. *Stonewall Jackson at Fredericksburg—The Battle of Prospect Hill, December 13, 1862*. Baton Rouge LA: LSU Press, 1993.

O'Reilly, Robert. *The Cavalry Battles of Aldie, Middleburg and Upperville: Small but Important Riots*. Lynchburg VA: H. E. Howard, 1993.

Pfanz, Harry W. *Gettysburg, the Second Day*. Chapel Hill: University of North Carolina Press, 1987.

Phillips, David L. *War Diaries: The 1861 Kanawha Valley Campaigns*. Leesburg VA: Gauley Mount Press, 1990.

Pollard, Edward Albert. *Southern History of the War: The Third Year of the War*. New York: Charles B. Richardson, 1965.

Priest, John Michael. *Before Antietam: The Battle for South Mountain*. Shippensburg PA: White Mane Publishing, 1992.

Reese, Timothy. *High-Water Mark: The 1862 Maryland Campaign in Strategic Perspective*. Baltimore MD: Butternut and Blue, 2004.

Rhea, Gordon C. *The Battle of the Wilderness*. Baton Rouge LA: LSU Press, 1994.

_____. *Cold Harbor, Grant and Lee, May 26 – June 3, 1864*. Baton Rouge LA: LSU Press, 2002.

_____. *To the North Anna River, Grant and Lee*. Baton Rouge LA: LSU Press, 2000.

Schaff, Morris. *The Battle of the Wilderness*. Boston: Houghton Mifflin, 1910.

Sears, Stephen. *Landscape Turned Red: The Battle of Antietam*. New York: Ticknor and Fields, 1983.

Seymour, Digby Gordon. *Divided Loyalties*. Knoxville TN: East Tennessee Historical Society, 1963.

Smedlund, William S. *Camp Fires of Georgia's Troops, 1861–1865.* Kennesaw GA: Kennesaw Mountain Press, 1994.

Smith, David C. *Campaign to Nowhere.* Strawberry Plains TN: Strawberry Plains Press, 1999.

Smith, Gerald J. *One of the Most Daring of Men: The Life of Confederate General William Tatum Wofford.* Murfreesboro TN: Southern Heritage Press, 1997.

Smith, George G. *The Boy in Gray: A Story of the War.* Macon GA: Macon Publishing Company, 1894.

Steere, E. *The Wilderness Campaign.* New York: Bonanza Books, 1989.

Stokes, William. *Saddle Soldiers: The Civil War Correspondence of General William Stokes of the 4th South Carolina Cavalry.* Edited by Lloyd Halliburton. Orangeburg SC: Sandlapper Publishing Co., 1993.

Switlik M. C. *The More Complete Cannoneer.* Monroe MI: Museum & Collector Specialties Company, 1990.

Temple, Sarah. *The First One Hundred Years: A Short History of Cobb County.* Atlanta: Brown, 1935.

Thomas, Emory M. *Bold Dragoon: The Life of J. E. B. Stuart.* New York: Harper & Row, 1996.

_____. *The Confederacy as a Revolutionary Experience.* Columbia: University of South Carolina Press, 1971.

Trout, R. *They Followed the Plume: The Story of J. E. B. Stuart and His Staff.* Mechanicsburg PA: Stackpole Books.

Trudeau, Noah Andre. *Bloody Roads South: The Wilderness to Cold Harbor.* Toronto and London: Little, Brown and Company, 1989.

_____. *The Last Citadel, June–April 1865.* Boston, Toronto, and London: Little, Brown and Company, 1991.

Walsh, G. *Damage Them All You Can: Robert E. Lee's Army of Northern Virginia.* New York: Forge, A Tom Doherty Associates Book, 2002.

Ware, W. H. *The Battle of Kelly's Ford, Fought March 17, 1863.* Newport News VA: Warwick Printing Co., 1922.

Wellman, M. *Giant in Gray: A Biography of Wade Hampton of South Carolina.* New York: Charles Scribner's Sons, 1949.

Wells, Edward L. *Hampton and His Cavalry.* Richmond VA: B. F. Publishing Co., 1899.

Wert, Jeffry D. *From Winchester to Cedar Creek: The Shenandoah Campaign of 1864.* Mechanicsburg PA: Stackpole Books, 1989.

Wiley, Bell Irvin. *Johnny Reb, the Common Soldier of the Confederacy*. New York: Doubleday, 1943.

Wilkinson, Warren. *Mother May You Never See the Sights I Have Seen: The Fifty-Seventh Massachusetts Veteran Volunteers in the Last Year of the Civil War*. New York: Harper & Row, 1990.

Wise, Jennings. *The Long Arm of Lee: Chancellorsville to Appomattox*. Lincoln: University of Nebraska Press, 1991.

Wittenberg, Eric J. *Glory Enough for All: Sheridan's Second Raid: The Battle of Trevilian Station*. Dulles VA: Brassey's, Inc., 2002.

7. Theses and Dissertations:

Hendricks, H. "Imperiled City: The Movements of the Union and Confederate Armies toward Greensboro in the Closing Days of the Civil War in North Carolina." M.A. thesis, University of North Carolina at Greensboro, 1987.

Mahan, J. B., Jr. "A History of Old Cassville 1833–1864." M.A. thesis, University of Georgia, 1950.

8. Articles:

Alexander, Joseph H. "Defending Marye's Heights," *MHQ: The Quarterly Journal of Military History*. 9/3 (Spring 1997) 86–97.

Anderson, Jimmy. "The Life and Times of Gen. Harrison W. Riley." Unpublished. Dahlonega GA: 2000, 166–78.

"The Breath of Hell's Door: Private William McCarter and the Irish Brigade at Fredericksburg." Edited by Kevin O'Brien. In *Civil War Regiments: A Journal of the American Civil War* 4:47.

Coffman, Richard M. "A Vital Unit (Phillips Georgia Legion)," *Civil War Times Illustrated*. 20 (January 1982) 40–45.

Dodgen, Lily Milhollin. "Grandma's War Memories," *The Bartow* (GA) *Herald* 9 April 1931.

McWhirter, A. "Gen. Wofford's Brigade in the Wilderness," *Atlanta Journal* 21 September 1901.

INDEX